M. P. K. SORRENSON (Ngati Pukenga, Pakeha) is one of New Zealand's most important living historians. He began as a junior lecturer in the University of Auckland history department in 1958, and completed a DPhil at Oxford and further research in East Africa, before returning to Auckland in 1964. He taught there for the next 31 years. He was president of CARE in the 1970s, sat on the council of the New Zealand Historic Places Trust for a decade and was a leading member of the Waitangi Tribunal for 25 years. He is author or editor of numerous books on African and New Zealand history, including *Maori Origins and Migrations: The Genesis of some Pakeha Myths and Legends* (AUP/OUP, 1979) and the three-volume work *Na To Hoa Aroha, From Your Dear Friend: The Correspondence between Sir Apirana Ngata and Sir Peter Buck, 1925–1950* (AUP, 1986, 1987, 1988), both of which have recently been launched as ebooks by Auckland University Press.

M. P. K. SORRENSON

KO TE WHENUA TE UTU
LAND IS THE PRICE

ESSAYS ON MAORI HISTORY, LAND AND POLITICS

AUCKLAND
UNIVERSITY
PRESS

First published 2014

Auckland University Press
University of Auckland
Private Bag 92019
Auckland 1142
New Zealand
www.press.auckland.ac.nz

© Keith Sorrenson

ISBN 978 1 86940 810 7

National Library of New Zealand Cataloguing-in-Publication Data
Sorrenson, M. P. K.
Ko te whenua te utu = Land is the price : essays on Maori history, land and politics /
M.P.K. Sorrenson.
ISBN 978-1-86940-810-7
1. Maori (New Zealand people)—History. 2. Land tenure—New Zealand—History.
3. New Zealand—History. [1. Kōrero nehe. reo 2. Whenua. reo
3. Taipūwhenuatanga. reo] I. Title.
993—dc 23

This book is copyright. Apart from fair dealing for the purpose of private study,
research, criticism or review, as permitted under the Copyright Act, no part may be
reproduced by any process without prior permission of the publisher.
The moral rights of the author have been asserted.

Cover design: Kalee Jackson
Cover image: Georgina Burne Hetley, *Surveying Party near Whangarei*, c. 1870. Watercolour,
254 x 447 mm. B-121-018, Alexander Turnbull Library, Wellington, New Zealand

Printed by 1010 Printing International Ltd

Contents

Acknowledgements		vi
Introduction		1
1	The Whence of the Maori: Some Nineteenth-century Exercises in Scientific Method	9
2	Treaties in British Colonial Policy: Precedents for Waitangi	40
3	How to Civilise Savages: Some 'Answers' from Nineteenth-century New Zealand	55
4	Folkland to Bookland: F. D. Fenton and the Enclosure of the Maori 'Commons'	68
5	Land Purchase Methods and their Effect on Maori Population, 1865–1901	90
6	The Maori King Movement, 1858–1885	106
7	Polynesian Corpuscles and Pacific Anthropology: The Home-made Anthropology of Sir Apirana Ngata and Sir Peter Buck	126
8	Colonial Rule and Local Response: Maori Responses to European Domination in New Zealand since 1860	145
9	Maori Representation in Parliament	157
10	Towards a Radical Reinterpretation of New Zealand History: The Role of the Waitangi Tribunal	217
11	Giving Better Effect to the Treaty: Some Thoughts for 1990	238
12	The Waitangi Tribunal and the Resolution of Maori Grievances	256
13	Waitangi: Ka Whawhai Tonu Matou	273
Epilogue		292
Notes		304
Index		329

Acknowledgements

I am grateful to my wife Judith, my sons Richard and Julian, and grandsons Peter and David for help with computing; to Sam Elworthy and Anna Hodge at Auckland University Press and Mike Wagg for their care in editing and formatting; and to the following journals and publishers for permission to reproduce the essays in this collection: *The Journal of the Polynesian Society*; *The New Zealand Journal of History*; *The Journal of Imperial and Commonwealth History*; *The British Review of New Zealand Studies*; Paul's Book Arcade; the Government Printer; Oxford University Press; and Otago University Press.

Introduction

The essays in this collection have been published over a period of 56 years and most of them have long been out of print. That longevity might well suggest that many of the essays are no longer relevant. Yet, oddly enough, the first of the essays to be published, 'Land Purchase Methods and their Effect on Maori Population, 1865–1901', which was based on my 1955 Master's thesis, 'The Purchase of Maori Lands, 1865–1892', has been the most cited of all.[1] In recent years it has been used to support numerous research reports and submissions for Waitangi Tribunal inquiries, often in my presence and to my embarrassment while I was sitting as a member on various Tribunal inquiry panels. If the other essays have received less notice, they provide a progression of my thoughts on various aspects of Maori history, more especially in relation to Maori losses of land and their political responses to those losses as, in the face of remorseless Pakeha colonisation of New Zealand, they became a minority in their own country. Indeed, the title of this collection, *Ko te Whenua te Utu*, uses one of the meanings of utu to signify that land was the price Maori had to pay for signing the Treaty of Waitangi, accepting British sovereignty and allowing European colonisation to proceed.

New Zealand race relations, and more particularly Maori–Pakeha relations, have often been acclaimed (though not by me) as an object lesson to the rest of the world. One of my mentors and a former colleague, Sir Keith Sinclair, simply accepted that assumption before going on to explain why that was so.[2] Several of the essays in the collection do discuss race relations — or Maori–Pakeha relations, as I would prefer to call them — but others are more concerned with examining the evolution of racial thought as a background to assessments of Maori and their placement in racial hierarchies of the day. One of them, 'Polynesian Corpuscles and Pacific Anthropology', examines those ideas as filtered through the minds of two of our greatest Maori scholars, Sir Apirana Ngata and Sir Peter Buck. Such ideas are but a brief sample from their wide-ranging correspondence on Maori affairs during the inter-war years that

I subsequently edited for publication in three volumes by Auckland University Press in 1986–88.[3]

The essays are not arranged in order of publication but mainly in so far as they fit into a chronology of Maori history, land and politics. Some, however, cover the whole of the period, while the last four, all of them inspired by Waitangi Tribunal associations, represent my contributions to various Treaty and Tribunal occasions. They are a small contribution to the 'Treaty industry' which, to the annoyance of some historians, has captured too much attention in recent years. But I make no apology for my involvement. It has been the crowning climax of my life as a professional historian and brought me into contact with the lively minds and memories of numerous distinguished kaumatua and kuia, lawyers and fellow historians. Through Maori elders, their history has come alive and been relived in many a Tribunal hearing; reminding us that there are essentially two histories of Aotearoa. First, a long Maori history, beginning with their Pacific origins, continuing through their arrival in Aotearoa and intensifying with the arrival of Pakeha, those strangers who were very different from the tangata maori, the ordinary people. And secondly, there has been a history of Pakeha colonisation and takeover of Aotearoa, not always taking much note of the tangata whenua, the people of the land, but never able to totally ignore them. The two narratives have been repeatedly stitched together in short and long histories of New Zealand.

The question of 'Maori history' has at times been the subject of controversy since in recent years some Maori have said that only Maori can write it. That notion is not new: as seen in my 'Polynesian Corpuscles' essay, Ngata and Buck held a similar view of their contemporary Pakeha scholars. As Ngata put it, 'chaps like [Felix] Keesing & others cannot get very far in'. And, in discussing the work of another anthropologist, Raymond Firth, Buck said, 'We have got to ... [make] the most of any natural assets we may have through our blood.' In discussing Firth's 1929 publication, *The Primitive Economics of the New Zealand Maori*, Ngata said that he had failed to penetrate 'the psychological strata of Maori life and thought'.[4]

My own position has been somewhat ambiguous. Sometimes, because of my Ngati Pukenga ancestry, I am included in the fold; at other times, because of my larger Pakeha ancestry, I am excluded. The whole argument has been rather silly, especially when we remember that the most outstanding Maori history written in recent years has been by my late colleague Judith Binney who was not Maori at all, except by adoption. But I also get some wry pleasure from the fact that my Maori ancestry comes from a marriage between Katerina Te Atirau of Ngati Pukenga and a Jewish trader, David Asher; a marriage, we might say, that was made not quite in heaven but in the Old Testament. As I point out in chapter 3, 'How to Civilise Savages', the missionaries were always telling Maori that they were one of the lost tribes of Israel; tribes that were united, in my case, through Katerina and David (and through a good many other Maori–Jewish marriages). In fact my earliest essay in what could be described as Maori history (though the term was hardly used at the time) — the study of the Maori King movement (or Kingitanga), with its particular emphasis on Maori conceptions of their kingship — was published as long ago as 1963. Maori history has come of age recently with the formation of a Maori historians' network, Te Pouhere Korero, which has published a journal with that title since 2006.

My involvement in the long-vexed question of Maori origins is represented by the first essay in the collection, 'The Whence of the Maori'. This was a preliminary review of that question which I followed up in 1978 in my three Macmillan Brown lectures, published the following year as *Maori Origins and Migrations*.[5] It has been my most successful book and has been reprinted several times, which suggests that there is something to be said for brevity. As I explain in my Epilogue, the quest for Maori origins has been continued vigorously by others since the publication of my book.

The arrangement of the essays to fit into a chronology of Maori history, rather than by date of publication, might imply that I have been historiographically calcified over my long career. I would plead that that is not quite true; but rather that I have usually ridden the waves of fashion and perhaps on one occasion been slightly ahead. My *Maori Origins and Migrations* was recognised by Simon During, in the Australian literary journal *Meanjin*, for 'demystifying the construction of Maori mythology',[6] a 'mythology' that had been constructed by Pakeha scholars. That 'demystifying' was soon to be known as 'Deconstruction' though I saw no need to become a convert since I regarded it as a new name for what historians always try to do — examine what intellectual ingredients go into the making of texts.

As a historian, I came of age as a Master's student in the History Department of Auckland University College where I was mentored by a curious mix of fine scholars. They included the constitutionalist James Rutherford, struggling with the headship of the department while also trying to finish his *magnum opus*, the biography of Sir George Grey. (As a research assistant in the department, I was his hapless Lucky Jim, asked to check his footnotes.) Perhaps more influential, so far as Master's students were concerned, was Rutherford's offsider, the Marxist Willis Airey, who supervised many of the Master's theses, though he never sought to make converts. Many of us, however, became advocates of the economic interpretation of history in the Tawneyian tradition. Then there was the lively, upcoming Keith Sinclair who was completing his own doctorate, soon to be published as *The Origins of the Maori Wars*, in my view the best of his books and soon to influence my approaches to Maori history. He did not become my supervisor — he was on leave at the time — but he did suggest a field. Since he was working on the pre-New Zealand wars period, he suggested that I might look at the then neglected post-war period. I refined my topic into an examination of the alienation of Maori land under the operations of the Native Land Court and the Native Lands Acts from 1862. But I could hardly deny that there was a personal motive behind it, since I had been nurtured on stories of the alienation of the last remnants of my mother's Maori land. As I worked on my thesis, I became greatly impressed by the Report of the 1890 Native Land Laws Commission, headed by the radical Liberal, W. L. Rees, with its devastating condemnation of the previous 30 years' native land legislation. That report provided a useful closure to my own Master's thesis, though I also looked beyond the alienation of Maori land to the effects of that alienation on Maori social conditions and population, the subject of my first published essay which is reproduced here as chapter 5, 'Land Purchase Methods and their Effect on Maori Population, 1865–1901'.

Having completed my Master's degree, I had the good fortune to spend over three more years in the History Department, first as a research assistant to Professors Rutherford and Rodwell (from Economics), who were editors of a proposed, if never completed, History of the Auckland Province; and then as a junior lecturer when, amongst other things, I had the benefit of being required to deliver a course of lectures on New Zealand history to students at Ardmore Teachers' College. I went to Oxford with considerable experience in historical research. My experience at my college, St Antony's — then a new postgraduate college — and Oxford in general could be described as a second coming. Here, I got onto a new bandwagon: African history, though the Oxford dons, still mired in imperial history of Africa, were not leading the way. The leadership was coming from elsewhere in the United Kingdom and especially from Roland Oliver (at London) and J. D. Fage (at Birmingham). Now the emphasis was on the history of Africa and Africans, rather than that of their imperial rulers, since imperial rule was quickly coming to an end, with one country after another becoming independent. The year 1960 was hailed as 'Africa Year' and at Oxford there was a constant stream of budding African leaders who spoke to enthusiastic audiences. It was in that atmosphere that I took a little time from my African studies to answer a request from Keith Sinclair for a contribution to a *festschrift* for Willis Airey. The result was my essay on the Maori King movement, the sixth in this collection. I cannot pretend that it was not influenced by the efflorescence in African studies that surrounded me. My first exercise in Maori history, as it would now be called, would be my attempt to do for New Zealand history what was hurriedly being constructed for African history. Since then others claimed to have pioneered the subject. My return to the Auckland History Department in 1964 meant that I could resume my activity in New Zealand history, while also pursuing a second string to my bow in African history. But it was the former that remained the main focus of my research and publications.

Over the years, there was a gradual shift in my interests from race relations (especially Maori–Pakeha relations) to the origins and developments of race theory. During sabbatical leaves at Cambridge (in 1973–74) and in London (in 1982) I was able to read my way through the major works, but always with the wonder of how such works might have influenced thought about Maori. My essays 'How to Civilise Savages' and 'Maori Responses to European Domination' (chapters 3 and 8) were first conceived during these sabbaticals. The first was presented to a somewhat puzzled imperial history seminar at Cambridge that was run by Professor J. A. Gallagher, the co-author of a recent classic, *Africa and the Victorians*; the second to a seminar run by Professor Sanderson at the Institute of Colonial Studies in London and sporting the title 'Colonial Rule and Local Response'. Such seminars were preoccupied with Africa and India and it required a stretch of imagination (as well as a need to explain a good deal that was common knowledge to New Zealand students) to provide something relevant about the fate of Maori in this remote corner of empire. There was also the problem that the approach, whereby local natives always responded to European initiatives, was becoming antiquated. Perhaps it was just as important to see how Europeans responded to Indian, African — or Maori — initiatives.

In the early 1980s I finally came to grips with the considerable task of editing the correspondence between Ngata and Buck.[7] That provided me with an opportunity to discuss their attitudes to race theory and the place of Maori in Pakeha assessments when I was invited to deliver the Beaglehole lecture at a conference of the New Zealand Historical Association in 1981. A grand occasion one might well say, but what gave it an added piquancy was that the All Blacks were playing the Springboks in Wellington the next day. Having made some off-the-cuff remarks on how Ngata and Buck may have regarded such an occasion,

I duly delivered the lecture but next day deserted the conference to join the protesters in the streets. My African interests (which had earlier included opposition to apartheid through presidency of the Auckland-based Citizens' Association for Racial Equality) had come full circle with my Maori interests. But it was not until I reached London, on sabbatical leave, in February 1982, that I revised the lecture for publication. It was published in *The Journal of the Polynesian Society* later that year.

My career as an academic historian took a new turning in 1985. In that year the Waitangi Tribunal was given retrospective jurisdiction to examine Maori claims of breaches by the Crown of the principles of the Treaty of Waitangi since it was signed in 1840. It seemed that my previous research on the alienation of Maori land could be valuable for the Tribunal and I was appointed initially as a deputy member (a deputy to a retired judge) but subsequently as a full member to the Tribunal. Over the next 24 years I sat on numerous Tribunal panels that investigated Maori historical claims, and contributed to their reports. The Tribunal experience reinvigorated my university teaching since I replaced a paper on race theory with one on the Treaty and the Tribunal, a paper that went beyond New Zealand to examine treaties (or the lack of them) in other jurisdictions such as Canada, the United States and Australia, as lawyers on the Tribunal or in academic institutions had been doing in Treaty litigation. Since I had not previously studied Native American history, I took the opportunity during a sabbatical leave in 1989 to contact scholars working on Canadian Indian history at Vancouver and spend an extended period reading my way into American Indian history at the McNickle Center for American Indian History at the Newberry Library in Chicago, the largest such collection in the United States. For me, as a New Zealander, there was always the puzzle of why the Native Americans got some 370 treaties, which were largely ignored during the European occupation of their continent, though some large isolated reserves had remained, whereas New Zealand's single Treaty of Waitangi had been forever present, if not always observed. During that and on subsequent sabbatical leaves and at conferences at home and abroad, I now took the opportunity to read papers on our Tribunal and its activities. Chapter 12, 'The Waitangi Tribunal and the Resolution of Maori Grievances', was presented to the New Zealand Present and Future Conference at Edinburgh in May 1994. Chapter 13, 'Waitangi: Ka Whawhai Tonu Matou', had an even more exotic genesis. I prepared it while I was Visiting Professor to the Center for Australian and New Zealand Studies at Georgetown University in Washington DC in 1998 — on the understanding that, like my predecessor in the fellowship,

I would deliver it at the New Zealand Embassy on Waitangi Day. In view of my already considerable experience on the Waitangi Tribunal, I assumed that I was well qualified to deliver such a lecture. But for reasons unknown to me, the then ambassador decided to close the embassy for the day. However, I was invited to Penn State University where I gave the lecture to an appreciative audience. In a final ironic twist, it was published as one of the ANZAC Lectures and Waitangi Addresses ostensibly delivered at the Georgetown Center. I must leave readers to decide whether what I regarded as a mild, appreciative review of the Treaty settlement process was subversive. Historians, who are forever making history in their musings, sometimes become footnotes to that history.

My Tribunal work had scarcely got under way when I was invited by Mr Justice Wallace, chairman of the 1986 Royal Commission on the Electoral System, to prepare a paper on the History of Maori Representation in Parliament. That history, the longest essay in this collection, was published as an appendix to the Commission's report. It explains how the four Maori seats were created in 1867 and why they were still in existence in 1986. The fate of the seats, subsequently increased to seven following the Commission's report, is picked up again in my final chapter. But Maori politics were not confined to their minority representation in the Pakeha parliament, since they long pursued various notions of political separation, or mana motuhake, as emphasised in chapters 6 (on the King movement) and 8 (on Maori responses to European domination).

Needless to say, the essays do not represent final conclusions on any of the subjects discussed. Rather, they should be regarded as my contribution to an ongoing dialogue that has been much stimulated by my long involvement in teaching and researching in the History Department at the University of Auckland; generous provision by that university of overseas sabbatical leave, with opportunities to connect with scholars particularly in the United Kingdom, North America and Africa; and my association with the Waitangi Tribunal processes that have provided a home for my thoughts for a third of my life.

In one way or another, all of the essays are a reflection of the intellectual environment in which they were conceived. They illustrate that historians, no matter how fully committed to objectivity, cannot achieve that long-sought-after dream of the great German historian Leopold von Ranke, of mastering the subject, once and for all, by revealing all that needs to be known. History is forever and historians are always remaking it according to their own lights. Others can refashion mine.

A note on the text

Apart from minor amendments and corrections, the essays in this collection are reproduced substantially in their original form, including orthographical conventions of the day such as italicisation of Maori and various other non-English words in earlier texts, and macronisation in later ones. While there are inconsequential style variations between individual essays, care has been taken to ensure consistency of presentation within each. Similarly, all sources are provided in full in the respective chapter endnotes rather than in a separate bibliography.

Abbreviations

ATL	Alexander Turnbull Library, Wellington
AJHR	*Appendices to the Journals of the House of Representatives*
NA	National Archives of New Zealand
NZPD	*New Zealand Parliamentary Debates*
JPS	*The Journal of the Polynesian Society*
NZJH	*The New Zealand Journal of History*
T&PNZI	*Transactions and Proceedings of the New Zealand Institute*

1

The Whence of the Maori:
Some Nineteenth-century Exercises in Scientific Method

This essay does not attempt a final solution of that consuming passion of New Zealand scholars, the whence of the Maori. Rather, it is an examination of the quest itself, and an assessment of the influence of ideas on the origin of Maori on contemporary attitudes to Maori and their supposed capacity for civilisation. Some theories on the origin of Maori were patently absurd, yet these cannot be scathingly dismissed, for even the wrong ideas tend to have a currency that outlasts their exposure before the plain light of scientific reason.

It is well known that the voyages of Pacific discovery in the late eighteenth century provided a new testing ground for science and stimulated thought on man and his place in nature.[1] In the nineteenth century there was a shift in focus from the oceans to the continents, and particularly to tropical Africa where the discovery by European explorers of apparently primitive African societies emphasised the great disparity between races and seemed to validate the social Darwinist theories of the period. In the Antipodes similar theories were to gain currency, though for slightly different reasons. Here the progress of commerce, Christianity and European colonisation were to reveal differences between Europeans and aborigines that also seemed to validate an assumption of the innate superiority of the white or Caucasian race. Developments in anthropology, linguistics, folklore and archaeology were used by historians — who were themselves beginning to regard their subject as a science — to extend their

Originally published in *The Journal of the Polynesian Society*, vol. 86, no. 4 (1977), pp. 449–78.

quest back in time beyond the range of written documents. Eighteenth-century reason and doctrines of nature were to leave Maori in a somewhat ambiguous position; the nineteenth century was to give them a more assured place, and not merely because scientific inquiry placed them higher in the hierarchy than other races. Christian dogma which eschewed the progressive theory also ranked Maori highly.

Eighteenth-century Voyages of Discovery

The quest for the origin of Maori began in the eighteenth century, if not the seventeenth. Tasman, having lost four men on the New Zealand coast in 1642, did not land or speculate on the origin of the people who had treated him so savagely. But Cook, on first making contact with Maori of the East Coast in 1769, realised that they were related to other Pacific peoples. Cook had previously visited Tahiti where he had taken on board an interpreter, Tupaia, who had little difficulty in conversing with Maori. This happy fact was noted at the time[2] but it was not until they were preparing to leave New Zealand that Cook and his naturalist companion, Joseph Banks, paused in their journals to sum up on the Maori and speculate on their origins:

> Having now given the best account in my power of the customs and opinions of the inhabitants of New Zealand, with their boats, nets, furniture, and dress, I shall only remark, that the similitude between these particulars here and in the South Sea islands is a very strong proof that the inhabitants have the same origin; and that the common ancestors of both, were the natives of the same country. They have both a tradition that their ancestors, at a very remote period of time, came from another country; and, according to the tradition of both, the name of that country was HEAWIJE; but the similitude of the language seems to put the matter altogether out of doubt.[3]

To emphasise the point a vocabulary of over 40 words in Maori and Tahitian was added.

Here Cook and Banks had initiated three methods of inquiry that were to be used with increasing confidence in later years: a comparison of customs and material culture, philology, and oral traditions. Yet they retained a caution that was not to be so evident in later estimates: 'But supposing these islands, and those in the South Seas, to be peopled originally from the same country, it will perhaps for ever remain in doubt what country that is....'[4] They did not believe that the country was America or even the Southern Continent — for they were now very doubtful whether this existed at all — so they simply concluded that the ultimate source of both peoples was somewhere in the west. Neither Cook nor Banks speculated on how Maori might have reached New Zealand, but it is notable that Sydney Parkinson, the artist on the *Endeavour*, held that the canoes they had seen were unsuitable for oceanic navigating. He went on to propose the unlikely theory that Tahiti had been colonised from New Zealand.[5]

Cook's second voyage was to add further speculation on the problem. This time the main source of speculation was John Reinhold Forster who had replaced Banks as naturalist. Forster had with him his son George who wrote up and published the father's diary of the voyage.[6] Having come to New Zealand from Tonga, the Forsters noted that the New Zealanders' dialect was much the same as that of the Tongans. But J. R. Forster was interested in far more than simple linguistic comparisons. He had spent most of his life in Europe and was well acquainted with Continental philosophy and anthropology, particularly the work of J. F. Blumenbach, often described as the father of anthropology. A year after George had published the diary of the voyage, J. R. Forster brought out a rather more ambitious work, *Observations made during a Voyage round the World, on Physical Geography, Natural History, and Ethic Philosophy*. . . . 'My object,' Forster wrote, 'was nature in its greatest extent; the Earth, the Sea, the Air, the Organic and Animated Creation, and more particularly that class of Beings to which we ourselves belong.'[7] He did not quite achieve this soaring ambition; his comments on peoples were confined largely to those he had observed on the voyage. Forster's views on race were orthodox. He accepted the ruling Christian doctrine of monogenesis, *'that all mankind, though ever so much varied, are, however, but one species . . . . descended from one couple'*.[8] He accepted Blumenbach's classification of races and his view that racial differences had been caused largely by environmental factors. Though Forster accepted the philosophical notion that nations progressed from animality to savagery to barbarism and eventually to civilisation, he did believe that climatic factors could bring about degeneration. In a theory, which he appears to have confined to the Southern Hemisphere, Forster held that the natives inhabiting the frozen extremities appeared to be 'degenerated and debased from that original happiness, which the tropical nations more or less enjoy. I was first persuaded into this belief, from the state in which we found the inhabitants of Tierra del Fuego and New Zealand, and by comparing their situation, with that of their neighbours.'[9] Forster thought that even within New Zealand there were considerable differences between the apparently primitive Maori that Cook's expedition had come across in Dusky Sound at the south of the South Island and the more advanced Maori in the North Island. This division of the peoples of the Pacific into hard and soft primitives had some support in eighteenth-century thought, but it was not to endure. Nineteenth-century theorists were more inclined to reverse the climatic factor and favourably to compare the energetic Maori of temperate New Zealand with their 'slothful' cousins of tropical Polynesia.

Some of Forster's other theories were to have rather more lasting significance. He anticipated the division of the peoples of the South Pacific into Melanesians and Polynesians; the former a dark-skinned, small-framed people confined mainly to the western Pacific; the latter a handsome, lighter-coloured, large-limbed people inhabiting the eastern Pacific. The theory did not rely only on physical features since it was also supported by linguistic evidence. Forster assumed that the Polynesians had come into the Pacific by a process of island-hopping from Malaya. He went on to apply the two-race theory to New Zealand. In a passage that was confused by an infusion of his environmental theory, Forster spoke of Malay immigrants who had absorbed an earlier aboriginal people and formed 'a coalition of customs, wherein many points of civilization were totally lost, though the language was taken from the newcomers, and preserved blended with some words of the aboriginal tribe'.[10] The idea of an aboriginal, pre-Maori race, perhaps Melanesian in origin and certainly inferior to Maori, was to linger in the ethnological record.

Nevertheless it was not so much the Forsters as Joseph Banks who was to put the Polynesians into the mainstream of European anthropology. Like Forster, Banks was acquainted with the great Blumenbach whose treatise *On the Natural Variety of Mankind* (1775) had maintained that mankind was one species which was divided into four races — Caucasian, Asiatic, American and Ethiopian. Then, after meeting Banks, Blumenbach added a fifth race to his second edition of 1781: the Malays (who included the Pacific Islanders).[11] The work was further modified for its third edition of 1795 which was dedicated to Banks. Now the races were graded as well as classified. Blumenbach allotted the 'first place' to the Caucasian, the primeval race. This had diverged in two directions — the Ethiopian and the Mongolian. He regarded the Ethiopians who inhabited most of Africa as the most removed from the Caucasians, though he strenuously denied assertions that the Ethiopians were a separate species. The Americans occupied an intermediate position between the Caucasians and the Ethiopians. Finally, it can be noted that Blumenbach, like Forster, was aware of differences among the Pacific Islanders who varied from the 'tawny colour of the Otaheitans . . . to the tawny-black of the New Hollanders'.[12] Subsequent authorities were sometimes to vary the number and names of races, but this basic classification and ranking of the races was to be accepted throughout the nineteenth century; indeed fragments of it still remain in popular usage. The Maori, as members of the Malay race, were quite well placed, since they were not far removed from the 'superior' Caucasians. Later, scholars were to devote much intellectual energy to formulating a more direct connection.

In contrast to the lavish productions which followed from Cook's visits to New Zealand and the Pacific, very little was to be published on the voyages of his French contemporaries. Only a brief summary of de Surville's journal was published — twelve years after his visit to New Zealand. Marion du Fresne's journals were not published, though Lieutenant Crozet's was in 1783, after considerable editorial amendment by Abbé Rochon, as *Nouveau Voyage à la mer du Sud*. Crozet had taken command of the expedition following the death of Marion and 26 of his men at the Bay of Islands in 1772, and his journal is studded with *ex post facto* wisdom. Nevertheless it does contain much useful ethnographic information. Though the French had no interpreter with them, they did have a Tahitian vocabulary and were able to use this to converse with Maori. It is notable that Crozet thought that the New Zealanders were composed of more than one race; indeed in his view there were three: 'true aborigines' with a yellowish-white skin, tall stature and straight black hair; a swarthy, shorter variety with curled hair; and 'true negroes', short and broad in physique and with woolly hair.[13] In a later passage he referred to the 'whites, blacks and yellows', the yellows being a mixture of the whites and the blacks.[14] Some of the whites, he added, were no darker than the French sailors. The assumption that the New Zealanders were composed of two if not three races was to persist. In publishing an English translation of Crozet's journal in 1891, H. Ling Roth said that Crozet was 'very correct', there were two races in the make-up of the New Zealanders, the black or Papuan, and the yellow or Malayo-Polynesian.[15] By the late nineteenth century this was accepted dogma.

During the years between the explorers of the 1770s and the introduction of missionaries into New Zealand by Samuel Marsden in 1814, the published record on New Zealand is slim indeed. There was a good deal of commercial contact, most of it arising from the convict settlements at Sydney and Hobart, and including an intermittent trade in spars, sealing on the shores of the South Island, and a beginning of whaling. But the men who visited New Zealand were not of the kind who would make patient scientific observation of Maori, let alone speculations on their origin. Only one book directly relating to New Zealand was published in the period: Dr John Savage's *Some Account of New*

Zealand (1807) and this does not speculate on the origin or racial characteristics of the Maori. This *Account* probably helped to dispel the Maori reputation for savagery that had stuck to them following the massacre of Marion and his crew; but within a year of the publication of the *Account*, most of the crew of the *Boyd* were massacred at Whangaroa, and it seemed that the Maori reputation was deserved after all. Commercial contacts were reduced and Marsden had to postpone plans for the establishment of a Christian mission.

Missionary Ethnology

Marsden achieved his ambition in 1814 when he proceeded to the Bay of Islands with a 'perfect resemblance to Noah's ark',[16] preached the first sermon on Christmas Day, and left behind three missionaries — Thomas Kendall, John King and William Hall — and their families. The foundation and early history of the mission have been frequently described; here it is sufficient to note the contribution of Marsden and his missionaries to discussion on the origin and racial characteristics of Maori. Needless to say, the missionaries did not approach this task in the spirit of cool and detached scientific inquiry characteristic of the eighteenth-century voyagers. The missionaries came to civilise and convert the savage heathen, not to preserve what they regarded as degraded, inhuman and often obscene customs. Missionaries learnt the Maori language, inquired into their religion, their myths and legends, their systems of *tapu* and their social customs largely as a matter of expediency — so that they could replace them with the 'truths' of Christianity and the moral habits of civilisation. But even this form of inquiry had its dangers: too close an acquaintance with the 'obscenities' of Maori beliefs and behaviour was likely to bring about the fall of the missionary. Such was the fate of Thomas Kendall, who tried earnestly to understand Maori religion but who also had an affair with a Maori girl and traded in muskets.[17] Marsden dismissed him for his sins. However, there were several missionaries who wrote useful accounts of Maori culture: William Yate, William Colenso and Richard Taylor, among the Anglicans; the Wesleyan, Thomas Buddle; and the Catholic, Catherin Servant. Nevertheless the missionary journals, or at least those portions of them that reached the public through the mission periodicals, are poor sources of Maori ethnology. They are, for the early years, a record of missionary trials and tribulations at the hands of truculent heathens, and later of hopeful signs and quickening achievements in the civilisation and conversion of the Maori. Too often Maori customs are not described but simply dismissed as expressions of the domination of Satan.

The role of the missionary in creating the Ignoble Savage needs further investigation, at least in relation to Maori. Certainly it was part of the missionary creed that the Maori, like other heathen, was a fallen if not an irredeemable savage.[18] Because of their firm belief in monogenesis and specifically the Mosaic account of creation, missionaries considered that mankind was one species, though some races, like Maori, had fallen or degenerated since they had dispersed from the biblical cradleland. Such Christian doctrine was bound to be applied to Maori; what was to be important in New Zealand was the way in which it was applied by Marsden and the missionaries.

In New South Wales Marsden had tried, but was rebuffed in his attempts, to civilise and convert the intractable Aborigine.[19] He turned with renewed optimism to the more promising New Zealand Maori. Long before he established the New Zealand mission, Marsden had met and entertained New Zealand chiefs in Sydney; he was impressed by their proud demeanour, their intelligence and their enterprise. In almost every way the Maori seemed to be superior to the Australian Aborigines who were already coming to be classed as one of the lowest races known to mankind. Indeed those who accepted the doctrine of a Chain of Being had begun to classify Aborigines, along with the hapless Hottentots, as the last links between man and the apes. Christian doctrine would not allow them to be set aside as a separate species, but it did group them with the coloured sons of Ham who were forever cursed and required to serve the white man.[20] In contrast, Maori were classified by Marsden and the missionaries as having descended from the sons of Shem.

By suggesting that the Maori had sprung from dispersed Jews who had somehow got from Asia to New Zealand, Marsden was to lay the scent for one of the great nineteenth-century hunts for the whence of the Maori. Marsden's case for the Semitic Maori was based mainly on biblical precedents; he was able to find numerous points of comparison between Maori customs and those of the Jews of the Old Testament. When Maori went to war their priests addressed them in language similar to that of the Jewish high priests (Deuteronomy: XX,2,3,4); when a chief fell in battle, Maori cut off his head and preserved it as a trophy, as David did with Goliath's head or, as was done with Ahab's sons when Jehu rebelled against him (Second Book of Kings: X); the burning of the bodies of Maori chiefs was like the burning of Saul and his sons when they were killed by the Philistines (First Book of Samuel: V,11,12). Maori cannibalism displayed in the drinking of blood and eating the flesh of vanquished chiefs could, in Marsden's view, have been 'derived from Divine revelation. Our Saviour told the Jews: "He that eateth my flesh and drinketh my blood dwelleth in me and I in him'". It was a rather dangerous precedent to let loose on the lively intelligence of Maori; one day it would boomerang on the missionaries. Nor was Marsden content to rest on biblical precedents. As one who was not lacking in the commercial instinct, he was quick to note a similar facility in Maori, though this too was attributed to their Semitic origin. Like the Jews, Marsden wrote, Maori had a 'great natural turn for traffic; they will buy and sell anything they have got'.[21] Marsden was not to be alone in the quest for a Semitic Maori.

J. L. Nicholas, who accompanied Marsden on his first voyage to New Zealand, expounded the same theory. Nicholas thought the Maori had descended from a people familiar with the Mosaic account of creation and, having spent a period in India, had since degenerated from a high state of civilisation into barbarism. Like Marsden, Nicholas was able to find biblical precedents for various Maori customs and beliefs — for instance their belief that the first woman was formed from the ribs of man; their custom of sprinkling children with water on naming them.[22] And, on a slightly different but no less significant tack, Nicholas suggested that certain Maori words could be derived from Sumatra and ultimately from Sanscrit.[23] With the growth of Aryan studies in British India, Britain and Europe in the nineteenth century, there was much to encourage New Zealand exponents of the genre to expand on Nicholas's suggestion. But in the meantime it was the pursuit of the Semitic origins of Maori that held the field.

It is unnecessary to follow all the ramifications of the Christian comparative anthropology set off by Marsden's speculations. It is sufficient to note that in the next 20 years or so many who published works on the Maori were to take up and illustrate the theme. Craik, Marshall, FitzRoy, Polack, Dieffenbach and Mundy are notable examples.[24] But undoubtedly the most persuasive advocate of all was the Anglican missionary Richard Taylor, who was perhaps the best and certainly the most enthusiastic of the missionary ethnologists. Taylor's *Te Ika a Maui* (1855) was an attempt 'to rescue from that oblivion into which they are fast hastening, the Manners, Customs, Traditions, and Religion of a primitive race'.[25] A critic of the 'progressive development doctrine' — soon to receive the *imprimatur* of Darwin — Taylor saw in the history and traditions of Maori proof of the alternative theory of degeneration, reflected in their language, their material culture and their religion. The 'beautiful parable' of the prodigal son had its

> literal fulfilment in the history of the New Zealand race; in it may we not behold one of the lost tribes of Israel, which, with its fellows, having abandoned the service of the true God, and cast aside his Word, fell step by step in the scale of civilization; deprived

of a fixed home, become nomadic wanderers over the steppes of Asia, a bye-word and a reproach among the nations, and gradually retreated until in the lapse of ages they reached the sea, and thence, still preserving their wandering character, from island to island driven by winds and currents, and various causes, they finally reached New Zealand, and there fallen to their lowest stage of degradation, given up to the fiercest passions, consumed, and being consumed, they are enabled to reflect, repent, and amend, and resolve to arise and go to their Father.[26]

Taylor reiterated these points in a second edition of the book in 1870 but the assumption of a Jewish ancestry for Maori was already coming under criticism on a number of fronts. Those who, like Taylor, took up the study of language, material culture and religion were still to trace Maori back to the East, but in the later nineteenth century most were to provide them with an Aryan rather than a Semitic ancestry.

There has always been a tendency to assume that remote New Zealand was an intellectual backwater, completely out of touch with the latest developments in the arts and science; but this has never been particularly true, even in the early days of the colony when it took at least ten weeks for ships to reach the country from Britain. Many of the early colonists were highly educated men who in New Zealand continued to take *The Times* and the literary and scientific reviews. They were quick to form Mechanics Institutes (which in New Zealand, as in Britain, tended to be patronised by the middle class), and philosophical and debating societies. Darwin's *Origin of Species* was soon serialised in colonial newspapers and his theory of evolution was debated as keenly in New Zealand as it was in Britain.[27] New Zealand and its Maori were still regarded as admirable fields for the cultivation of the arts and sciences, not least that budding science of anthropology. But this had not yet come under the sway of Darwinian evolution. Indeed it was to remain for some time under the influence of speculative historians, folklorists, and comparative anthropologists who saw in the collection of myths and legends, random information on ancient institutions, and in the customs of contemporary savages a means of arriving at an estimate of mankind in its chrysalis stage.[28] New Zealand Maori provided numerous examples for the armchair anthropologists, just as their theories and techniques were eagerly applied by New Zealand colonists to the problem of the origin of the Maori. The most notable developments from the mid-century were in physical anthropology (now being influenced by phrenology), folklorism, philology and archaeology; all of them tended to upset the missionary view of the Semitic Maori.

Physical Anthropology

In the early nineteenth century physical anthropology was based largely on casual observation. Visitors to New Zealand in the first two or three decades of the nineteenth century were usually content to reiterate or elaborate the observations of the British or French explorers. Thus Dumont d'Urville, the French navigator who visited New Zealand three times between 1824 and 1840, followed Crozet in asserting that the New Zealanders were made up of three racial groups. He did add that the 'whites had come last and conquered the existing inhabitants' — an assumption that was to have later nineteenth-century echoes. And d'Urville seems to have been the first to divide the Pacific Islanders into Polynesians, Melanesians and Micronesians, a division that was in general usage by about 1830 and is accepted today.[29] The trader J. L. Polack, though familiar with Crozet, reverted to the two-race theory of Forster so far as Maori were concerned: a superior race, Malay in origin, an 'olive, or copper-coloured race . . . a noble people, often above six feet in stature . . . . of dignified appearance . . . . the hair glossy, black, and curling, and the features approaching to the European'; and an inferior race, Papuan in origin, and seen particularly on the East Coast, 'short in stature; hair lank, or frizzly; complexion brown, approaching to black, and the expression of the features often insidious'.[30] Physical anthropology had not advanced far beyond Linnaeus and Blumenbach; races were still judged by the extent to which their appearance and especially skin colour approached the superior Europeans. In the circumstances some at least of the Maori almost made the grade. But Polack, like others of his time who also applied this conventional wisdom on race, tended to confuse race with class. Though he spoke of the 'inferior' race being common on the East Coast, he and others also thought that the slave class was made up of the 'inferior' race, an assumption that was probably based merely on the unkempt appearance of the slaves. Yet the two-race theory was to survive the nineteenth century; later observers were to bolster it with scientific data.

Not all of these later observers need be discussed, though one or two who added something to the pursuit are worth mentioning. Ernst Dieffenbach, the New Zealand Company naturalist, divided the peoples of the South Seas into Malay-Polynesians and Austral-Negroes and found traces of both in New Zealand. The former were the superior race, light-skinned and 'Caucasian' in their features; the latter were inferior and generally burdened with the heavy work. But Dieffenbach did not rest his case on casual observation. He called in the findings of phrenology. The Maori of the superior Malay-Polynesian race, in addition to being tall, muscular and handsome, had a cranium that 'often approaches in shape the best and most intellectual European heads'. Though the heads were 'showing a great amount of animal propensities' these were not 'in undue preponderance over the intellectual'.[31] The phrenological craze had hit New Zealand and was to be taken up with enthusiasm though no more enlightenment by the likes of William Brown, a prominent early settler and politician in Auckland, and even the hapless Governor FitzRoy.[32] Nevertheless it would seem that neither phrenology nor its rather more 'scientific' cousin, craniology, made much progress in New Zealand or the Pacific.

One who did attempt to apply the latest techniques in craniometry was A. S. Thomson, who spent eleven years in New Zealand as surgeon to the 58th Regiment. As befitted a man of science, Thomson conducted precise measurements:

> It was ascertained, by weighing the quantity of millet seed skulls contained and by measurements with tapes and compasses, that New Zealanders' heads are smaller than the heads of Englishmen, consequently the New Zealanders are inferior to the English in mental capacity. This comparative smallness of the brain is produced by neglecting to exercise the higher faculties [sic] of the mind, for as muscles shrink from want of use, it is only natural that generations of mental indolence should lessen the size of brains. In support of this inference, intelligent travellers [he cites in a footnote Sir Charles Lyell, the geologist] have already detected that the heads of the negro race in the United States are becoming more developed from the intellectual career they are now pursuing.[33]

It seems scarcely necessary today to add that Thomson's conclusions were completely unfounded, since mental capacity does not depend on brain size. What must be said for Thomson is that he was applying in New Zealand the best of conventional scientific wisdom. The same kind of experiments had been carried out in Britain and the United States, with the same kind of results, and the same inferences drawn; the Anglo-Saxon skull was always the largest; the negroid (and in some experiments, the Aboriginal) skull was always the smallest. What tended to be overlooked were the tremendous variations in the number of skulls chosen to 'represent' each race — often from fewer than ten of one kind compared with over 100 of another — and that there was no control over the number of female or juvenile skulls included in some of the samples. Even then it often turned out that no two measurers could come up with the same measurements for the same skull.[34] Thomson's experiment was probably just as unsound since he gave no details of the number of skulls used; and, as has been suggested, even if it had been perfectly conducted, his inferences would still have been invalid.

Thomson carried out two other scientific experiments that are of interest. Using a sample of 100 men from his regiment and another 100 Maori men, he tried to test their bodily strength. He found that on an average the Maori men were able to lift 367 lb an inch from the ground, whereas the Englishmen could lift 422 lb. Thomson attributed the defeat of the Maori to the large amount of potato in their diet. In the other experiment he found that the Maori were faster over 100 yards but that the English won easily over a mile. He seems to have been quite pleased with the results: 'Persons who delight in thinking that the human race degenerates physically after ages of civilization, will be surprised to learn that the New Zealanders are not equal to the English in bodily strength.'[35] Thomson was viewing the Maori 90 years after Cook, and was well aware that his assessment of their physical and mental capacity was less favourable than that usually given. But he was writing in the year of *The Origin of Species*, and it would not be long before his scientific measurements, like Darwin's, would be called in to explain the passing of the Maori as a consequence of 'the survival of the fittest races'. But in New Zealand few were to follow Thomson's lead in scientific anthropology, though photos of Maori heads were sometimes used to illustrate texts in craniology.

The only notable case before the end of the century was Dr J. H. Scott's 'Contribution to the Osteology of the Aborigines of New Zealand and of the Chatham Islands'. Scott was Professor of Anatomy at Otago University's medical school and was familiar with overseas developments in craniology. His paper was replete with the forbidding terminology that had developed in the subject: he provided, among other things, measurements of the cranial capacity, the facial angle and the cephalic index of 83 Maori skulls from museums and private collections. He claimed that these (and measurements from skulls in other collections) proved that the Maori were of mixed Polynesian and Melanesian stock, the former characterised by heads that were 'shorter and broader, with orthognathous faces', the latter 'long and narrow, high in proportion to their breadth, prognathous, and with wide nasal openings'.[36] But physical measurements of living specimens were not so easy: after all, no important chief would willingly submit his *tapu* head to the craniologist's tape measure. At the turn of the century S. Percy Smith lamented that no comprehensive study of the craniology of the Polynesian race had yet been made.[37] So far as the Maori were concerned, nothing was done until another product of the Otago Medical

School, Te Rangi Hiroa (P. H. Buck), obtained a captive sample of men in the Maori Battalion in 1919 to produce the first comprehensive exercise in Maori somatology.[38]

Folklore

Maori oral traditions, myths and legends offered another promising means of inquiry. Here at least the Maori readily — some would say, too readily — co-operated with European inquirers. As has been noted, Cook and Banks picked up a tradition that the Maori had come to New Zealand from 'Heawije' (Hawaiki), the mystical homeland in the Pacific which was to figure in all later migration traditions. John Ledyard, who was with Cook on the third voyage, said that 'after a laboured enquiry' Maori informants had admitted that their forefathers had come at a remote period from 'Hawyjee'.[39] But the missionaries, with one or two notable exceptions, do not appear to have been interested in collecting oral traditions. As Edward Shortland, a pioneer collector of such traditions, pointed out: 'They came to teach a religion, and not to learn the principles of superstitions, which, however valuable in reference to matters of ethnological interest, they regarded as having for their author the great enemy of mankind.'[40] What inquiry had been conducted was largely designed to establish the Maori connection with the Mosaic record: 'Some persons have imagined that they could trace in the traditions of the New Zealanders vestiges of the principal historical facts recorded by Moses. But I must confess, that my inquiries on these subjects have led me to arrive at very different conclusions.' Thus he noted how a certain missionary claimed to have discovered from the Maori a tradition of the Deluge but Shortland, on questioning the same people, found 'that the Deluge of his imagination was no more than a remarkable flood, which had overwhelmed a village several generations ago'.[41] But the missionaries were not the last eager inquirers whose leading questions produced the answers they expected.

For reasons that still remain obscure, detailed oral traditions of the Maori migration from Hawaiki began to appear on the eve of European colonisation of New Zealand. Probably the first to gather such traditions was the missionary James Hamlin who, in the course of a journey south of Auckland in 1838, picked up information on four canoes from Hawaiki — *Tainui*, *Arawa*, *Mataatua* and *Kurahaupo*.[42] Then in 1840 Horatio Hale, a member of the United States Exploring Expedition, obtained more detail from some old men at the Bay of Islands. They gave him a list of the principal chiefs and their canoes. The list included two canoes mentioned by Hamlin, *Tainui* and *Te Arawa*, and two new ones, *Horouta* and *Takitimu*, but it did not include *Mataatua* and *Kurahaupo*.

Hale was also given information on the landing places of the canoes in New Zealand, and was told something of their journey:

> A fleet of canoes . . . set sail (we may suppose) from Savaii to Tonga, between which places a constant communication has been kept up from the earliest times. Before they reached their destination, a gale in the direction of the southeast trades struck them and obliged them in order not to be driven towards the Feejee Islands, to lie up to the southwest. In this way they were carried into the zone of the westerly winds south of the tropics, and finally brought to New Zealand.[43]

This is an interesting statement, since it contains the ingredients of much later controversy. Hale is probably the first to have suggested that the Maori migrated to New Zealand in a 'fleet', an assumption that was apparently confirmed in later and more detailed collections of oral tradition. But Hale also said that there was an element of accident in Maori voyaging, a theory that had already been suggested by the Rev. J. D. Lang in 1834 and was to be more persuasively advanced by Andrew Sharp in 1956.[44]

After 1840 the collection of oral traditions became a matter of some urgency and lists of migration canoes were commonly appended to discussions of the early history of the Maori. Dieffenbach, writing in 1843, urged all travellers to collect Maori traditions before they were lost forever; otherwise it would be difficult to trace Maori history back to Malaya. He collected some traditions relating to the *Arawa*, *Tainui* and *Mataatua* canoes.[45] In 1846–47 John White obtained information on the first Northland canoe to be mentioned so far, *Matahoura*. He was to go on collecting oral traditions for the rest of his life, and in the 1880s was to publish a massive six volumes of *The Ancient History of the Maori* (and much more was to remain unpublished). Then there was Edward Shortland who, as a Sub-Protector of Aborigines, had to represent Maori interests in some of the land claims inquiries in the early 1840s. He was involved in Colonel Godfrey's inquiry into South Island land claims in 1843–44 and collected a mass of genealogical information going back some fifteen or sixteen generations. Shortland was so confident in the accuracy of these traditions that he proposed a Maori history of the South Island: 'The history of the migrations, and wars, and losses, and triumphs of the tribe, generation after generation, seemed to be preserved in their retentive memories, handed down from father to son nearly in the same words as originally delivered.'[46] Shortland also served in the Bay of Plenty and once more took the opportunity to gather oral traditions, this time from tribes descended from the *Tainui*, *Arawa* and *Mataatua* canoes. On the basis of this material and the traditions he had collected in the South Island, Shortland concluded that the Maori had come to New Zealand some eighteen generations or 500 years earlier.[47] It was probably the first use of the genealogical method which was to become the main means of dating Maori migrations. Finally, Shortland tried to locate Hawaiki, but he fell into the temptingly simple trap of accepting Hawaii, as the Sandwich Islands were now coming to be called. He assumed, without explanation, that the Maori had navigated over almost 4000 miles of the Pacific Ocean from Hawaii to New Zealand.

Despite Shortland's pioneering work, the most notable collector of oral tradition, myths and legends in the mid-nineteenth century was Sir George Grey, Governor of New Zealand from 1845 to 1853 and 1861 to 1867. For Grey the collection of Maori folklore was more than a hobby. On his arrival Grey found that the Maori were in revolt in various parts of the country. He decided that he could neither control nor conciliate 'a numerous and turbulent people, with whose language, manners, customs, religion, and mode of thought I was quite unacquainted'.[48] So, Grey continued, he felt compelled to learn the language, myths, proverbs and customs of the Maori. Whenever he consulted chiefs in an official capacity he also took the opportunity to question them on myths and legends, and he made a habit of keeping chiefs in residence with him at Government House. Grey's first collection was destroyed by fire, but he started again and, on his first departure from New Zealand, he published *Ko Nga Mahinga a Nga Tupuna Maori* (1854). This was to reappear in translation as *Polynesian Mythology and the Ancient Traditional History of the New Zealand Race, as furnished by their priests and chiefs* (1855). As Grey's subtitle implies, this was more than a collection of mythology. It included oral traditions relating to Hawaiki, the discovery of New Zealand by Ngahue and Kupe, preparations for the migration to New Zealand, and the voyages of several of the canoes to New Zealand. *Polynesian Mythology* was to go through numerous editions and establish Grey in the front rank of colonial folklorists; it became a standard source for collected editions of 'savage' folklore. Some of the leading evolutionary anthropologists like E. B. Tylor were in touch with Grey and drew on *Polynesian Mythology* for material on Polynesian migrations and distribution. Max Müller, the Sanscrit scholar who held a chair of comparative linguistics at Oxford, called on it for material on solar myths — comparing the Maui myth with those of the Greeks and the Aryans.[49] These European scholars were primarily interested in Maori and other 'savage' folklore in their quest for comparative evidence of the early history of the Aryans in Europe; later, New

Zealanders including Edward Tregear, S. Percy Smith and J. Macmillan Brown were to take up their techniques to unravel the supposed relation of Maori to the eastern branches of the Aryans.

Grey was aware that Maori myths and legends contained a large element of fiction but he considered them in no way inferior to those of the Scandinavians, Saxons and Celts. 'It must further be borne in mind,' Grey added, 'that the native races, who believed in these traditions or superstitions are in no way deficient in intellect, and in no respect incapable of receiving the truths of Christianity ....'[50] Grey saw in the collection of Maori myths and legends a means of understanding and more effectively governing Maori; and in the replacement of their former superstitions by the truths of Christianity the fulfilment of the civilising mission. The Rev. Richard Taylor had a similar aim. He hoped that knowledge of Maori myths and legends, manners and customs would help to induce respect for Maori. And he saw in mythology 'an important aid in ascertaining the locality, from whence it [the Maori race] originally sprung'.[51] He went on to list Maori gods, denying that they had knowledge of a Supreme Being, and then passed to Maori legends, listing thirteen canoes by which the Maori migrated to New Zealand. Though there were discrepancies in the canoe traditions, Taylor claimed that the main stories were known in every part of the country; 'we have a sure proof that the general tradition is correct, and that the natives have a more accurate account of the founders of their race than either the English or Spanish have of theirs in America'.[52] Taylor also appealed to linguistic evidence, noting some affinities between Maori and Sanscrit and, as had been pointed out, to the Mosaic record.

Once more it was Thomson who in the 1850s provided the most satisfactory synthesis of evidence on the origin of Maori. He applied a necessary scepticism to the theories that had been expounded:

> In the mythology of the New Zealanders classical readers may trace chaos; biblicists many texts in Genesis, and geologists forces which have given the earth its present formation.
>
> There are many who see in the fishing up of the land from the sea by Maui a type of the flood, detect a resemblance between the names of Noah and Maui, and a similarity between many Scriptural and Maori customs. In the transmigration of souls to certain animals, in the wooden images of the New Zealanders, and in some of the attributes of their gods, a faint indication is given, which becomes more clear when connected with other things, that the New Zealand race have had intercourse with men holding the Hindoo faith.[53]

Thomson accepted the now widely held view that the Polynesians had migrated to the Pacific from Malaya, though he added that they must have left the mainland before 1278 when Islam arrived and Arabic words began to be absorbed into the Malay language. Though no such words were to be found in Polynesian dialects, these and Malay had similar roots and structure. Thomson made a better guess at the location of Hawaiki than the other writers of the period, suggesting Savai'i of the Samoan group, but adding that the canoes must have come through the Cook Islands. Like Hale, Thomson spoke of a fleet of canoes which started together but which was subsequently scattered by a storm. Though Thomson was aware of the claim that Polynesian voyagers could navigate by the stars, he also noted accounts of canoes on inter-island journeys being driven off course by storms. Thomson also tried to establish an accurate chronology. On the basis of available genealogies he calculated that the fleet had arrived in New Zealand some 20 generations before. Using an English regnal chronology, dated from William the Conqueror, which gave an average reign of 22.1/35 years, Thomson concluded that the Maori fleet had arrived in New Zealand in 1420.[54] The method, subject to variations in the length of the Polynesian generation, was to be used by several later authorities. Finally, Thomson added another calculation to support his genealogically based chronology. Assuming that the fleet had carried some 800 Maori and that their population had doubled itself every 55 years, he calculated that they would have numbered some 100,000 souls by the time of Cook's visits. As Thomson pointed out, this was the number estimated by Forster. Further inquiries into Maori oral traditions and further exercises in the genealogical method, especially by Smith, were apparently to confirm Thomson's findings.

Yet there were some nagging doubts even to those who were primarily concerned with oral traditions. Hochstetter, for instance, quoted the work of C. Schirren on Polynesia to the effect that oral traditions did not convey historical truth, but mythology.[55] Hawaiki was the place from which their fathers came and to which spirits departed. Maui, god of these nether regions, was also the first man; so also the first migrants to New Zealand (or other Polynesian islands) hailed from Hawaiki. Each tribe endeavoured to trace its descent from one of the mythical heroes to establish a claim to this or that piece of country, a point that was soon to be borne out in Maori claims for land argued before the Native Land Court. Moreover, oral traditions which were the remembered history of the conquerors were not a very reliable guide to earlier people who had been vanquished or absorbed by the 'fleet' Maori.

Archaeology

Archaeology provided another kind of information on this problem. This new mid-nineteenth-century science was quickly applied in New Zealand to the whence of the Maori. It arose largely as a by-product of that other great quest of nineteenth-century science in New Zealand, the search for the moa.[56] Fossil remains of a giant bird were discovered by several missionaries and Polack in the late 1830s. On the basis of their reports, the distinguished geologist and palaeontologist Professor Owen read a paper in London in November 1839. He claimed that 'there had existed and perhaps still existed in New Zealand a race of struthious birds of larger and more colossal size than the ostrich or any known species'. Owen produced a sketch of remarkable accuracy. Copies of his paper were soon available in New Zealand and added stimulus to the hunt for the moa or its remains. Maori co-operated in the search readily enough, providing enthusiastic European collectors with moa bones, and with information on midden sites. (One story, perhaps apocryphal, says that the name is not derived from the common Polynesian term for the domestic fowl, but merely from the urgent European demand for 'more bones, more bones'.) But there seems to have been little if any reference to the moa in Maori oral traditions and legends, though in response to urgent European inquiries numerous stories gained currency that the Maori had indeed known the moa.[57] These can be discounted, since Maori were adept at obliging their interrogators, and not above taking some wry satisfaction from garnishing their tales; the story-teller should be worthy of his hire. But what could not be discounted was evidence which came to light of an archaeological association of man and the moa. In 1843 Taylor came across moa bones in association with what looked like Maori ovens and artefacts in southern Taranaki. W. B. Mantell examined the site and supported Taylor's conclusions. Similar evidence was revealed at Opito (Coromandel Peninsula) in 1850, Sumner (near Christchurch) in 1851, Awamoa (South Canterbury) in 1852, and at numerous other South Island sites in the next 20 years. At some of these sites enormous quantities of moa bones were uncovered and, since no live moa were discovered, despite the extensive exploration of the South Island during the gold rushes of the 1860s, it seemed probable that the moa had been exterminated by the people who had hunted it.

These were exciting discoveries but they did not in themselves clear up the mystery of the pre-fleet inhabitants. Archaeology in New Zealand, as in Europe, had not developed far beyond the fossicking of antiquarians. Progress in geology had encouraged closer attention to stratigraphy, but there were as yet few controls over excavations, let alone precise methods of dating. There was great danger that sites would be ruined by careless digging up of fossils for private or museum collections. Fortunately, in Julius von Haast, New Zealand had one archaeologist who was able to rise above these temptations. In a series of carefully controlled excavations in the South Island in the 1860s and 1870s, notable for a careful attention to stratigraphy, von Haast came close to establishing what was ultimately to be accepted as the basic story of the 'Moa Hunters', as he called these early New Zealand inhabitants. Mainly as a result of his Rakaia excavations, von Haast concluded that the Moa Hunters had extinguished the moa long before the arrival of the fleet Maori; so long ago, in fact, that no reliable traditions relating to the moa had survived. The Moa Hunters were regarded as being of a lower civilisation than the fleet Maori, but were, nevertheless, of Polynesian origin, and had perhaps descended from a canoe-load accidentally driven off course in a storm. Eighty years later Roger Duff, following exhaustive excavations at Wairua bar, concluded in *The Moa-Hunter Period of Maori Culture* (1950) that the Moa Hunters were indeed of Polynesian stock. But in the meantime von Haast's theses had been contradicted by other authorities and he had recanted. Walter Mantell, Sir James Hector and, in 1891, the president of the New Zealand branch of the Royal Society, Sir James Hutton, laid down that the moa had been exterminated soon after the fleet Maori had occupied New Zealand. As L. M. Groube has pointed out, this decision was based on the genealogical not the archaeological record;[58] archaeology, instead of providing a corrective of oral traditions, was merely being called on to buttress their apparent truth. It was to take archaeology 50 years to recover its proper role in New Zealand prehistory.

Oral Traditions and the Genealogical Method
The later nineteenth century was to witness a great flowering of Maori oral tradition. As has been suggested, Grey, Shortland and Taylor laid the foundations for collecting oral traditions, myths and legends in the 1850s. Numerous other Maori and Pakeha were to build on their work. Shortland had found the sorting out of Maori oral traditions on their colonisation of New Zealand a necessary means of settling Maori land claims: a method that was akin to the searching for a good root title in English conveyancing.[59] The method was to be considerably expanded with the establishment of the Native Land Court in 1865. The court was presided over by European judges, assisted by Maori assessors. It was to adjudicate ownership of land according to Maori custom and decided to award titles on the basis of occupation in 1840, when New Zealand became a British colony. This was not as simple a matter as it seemed since

occupation was not always clearly established by 1840 and there were invariably several contending claimants. The court became involved in hearing and adjudicating on long and conflicting recitals of tribal history going back to the founding canoes and beyond; a history that was much laced with genealogy. Since the evidence was carefully written down, the Native Land Court minute books became vast repositories of oral tradition, and the judgments that were founded on them significant exercises in historical interpretation. This great body of material has never been thoroughly scrutinised by historians, but it cannot be accepted at face value. The evidence itself was often distorted by the determination of Maori witnesses (and their European backers) to persuade the judges to accept their claims; and the judgments, however objective in intent, were merely designed to ascertain the valid claimants in 1840.[60] Thus, in so far as the judgments were a record of history, they suffered from the same faults of other oral traditions — they recorded the history of the successful. In 1840 these were the tribes which, like Ngapuhi, had earliest access to muskets and did well out of the wars that followed; several of the other successful tribes were descended from canoes of the 'fleet'. Not surprisingly, some of the judges of the court became experts in Maori oral traditions and enthusiasts in the pursuit of the whence of the Maori. F. D. Fenton, the first Chief Judge, published a collection of *Important Judgements Delivered in the Native Land Court, 1866–1879* and in 1885 some *Suggestions for a History of the Origins and Migrations of the Maori People*. The latter was a curious work which gave the Maori a Chaldean origin; it was more in keeping with the early nineteenth-century theories that classed the Maori as Semites. But most of Fenton's contemporaries now concluded that the Maori were of Aryan origin. Another judge, J. A. Wilson, published *Sketches of Ancient Maori Life and History* in 1894 while Colonel Gudgeon, who had been a judge in the Compensation Court, established to hear Maori claims arising from the confiscations during the wars of the 1860s, and went on to become administrator and a judge in the Cook Islands, wrote a series of articles on the whence of the Maori.[61] Gudgeon, his brother-in-law Elsdon Best, and above all Percy Smith were to co-ordinate and direct the search for the Polynesian cradleland when they formed the Polynesian Society in 1892. Smith became and remained until his death in 1922 the editor of the society's journal, which under his editorship devoted much of its space to the quest. Several of Smith's major contributions, including *Hawaiki* and *The Lore of the Whare Wananga*, were first published by the *Journal of the Polynesian Society*.[62]

Earlier in the century oral traditions had been collected to help to preserve a record of what was thought to be a fast-dying culture. This remained an objective but in the later nineteenth century rather more was expected of Maori oral traditions. For instance, the Rev. J. F. H. Wohlers suggested in 1874 that: 'Ethnology might be assisted if all who are in a position among uncivilized races to do so, would make themselves acquainted with their mythology and ancient tales, and then communicate the results to scientific men, who might thereby trace the development and migration of the races.'[63] Could oral traditions, and beyond them myths and legends, provide scientific men with the keys to the ultimate origin of the Maori? Certainly some of the older hands like the veteran collector and former missionary printer, William Colenso, were sceptical. Some writers, he complained in 1865, had stated their 'full belief' in Maori migration traditions and, 'believing, of course, *all* their genealogical statements' had gone on to assume that Maori had been in New Zealand for no longer than 500 years. Nor did Colenso accept the tradition that Maori explorers like Kupe, having discovered New Zealand, returned to Hawaiki and sent out emigrants:

> In all this mythical rhapsody there is scarcely a grain of truth; and yet some educated Europeans have wholly believed it! The New Zealanders themselves however, never did so. The names of the canoes and of the leaders are nearly all figurative names suitably coined in the New Zealand tongue, and given after the event; several of the latter being also the names of ideal beings in their mythology. . . . Their adventures on the way . . . (excelling those of Munchausen, or Gulliver), are suited, perhaps, for the region of romance, but ought to have no place in any reasonable enquiry.[64]

Another sceptic, W. T. L. Travers, said that the migration traditions 'are, so far as they pretend to give historical accounts . . . pure fictions; and . . . so far as they represent events at all, they only represent comparatively recent occurrences, which have been engrafted upon the leading idea by some imaginative minds.'[65] But such warnings were unheeded. Later recorders of Maori traditions, like Smith and his protégé Elsdon Best, came to have such unbounded faith in their Maori informants that their information was regarded as historical truth. To Smith the genealogical method was the key to the whence of the Maori.

The most significant and influential example of his work was *Hawaiki: The Original Home of the Maori; with a sketch of Polynesian History*. It was not based solely on the oral traditions of New Zealand Maori. Smith collected many traditions and genealogies from Te Ariki-tara-are, one of the high chiefs of Rarotonga, in 1897. Indeed it was largely on the basis of the Rarotongan traditions that Smith was able to trace the Polynesians back to India, though he admitted that the Indian side of it was 'weak' through lack of books on India itself.[66] Smith says little about his genealogical method. He regretted that European ethnologists were apt to discredit oral traditions but to him it was 'an axiom that all tradition is based on fact — whilst the details may be wrong, the main stem is generally right'.[67] Since the Polynesians had no sense of chronology, Smith decided to add dates calculated from the collected genealogies. Here he was following the example of earlier writers like Thomson, though none of these had attempted to construct so precise and lengthy a chronology as Smith. He also had before him Fornander's massive study, *The Polynesian Race* (1878), based mainly on the oral traditions of Hawaii. Fornander had adopted a European model in averaging the generations at 30 years but Smith used a 25-year generation on the ground that the Polynesians married earlier than Europeans. He worked back in time, starting from New Zealand. On the basis of some 50 genealogies he calculated that the Maori of the great fleet had come to New Zealand 21 generations before, in 1350, a date that was to become as firmly fixed in the chronology of New Zealand history as 1642, 1769 and 1840. Next Smith compared genealogies from New Zealand, Rarotonga, Tahiti and Hawaii and noted that all had several common ancestors like the Maori Whiro (or, as he was called in other dialects, Hiro or Iro) and his brother Hira. Smith concluded that the brothers had lived about 100 years before the fleet had left for New Zealand. His calculation of the earlier dates for Polynesian migration was based on Rarotongan material, though Smith admitted that this was not reliable beyond 40 or 50 generations. Nevertheless he felt able to date the Polynesian departure from India, which he regarded as their original homeland, at about 450 BC. At the end of his book he printed a chronological table of Polynesian migration:

450	BC	India
65	"	Java
450	AD	Fiji-Samoa
650	"	Hawaii
675	"	Marquesas
850	"	Maku visits New Zealand
1150	"	Toi visits New Zealand
1175	"	Moriori to New Zealand and Chathams
1250–1325	"	Voyages to New Zealand of Paoa, Tumana, Kupe, Ngahue et al.
1350	"	Voyage of the Great Fleet to New Zealand

Later, in his *History and Traditions of the Taranaki Coast* (1907), Smith modified his pre-fleet chronology for New Zealand to make Kupe the discoverer of the country in 925.[68]

Smith's dates were long to remain as the accepted chronology of early New Zealand history. Their authenticity was reinforced by his publication of *The Lore of the Whare Wananga* in 1912–15. This was based on the oral traditions recited by two old *tohunga*, Te Matarohanga and Nepia Pohuhu, and taken down by a part-European scribe, Whatahoro Jury. The tangled history of this lore has only recently been unravelled by D. R. Simmons who has pointed out that the process of recording, transcribing and interpreting the traditions by Jury and then Smith had added a considerable amount of 'rationalisation' to the originals; and in particular that the idea of a precise chronology which included a great fleet was more the product of fertile European imagination than genuine Maori traditions.[69] Though Smith cannot be accused of having invented the great fleet, he did give it a spurious authenticity with his scientific genealogical methods.

In tracing the Polynesians back to India Smith was in accord with the bulk of contemporary opinion on their ethnic origin.[70] For by the end of the nineteenth century most authorities believed that the Polynesians were of Aryan stock. Smith thought that they had come from a people similar or akin to the Nagas. Both peoples were originally of Aryan or closely related stock. As Smith put it, the Polynesians were 'generally acknowledged now to be a branch of the Caucasian race'. He thought it probable that 'the handsome, tall, oval-faced, high browed, lithe, active, light brown, black straight-haired, black or very dark-brown-eyed, cheerful, dignified individual so frequently met with, is the nearest to the true Polynesian'.[71] It was a type that was most commonly found in Samoa, and in fewer numbers everywhere else; a type, one might add, that bore many of the characteristics usually attributed to the Aryans of the West.

Smith believed that the Polynesians had acquired other physical characteristics and customs on their journey to the Pacific; these included Papuan and Melanesian features and the practice of cannibalism which Smith thought Maori, Rarotongans, Tuamotuans and Marquesans had picked up from Fiji. The Melanesian strain, he thought, had been introduced to New Zealand by pre-fleet Polynesians who were generally confined to the Urewera and the so-called Moriori of the Chatham Islands. The fleet Maori, by contrast, were a purer strain; they became an 'aristocracy' which traced descent from one or other of the fleet canoes. Later Smith was converted to Elsdon Best's theory that Melanesians had actually reached New Zealand where they were absorbed into the ranks of the Polynesians of the fleet.[72] But whatever way the so-called Melanesian strain was introduced it was generally agreed that this inferior type had been virtually wiped out or absorbed by the more advanced and militarily superior fleet Maori. A typical example was seen in the fate of the Moriori the last of whom were almost completely annihilated by a party of Te Atiawa and Ngati Mutanga, armed with muskets and transported to the Chathams on a European ship in the 1830s.[73] Though long accepted, Smith's and Best's theories of a Melanesian strain, and even the idea of the Moriori as a separate race, have been abandoned by recent scholarship which holds quite simply that the pre-fleet inhabitants were Maori.[74]

Comparative Mythology

The idea of the Aryan Maori rested on rather more than Smith's exercise of the genealogical method and speculations in physical anthropology. Here it is worth turning from Smith to that other advocate of the Aryan thesis, Edward Tregear:

> To learn that many nations, separated by distance, by ages of strife and bloodshed, by differing religious creeds, and by ancient customs, yet had a common source of birth, that their forefathers spoke the same tongue, and sat in the one council-hall, was as delightful to the man of pure intellect, as it was valuable to the student of history. New fields of thought, endless paths of inquiry, opened before the feet of the worker, bringing reward at every mental step, and promising always new delights beyond. Comparative Philology and Comparative Mythology are the two youngest and fairest daughters of knowledge.[75]

Needless to say, Tregear was too easily seduced by these fairest daughters of knowledge; and he was not alone. W. H. Blyth, for instance, had so much faith in comparative mythology and was so little deterred by his own ignorance of Maori lore that he was prepared to risk the 'critical displeasure' of authorities like Colenso and boldly assert the Aryan or Turanian origin of the Maori.[76] After all, there were better authorities than Colenso to fall back on, including the great Max Müller, whose works invariably found their way into the footnotes of New Zealand's amateur exponents of the comparative mythology and philology. Thus we have Blyth comparing a Maori poem of creation (from Taylor's *Te Ika a Maui*) with a Hindu hymn (from Müller's *Chips from a German Workshop*); and then he compares a Maori invocation to Pani with a hymn from Müller's translation of the Rig-Veda; and the spell of Tawaki with Müller's Hymn to Varuna. Nor was Blyth content with comparison; he asserted that there was a connection. Thus, to mention but one connection, he saw in legends of Tane a relationship with the phallic worship of India. Enmeshed in Maori cosmological and other legends were remnants of ancient Turanian and Phallopantheistic beliefs. Here was one of the core beliefs of the new comparative sciences — that survivals of this earlier connection had become embedded, or, to use Tregear's favourite word, 'embalmed', in the mythology and language of contemporary savages, though knowledge of the original connection and meaning had long since been lost. The exponents of the method had unbounded faith in it. Thus Blyth concluded his essay by asserting that unless the 'coincidences' could be proved false the comparative method would have to be regarded as the only effective means of solving the problem of the whence of the Maori.

Though Tregear was mainly interested in comparative philology he often ventured into comparative mythology, mainly to provide additional support for his linguistic theses. He thought 'the evidence given by common religious belief, by common superstitions, hopes, and fears must be of the utmost value in trying to trace the descent and follow the footsteps of a people'.[77] In support Tregear was able to find in the *taniwha* of Maori legends an 'embalmed knowledge' of Sanscrit or other Aryan monsters. Thus the Maori Hotupuku ('Panting Belly') could be related to the Hindu demon Vritra, the Norse giant Fafnir and the Greek snake Python. Not content with monsters, Tregear went on to embalmed customs, finding in the Maori use of *tapu* a connection with the tapas which had long been known in India. He concluded by promising more samples of comparative mythology, a promise that was duly fulfilled in the pages of the *Transactions and Proceedings of the New Zealand Institute* and *The Journal of the Polynesian Society*.[78] Smith employed the same technique. After one such exercise, in which he compared Polynesian sun worship with that of the ancients in the best Müller style, he concluded:

> If we compare the Mythology of the Polynesians with those of the ancient mythologies of the old world ... there are sufficient points of similarity to hazard the conjecture that the race is the remnant of one of the most ancient races of the world, who have retained in its primitive forms, much of the beliefs that gave origin to the mythology of Assyria and Egypt.[79]

It is evident that the exponents of comparative mythology knew no bounds.

Others who worked this rich vein could be quoted, but it will be sufficient to rely finally on J. Macmillan Brown, the former professor of English at

Canterbury University College, who lent erudition and academic respectability to the quest for the Aryan Maori. Brown had more strings to his bow than comparative mythology but he found in this useful corroborative evidence for other theories. He too explored solar mythology and found that many of the Maori heroes and demigods resembled those of the Aryans, and in particular their Vedic system; but he was not content to remain in India. Like Tregear he found Greek, Celtic, and especially Scandinavian models for the Polynesian gods. He found in the demigod voyagers in Polynesian traditions — in Whiro, Kupe, Turi and Tangiia, for instance — a reminder of the 'half-mythical Scandinavian vikings who sailed to Iceland and Greenland and Vinland'.[80] Long before Te Rangi Hiroa was induced to use the title, Brown had discovered the Vikings of the Pacific. What more reputable a pedigree than this could have been devised for Maori?

Comparative Philology

But what of that other fair daughter of knowledge, Comparative Philology? She was, to continue the metaphor, Tregear's greatest passion; 'the discovery of a new world', a quotation which Tregear attributed to 'a great German thinker' (Müller, no doubt).[81] In some respects comparative philology was not new. As has been noted above, the early explorers and their scientific companions commonly appended comparative vocabularies to their published journals. Moreover, they were aware that the Polynesians spoke different dialects of the one family of languages. It was also in the late eighteenth century that Sir William Jones had provided, through his study of Sanscrit, the key to the Aryan family of languages. For a century lesser lights were to follow in his footsteps and, more dangerously, to assume that there was a connection between language and race. Though most of the effort was concentrated on the westward and especially the northern European branches of the Aryans, a few enthusiasts used comparative philology to trace the eastward movement of Aryan peoples. Just as the study of Sanscrit had provided the key to unlock the philological problems of the Aryan nations, so, to quote Blyth, Turnbull Thomson's 'happy discovery of the linguistic and ethnological relationship of the Maori races to the aboriginal Turanian races of Peninsular India, or Bharata, forms the key to the solution of this interesting question'[82] — that is, to the whence of Maori. This was the voice of an enthusiast who was, needless to say, prepared to ignore the advice of the sceptics. As long ago as 1834 that querulous Presbyterian, the Rev. J. D. Lang, had warned that the 'eminent orientalist', Jones, was 'perhaps overfond of referring everything to the Sanscrit'.[83] Lang would not be seduced into believing that Sanscrit provided the key to the Polynesian languages. But he went off in pursuit of an even more unlikely relationship: William Marsden's assertion that the Malay and Polynesian tongues were derived from Chinese Tartary. The choleric William Colenso complained that the exponents of comparative philology had not even bothered to learn Maori properly: 'Some Europeans have ventured to write "learnedly" upon it! using (without acknowledgement) the material obtained by others and racking and distorting by turns Hebrew, Sanscrit, Arabic, Greek, Coptic, Spanish, and many others; never once suspecting their own ignorance of that of New Zealand!'[84]

Tregear could hardly have been deterred by such advice since he was something of a lexicographer; he was later to publish a *Maori–Polynesian Comparative Dictionary* (1891). But to him lexicography led on to comparative philology and in turn to the discovery of the whence of the Maori. Indeed Tregear prided himself in being 'the first to apply the scientific method to the Maori language, and to prove the fellowship of the Polynesian with the races of Europe'.[85] His major contribution was *The Aryan Maori*, published in 1885. In this Tregear concluded that Maori were Aryan; that their language and traditions proved them to be descended from a warlike pastoral, migratory people; that their language had preserved, 'in an almost inconceivable purity', the speech of their Aryan forefathers; and that their language had 'embalmed' the memory of animals and implements, the actual sight of which had been lost for centuries. Tregear thought it possible that the ancestors of Maori had left India some 4000 years ago and had been in New Zealand almost as long — a very much longer time than Smith and others were to allow.

Though he explained little of his method, Tregear seems to have worked on the assumption that parallel words, or paronyms, could have a common ancestor, usually a Sanscrit root. His book discusses over 80 examples but one will be sufficient to illustrate his method. From the Sanscrit *tu*, to grow, Tregear derived the Maori *tupu* 'to grow', *katua* 'full grown', *matutu* 'to grow healthy', *tutu* 'to assemble', *whaka-tupu* 'to nourish', *turuki* 'to grow up', and *tuhea* 'overgrown'. In addition Tregear argued that there were many points of resemblance in the grammars of Maori and Sanscrit; he appears to have overlooked the fact that the missionaries had applied rules of grammar from European languages to Maori.

Yet, as has been suggested, Tregear went much further than trying to establish links of vocabulary and grammar. He thought he had found in Maori an embalmed memory of Aryan animals and customs. His paronyms were not, as one might have expected, nouns, but mainly verbs. Thus the patterns of behaviour relating to Aryan animals had become embalmed in the Maori language. Again, one sample of Tregear's technique will be sufficient, that of the cow, for the Aryans but not the Maori were cattle-keepers. In this the Sanscrit *gau* 'cow' survives in the Maori *kahui* 'herds', *kahurangi* 'unsettled' (in the sense of 'sky-cow', or moving clouds), *kakahu* 'clothes' (which the Aryans made from leather), *kauruki* 'smoke' (the Aryans burnt dung), and so on. The Sanscrit *go-pala* 'herdsman' becomes embalmed in the Maori phrase *kahu o te rangi*, translated by Tregear as 'cow of heaven', which he says was also a familiar phrase in Aryan works. Nor was Tregear content to rely on Sanscrit; Greek and Latin were equally suitable for providing paronyms. Thus the Latin *taurus* 'bull' became the Maori *tara* 'courage'. From such exercises Tregear argued that the Maori had once known the cow and the bull. He wrote in triumph:

> If some great European philologist would now undertake the task of rescuing the fast-fading *older* word-types of the languages spoken in these Southern Seas, he will have reward as he works, and fame for his guerdon.
>
> These uncivilized brothers of ours have kept embalmed in their simple speech a knowledge of the habits and history of our ancestors, that, in the Sanscrit, Greek, Latin, and Teutonic tongue, have been hidden under the dense aftergrowth of literary opulence.[86]

If no great European philologist took up the challenge, another New Zealand amateur, A. S. Atkinson of Nelson, did do so. His 'Aryo-Semitic Maori', published in the august pages of the *Transactions and Proceedings of the New Zealand Institute*,[87] was for the most part an ingenious spoof. He began in all seriousness by claiming that Tregear had tried to bridge the chasm, which none before him had bridged, between the Polynesian and Aryan languages. Though Tregear had said little about his method, this was found wanting on no fewer than ten counts: all of them sound and serious points, it would seem, in Atkinson's favour. Philology, in Tregear's hands, was not an exact but an 'intuitional science'.[88] And, as for the embalmed memory of animals, the curious were invited 'to watch whilst, under Mr Tregear's guidance, the whole Aryan menagerie files out of this ancient, but hitherto unsuspected, Noah's ark — the Maori language'.[89]

Atkinson went on to add some samples of his own to Tregear's menagerie. However, he reversed Tregear's procedure by using Maori words to throw light upon Aryan ways, to explain some common but obscure passages in modern Aryan languages — English especially — and as 'proof' that the Maori, after discovering New Zealand, returned to their ancient Aryan homeland before settling back in New Zealand:

> The saying explained is: 'a cock and bull story'; and the word which explains it is *kakapo*. This last word is, as you know, the name of a large ground-parrot . . . . Its name was hitherto thought to signify 'night parrot', in accordance with its nocturnal habits — a satisfactory explanation till the new method revealed the truth. For *kaka*, it appears, is the Sanskrit form of our word 'cock'; *po* is 'a bull': *kakapo*, therefore, will mean 'the bull-like *kaka* or cock'. But the Aryan bull was not so much physically large as morally terrible; and hence, under its Maori name, was, as Mr Tregear points out, the etymon of our English word 'Bo-gey, the demon of darkness'. Now, remembering this, and coupling with it the saying I have quoted, what does this word *kakapo* reveal, even to the amateur philologist? First, there become visible, the adventurous few of those primeval navigators peering into the gloomy recesses of the New Zealand forest, and there for the first time seeing in the dusk this strange bird: not flying, but uncannily marching; not cracking nuts, or eating fruits like a reasonable parrot, but nibbling the grass and herbage like a quadruped; 'grunting while so doing, if satisfied', or 'uttering a discordant shriek, if irritated'; big naturally, but looking far bigger in the uncertain light; in all ways most impressive to the primitive imagination. Then our voyagers are seen, returning to the family home in Asia; and when they relate there all they have seen, and how, among other strange and wonderful things, there was a *kaka-po*, 'a cock just like a bull', what wonder if those who had stayed at home, including our Teutonic ancestors, received the narrative with incredulity and ridicule, and so took with them to the West the dim remembrance of this story about 'a Cock and a Bull', as the very type of a traveller's tale.[90]

With this delicious sample of the comparative philologist's art we can leave Atkinson, though it is worth noting that he went on to apply Tregear's method to locate the Maori cradleland in Mauretania, on the assumption that Maori was a paronym for the Arabic *mauri*, and thereby to make the Maori Semites rather than Aryans.

Tregear hardly recovered from Atkinson's stunning ridicule. He replied sourly, accusing Atkinson of mocking the New Zealand Institute by presenting a paper without any serious discussion in it.[91] Though he continued to produce papers on comparative philology and comparative mythology, Tregear no longer commanded conviction. When he published his large survey, *The Maori Race*, in 1904 he was content to admit that the whence of the Maori was a controversial subject, and to fall back on Smith's genealogically based thesis.

Yet, even if a convincing method of proof was lacking, the assumption that the Maori was of Caucasian stock remained generally accepted. Macmillan Brown gave it comprehensive support in his *Maori and Polynesian* in 1907, adding through his theory of stone megaliths yet another 'embalmed memory' of the Maori's path through Asia and the Pacific. There is no need to follow every hare-brained thesis to its logical but erroneous conclusion; it is sufficient to accept that the myth of the Aryan Maori existed, and this in itself was significant. For Maori were made into Aryans by the same processes that built up the Aryan myths of western Europe and where the Anglo-Saxon races in particular were assumed to have become the finest expressions of mankind. New Zealand was not unaffected by the excesses of Anglo-Saxon racism that were evident elsewhere, though in New Zealand it was reflected largely in the vicious anti-Chinese campaign that led ultimately to the imposition of a 'White New Zealand' immigration policy.[92] But Maori, who were no longer a military threat to the Europeans, escaped much of this stigma. Was this because 'our' Maori were Aryans after all? In this respect it is worth quoting Tregear again. Like many of his contemporaries, he held that 'the degraded Natives who hang about our towns have little of the appearance of character of the true Maori'. But among the tribes there were 'noble specimens of the human race. . . . The ordinary European who counts in his ranks the Bengalee, the Savoyard and the Portuguese as Aryans, need not blush at his own brotherhood with the beauties of Hawaii or the heroes of Orakau.'[93] Then he added that, just as some Aryans had migrated into western Europe, others had gone eastwards: 'No free-booting Huns or Vandals, made for plunder and the sack of towns, were they, but colonists seeking new homes beneath strange stars. We of Europe have set out on the same quest. Encircling Africa, the two vast horns of the Great Migration have touched again . . . the Aryan of the West greets the Aryan of the Eastern Seas.'[94] What better myth could there be for a young country struggling for nationhood and for the amalgamation of its races than this reunification of the Aryans?

Conclusion
Such were the romantic ideals that were founded on the scientific methods of the late nineteenth century. It required another generation of observers, schooled in newer scientific methods, to clear away the myths. This was to be seen in the work of Cambridge-trained H. D. Skinner, who led the attack on the diffusionist, comparative anthropology of the later nineteenth century, and whose early attempts to publish were obstructed by Smith's control of the

Journal of the Polynesian Society. There was also to be a new scepticism in the interpretation of oral traditions, perhaps first seen in Te Rangi Hiroa's questioning of the tales of Te Matorohanga and Nepia Pohuhu, though Te Rangi Hiroa himself believed the Maori were Caucasians.[95] In archaeology, there was to be a much stricter control over stratigraphy and precision in interpreting evidence, most notably in Duff's work on the Moa-Hunter Maori in the late 1930s. And finally, with Andrew Sharp's *Ancient Voyagers of the Pacific* (1956), the theory that the Maori had come to New Zealand by accidental voyages, occasionally mentioned in the nineteenth century, and not by a deliberately planned great fleet, was convincingly expounded. But the precise location of Hawaiki, and the original homeland of the Maori, remain mysterious, and continue to fascinate amateur and professional scholars alike. Yet the solution was not as important as the quest itself, for the endeavour to give the Maori a respectable ancestry, whether Semitic or Aryan, helped to make them a suitable subject for amalgamation with their long-lost Pakeha 'brothers'.

2

Treaties in British Colonial Policy:
Precedents for Waitangi

In his 1990 essay for the *New Zealand Herald* Professor Sir Keith Sinclair took the Chief Judge of the Maori Land Court, Eddie Durie, to task for saying that, without the Treaty of Waitangi, there would be no lawful authority for the Pakeha presence in New Zealand. 'Pakehas,' Sinclair continued, 'did not need any "lawful authority" to be here; they just needed a chief or tribe willing to accept them. There was no government to possess sovereignty or to negotiate a treaty.'[1] Bishop Manuhia Bennett then took issue with the Professor, saying in a letter to the editor of the *Herald*, that 'no [British] subject could establish a colony without the licence of the Crown; that the Crown acknowledged the sovereign title of the Maori; and that there would be no annexation of New Zealand without Maori consent'. And the Bishop went on to ask: 'How then is the unauthorised occupation of a few to be seen as the source of authority . . . ? Sir Keith's article gives scant weighting to Crown Policy and the Maori view.'[2] So far as the *Herald*'s columns were concerned, that was the end of the controversy.

In my view the Bishop and the Chief Judge were right. Professor Sinclair seems to believe that the Treaty of Waitangi was a unique development in British colonial policy and a consequence of a recent bout of humanitarian conscience as seen in the 1837 Report of the House of Commons Committee on Aborigines. That Committee said that it was 'inexpedient' to enter into

---

Originally published in W. Renwick, ed., *Sovereignty & Indigenous Rights: The Treaty of Waitangi in International Contexts*, Victoria University Press, Wellington, 1991, pp. 15–29.

treaties with aboriginal peoples who could too easily be disadvantaged by 'the ambiguity of language' of such treaties and 'the superior sagacity which the Europeans will exercise in framing, in interpreting and in evading them' — advice that was most certainly ignored at Waitangi.[3] Unlike Sinclair, I think the Treaty was an expression of a much older colonial policy that had been applied in various parts of the British empire. Indeed, I would go further and say that there is very little in the Treaty, at least in its English text, that had not already been expressed in earlier treaties or statements of British colonial policy. The only thing about Waitangi that was unusual was its Maori text which I shall discuss briefly at the end.

The first point to be made is that treaties between European and non-European, even tribal peoples like the Maori, were not at all unusual. As Paul McHugh has ably demonstrated,[4] European nations had been concluding treaties with non-Christian societies since the fifteenth century — in Barbary, the Levant, in India and, with the opening up of the New World, in the Americas, Africa, South-east Asia and the Pacific. Most of these were originally commercial treaties, designed to safeguard and promote the trade of European merchants in foreign countries. But activities that had begun in this way quite often led on to an assertion of *imperium* or even *dominium*, by negotiation or conquest, as individual traders or trading companies gradually asserted their control over forts and factories and often the surrounding territory and their peoples as well. Inevitably, in many instances, the British Crown was dragged in: extra-territoriality in a foreign country had to be replaced by a declaration of a protectorate, or even formal annexation. Consuls, who could no longer cope, were replaced by residents and, with annexation, governors.

In India the East India Company moved from coastal factories — a model, it will be recalled, that Hobson, who had served in the East, initially recommended for New Zealand — to the annexation or conquest of increasingly large territories, or involvement by way of treaties with princely states. In the end the Company was succeeded in its *imperium* by the British Crown.

In West Africa the process was similar, though here Britain's European rivals maintained a greater share of the booty than in India. In the end the continent was partitioned between them during the late nineteenth century. Originally, the forts and factories were established around the West African coast to facilitate the Atlantic slave trade. But in the early nineteenth century, as that trade was curtailed, they were used as springboards for the development of 'legitimate' trade and, in due course, imperial expansion. The West African societies at this time were, like Maori society, essentially small-scale tribal societies with chiefly rulers, though some chiefs who had waxed rich on the slave trade were more grandiloquently titled. Accordingly, it is instructive to look at treaties concluded with some of these rulers in the years leading up to Waitangi. Although most of these treaties were concerned with the suppression of the slave trade and the development of legitimate commerce, some were treaties of cession.

The most interesting of all is the British–Sherbo agreement of 1825, one of several negotiated with tribal rulers on the Gambia around this time. Professor Sir Kenneth Keith has recently resurrected this agreement and pointed out its kinship with Waitangi. I follow his summary. Like Waitangi, the agreement has three operative provisions: the King of Sherbo, with the advice and consent of various people who are named, ceded sovereignty; in return they received the protection of the British government and the rights and privileges of British subjects; and they were guaranteed 'the full free and undisturbed possession and enjoyment of the lands they then occupied'. That, apart from the ordering of the provisions, and the failure to guarantee forests and fisheries, is virtually identical with the three articles of Waitangi. As Keith adds, 'some of the very same verbs, adjectives and nouns are used'.[5] It is tempting to conclude that Hobson and Busby had a copy of this agreement with them at Waitangi. But if not they probably knew of it, or similar agreements, since both had been briefed at the Colonial Office not long before the Treaty of Waitangi was drawn up. And there were several other West African agreements or treaties, using the same language, which were signed in the years before Waitangi. There was even a treaty in 1840 that has some resemblance to Waitangi. This was a treaty with King Combo of the Gambia who, in return for $100 worth of merchandise, ceded to Her Majesty 'all claim, title, and right to the sovereignty of the territory ... Provided always that the individuals in possession of any property ... shall in nowise be disturbed in the enjoyment of the same'.[6] We have here, I think, what one might call a treaty language that was in fairly widespread use, ready to be applied wherever a crisis on one of the frontiers of empire needed to be resolved by the last resort of a treaty of cession. There is no need to attribute the expressive terms of the Treaty of Waitangi to Busby's verbosity.

It is not necessary to examine the rest of Africa in similar detail since it is likely to be less fruitful in Waitangi precedents. The subject appears not to have been researched at all. The most likely parallel with New Zealand, since it was a settlement colony, is South Africa, but there appears to be no precedent for Waitangi there. Perhaps that is not surprising since the original Dutch East India Company and the Trekboers of the frontier were not in the habit of signing treaties of cession with the Khoi, the San or the Bantu-speaking tribes of the eastern Cape. Nor was there any substantial change when the British took over the Cape from the Dutch, and additional territory on the frontier was added to the colony. In the mid-1830s D'Urban and Strockenstrom, on Glenelg's instruction, imposed a brief but unpopular treaty policy on the Xhosa beyond the eastern Cape frontier. Under treaties Stockenstrom negotiated in 1836, the Xhosa paramounts ceded territory but were guaranteed their remaining land 'in perpetuity', provided they were not involved in further hostilities, and provided the British were allowed to locate troops, forts and agents in the Xhosa territory.[7] That was a situation bristling with potential conflict and, when there was yet another 'Kaffir war', the British proceeded to acquire territory by conquest, using treaties and proclamations to assert their sovereignty over the annexed territories, and to set aside reserves for the Xhosa and other tribes. That policy was continued through the century as southern Africa was gradually partitioned between the British colonies and the Boer Republics, and the Africans were penned into reserves. The situation was not unlike that which developed in North America at the same time. But there were some exceptions in South Africa, for instance with the Basuto, Tswana and Swazis who were able to gain protectorate status. Otherwise treaties, where they were used at all, were a record not of voluntary cession but of conquest. It was not long before Waitangi was being quoted as a precedent to avoid. When Governor Smith of the Cape Colony declared the Crown's sovereignty over the Orange River Sovereignty in 1848 the Attorney General, Porter, considered a treaty of cession with the Griqua chiefs but concluded: 'Another Waitangi treaty would have been another mockery....'[8]

As the scramble for Africa speeded up in the later nineteenth century, empire-builders staking out territory tried to give credibility to their claims by negotiating treaties with local potentates. Leopold of the Belgians led the way, using his agents to collect a whole shaft of treaties by which the African rulers of the Congo 'voluntarily ceded all their sovereign rights'.[9] Such treaties were accepted by other European powers who were themselves busily acquiring treaties to back their claims to territory. As Lugard, one of the leading British empire-builders, put it:

> The civilised nations entered for the competition with avidity. Treaties were produced by the cartload in all the approved forms of legal verbiage — impossible of translation by ill-educated interpreters. It mattered not that tribal chiefs had no power to dispose of communal rights, or that those few powerful potentates who might claim such looked on the white man's ambassador with contempt, and could hardly be expected to hand

over sovereignty and lands and other assets had they understood what was asked of them.... The treaties were duly attested with a cross, purporting to convey the assent of the African chief, and this was sufficient. In some cases, it is said, the assent had been obtained by the gift of a pair of boots, or a few bottles of gin....[10]

That looks a bit like giving blankets for signatures to Waitangi. But in tropical Africa during the 'Scramble', such treaties of cession were intended to give credibility in Europe to claims of 'effective occupation' which the Berlin Conference of 1884–85 laid down as a necessary prerequisite to valid territorial claims. Most of them had no subsequent significance. An interesting exception was the Buganda agreement of 1900, which has much in common with the Treaty of Waitangi and, like Waitangi in New Zealand, had a very considerable influence in the subsequent history of Uganda.

What has been said for Africa can also be said for the Pacific, as Tom Bennion has recently demonstrated.[11] Once again, the great powers of Europe had few qualms about negotiating treaties with what were often small-scale tribal societies, and regarding them as binding in international law. Initially, a lot of these were treaties of friendship to promote commerce and Christianity. But, as the nineteenth century advanced, there were some treaties of cession, of which Waitangi was the most important, though Fiji's Deed of Cession of 1874 was scarcely less so. As in Africa, annexation of formal colonies tended to be a last resort. It was often brought on by a large influx of Europeans threatening indigenous land and other resources, and was usually confined to the larger island groups: New Zealand, New Caledonia, Samoa, Hawaii and Papua New Guinea. The others tended to be left with protectorate status, though by the end of the century there were scarcely any island groups that were still fully independent. But, as Bennion has pointed out, there were not many cases in the Pacific where island groups became colonies or protectorates without some kind of a treaty with the indigenous authorities; the doctrine of *terra nullius* was hardly applied at all.[12]

In searching for Waitangi precedents, it is also important to turn to North America. Here the story is different, though no less significant. One major difference from Waitangi must be admitted at the outset. Sovereignty over the North American continent was not acquired by European states by treaties of cession with the Indians. The Europeans gained sovereignty by right of discovery, followed up by occupation, and by treaties between themselves at the conclusion of wars. Notable cases are the transfer of the French territories, including French Canada and Nova Scotia, to Britain at the first Treaty of Paris in 1763, after the Seven Years' War; and the transfer of sovereignty over the rebellious American colonies at a second Treaty of Paris in 1783, after the War of Independence. Thereafter the independent American nation extended its sovereignty across the continent by a combination of occupation and warfare, culminating in the acquisition of Texas and California after the war with Mexico in 1847. Of course that expansion was often achieved by warfare with the native Indian tribes, and Indian wars were usually concluded by treaties. But these treaties did not cede sovereignty, merely land and sometimes other rights, like freedom of passage through the Indian reservations.

However, in some other ways the Americans gave their Indian treaties more status than Waitangi was to receive in New Zealand. The existing Indian treaties, most of them drawn up by the British, were protected under Article IV of the federal constitution as part of the 'fundamental law' of the United States. And subsequent treaties, which the federal government went on concluding for almost a hundred years, received similar status once ratified by Senate. This meant that they had standing in the Supreme Court, something Waitangi has never had in New Zealand's courts. Moreover, the treaties were meant to protect Indians in their reservations from predations by the states; only the federal government, and the Supreme Court in interpreting the Constitution, had plenary or judicial authority to override the 'sovereignty' of the Indian reservations. They were, in Mr Chief Justice Marshall's famous words of 1831, 'domestic dependent nations'.[13] The Americans, in their treaty relations with such 'nations', have accepted a degree of divided sovereignty that has never been acceptable in New Zealand where the Maori cession of sovereignty in Article 1 of the English text of Waitangi has always been used to promote a domestic sovereignty that is one and indivisible. By the same token we have never seriously considered the notion that Article 2 of the Maori text of the Treaty might well have preserved for the Maori, in their 'tino rangatiratanga o o ratou wenua', the status and authority of a 'domestic dependent nation'.

But if we turn to the English text of Article 2, where that 'tino rangatiratanga o o ratou wenua' is expanded into the 'full exclusive and undisturbed possession of their lands', then we can find important precedents in North America as well as West Africa. Perhaps the most notable statements of British policy came at the end of the Seven Years' War with France when the British were keen to conciliate their Indian allies. Thus the Earl of Egremont advised the Lords of Trade on 5 May 1763 that it might be necessary to erect forts in Indian country, 'with their consent' and to protect their

Persons and Property and securing to them all the Possessions, Rights and Privileges they have hitherto enjoyed, and are entitled to, most cautiously guarding against any invasion or Occupation of their Hunting Lands, the Possession of which is to be acquired by fair Purchase only.[14]

This instruction paved the way for the Royal Proclamation of 7 October 1763 which laid down the basic policy towards Indians and their lands in the territories ceded by France and Spain, and also for Britain's other North American colonies and much of their hinterland. Amongst other things, the Proclamation stated:

And whereas it is just and reasonable, and essential to our interest and the security of our colonies, that the several nations or tribes of Indians with whom we are connected, and who live under our protection, should not be molested or disturbed in the possession of such parts of our dominions and territories as, not having been ceded to or purchased by us, are reserved to them . . . as their hunting grounds . . .

The Proclamation went on to 'reserve under our sovereignty, protection, and dominion' for the use of the Indians 'all land not within the said colonies' (of Quebec and East and West Florida) or the territory granted to the Hudson's Bay Company and falling within the headwaters of rivers which fell into the Atlantic Ocean — a provision which eventually excluded the north west and western provinces of Canada from the protection of the Proclamation. Finally the Proclamation asserted what amounted to a Crown right of pre-emption to purchase Indian lands:

We do . . . strictly enjoin and require that no private person do presume to make any purchase from the said Indians of any lands reserved to the said Indians . . . but that if any time the said Indians should be inclined to dispose of said lands, the same shall be purchased only for us, in our name, at some public meeting or assembly of the said Indians, to be held for that purpose by the Governor or commander in chief . . . .[15]

This was no new departure in British North American policy since a Crown right of pre-emption to acquire land from Indians and grant title to colonists had been asserted from early in the settlement of the eastern seaboard. Paul McHugh has pointed to a whole battery of laws, starting as early as 1609 in Virginia, which recognised Indian titles to land, placed restrictions on private dealings with Indians, and affirmed that patents or titles could only be granted by the Crown. In 1634 the General Court of Massachusetts Bay prohibited the purchase of land from Indians without its permission. McHugh continues:

> During the mid-seventeenth century, similar legislation was passed in Plymouth, Rhode Island, New Hampshire, New Haven and Connecticut. Likewise the colonial authorities of the other British colonies, New York, Maryland, New Jersey, Pennsylvania, North and South Carolina, and Georgia reserved the exclusive power to extinguish the tribal title.[16]

And he went on to note that the 1763 Royal Proclamation, which applied to the existing colonies as well as Britain's new acquisitions from France, 'gave the principle uniformity throughout British North America'. Moreover, as McHugh also points out, the Crown's exclusive right to extinguish Indian title was being termed by the end of the seventeenth century a 'pre-emptive right', which is of course the way it was used in the Treaty of Waitangi.[17]

The historical development of this principle was ably summed up by Marshall CJ in his famous judgment in *Johnson v M'Intosh* (1823).[18] This was well known in British legal circles around the time of Waitangi (and it was used by Martin and Chapman in the New Zealand case *R v Symonds* in 1847).[19] More importantly — and once more I am indebted to McHugh — Busby knew about the North American precedent, as he explained in 1858:

> the word [pre-emption] in the English version of the Treaty, is used in the technical sense, in which it has always been used in dealing with the American Indians . . . that is, as an exclusive right to deal with them for their lands . . . .[20]

Busby returned to the subject again in some remarks on Sir William Martin's pamphlet, *The Taranaki Question*, which were published in the *Appendices to the Journals of the House of Representatives* in 1861, saying that the Treaty of Waitangi had 'established in New Zealand . . . a power which not only Great Britain, but all other colonizing powers had previously assumed, of preventing the transfer of an aboriginal title to a subject'.[21] These statements of Busby's indicate, I think, a familiarity with Marshall's judgment in *Johnson v M'Intosh*, which has numerous statements similar to Busby's — for instance: 'all the nations of Europe, who have acquired territory on this continent, have asserted in themselves and have recognized in others, the exclusive right of the discoverer to appropriate the lands occupied by the Indians'.[22] And, as McHugh adds, Hobson was also familiar with North American precedents since he had been elaborately briefed on them in London and in Sydney (by Gipps) before he came to New Zealand.[23]

The root problem that led to the assertion of the pre-emptive right in New Zealand — the mad scramble by European speculators to buy up land in advance of the declaration of British sovereignty — was nothing new in colonial history. It had been going on for years, indeed centuries, in British North America. Marshall pointed to a 1779 Act in Virginia declaring an 'exclusive right of pre-emption' to acquire Indian lands within the colony and an annulment of all deeds between Indians and private buyers;[24] a situation that was to be reiterated by Hobson's proclamation of 30 January 1840, prohibiting further purchases of Maori land, and the second part of Article 2 of the Treaty of Waitangi. Even more relevant was the contemporary problem in Upper Canada where, ever since the 1763 Royal Proclamation, the Crown had been trying to prevent settlers from buying or squatting on Indian land, a problem that was examined by the 1842 Commission on Indian Affairs.[25]

There was little sign of this problem in Australia, for the simple reason that for a long time no one acknowledged that the Aborigines had a title to land at all. How, one might ask, could such an attitude, so at odds with British policy in North America, develop when settlement began in Australia a mere 25 years after the Royal Proclamation of 1763?

Those who like to claim a unique character for the Treaty of Waitangi usually look across the Tasman and remind us that the Aborigines did not get a treaty, or even any recognition of a title in land. But that hardly proves that Waitangi was unique. If anything, it was the Australian situation that was unusual, though hardly unique, since there were other places where aboriginal rights to land were ignored and there were no treaties.

Australian historians have gone to some trouble to explain why Aboriginal rights were ignored,[26] but I am still puzzled about it, though I failed to find anything new in my reading of the Colonial Office files for the early years in New South Wales, Western Australia and South Australia.

When James Cook was sent on his first expedition to the Pacific in 1769, just six years after the Royal Proclamation, he was instructed to get the consent of native inhabitants before taking possession of territory. But when he got to Botany Bay he simply took possession by right of discovery, as he did on several later occasions as he sailed up the coast (and indeed as he had done in

New Zealand), nowhere attempting to get the consent of existing inhabitants. Thirty years later the British authorities were still going through the motions of requiring Aboriginal consent before extending sovereignty over other parts of Australia. Thus, when Portland instructed Governor King to send an expedition to the southern coasts of Van Diemen's Land, recently revealed to be an island, it was to take possession in His Majesty's name 'with the consent of the inhabitants, if any'.[27]

It was of course Cook's discovery of Botany Bay, and various descriptions of its timid inhabitants, that led Britain nearly 20 years later to select it as a site for a convict colony, while New Zealand, thanks to its ferocious aborigines, was spared that shameful beginning. However, it was Banks's rather than Cook's views that were influential. His appearance before the Beauchamp Committee on Transportation in 1785 clinched the decision.[28] Here he distorted the record by underestimating the number of Aborigines at Botany Bay and passing them off as a nomadic people, devoid of political authority, social organisation or religious belief. Asked if there was any possibility of obtaining land from them by cession or purchase, he said: 'No. There was nothing we could offer that they would take except provisions & those we wanted for ourselves.'[29] When approached, the Aborigines would retire, being unwilling to trade or fight. James Matra, who also travelled with Cook on the first voyage, had proposed the establishment of a settlement at Botany Bay in 1783, saying that Cook had found an immense tract of country, 2000 miles in length, and 'peopled only by a few black Inhabitants, who in the rudest state of society, knew no other arts than such as were necessary, to their mere animal existence, of which was almost entirely sustained by catching fish'.[30] Before deciding on Botany Bay, Britain considered various places around the African coast — at the Gambia, Das Voltas Bay, Madagascar — but always had assumed it would be necessary to purchase the land required.[31] Perhaps Banks's assurance that it would not be necessary to buy land was a reason for finally choosing Botany Bay.

Though Robert King has suggested that the precedent of the 1763 Royal Proclamation was not wholly absent during the discussions on selecting Botany Bay, it dropped out of mind during the drafting of Phillip's Instructions, 'probably because of the impression given by the *Endeavour* voyages that the Natives of New South Wales had no idea of property rights, or of commercial transactions'.[32] Thereafter the British assumed it was not necessary to purchase land. Australia was a *terra nullius* and its Aborigines, in Vattel's phrase, were 'wandering savages' who had no title in the soil and could be confined to 'narrow bands'.

Thus Australia could become a colony of settlement, without any perceived need for cession or conquest, and aboriginal rights, a doctrine readily recognised in North America, could be put out of mind and out of sight in the historical record — until recently. Even James Stephen, later to have a fit of conscience over the Australian Aborigines, could say in 1822 that Britain had acquired New South Wales 'neither by conquest nor cession, but on the mere occupation of a desert or uninhabited land'.[33] Botany Bay a desert? Hardly. Nor was it uninhabited. Indeed Phillip soon found, rather to his surprise, that it was quite thickly inhabited by some 2000 people, at least until that population was decimated by a smallpox epidemic in 1790. He also admitted, in his first dispatch from Botany Bay, that he had gained a 'much higher opinion' of the Aborigines than he had got from Cook's journals. 'Their confidence and manly behavior made me give the name Manly Cove to this place.'[34]

Phillip's Instructions[35] were mainly concerned with the management of convicts and said very little about the Aborigines. He was to 'endeavour by every possible means to open an intercourse with the Natives [an earlier draft had used "savages"] and to conciliate their affection, enjoining all our subjects to live in amity and kindness with them'. That was asking a bit much of His Majesty's convicts, as was soon to be demonstrated. The Instructions went on to advise Phillip to punish 'any of our subjects who wantonly destroy them, or give them any unnecessary interruption in the exercise of their several occupations'. Finally, he was to make a census and report 'in what manner our intercourse with these People may be turned to the advantage of this country'. There was no suggestion of negotiating for land, let alone a treaty of cession. But the Instructions did say how Phillip was to provide land for emancipated convicts, military officers and free settlers. And in later years, as Crown land regulations were introduced and amended from time to time, it was simply assumed that the Crown had an unencumbered title to all waste lands, indeed all land. Even when the Aborigines around Sydney soon began to pick off stock and burn crops, no one in authority ever admitted that they might be asserting a title to the land the British had occupied. And when these 'depredations', as they were called, were put down by military force, no one ever admitted that this amounted to a 'conquest', since this would spoil the legal fiction that the Europeans were settling a *terra nullius*.

The mind-set that was established in New South Wales was passed on to other colonies in Australia. Phillip's Instructions, which had done service for his successors in that colony, were remodelled for Captain Stirling in Western Australia in 1828. Indeed his Instructions dropped all reference to Aborigines. They really did make the new colony a *terra nullius.*

But by the mid-1830s, when preparations were being made for a colony that was to be different — non-convict, Wakefieldian South Australia — winds of change were beginning to blow through colonial policy. It was necessary to attune the propaganda to a humanitarian climate of opinion. So the promoters of the South Australia Association promised to regulate the intercourse between the colonists and the Aborigines, providing the latter with peaceful security and enjoyment of their 'rights as men'.[36] A draft of the Letters Patent for the new colony promised to protect 'the rights of any aboriginal Natives . . . to the actual occupation or enjoyment . . . of any lands . . . now actually occupied or enjoyed by such Natives'.[37]

That seemed like a considerable advance on anything that had been recognised in New South Wales or Western Australia. But was it? That depended on who decided whether the Aborigines occupied or enjoyed any land at all. As it turned out, the South Australia Association was allowed to draft its own Act which was dutifully passed by Parliament. This presupposed that South Australia was a vacant territory and, though it recognised the *dominium* of the Crown, granted the proprietary right to the soil to the Association's commissioners and colonists who purchased land from them.[38]

Stephen, who had just become Permanent Secretary at the Colonial Office, and who had begun to revise his ideas about Aborigines' rights in Australia, realised too late that he had lost control. He tried to limit the damage by considerably restricting the boundaries of the new colony. In an official letter of 15 December 1835, which Stephen drafted, Torrens was warned that if the new colony extended far into the interior it 'might embrace in its range numerous Tribes of People whose Proprietary Title to the soil we have not the slightest ground for disputing'. Before His Majesty would sanction any transfer of land to colonists he would need to be satisfied he was 'not about to sanction any act of injustice towards the Aboriginal natives'.[39] Torrens was also told that in 'drawing the Lines of demarcation for the province . . . the Commissioners, therefore, must not proceed any further than those limits within which they can show, by some sufficient evidence, that the Land is unoccupied, and that no earlier and preferable title exists'.[40]

For Australia that was a language of aboriginal rights the like of which had not been heard before. Spokesmen for the Association had to tread carefully to get round it. Torrens promised to protect the Aborigines' food supplies, to establish dispensaries and even to encourage them to send their children to school, but he also stuck adamantly to the terms of the South Australia Act which had granted the Association title to all land within the province. 'In the colonization of Australia,' he reminded Grey, 'it has invariably been assumed as an established fact, that the unlocated tribes have not arrived at a stage of social improvement in which a proprietary right to the soil exists.' This had been the case in New South Wales, Van Diemen's Land and Western Australia. Why should South Australia be different? But if their land commissioners did find some Aborigines 'occupying, or enjoying or possessing any right of property in the soil', their land would be withheld from colonisation. He invited the government to insert a condition to this effect in the Letters Patent for the new colony.[41] This was done. But even though a Protector of Aborigines was appointed and he managed to set aside some Aboriginal reserves, South Australia's record on Aboriginal rights was scarcely any better than those of the earlier colonies. Yet it has some relevance to New Zealand since it would seem that the failure there made Stephen all the more determined to succeed across the Tasman.

There is one other Australian development that needs to be noted, since it also has some relevance to New Zealand: the rather odd case of the Batman 'treaty' at Port Phillip, sometimes regarded as the only treaty that the Aborigines nearly got. It was odd also because it may have been the only time that a settler thought he should buy Aboriginal land. Otherwise they just took it, conveniently assuming that it was ownerless. So did the Crown, which assumed that the only problem was how to deal with these 'squatters' on Crown land. They needed to be brought under the Crown land regulations. Stephen referred to the problem in a letter to the South Australia Colonization Commissioners in 1836 in reply to their complaint about Batman and his unauthorised settlement at Port Phillip. 'For some years past,' Stephen wrote, 'HM Govt. have steadfastly enforced the rule, which forbids the alienation of wild lands in New Holland, except by Sales and Public Auction at a fixed Minimum Price.' But there had been difficulty enforcing this on the frontiers. 'In NSW,' he continued, 'the "squatters" (to employ the significant local term) find in the high upset price of land, some of those advantages which a smuggler in other countries derives from a high rate of duty.' Stephen noted how Batman's Port Phillip Association had taken 'possession of considerable tracts of land under grants from the neighbouring Chiefs. With this semblance of a title they readily attracted new settlers . . . .' He described how the New South Wales administration had brought Batman and his settlers under the existing land regulations — or, rather, how they had relaxed these to accommodate them, since it was impossible to coerce them into full acceptance by force of arms.[42] In fact Batman's treaty, which was like some of the pre-1840 land purchase agreements with Maori in New Zealand, was promptly disallowed by a proclamation from Governor Bourke of 26 August 1835, along with any other such transactions that might be entered into anywhere in New South Wales. These were to be regarded as 'void, as against the rights of the Crown; and . . . all persons who shall be found in possession of any such lands without license or authority of Her Majesty's Government will be considered as trespassers, and liable to be dealt with in like manner as other invaders upon the vacant lands of the Crown'.[43] In other words, the North American policy reiterated, except that there was never any suggestion that Aborigines might have a prior right to land which the Crown needed to respect.

But what, one might well ask, has all this got to do with New Zealand and its Treaty? In the first place, the authorities in New South Wales were already aware that some of their colonists, involuntary and free, were creating many more problems in dealing with Maori for land than Batman and his friends had with the Port Phillip Aborigines. In due course Gipps was to deal with them in the same way — with his proclamation against further purchases of Maori land of 14 January 1840. Secondly, as I have indicated, I think the South Australian experience made Stephen and the Colonial Office authorities much more careful when another Wakefieldian organisation, the New Zealand Association, attempted to colonise New Zealand. This Association was not allowed to put its own Act through Parliament, was instructed to turn itself into a commercial company and, when it sent a land-buying expedition to New Zealand in May 1839, the Colonial Office moved quickly and decisively to send Hobson to negotiate a cession of sovereignty from the Maori, to impose Crown pre-emption over future land purchases, and to investigate all previous purchases, including any negotiated by the New Zealand Company. In this way the experience of belatedly attempting to protect Aboriginal rights in Australia was linked to the recent West African policy of negotiating sovereignty with local chiefs and a much older North American policy of imposing pre-emption to stop private dealings of colonists with the natives. Indeed, it was the atrocities in Australia that were referred to in the House of Commons debate in 1845 as being one of the 'chief causes of the national reassertion of the old and righteous principle in the case of New Zealand'.[44] The recent Report of the Aborigines Committee may have lent some urgency to the attempt to protect Aboriginal and Maori rights, and some of its sentiments entered into policy, even the preamble of the Treaty of Waitangi, but the three articles of the Treaty are deeply embedded in an older colonial policy, drawn from various corners of the empire. They were cobbled together as a typically pragmatic response by the Colonial Office to yet another crisis on a far-flung imperial frontier.

It is true of course that Busby 'wrote' the Treaty, on the basis of notes provided by Hobson and Freeman. But the gist of it is there in Normanby's Instructions and in their briefings in the Colonial Office. So they wrote the English text in the treaty language of their day, adding very little that had not been spelled out in previous treaties, most notably the British–Sherbo agreement of 1825. But if they did not create a unique treaty, Henry Williams certainly did in his creative reworking of the main English provisions into a saleable Maori text. Of course bilingual treaties were common enough in European diplomacy, but they seem to have been fairly rare elsewhere. They were not used in North America where the Indian treaties were written in English, though presumably these were translated orally. So far as I know, it was the same in Africa and Asia. But there seem to have been a few treaties in the Pacific in the indigenous languages as well as English; for instance two British treaties or conventions with the Sandwich Islands in 1843 and 1846.[45] Interestingly, the Fijian Deed of Cession of 1874, which is the closest of the Pacific treaties to Waitangi, was written in English though a note on it by the Chief Interpreter, D. Wilkinson, says he wrote out an interpretation in the Fijian language which he read to the Tui Viti and the other ceding chiefs who approved it. However, they signed the English text.[46] As if to say, Waitangi's Maori text was a precedent to be avoided. And indeed this was to be the case in New Zealand, at least for Pakeha who, except for the last 20 to 30 years, have remained oblivious to it. It is the Maori text that gives Waitangi its most distinctive quality. We in New Zealand have not yet come to terms with that.

3

How to Civilise Savages:
Some 'Answers' from Nineteenth-century New Zealand

> It is not to be doubted that this country has been invested with wealth and power, with arts and knowledge, with the sway of distant lands, and the mastery of restless waters, for some great and important purpose in the government of the world. Can we suppose otherwise than that it is our office to carry civilization and humanity, peace and good government, and, above all, the knowledge of the true God, to the uttermost ends of the earth?
> — *The Rev. W. Whewell's sermon to the Trinity Board, quoted in the* Report . . . on Aborigines, *1837*[1]

This essay is an examination of the British civilising mission in Antipodean New Zealand, and in particular of the role attributed to those vital agents of civilisation — commerce, Christianity and colonisation. These were confidently expected to bring about what Europeans in the nineteenth century called the amalgamation of the races. Civilised Maori were ultimately to be absorbed or assimilated into the European population. Perhaps to a greater extent than any other British colony New Zealand was, and has remained, a monument to the evangelicals and the utilitarians. But in New Zealand the civilising mission was

---

Originally published in *The New Zealand Journal of History*, vol. 9, no. 2 (1975), pp. 97–110, as a revised version of a paper first read to Professor Gallagher's seminar at Cambridge in 1974 while I held a Smuts fellowship. I am aware that much of the language of this paper is more suited to the nineteenth than the twentieth century and that the 'answers' are more varied and complex, especially in terms of Maori motivation, than those discussed here.

continued — by British colonists — through the later nineteenth century (and indeed into the twentieth) when it was being tempered or abandoned in other parts of the colonial empire for segregation or differentiation. This essay will explain why New Zealand was different.

The continued pursuit of assimilation in New Zealand owed a good deal to assessments of Maori and their capacity for civilisation. Indeed Maori had the good fortune to be ranked higher than most other 'savages'. Exponents of the old theory of a Great Chain of Being invariably put Maori somewhat above the unfortunate Hottentots or Australian Aborigines who were usually placed as the last links in the chain between man and the apes.[2] It was much the same if a more modern though still pre-Darwinian evolutionary scheme was used, for Maori, with their sedentary agriculture and skilled arts, were usually placed on the border between savagery and barbarism and assumed to be capable, with proper guidance, of graduating to civilisation.[3] It is true that some Christian diffusionists saw Maori as having degenerated from a higher stage, but they had little doubt that the process could be reversed. Moreover, they believed that Maori had descended from one of the lost tribes of Israel:[4] these Polynesian sons of Shem could at least escape the stigma that was attached to the African (and Australian)[5] sons of Ham. Maori were well treated by the early exponents of anthropology.

Nevertheless, Maori who emerge from the pages of early publications on New Zealand were no Noble Savages: that reputation, so far as Polynesians were concerned, was reserved for the more compliant Tahitians.[6] Maori gloried in war and indulged in cannibalism. They dealt some savage and apparently treacherous blows to incautious explorers and traders: Tasman lost four men; Cook on his first voyage was repeatedly greeted by aggressive behaviour and often opened fire; on Cook's second voyage the *Adventure*, commanded by Furneaux, lost ten men; and in the same year the French explorer, Marion du Fresne, who apparently did regard Maori as Noble Savages, was killed along with 26 of his crew. The victims were eaten. But this savage behaviour had one beneficial result: New Zealand was spared from becoming a convict settlement.[7] Ships from the convict settlement that was established in Australia were soon frequenting New Zealand waters and some of them — the most notable was the *Boyd* in 1809 — were cut off and their crews killed. Maori remained dangerous and apparently treacherous savages.

Yet this was not the only aspect of their behaviour that attracted notice. Maori had quite an advanced form of agriculture, sophisticated fishing gear, skilfully woven garments and elaborately carved artefacts; these were clear evidence of industry and ingenuity.[8] Moreover, Maori were quickly alive to the possibilities of commerce; they were willing, after an initial display of defiance, to barter fresh fish, artefacts, and, with more hesitation, women, for cloth, bottles, spike nails and iron. This could become the seed of a valuable commerce since New Zealand, as Cook found, was rich in products like hemp and spars that were useful to a naval and mercantile power. Yet there remained a problem of how to discipline and guide Maori into peaceable and reliable trading partners, and of persuading them that they would gain more by open-handed exchange than by attempting to 'pluck the Pakeha' or steal their goods. There was also a good deal that Europeans had to learn about Maori culture and behaviour. Cook and his companions began to unravel some of the apparent irrationalities of Maori savagery. They inquired closely and persistently into the nature of Maori cannibalism and found — correctly, as it turned out — that this was a means of utu, of taking revenge upon one's enemy.[9] Though Maori were fierce and unrelenting in dealing with their enemies, their treatment of kin was marked by tenderness and affection. As Cook, Banks and others soon found, friendship and hospitality could be extended to strangers once initial suspicion had been overcome and other proprieties observed. Cook summed it up by noting that: 'Notwithstanding they are *Cannibals*, they are naturaly of a good disposission [sic] and have not a little share of humanity.'[10] Europeans still had to learn to respect the laws of tapu and the mana of chiefs; it was probably their failure to do so that provoked the massacres of Marion du Fresne and some of his crew, and the crew of the *Boyd*. Such affrays emphasised the dangers of commercial contact with the Maori, but such was their demand for European goods and particularly military hardware that the Maori soon accommodated themselves to even the most outrageous behaviour of Europeans. For a period after 1815 New Zealand offered merchants and whalers lucrative cargoes of whale oil, flax (scraped by hand by Maori women at a ton per musket) and timber, cheap provisions and ample pleasures.

The details of this burgeoning commerce cannot be measured here; my concern is with commerce as an agent for civilising Maori. Though there was much criticism of the activities of unscrupulous traders and the ill effects of unregulated trade in muskets and spirits, few European observers doubted the ultimate beneficence of properly conducted commerce. Take for instance that pioneer of commerce and Christianity in New Zealand, the Rev. Samuel Marsden, chaplain to the convict settlement at New South Wales and founder of the Anglican mission to New Zealand. He indulged in the New Zealand trade (though not, be it added, the musket trade) for his personal profit, distributing agricultural implements in the rather naive hope that they would be used solely for agricultural purposes: 'as the comforts of the natives increase so will their civilization be proportionately improved. . . . They neither want industry nor natural ability of mind nor strength of body. All these they possess, perhaps, in superior degree to any other barbarous race upon earth. And as their climate and soil are suitable for agriculture they no doubt will make a very rapid progress in the attainment of the necessary comforts of civil life.'[11] Thanks to the patient instruction of Marsden's lieutenants — and also to an insatiable demand for iron wares — Maori did make rapid progress in agriculture, and in the barter of agricultural produce with visiting ships. Marsden saw in agriculture and trade the first steps in civilisation and, in turn, the adoption of Christianity; for Maori, they provided the wherewithal for war. Certainly Hongi Hika, the Ngapuhi chief who was the first to obtain a supply of muskets, was to demonstrate in his career of conquest in the 1820s that trade provided the sinews of war. Other chiefs quickly followed suit. Yet there was always hope that commercial activity would eventually provide a substitute for war. Thus Augustus Earle, an itinerant artist who visited northern New Zealand in the late 1820s, hoped that commerce would replace barbarous rites. After a visit to the Hokianga river where he noted the Maori keenly working in a European boat-yard, Earle described boat-building as 'the best method of civilizing a savage'.[12] And, as J. S. Polack put it, 'however simple the wants of people may be, yet no sooner are they possessed of the article of European manufacture, the possession of it begets additional requisites; thus, slowly, but nevertheless eventually, progresses their civilization'.[13] Polack was writing in the year of New Zealand's annexation when there was widespread optimism that Maori had at last found in agriculture and trade a substitute rather than the means for war: 'The most pleasurable devotion of time, is no longer the dance of love or war; but barter .... This new passion with the New Zealander, may be regarded as the primary cause of his progression, from uncivilization to a new moral state of existence.'[14] Another observer saw Maori as having become 'irrevocably enslaved by wants which were unfelt by their ancestors'.[15]

European optimism was to continue in the first two decades of colonisation, despite the setbacks of military conflict in the New Zealand Company settlements and Heke's war in the north, for Maori continued to supply the colonists with agricultural produce, labour and other services. By the early 1850s Maori agriculture was so advanced that they were able to supply the bulk of New Zealand's exports to the Victorian goldfields. Sir George Grey, who as governor had effectively ended the conflicts in the Cook Straits settlements and in the north and done much to encourage Maori agriculture and commerce, left the country in peace and prosperity in 1853, confidently asserting that the amalgamation of the races was rapidly being achieved.[16] By 1859, when A. S. Thomson published his *Story of New Zealand . . . Savage and Civilized*, the progress was even more impressive:

> tattooed natives are seen between the plough handles, and men congregate around the evening fire to talk about the appearance of the crops. The sound of the flail is heard in the huts; and beggars, the constant attendants of the enlightened civilisation of Europe, are unknown. The engrossing subjects of conversation are the relative value of mills, vessels, horses, and bullocks, with the best means of raising money for purchasing these articles. . . . But the amount of free-labour produce exchanged for articles of usefulness and gratification is the best measure of this progressive civilisation . . . idleness, the besetting sin of savages and the root of all evil, is fast giving way to industry.[17]

Within a year this idyllic condition was being destroyed by war between the races. But discussion of this crisis in the civilising mission needs to be postponed until the roles of Christianity and colonisation have been more fully discussed.

In the New Zealand case the precise relationship of commerce and Christianity as agents of civilisation was subject to some confusion. Marsden assumed that it was necessary to civilise before attempting to convert the heathen. So he started his New Zealand mission with godly mechanics rather than ordained priests. Kendall, the first head of the mission, was a schoolmaster; he was accompanied by a blacksmith and a carpenter; and a little later, in response to Hongi's persistent requests, Marsden sent over George Clarke, a gunsmith. But the godly mechanics made no progress whatsoever in converting the Maori. Their predicament was neatly if cruelly summed up by the ungodly Earle: 'I once saw a sturdy blacksmith . . . sitting in the midst of a group of savages, attempting to expound to them the mysteries of our holy redemption — perplexing his own brains, as well as those of his auditors, with the most incomprehensible and absurd opinions.'[18] In fact the local missionaries were gradually rectifying Marsden's error. The arrival of the Williams brothers in the mid-1820s had provided a new and effective leadership. Henry, a former naval officer, became head of the CMS mission, earned the respect of the proud and turbulent chiefs as a man of mana, and began to emerge in the late 1820s as a successful peacemaker. William was a scholar who gave a lead to the translation of Christian texts into the Maori language and later produced the first useful Maori dictionary. The missionaries now reversed Marsden's priorities and concentrated on Christian instruction and conversion before civilisation. They were soon to be justified: in the 1830s there was first a trickle and then a flood of 'conversions'. It was now generally agreed — even by Marsden's first biographer — that the missionaries had been right and Marsden wrong.[19] As the historian Herman Merivale argued, the only experiments in civilisation which offered the remotest chance of success were those which commenced with religious instruction.[20] Others, not too concerned with priorities, were content to equate the two. Thus, according to G. L. Craik, the Maori had been 'brought at least into contact with the light of knowledge and of religion .... Christianity, emphatically the religion of civilization, goes forth among them ....'[21] Christianity, the religion of civilisation: that was a phrase that would reverberate through the mission records;[22] Christianity would do for the Maori what it had done for the barbarous inhabitants of Britain.[23]

For some years the mission stations, with their neat cottages and cultivations, their regular religious observances, their prim morality and their pious converts, were islands of Christian civilisation in a barbarous sea.[24] Yet, as the missionary W. Yate noted in 1835 in discussing one of those 'hopeful deaths' that so encouraged the mission camp, 'the New Zealanders are neither too ignorant nor too savage to be made the subjects of the saving and sanctifying influence of the Gospel.... [T]he time is not far distant, when the nation will be acknowledged as a Christian nation ....'[25] He was right; the heathen tide was beginning to recede. By 1847 G. F. Angas, another itinerant artist, could announce that 'the change from barbarism has been rapid ... and complete'.[26] He went on to contrast the scene with that of eight years ago when at J. Morgan's mission station in the Waikato 'cannibals held banquets of human flesh at his door' before a terrified Mrs Morgan. Fortunately the 'cannibal banquet' was a thing of the past, and within about ten years the bulk of the Maori population had become professing Christians or, as they called themselves, mihinare Maori. Most of them had joined the mission camp.

Whether they had been genuinely converted — made over in body and soul to Christ — has been much debated,[27] for it often seemed that Maori had taken over the external expressions of Christian civilisation without its inner religious conviction. Thus the Maori demand for literacy could, since all the texts were religious, be interpreted as a Maori thirst for Christian instruction; but it was to a large extent merely an urge to learn to read and write.[28] The same sort of point could be made about mission-promoted agriculture and even Victorian social practices: Maori motives in adopting these did not necessarily coincide with missionary objectives. Though there were a few contemporary cynics, most observers were content to laud the missionary achievement in converting and civilising the Maori, at least until the wars of the 1860s brought about a massive Maori rejection of the missionaries (if not of their message). Prior to that, Maori backsliding could usually be attributed to the influence of degenerate whites. By the late 1830s it had become evident that hopes of a mission-dominated theocracy were being destroyed by a rapid influx of lawless settlers, many of them escaped or ex-convicts or ships' deserters. Such uncontrolled colonisation by 'the veriest refuse of civilized society'[29] was unlikely to promote civilisation but destroy the progress that had been made. On this point the missionaries and the colonial reformers led by E. G. Wakefield were in agreement.

Before examining the contribution of systematic colonisation to the civilisation of Maori, it is worth pausing briefly to see if anything can be said for what Robert FitzRoy, later a governor of New Zealand, called these 'democratic seceders from regular government',[30] the Pakeha-Maori. Though these pre-1840 settlers had many critics, they also had a few defenders. The exuberant Earle, having earned missionary disapproval by living with a Maori girl, claimed that the whalers had done more to civilise the Maori than the missionaries: 'To the courage and enterprise of the commanders of whalers all credit is due for working the rapid change in these once bloody-minded savages.'[31] In later years some of the old settlers managed to make themselves into a legend. According to W. Brodie, anxiously promoting the land claims of the old settlers, 'We, by personal sufferings and exertions, laid the foundations of an empire; we civilized and Christianized the savage.'[32] In 1862 F. E. Maning, the most famous Pakeha-Maori of them all, immortalised his kind in *Old New Zealand*, a book which has undeservedly become a local classic. Not surprisingly, it was not Maning but the historian Thomson who attempted an objective assessment of the role of the old settler. Thomson was no missionary-baiter and gave proper recognition to the achievements of Marsden and the missionaries. He had no time for the beachcombers, but he staunchly defended the Pakeha-Maori traders and the whalers: 'Impartial witnesses, in 1840, admitted the civilisation introduced by these men to be more practically useful than that around the missionary stations.... The truth is, their evil doings, which were neither few nor small, were loudly proclaimed, while their good deeds were unrecorded.... [T]hey taught the natives to trust white men, and encouraged industry, the promoter of peace and civilisation, by opening up a steady market for flax and potatoes; their half-caste children were hostages for good behaviour, and stepping-stones to health and progress.'[33]

Thomson could have said more, for he was on the point of drawing an important contrast between the approach of missionaries and Pakeha-Maori to the civilising mission. The missionaries tried to promote the civilisation of Maori while also retaining a considerable measure of social separation; they tried to turn Maori into brown-skinned Pakeha, but, apart from rare sinners, they did not take Maori wives or even encourage their sons to do so (and for their daughters to take Maori husbands would have been unthinkable). But Pakeha-Maori had no hesitation in taking Maori mistresses; and the Dane, Phillip Tapsell, even persuaded the missionaries to give him a Christian marriage. They were therefore the real pioneers of the amalgamation of the races. Yet, as Thomson concluded, the 'golden age' of the Pakeha-Maori trader did not long outlast the coming of systematic colonisation. He was no longer needed once a numerous body of settlers had been established since Maori could deal directly with them. But there was more to the decline of Pakeha-Maori than that. Like the missionaries, the colonists brought wives with them, or made up the shortfall by importing seamstresses and servant girls. The social distance of the mission stations was perpetuated in the colony at large and the rate of miscegenation slowed. New Zealand was to be no Portuguese colony. Yet it is important to emphasise that there was no formal segregation, nor any significant demand for it: colonial New Zealand remained committed to the amalgamation of the races.[34]

With annexation and the beginning of systematic colonisation under the auspices of the New Zealand Company the civilising mission gained a new lease of life. According to Wakefield and Ward, the plans of their organisation were 'altogether new ... for, though professions of a desire to civilize barbarians have often been used as pretexts for oppressing and exterminating them, no attempt to improve a savage people, by means of colonization, was ever made deliberately and systematically. The success of such an experiment must in a great measure depend on the natural capacity of the inferior race for improvement.... [I]n this respect, the native inhabitants of New Zealand are superior to most, if not all thoroughly savage people.'[35] Company spokesmen deemed it expedient to use the language of the humanitarians. Historians have come to treat with a grain of salt the exalted promises of Wakefield and his fellow propagandists. But their plan for civilising the Maori should not be too cynically dismissed for much of the programme of the New Zealand Company became the common property of the colony when the settlers achieved self-government.

At the heart of the Company plan were the proposals to deal with Maori land. The Company proposed to buy land for colonisation from the Maori owners but considered it unnecessary to pay a high price, since the 'real payment' was to be 'the conferring on them of the great boon of civilization'.[36] Then, every eleventh allotment in each settlement was to be reserved for the Maori chiefs from whom the land had been purchased, and allocated to them in the lottery by which the remainder of the land was allotted to European colonists. Wakefield hoped to create a Maori landowning gentry interspersed among the European gentry, an early exercise of 'pepper-potting'. Just as the European colonists would employ Company labourers, so the Maori landowners would employ Maori labour recruited from the lower ranks of the tribe. It was a system which Jerningham Wakefield said would preserve the chief in his high station among his own people and, through social alliances with the settlers, promote amalgamation — 'perhaps the wisest and most charitable devices for the gradual amelioration of the barbarous races ... that have been known in the history of the world'.[37] '[T]here is good reason to hope,' said his father, 'that ... future generations of Europeans and natives may intermarry and become one people.'[38] And this was far better than segregating the Maori on large and remote reserves like the Indian reserves of Canada where 'the defective habits and inclinations of the savage are preserved, and his existence as an isolated and inferior being is encouraged and perpetuated'.[39] Moreover, Maori were thought to be manageable. Divided into hostile tribes and thought to number some 115,000 in the early 1840s,[40] they constituted no long-term barrier to colonisation. It was true that their warrior reputation meant that they could not be shot off like vermin — like the Australian and Tasmanian Aborigines — and if further warning was needed it was delivered with the Wairau massacre in 1843; there were no more settler commandos. The methods of the South African and Australian frontiers could not be easily applied in New Zealand. Nor was there any need to apply the segregation policies of those colonies since the Maori continued to display a capacity and apparently a desire for civilisation. Amalgamation remained a possible goal.

There is no need to examine the detailed working of the Company plan. It was hopelessly bungled through dishonest and incomplete purchases and haphazard administration.[41] Many legitimate Maori claimants were left out of the original purchases and even those whose rights were recognised were often unhappy with the reserves that were allocated to them, since these seldom coincided with existing villages. Though a few of the chiefs were carefully patronised by the Wakefields and went, top hats, morning suits and all, to Company levees, for most Maori systematic colonisation under the Wakefield system proved a disillusioning experience that boded ill for their future. Yet that future rested more in the hands of the government than the New Zealand Company which was soon forced to abandon its colonising role.

Under the Treaty of Waitangi of 1840 Maori rights to land were recognised, and the Crown was accorded a right of pre-emption to purchase such lands as the Maori owners were willing to sell. The Crown thus played a vital role in the continuation of colonisation. If plenty of Maori land was purchased and made available for settlement the colonists were relatively content; if not, they pressed for the abolition of pre-emption and the right to purchase land directly from Maori. This was conceded by the hapless Governor FitzRoy in 1844, but his successor, Grey, resumed pre-emption. He embarked on a vigorous programme of purchase and managed to acquire land well in advance of the needs of settlement in many parts of the country. However, neither Grey nor his successor, Browne, was able to purchase much land in Taranaki or Waikato, two of the most fertile and desirable districts in the North Island. In particular there was a bitter dispute over the Waitara block in Taranaki. Governor Browne's attempt to purchase part of this block from a minor chief, in defiance of the leading chief and the bulk of his tribe, and the occupation of the disputed land by military force led to the outbreak of war in 1860.[42] The war soon spread to Waikato and other districts; it continued intermittently for more than ten years. As a consequence of settler criticism of the government bungling of the Waitara purchase, the Crown's right of pre-emption was abolished once more by the Native Lands Act of 1862. A second Native Lands Act in 1865 provided for a Native Land Court to adjudicate Maori titles and allowed settlers to purchase land belonging to the individuals named in the court's orders. The system of 'free trade' in Maori lands thus initiated was to continue for many years.[43]

This brief recital of the main facts relating to the conflict over land and the outbreak of war needs to be related to the continuation of the civilising mission. For the Crown purchase regime had continued some of the leading features of the Wakefieldian system. As Grey and the chief land purchase commissioner, Donald McLean, never tired of telling the Maori, it was not the low price that was paid that would be their real benefit, but the settlement in their midst of civilised colonists.[44] Civilisation would spread to the Maori like a benevolent infection. And something like the Company 'tenths' system was continued in some of the Crown purchases in that provision was made for the establishment of small Maori reserves or endowments for supporting schools or hospitals. Little practical effect was given to these provisions. For Maori who had sold land the future was by no means as bright as the purchase agents had pretended. The shiny gold sovereigns paid for the land were soon spent, but the land was gone forever. And as the Maori landed estate decreased, colonists continued to pour into the country: in 1858 the European population passed that of Maori whose numbers were declining. The progress of colonisation was being achieved by the dispossession, possibly the extermination, of Maori. This much became evident with the great pressure that was exerted on the Waitara and Waikato tribes. Their progressive advance in agriculture — in civilisation — brought forth the admiration and the envy of the settlers; but in resisting the European seizure of their lands in the wars they were described as rebels and suffered the confiscation of their land. Yet even confiscation could be justified by an appeal to the civilising mission; it was necessary, said Premier Domett in 1863, to confiscate the land of the rebel Maori to force them into civilisation, since peaceful methods had failed.[45]

It is rather too tempting to see in the settler use of their civilising mission a cynical attempt to possess Maori lands, by fair means or foul. But there was rather more to it than that. There was the equally important question of law and order.[46] Ever since the Treaty of Waitangi had transferred sovereignty from Maori chiefs to the Queen, and New Zealand had become a British colony, the governors and, after them, settler politicians, had set their faces firmly against any independent exercise of sovereign powers by Maori chiefs, let alone the Maori King who was set up by the Waikato tribes in 1858. Despite the urging of the Colonial Office and a special provision in the 1852 Constitution Act to set aside districts beyond the European settlements where Maori law and custom would prevail, no such districts were ever established. It was the consistent object of successive New Zealand governments to bring Maori and their property within the scope of English civil and criminal law, including locally enacted laws. This could be seen as upholding not merely the first article of the Treaty of Waitangi (which related to the transfer of sovereignty) but also the third, which promised Maori the rights and privileges of British subjects. The Maori were to have equality before the law, reiterated in successive pieces of legislation, including the Native Rights Act 1865. At the height of the war there were some infringements of this principle, notably with the New Zealand Settlements Act of 1863, which provided for the confiscation of the 'rebels' land', and the Suppression of Rebellion Act, also of 1863, which permitted trial by court martial and the suspension of *habeas corpus*. Yet these were seen as temporary expedients, necessary to bring the 'rebel' Maori under law and order. And while military suppression of the 'rebellion' continued, legislation designed to bring about a long-term peace was being passed.[47] The Native Rights Act and the Native Lands Acts were part of this. So too was the Maori Representation

Act of 1867 which provided for the election — by adult male franchise — of four Maori to the House of Representatives. When the 1852 Constitution Act was framed it was assumed that Maori would exercise the franchise along with Europeans, on a common roll. A few did in fact do so, but the courts decided that Maori property, being communal, could not be used as a qualification; they needed individual freehold or leasehold titles. The Native Lands Acts made provision for such titles but little land had been individualised and few Maori electors registered when the Act of 1867 was passed. The government of the day had decided that Maori representation was a useful expedient to balance an increase in South Island representation to enfranchise the gold diggers. Separate Maori representation was expected to be temporary; it has remained to this day because Maori have been unwilling to give it up.

Several other aspects of government policy of the 1860s need to be mentioned since these reinforced the drive to assimilate Maori. Thus the Native Schools Act of 1867 provided for village primary schools to replace the now-deserted mission schools; these soon came to be regarded as a prime agency in the Europeanisation of Maori children, even to the extent of prohibiting the use of the Maori language. But they were not segregated schools since they admitted local European children. Then there was the continued introduction into largely Maori districts of resident magistrates. Unlike his counterpart in British territories in Asia and Africa, the RM was not an agent of indirect rule, but a key figure in displacing Maori law and custom by English criminal and civil law. The RM, the Native Land Court judge, the village schoolteacher and the Native Medical Officer, had succeeded the merchants and the missionaries as the prime agents of civilisation.

It is time to return to the question posed at the beginning: Why was the policy of assimilation continued in New Zealand when it was being tempered or abandoned elsewhere?

Clearly, the main reason was that assimilation could be equated with settler interests, notably in relation to the acquisition of Maori land. It was hardly coincidental that legislation was passed to individualise Maori land titles and allow 'free trade' in Maori land, and to confiscate the land of 'rebel' Maori soon after the settlers took responsibility for Native Affairs in the early 1860s. The objective of the Native Lands Act, Henry Sewell told Parliament, was twofold: to amalgamate the Maori to the British social and political system, and to bring the bulk of the Maori lands within the reach of colonisation.[48] The legislation, said Frederick Whitaker, was necessary 'to break down the beastly communism of the tribe' which stood as a barrier to the assimilation of the Maori.[49] The 'free trade' policy was continued vigorously for the remainder of the nineteenth century and played a vital part in the opening up of the central North Island for European settlement, including those two last refuges of Maori independence, the King Country and the Urewera. Moreover, the policy could be pursued with a relatively free conscience, since Maori population was still declining and there was little likelihood that they would need the land.

Though the Native Lands Acts were clearly the most important weapon in promoting the assimilation policy, other aspects of the application of law were of importance. In particular there was the continuing settler demand that all Maori who plundered, assaulted or murdered settlers must be brought to justice — to British justice — and prevented from absconding to Maori districts. This remained a problem even when the wars were over, since Maori accused of such crimes were able to obtain refuge in the King Country (until about 1885) or the Urewera (until 1892, or, in some estimates, 1917).[50] Coupled with the settler drive to impose the British legal and judicial system was a determination not to recognise any independent Maori authorities whether these were village runanga (committees) or quasi-national political movements like the King movement or Kotahitanga, the Maori Parliament or Home Rule movement of the late nineteenth century. Maori had been granted representation in the European Parliament; this was their proper forum. At Waitangi in 1840 Hobson had announced: 'We are now one people.'[51] Thereafter settlers were to assume, with some satisfaction, that they were fulfilling this pronouncement when they were making of the Maori a British people.

Finally, and this is a matter of considerable importance that is not examined here, there remained in Maori responses in the later nineteenth century sufficient to persuade Europeans that assimilation was indeed coming about. It is true that there was apparently a reversion to savagery, even to cannibalism, with the Hau Hau movement during the wars; but the movement quickly petered out and was replaced by pacifist Christian cults. More important, in the later stages of the wars several Maori leaders allied with the Europeans in the pursuit of rebel guerrilla leaders. These faithful allies could not be excluded from the post-war settlement; several of them became Maori MPs. But the future did not rest entirely in their hands. At the end of the century a new Maori elite emerged from the church secondary schools and universities. Their efforts for Maori health and land reform coincided with a revival of Maori population in the early years of the twentieth century.[52] Again it was plausible for Europeans to believe that their assimilation policy was working; now it seemed to have the enthusiastic support of a new Maori elite.

4

Folkland to Bookland:
F. D. Fenton and the Enclosure of the Māori 'Commons'

My 1955 MA thesis and several more recent studies of the early years of the Native Land Court in New Zealand concentrated on the role of the court as an engine behind the alienation of Māori land. Sir Hugh Kawharu called the court an 'Engine of Destruction', as did David Williams, who named his book *Te Kooti Tango Whenua* ('The Land Taking Court').[1] This essay does not further examine that conclusion but returns to a precedent that I briefly noticed in my thesis: that the native land legislation and court had followed the precedent of the English enclosures of common land. I suggested that the English enclosure movement 'had completed the long transition from communal to individual property' and that the native land legislation and court had attempted to perform a similar task in New Zealand: 'Individual Maori property was expected to emerge from the application of "Enclosure laws", not altogether unlike those which had caused so much distress in England.'[2] This essay further examines that precedent and the role of its main exponent, F. D. Fenton, the first chief judge of the Native Land Court, in promoting it.

Since the completion of my thesis and particularly since 1985 there has been much research and publication on the legislation and the court, mainly in reports prepared for or published by the Waitangi Tribunal. In 1985 the Tribunal was given retrospective jurisdiction to examine claims by Māori of

---

Originally published in *The New Zealand Journal of History*, vol. 45, no. 2 (2011), pp. 149–66. I am grateful to Alan Ward and Paul Hamer who read a draft of this essay and made many valuable suggestions which I have adopted.

Crown breaches of the principles of the Treaty of Waitangi since the Treaty was signed in 1840. That extension of jurisdiction encouraged a flood of historical claims, many of which have been reported on in the Tribunal's published district reports. Several of these and the research reports commissioned by the Tribunal, claimants and the Crown for various enquiries are used for this essay.[3] All of the reports have, in turn, been heavily reliant on the work of Alan Ward, also referred to frequently below.[4]

Francis Dart Fenton belonged to a prominent Yorkshire legal family and received his legal training in his uncle's law firm in Huddersfield. He came to New Zealand in 1850, disembarked in Auckland and soon afterwards travelled to Waikato where he intended to buy Māori land with his cousin, James Armitage. Fenton described this journey in a letter to his mother, noting that his party had travelled some 200 miles 'to see the country & make a choice of our land'. He commented on missionary stations and Māori settlements along the lower Waikato river and added that: 'these natives wanted us very much to buy land there and settle amongst them but their character is no inducement for one to go and settle amongst them, they are very covetous and try to get all they can out of you'.[5] In this letter Fenton treated the purchase of Māori land as a perfectly normal, legal procedure even though private purchases were prohibited under the 1846 Crown Land Ordinance which reasserted the Treaty of Waitangi-based Crown right of pre-emption. Fenton and Armitage became squatters on Māori land at Paetai, near the mouth of the river and near the station of the Church Missionary Society missionary Robert Maunsell. However, their situation was fraught with danger since there were numerous disputes with Māori, soon to come to the attention of Fenton when he became a magistrate in Waikato, as wandering Pākehā-owned cattle destroyed Māori cultivations. Fenton had a ready solution, discussed more fully below: to fence off individual holdings, an integral requirement of enclosure. Though the two men ran sheep and cattle on the holding, Fenton himself was not much involved and left the day-to-day operations to Armitage, who remained there until he was killed by a party of Ngāti Maniapoto in September 1863 while he was organising supplies for the British military forces after the invasion of Waikato.[6]

Because of his legal qualifications Fenton soon gained several official positions. Governor Grey appointed him as clerk in the Registry of Deeds office in 1851. He was successively resident magistrate at Kaipara (1854–56); temporary native secretary in 1856; resident magistrate at Waipa and Waikato (1857–58); civil commissioner in Waikato (1861); assistant law officer at Auckland

(1859–62); Crown law officer (1862–65); and finally, from January 1865, chief judge of the Native Land Court until his retirement in 1882.[7]

Fenton's private and official experiences in Waikato were particularly important in the development of his ideas about the transformation of Māori customary land tenure into officially recognised land titles. In 1859 he published *Observations on the State of the Aboriginal Inhabitants of New Zealand*, a paper that ably summed up existing knowledge on the causes of Māori depopulation. This essay is not concerned with that analysis but rather with Fenton's remedy for the depopulation. He recommended that Māori be given 'security and permanence to the occupation and possession of land [which] will be achieved by the grand requisite of civilization, fixity of residence'. This would 'wean the Maoris from their present desultory plan of agriculture.... Permanent fences [and] cultivated grasses ... will maintain sheep to furnish an annual income from their wool, and cows, whose milk will supply a nutritious food to the young....'[8] Fenton appended to his *Observations* a 'Scheme for the Partition and Enfranchisement of Lands held under Native Tenure'. He described this as a 'simple scheme for settling the Native title to land somewhat analogous to the system pursued by our Anglo-Saxon forefathers'; a process 'of separating common titles and apportioning lands [that] is not yet completed even in England'.[9]

Though he had no official sanction to do so, Fenton was already trying to carry out an enclosure scheme with Māori land in the Waikato while he was supposed to be attending to his duties as resident magistrate. His activities were outlined in his journals of that magistracy, which were printed in parliamentary papers. As I note in my essay on the King movement, Fenton's attempts to interfere with Māori tenure and occupation of land, combined with his and Armitage's squatting on land at Paetai and their direct links with the 'Free Trade' in Māori lands movement in Auckland, heightened Kingite fears of land loss. Those activities contributed directly to their decision to elevate Potatau te Wherowhero to the kingship in 1858.[10]

Fenton's 'Scheme for the Partition and Enfranchisement' of Māori land envisaged a formal enquiry into ownership, prior to the Crown issuing a certificate of ownership and eventually a Crown grant. Fenton considered that Māori and the Crown should be jointly involved in this enquiry, a principle that had been recognised recently with the Native District Circuit Courts Act and the Native Districts Regulation Act. He was aware that it was 'very questionable whether the suspicions of the people will allow them to permit the adjudication of their lands in pureiy European Courts, or otherwise by purely

European machinery'. Though Fenton did not mention it, this procedure was also envisaged in a third measure: the Native Territorial Rights Bill.

According to Ward, Native Minister C. W. Richmond was 'the framer' of this legislation,[11] but it is so infused with Fenton's ideas that it is likely that Richmond, who had close links with Fenton,[12] took his recommendations into consideration. However, rather than promoting the idea of Māori self-rule, Fenton recommended using the machinery that had been employed in the English enclosure movement: 'No machinery can be invented more admirably adapted to the performance of the duty of investigation of the ownership and partition of the common lands of the country, than the species of Court Leet and Great Court Baron recently created by the Native [District] Circuit Courts Act 1858.'

Then, in terms reminiscent of the English enclosures, Fenton set out how the 'process of legalizing tenure' would follow with Māori land. A 'book of Record' for registering the names of recognised owners and the boundaries of their land was to be kept in each magistrate's courthouse. Once a request for an enquiry was received, a notice was to be registered in the court roll and posted on the door of the court. If any adverse claims were received that were likely to create a 'political difficulty' the matter was to be adjourned 'for the present'. Otherwise, at the appointed time, the court was to proceed with a hearing before a jury (provided for under the criminal jury provisions in the Native District Circuit Courts Act). The magistrate and jury were to take evidence from claimants and any opponents, 'as an enquiry before the Commissioners under an Act for inclosing [sic] lands of common would be conducted in England'. At the end of the hearing the jury, guided if necessary by the magistrate, would decide who was entitled to the land, or whether it should be subdivided between various claimants, when a partition would be carried out and boundary markers established. Then the verdict was to be entered on the court roll as evidence of native title. This was to serve as the title deed. Subsequent changes of ownership were likewise to be registered and entered on the rolls, with a fresh title being issued. 'Thus', Fenton continued, 'will be established a very tractable tenure resembling the copyhold or base tenure of England, each District of a Court representing a Manor.' Finally, Fenton provided for the alienation of the land to 'a pakeha' merely by the transfer of the court's certificate of title to 'the purchasing pakeha', who would then receive a Crown grant.[13] As Fenton noted, local juries, assisted by commissioners, played a large part in the management and enclosure of land during the English enclosures.[14] But it was a moot point whether Māori juries, under the guidance of magistrates like Fenton, could do likewise in New Zealand.

Although most discussions on the British enclosures refer to those in England, there were analogous developments in Ireland and Scotland that also had some influence in New Zealand. The Irish suffered confiscation of land for rebellion — as did Māori with the confiscations under the New Zealand Settlements Acts. In Scotland, the crofters lost their customary rights to land through the clearances of the highland estates for sheep-walks.[15]

Nevertheless, it was the English enclosures that were mainly in Fenton's mind. These started with the Norman invasion, when Saxon lands were reallocated in feudal titles to Norman barons, though these overlaid Saxon customary rights of occupation. Subsequent enclosures transformed most of those remaining customary rights into private ownership, usually with the sanction of Acts of Parliament. Two kinds of land were enclosed: dispersed strips of cultivated land which were consolidated; and the fallow and forested land, or commons, beyond that which was used for grazing livestock and gathering wild produce or wood. With consolidation of the cultivated land and the commons the landholders, including richer tenants, gained titles to individual holdings and the lesser tenants and cottagers were dispossessed of their customary rights.

After the Norman occupation, enclosures were resumed periodically. Statutes of 1235 and 1285 permitted landlords to enclose 'wastelands' on condition that they left sufficient land for their free tenants. Then, with the expansion of the Flemish wool trade in the fifteenth century, landlords found it profitable to turn cultivated land and unenclosed commons into pastures — a very early precedent for the pastoral occupation in New Zealand. Enclosures reached a peak in the late seventeenth century, tailed off in the early eighteenth century but were resumed dramatically in the second half of that century and in the early nineteenth century. Those enclosures and an accompanying rise in rents forced many smallholding tenants to migrate to the American colonies.[16] Much of the enclosure took place by agreement or was enrolled in Chancery Decrees and recorded in court rolls. But where agreement was not possible enclosures were validated by private Acts of Parliament, providing for enclosures on a parish-by-parish basis. The first such Act was passed in 1710,[17] and by the later eighteenth century some 100 private enclosure Acts a year were being passed. Then a General Enclosure Act of 1801 standardised the process and an Act of 1845 provided for the incorporation of all enclosures in a single Act for each year. By this time the movement towards general enclosure was largely completed and most common fields had been enclosed.[18] Common communal rights with reciprocal obligations had been replaced by the notion of private property by which, as E. P. Thompson put it, 'rights are assigned away from users and in which ancient feudal title is richly compensated in its translation into capitalist property-right'.[19] Those rights were reinforced by the requirement that the owners fence or hedge their individual properties. Landless cottagers and labourers who tried to continue their customary practices of hunting, gathering and gleaning on once common land were now trespassers on private property and, in the extreme cases, were transported to the convict settlements of Australia.

The enclosures in England and the highland clearances in Scotland facilitated an agrarian revolution whereby land became a commodity rather than a bundle of use-rights. In the process smallholders and landless labourers were removed and funnelled into industrial cities or migrated, mainly to North America and later to Australia. A trickle of immigrants came to New Zealand, where they hoped to acquire land in place of that they had lost in Britain. Everywhere they were motivated by the 'growing pervasiveness of private property'.[20] This quotation refers to the migrants who became small landowners in North America, but it applies equally to New Zealand, where there was a determination to acquire land in freehold title. In England land rights were based on a three-tier structure: manorial rights based on freehold; copyhold titles or tenancies and subtenancies based on various kinds of leasehold; and commonages, based on customary rights to cottages, cultivated strips and grazing and gathering from the commons.[21] Though the feudal theory of English land law was transplanted to the colonies, few of the appertaining rights were accepted. Settlers were reluctant to accept restrictions of freeholds, and revaluation of rentals on leaseholds was unpopular. As for the commonage, pastoralists in New Zealand, as in Australia, were notorious for squatting on and taking resources from Crown land, but it was the Māori who retained rights to the 'commonage' on land that remained in their ownership.

Notions of property rights, developed during the enclosure movement, were easily translated to the colonies. Just as English law that facilitated enclosures would take no cognisance of a communal personality, so in the colonies it would not recognise the rights of hunter-gatherer peoples. Locke, in his discussion of property, lamented that 'the wild Indian' knew 'no enclosure' and was still 'a tenant in common'.[22] As Thompson observed, the American Indian 'served as a paradigm for an original state before property became individuated and secure', and he quoted Locke's famous aphorism: 'In the beginning all the world was America.'[23] Locke's Indian was poor 'for want of improving' the land by his labour, which, for Locke, constituted the right to property, and thereby justified the taking of uncultivated Indian land by colonists. The same notions, Thompson continued, were used to justify the taking of Aboriginal land in Australia, but could not be so easily applied in New Zealand where there was ample evidence of Māori occupation and cultivation of land which was recognised in the Treaty of Waitangi. And that led Thompson to contemplate how Māori rights in land 'came to be cashed in law' and the communal rights of Māori hapū might be 'loosed for the market'. In support he used Henry Sewell's much-quoted dictum of the need to bring about the 'detribalisation of the Natives' and to destroy 'the principle of communism which ran through the whole of their institutions' and which stood in the way of amalgamation with the European social and political system.[24] It was this background of enclosures that Fenton and fellow colonists used as a precedent in their attempts to transform Māori customary tenure in New Zealand; a transformation that was necessary if, in the terminology of the time, the two races were to be amalgamated.

Behind the advocacy of enclosure lay a broader evolutionary philosophy, stemming from the late-eighteenth-century Scottish enlightenment philosophers such as Robert Chambers, but recently reinforced by Darwin. It was also implicit in the standard texts of mid-nineteenth-century legal authorities such as Palgrave and Hallam, who were quoted by Fenton,[25] and another advocate for Māori advancement, Sir William Martin, the first chief justice in New Zealand.

In Martin's view of Māori land tenure the absence of '*an individual claim, clear and independent of the tribal right*' was in accord with 'the natural and normal condition of a primitive Society'. He used Palgrave's *English Commonwealth* for an example from ancient Germany and Hallam's *Constitutional History* for his claim that 'the tribal right was even more strongly recognised than it is now amongst the New Zealanders'. Martin believed that Māori needed to follow the example of 'our Anglo-Saxon Fathers' and the example of the Irish in 'the transition from the earlier to the more advanced state of things — from Clanship to Nationality' (a transition that was taking place before his very eyes with the recent selection of a Māori king). He explained in summary and somewhat simplified terms how the transition had applied to land. Anglo-Saxon land was 'either *folkland* or *bookland*'. Folkland was held by customary title and might be occupied in common or possessed in severalty but could not be alienated in perpetuity; bookland was land that had been severed by act of the government from the folkland and was held by book or charter. It had been converted into an estate of perpetual inheritance and could be alienated. Martin then applied the analogy to New Zealand: 'Folkland ... corresponded to the Native Tenure; Bookland to the tenure under a Crown Grant.' Though he accepted that Māori customary rights had been guaranteed by the Treaty of Waitangi, a guarantee that had since been 'solemnly and repeatedly recognised by successive Governors', Martin did not comment on how that 'folkland' title might be transformed into a 'bookland' title.[26]

Fenton used the same approach, suggesting that the 'character attached by the English authorities to the wild lands of the colony . . . seems to resemble very much that of the folcland [sic] or public land of the Saxons'. Any transfer of Māori 'wild lands' would not be valid unless by way of grant from the Crown; a process that Fenton likened to the conversion in England of 'folcland into bocland [sic] or land of inheritance'.[27] A customary title was thereby transformed into a certificate of title. Fenton and Martin shared the common belief that if Māori were to progress in civilisation and adopt a settled, efficient form of agriculture (that would also make room for European colonists) they too would have to go through an enclosure movement. Another who shared that view was F. E. Maning, an early Native Land Court judge, and a pioneer settler whose *Old New Zealand* (1863) was to become a classic. He claimed that the court was bringing about 'a revolution . . . which must of necessity displace barbarism and bring civilization in its stead, for the difference between a people holding their country as a commonage and holding it as individualized real property is, in effect, the difference between civilization and barbarism'. He claimed that Māori in the north who had received titles from the court were enclosing and cultivating their land — as well they might since, as Maning admitted, there was little pressure from the Crown or Europeans to purchase their land.[28] As in England, enclosure was promoted as being in the public interest. When these notions were translated into law with the Native Lands Act 1862, the Christchurch *Press* compared the process set out by the Act with those described in Maine's *Ancient Law*.[29]

It is evident from the quotes from Fenton, Martin and others that the original Saxon communal tenures and systems of farming that were transformed by the process of enclosure were regarded as being similar to the Māori customary arrangements that settlers found in New Zealand, whereby land was cultivated in scattered plots and then fallowed, and the bush beyond was used for hunting and gathering. It is not surprising therefore that Fenton advocated the 'enclosure' of individual holdings that would be permanently occupied and fenced. During his circuits in 1857–58 Fenton was confronted with acres of abandoned cultivations in the Waikato, following the collapse of agricultural exports to Australia, and proposed that the Māori there sow grass, pasture sheep and erect fences. But he did not see this as inhibiting the sale of land to Europeans since the Māori 'enclosures' would free surplus land for settlement by European farmers. He wanted the Māori population to be gathered 'in a few well defined central positions' — he mentioned Rangioawhia, Whatawhata, Kirikiriroa, Rangiriri and Tuakau — after which, he assumed, the remaining land would be 'abandoned' to the Europeans.[30] In stressing the need for fixity of tenure and residence on fenced farms, Fenton was in line not only with the English enclosures but also with other colonial situations; for instance, in New England where fences were of pivotal importance in the taking and retaining of Indian land and in separating wandering stock from cultivations.[31]

It is necessary to return to Fenton's involvement with the native lands legislation. The Native Lands Act 1862 was the culmination of several previous attempts to abolish Crown pre-emption and allow direct settler purchase of Māori land. Governor FitzRoy did this with his 10/- and 1d per acre proclamations in 1844, though they were in breach of the Treaty of Waitangi, and Grey resumed pre-emption with his Native Land Purchase Ordinance in 1846. The 1858 Native Territorial Rights Bill was another attempt to provide for settler purchase of Māori land. It was part of a package of legislation that, according to Ward, was framed by Native Minister C. W. Richmond,[32] though it clearly incorporated ideas advanced by Fenton. Overall, as Donald Loveridge puts it, the Bills gave 'legislative form' to Fenton's proposals.[33] These were part of a larger scheme that was later called indirect rule whereby European officials, assisted by native assessors and juries, applied English law that was modified to include acceptable local customs. Thus a Native District Regulations Act authorised local councils, chaired by a Pākehā official, to make local by-laws. A Native District Circuit Courts Act provided for circuit court judges to sit with Māori assessors and juries to enforce such local by-laws and common law. The third measure, the Native Territorial Rights Bill, also envisaged using the circuit court judges and Māori juries to determine boundaries of land and award Crown grants of up to 50,000 acres a year in individual title. Such land could be alienated directly to settlers, on payment of a 10/- per acre tax. This use of circuit court judges and Māori juries resembled the arrangement whereby commissioners and local juries managed the enclosure of land in English parishes. The Bill breached the Crown pre-emptive clause of the Treaty of Waitangi, was referred to the colonial secretary and disallowed. Nevertheless, the central idea behind it, of a European official presiding over a

Māori committee for the individualisation of titles prior to alienation, was to survive in the Native Lands Act 1862.

In 1859, while the legislature was awaiting royal assent for the Native Territorial Rights Bill, four new Bills were drafted. These included a Native Land Partition Bill, which Loveridge described as 'simply Fenton's "Scheme for the Partition and Enfranchisement of Native Lands" . . . converted into a statutory format' and which was apparently drafted by Fenton himself. The scheme was to be administered by a tribunal or court, with a Māori jury or council presided over by a European magistrate or judge, again along the lines that Fenton had proposed in 1858.[34] Although the governor asked Sewell to prepare a Bill along these lines in 1861, the proposal did not survive a change of ministry later in the year.

With the outbreak of the Taranaki war in 1860, following the Crown's bungled Waitara purchase, there was a change of opinion in Britain in favour of direct settler purchase of Māori land. In a despatch of 5 June 1861, the Duke of Newcastle, secretary of state for the colonies, indicated that he would approve 'any prudent plan for the individualisation of native title' and for direct purchase by settlers under proper safeguards that the New Zealand Parliament may wish to adopt.[35] The proposal received further impetus with the return of Grey as governor late in 1861. Grey came armed with Newcastle's instruction. When a new session of Parliament opened in July 1862 the Fox Ministry brought forward a Native Lands Bill that Sewell had been asked to draft. But when Fox's Ministry was replaced in August by a Domett Ministry, the new minister of native affairs, F. D. Bell, replaced Sewell's Bill with a new draft.

Historians are not agreed on Fenton's role in drafting the new Bill. According to W. L. Renwick, who wrote the entry on Fenton in the *Dictionary of New Zealand Biography*, 'Fenton's skills as a law draftsman were called on by Governor Grey, particularly for the drafting of the Native Lands Act 1862'.[36] Renwick does not source these statements. Alan Ward, David Williams, Donald Loveridge and Richard Boast, who have written at length on Fenton and the Native Lands Acts, do not describe him as the draftsman, though Ward says that the 1862 Act was 'in accordance with principles first suggested by Fenton himself in 1858–60'.[37] Boast suggests that, although Fenton was one of the law officers in 1862, he 'had not been involved in the design of the 1862 Act'.[38] Loveridge describes Bell as 'definitely the principal author of the Bill', though he adds that Fenton's influence was 'obvious', particularly in the composition of the court (a European magistrate presiding over a Māori 'jury'), and in the granting of certificates of title which could be in the names of a tribe or individuals with powers of alienation.³⁹ Finally, I note that Alexander Brown, who has written a thesis on the subject, also concludes that Fenton did not draft the Bill. He quotes Fenton's own denial in 1885 that 'the Act was not mine'.⁴⁰ I accept this as conclusive. We can regard Bell as 'the principal author' of the Bill.

Discussion over the Native Lands Bill in Parliament was framed by the war and the assumption that it had been caused by Crown purchase methods, especially at Waitara. In introducing the second reading, Bell claimed that individualising titles through a Native Land Court and allowing Māori to sell their land directly to settlers would 'dispell [sic] the jealousy and distrust in the native mind' and strike 'at the root of the agitation by which many of the tribes had been seduced from their allegiance to the Queen'. It was not merely a matter of sentiment for Māori to owe allegiance to the Crown and submit to British law but 'a matter of material interest to them to do it [and] . . . they will infallibly become wealthy men'.⁴¹ Bell's Bill had overwhelming support in Parliament, where many of the representatives from pastoral districts in the northern provinces were already squatting on Māori land and wanted to legalise their titles. The only opposition came from the superintendents of Auckland and Wellington, who feared the loss of land funds derived from the sale of Crown land.⁴² Parliamentarians, obsessed with the need to obtain Māori land, paid little heed to how individualisation of titles might help Māori to develop land that they retained. If they were aware of Fenton's plan for enclosure, following individualisation, they said nothing about it.

The 1862 Act retained the arrangement from the 1858 Bill of using a European magistrate as presiding official and a Māori panel of leading chiefs. On the application of 'any Tribe Community or Individual' a court was to be convened to determine the interests of the applicants and other claimants, to define tribal rights and boundaries in a district, and to compile a register (or 'Doomsday Book') of tribal lands — as had often been proposed. If the tribes wanted partition into individual titles the court could be reconvened to do this. Once the title was endorsed by the governor and the land was surveyed, the court could issue a certificate of title and the land could be alienated, whereupon the purchaser would receive a Crown grant. Loveridge demonstrates that the draft Bill was considerably amended in the House and to a lesser extent in the Legislative Council and by Grey before it was submitted for imperial approval.⁴³

The Bill did not receive Colonial Office approval until March 1863, and this was notified by proclamation on 6 June 1863. Contrary to the opinion of most historians, Loveridge argues that the Act was brought into operation reasonably quickly: even before the end of 1863 at Kaipara, where J. Rogan was resident magistrate and soon to be appointed a Native Land Court judge. In 1864 there were several hearings around the Kaipara harbour, at Whangarei and the Bay of Islands, at Port Waikato and at Coromandel, mainly presided over by Rogan.[44] George Clarke Jnr and W. B. White were appointed in addition to Rogan as judges, along with several chiefs who were named as assessors or jurors. Loveridge, who consulted Rogan's journals, noted that Rogan was familiar with Fenton's thoughts on the use of juries during the English enclosures. Although Ngāti Whātua at Kaipara were said to be enthusiastic about the new system, their participation was prompted by previous dealings in land, as, for instance, with the 396-acre Otamatenui block at Henderson which had already been sold to John and Isaac McLeod. It was conveniently awarded to one person, Te Otene, who then legalised the sale to the McLeods. That was a portent of things to come.

On 24 November 1864 the Whitaker–Fox Ministry was replaced by the Weld 'Self-Reliant Ministry'. According to Weld, on that first day in office he asked Fenton to become chief judge of the Native Land Court.[45] Ward says that Fenton was reluctant to accept the position but he assumed that it would not be arduous and that he could continue with private practice, but he accepted because he 'wanted to show that the land of New Zealand could be judicially dealt with'.[46] In another statement Fenton said he had accepted the appointment because the Native Land Court could be 'founded upon my own principles'.[47] Fenton began work even before his appointment was announced on 9 January 1865. On 29 and 31 December 1864 proclamations were issued abolishing the five districts that had been established under the 1862 Act and declaring the whole country a single district — even though there was no provision for this in the Act.[48] Over the next few months Fenton continued to reshape the court along the lines that were to be validated when the replacement Native Lands Act came into force on 30 October 1865.[49]

Despite the doubts over Fenton's involvement with drafting the 1862 Native Lands Act, historians usually conclude that he drafted the 1865 Bill. According to Renwick, Fenton was responsible for 'drafting and administering' the Act.[50] Ward says that Fenton, on his appointment as chief judge of the Native Land Court, 'promptly drafted a new Native Lands Act'.[51] Boast concludes that the Act 'was not merely drafted but was designed by' Fenton.[52] Loveridge, however, qualifies the prevailing view, saying that 'the Native Land Court as it existed at the end of 1865 was not the product of Fenton's mind alone, as some writers seem to think'. He adds that Sewell, Bell and Rogan had done more than Fenton, or anyone else, to bring the court as far as it was by the end of 1865. Loveridge saw the 1865 Act and the court as the end products of an intense debate that had been going on for a decade.[53] As for Fenton himself, he said in September 1885 that he was 'the author, to a large extent, of the Act'.[54] He dropped the 'large extent' qualification in 1891, when he said that 'the Act of 1865 . . . was my Act'.[55]

Like the Native Lands Act 1862, the Act of 1865 was introduced as the third leg of a tripod of Bills intended to combat the spreading Māori rebellion, now fuelled by the Paimarire creed. In this respect the most important of the three Bills was the draconian Outlying Districts Police Bill, which Ward said 'added a new and sweeping ground for confiscation'.[56] Native Minister J. E. Fitzgerald feared that Māori might regard the Bill as an aggressive assault on their land, so he stressed that the other two Bills were designed to protect Māori and their lands under the law. Thus the Native Rights Bill reasserted the Treaty of Waitangi's promise in Article 3 that Māori would have the rights and privileges of British subjects. And the new Native Lands Bill, which had been framed 'with great care and labour, with the assistance of the Chief Judge of the Native Land Court', provided that native land 'shall be dealt with by our law'.[57] At least the members of Parliament must have been reassured since there was little further discussion of the Bills in either the House or the Legislative Council.

The new Bill embodied a change of mind by Fenton on the essential elements of the previous system. Ward attributes the change partly to Fenton's 'own ambition and vanity' and partly to 'the belief, now advanced most strongly by Fenton but also widely held among the settler community, that only a solemn legal tribunal would be respected by contending Maori claimants'. Ward adds that there was 'some justification for an authoritative tribunal' since demarcation of territory between two or more iwi or hapū was seldom clear-cut and uncontested.[58] Though Ward does not say so, the experience of the previous few years, following the eruption of the dispute over the Waitara purchase into war, may have led Fenton to conclude that Māori could not settle their interminable disputes over title to land without an overarching official authority.

As Ward noted, on his appointment as chief judge of the Native Land Court, Fenton 'was given virtually a free hand in reorganising the Court and making appointments, and promptly used it'.[59] But it was not so much in the terms of the new Act, which Fenton regarded as an 'amendment' of the 1862 Act with 'no new principle', but in his operation of it that there was an abrupt change. In place of a Māori-focused court, dominated by Māori jurors, a new tribunal emerged, 'organised along the lines of the Supreme Court, whereby a roving Judge could sit in any centre, summon witnesses, hear evidence and hand down a judgment with due pomp and formality'.[60] The new court became a formal court of record, and Fenton, in drafting the Bill, was careful to ensure that his own considerable salary of £800 a year was protected by the law. The role of Māori in the court process was reduced to that of assessors who were to advise the judges on Māori custom, but they held office 'during pleasure', while the judges were appointed to hold office 'during good behaviour' (section 6). A quorum for all judicial matters in the court was to be one judge and two assessors, and all had to concur in a judgment (section 120). This seemed to give assessors considerable authority, though Williams and others conclude that this was not so and that assessors who dissented were invariably ignored by presiding judges.[61]

It is necessary to discuss the main provisions of the Act. The preamble stated that its purpose was to ascertain the persons who, according to Māori proprietary customs, were the owners of land; to provide for the extinction of those customs and their conversion into titles derived from the Crown; and to provide for the regulation of descent for such land. The purposes were given effect by sections 21, 23 and 30. Section 21 allowed 'any Native' to apply to the court for ascertainment of title and a certificate of title. Section 23 allowed the court, after hearing evidence from the applicant and other claimants, to issue a certificate of title to those found to be entitled according to native custom. However, there was an important proviso to section 23: 'that no certificate shall be ordered to more than 10 persons; provided further that if the piece of land adjudicated upon shall not exceed 5000 acres such certificate may not be in favour of a tribe by name'.

The interpretation of this proviso, particularly by Fenton, caused much controversy, led to the dispossession of many Māori of their legitimate interests in land, and prompted important amendments to and eventually the replacement of the 1865 Act. Although section 23 clearly allowed blocks over 5000 acres to be awarded to tribes, Fenton and other judges seldom applied this provision. Fenton admitted in 1891 that there had been only two instances where the court had issued such titles. He was aware that the legislation required the court 'to refuse titles until the estates were reduced by division to ten', but admitted that the ten names were selected out of court 'by arrangement' with the Māori claimants and the European purchaser. They were then 'described to the Court as the owners, the object being to avoid the expense of divisional surveys'. Though Māori were required to have land surveyed before the court awarded title, the surveys were arranged and paid for by European purchasers, with those costs deducted from final payments when titles were awarded and alienation was completed. Clearly, it was in the interest of the European purchasers to avoid the cost of subdivisional surveys, which they did by purchasing the interests of the ten 'owners' of undivided land. Fenton assumed that the purchase money was then paid and 'divided amongst all interested', but he admitted he had no official knowledge of this. He further claimed that 'The Natives fell rapidly into this system'.[62] In all of this Fenton seems to have been affecting a judicial amnesia, since it was notorious that in the very transactions he was discussing, particularly the alienation of the Heretaunga and other blocks in Hawke's Bay, the system the court had blessed defrauded many legitimate claimants.

Fenton was unapologetic about this, writing in a comment on the working of the 1865 Act in 1867 that:

> The ultimate result of the operations of the Court will be the conversion of the Maori nation into two classes — one composed of well-to-do farmers and the other intemperate landlords. The intemperance and waste so noticeable amongst the Maori landlords of Hawkes Bay are ... much to be regretted; but ... it is not part of our duty to stop eminently good processes because certain bad and unpreventable results may collaterally flow from them, nor ... is [it] the duty of the legislature to make people careful of their property by Act of Parliament, so long as their profligacy injures no one but themselves.[63]

This acceptance of what would now be called 'market forces' was echoed by the two European commissioners, Richmond and Judge Maning, in their report on the transactions for the Hawke's Bay Native Lands Alienation Commission.[64]

In 1871 Fenton assured Donald McLean that the Hawke's Bay transactions 'were perfectly fair and honourable on the part of the European purchasers'.[65] Fenton was unconcerned that the land was being awarded to one or two chiefs, with the rest of the right-holders dispossessed, since he considered that the chiefs 'should have sufficient land secured to them to render certain their status as gentlemen'.[66] Gentlemen, I might add, who would profit from this enclosure of communal Māori land provided they did not squander the proceeds on extravagant living. When the Act came into force the chiefs were already heavily in debt to Hawke's Bay storekeepers and publicans. Runholders, squatting on Māori land on the basis of extra-legal leases, were able to use the Act to validate their titles, and within a few years little land remained in Māori ownership.[67]

The other main object of the 1865 Act was to provide for succession where an owner died intestate. In such a case, section 30 of the Act required the Native Land Court to decide who, as nearly as could be reconciled with native custom, were entitled to succeed. This led not so much to controversy as to confusion, since the court, having been instructed to convert customary titles into individual titles derived from the Crown, was required to allocate the hereditaments of intestate owners according to customary rules. The question was dealt with by Fenton in his judgment on *Papakura — Claim of Succession*. This concerned succession to Ihaka Takaanini's estate of 1120 acres of land near Papakura. In a convoluted judgment, Fenton began by saying that the Native Lands Act 1865 required the court to 'ascertain who, according to law, as nearly as it can be reconciled with native custom, ought ... to succeed to the hereditaments the subject of the investigation'. Though Fenton thought that the legislature intended that English law should regulate succession to Māori land, he allowed exceptions 'where a strict adherence to English rules of law would be very repugnant to native ideas and customs'. And, though he thought it would be 'highly prejudicial to allow tribal tenure to grow up and affect land that has once been clothed with a lawful title', he proceeded to do just that by declaring:

> The Court does not think the descent of the whole estate upon the heir-at-law could be reconciled with native ideas of justice or Maori custom; and in this respect only the operation of the law will be interfered with. The Court determines in favour of all the children equally.... Erina Takaanini, Te Wirihana Takaanini and Ihaka Takaanini ought to succeed to the hereditaments above mentioned in equal shares as tenants in common.[68]

This interpretation — or perhaps I should say misinterpretation — of customary rules of succession was to remain in vogue for many years. It created a form of tenure that was in accord neither with Māori custom nor with English law and was greatly to exacerbate the fractionation of Māori land. Instead of applying the English law of primogeniture for succession of intestate estates, the court, under Fenton, assumed that Māori custom required succession to be applied equally to all offspring, male and female.[69] Ironically, by providing for that form of equal succession, all offspring were entered on titles, thereby defeating Fenton's original plan to enclose land in the private ownership of a minority of chiefs. Moreover, equal succession was applied whether or not the heirs lived on the land, thus infringing the Māori custom that hereditary rights to land needed to be reinforced by occupation.

In 1867 a new Native Lands Act was passed to deal with some of the problems that had arisen from the 1865 Act. But it was not drafted by Fenton, who said that it was 'Mr Justice Richmond's Act, drawn up with Judge Prendergast's assistance'. Prendergast, the chief justice, had 'put in legal form what Mr James Richmond told him he wanted'.[70] The Act attempted to deal with the problem created by Fenton's interpretation of the 'ten owner rule' by laying down (section 17) that the court was to ascertain the right and title not merely of the applicant but of every other person or tribe interested in the land under claim. Though certificates of title were still to be issued to no more than ten persons, all others with interests were to be listed in the court records and a recital to this effect was to be entered on the certificate. However, section 17 did not automatically apply to all titles subsequently issued, and Fenton chose not to apply it since he believed that 'the true remedy was to compel the tribe to sub-divide ... until each ten of the tribe had got his share', irrespective of the costs to the owners of surveying those subdivisions.[71] But, as Fenton well knew, that had not occurred because of the expense of subdivisional surveys. Fenton made further comment on the Act in the Native Land Court at Auckland on 7 April 1868, when he said that the effect of the clause 'would be to make perpetual the Communal holdings of the Natives', since listing other names in the records of the court would create 'a system of concealed equities ... even if all the equitable interests could always be ascertained, which is a question open to grave doubts'. For this reason Fenton believed that the court had 'discretion' whether or not to apply the clause and, as Ward points out, 'he continued to issue Certificates of Title to ten owners as if they were the only claimants'.[72] Some other judges such as Rogan attempted to apply the provision, but they were usually defeated by the lack of 'satisfactory evidence', since Māori claimants had conveniently declined to name more than ten owners.[73]

If Fenton did not like the 1867 Act, he got his revenge when he drafted an amendment and, while temporarily a member, introduced it in the Legislative Council in 1869. He said that it was designed to correct 'several defects' in the Native Lands Acts, especially that of 1867. He did not explain the defects but assured the council that they were 'of a formal character, involving no principle'.[74] Subsequently Fenton said that he had drafted the Bill to overcome the problem of getting the assent of all listed owners required by the 1867 Act: 'Under the Act of 1869, which was mine, provision was made requiring the assent to a sale of the majority in value.' Fenton added that 'the Court in administering that [1867] Act found it practically impossible to discriminate between the values of individual Natives; and the shares of the owners were practically treated as equal, not because it was right, but because the Court could do nothing else'.[75] The 1869 amendment Act appears not to have been widely used and is not discussed by either Ward or Boast, though it is discussed briefly in the Tribunal's *Hauraki Report*.[76]

It was replaced by the Native Lands Act 1873, the most influential and enduring Māori land Act ever passed. Despite numerous amendments, it was to remain at the core of that legislation until Te Ture Whenua Maori Act 1993. The 1873 Act was largely a response to the report of the Hawke's Bay Native Lands Alienation Commission. This led some to assume, as Fenton put it, that the Act was 'the work of Mr Justice Richmond', who chaired the commission, but he had told Fenton he had 'nothing to do with it'. Fenton then said that the Act 'was Mr [H. T.] Clarke's', though he admitted that John Curnin had drafted it.[77] The role of Clarke is unknown. Though Martin and Fenton had previously written drafts of the Act, the one finally presented to the House was undoubtedly the work of Curnin. He was then in the Crown Law Office, and admitted that he had drafted the Act 'for Sir Donald McLean', who had given him 'definite instruction . . . to ascertain all the titles and have them passed by the Native Land Court', with the court listing all owners in a memorial of ownership. McLean, who was now Native Minister, hoped to overcome the difficulty of having all owners assent to an alienation by partitioning the land into individual lots, but Curnin admitted that this did not happen. However, Boast adds that the Bill was not based solely on McLean's instructions to Curnin and that it did incorporate some recommendations of the chairman of the Hawke's Bay commission, Justice Richmond.[78]

Unsurprisingly, Fenton did not agree with many of the provisions of the 1873 Act. Ward notes that he 'produced a long document claiming to show that many of the clauses of the Act were contradictory and unworkable, and he made no effort to make them work'.[79] Fenton was particularly opposed to the requirement that all with customary rights in a block of land be named in a memorial of ownership. He described the Act as an attempt 'to do celestial justice which I always believe to be impossible in this wicked world', and he thought requiring all named owners of a block to consent to alienations was going too far, since 'no one recusant should have power to lock up land'.[80]

The Act represented a final defeat for Fenton's ideal of awarding Māori land to an elite who would emerge from the enclosure of Māori land as a landowning gentry, like those who had succeeded in the English enclosures. It could be said to represent an alternative ideal favoured by McLean that all with customary rights must be included in the ownership, though McLean hoped to overcome the difficulty of getting the assent of all owners to an alienation by having the land subdivided into individually or family owned lots.[81] That was never achieved, and the court continued to take the easy way out by simply listing all who had customary rights of ownership in a single memorial of ownership.

It is tempting to regard the 1873 Act as a victory for McLean in his long-running battle with Fenton, and even to portray McLean, who was familiar with the fate of the Scottish crofters, as the champion of the small men, including Māori; as against Fenton, who was determined to create a landowning Māori gentry at the expense of all other right-holders. But such a scenario is simplistic. McLean, who hailed from the Outer Hebrides, was the son of a wealthy tacksman, or leaseholder, who, like many Scots migrants to New Zealand, improved his lot immensely by becoming a substantial landowner on land he had purchased from Māori.[82] Fenton, on his retirement from the bench, also settled on land, at Kaipara, that he had purchased from Māori, though this was soon transferred to his sons. He also busied himself with *Suggestions for a History of the Origins and Migrations of the Maori People*, published in 1885. That took Māori history well back from the narratives he had heard in court to an origin in the biblical lands of Arabia.[83] And, despite his persistent attempts to promote a Māori gentry, Fenton himself applied English equity rules to divide Māori land on inheritance equally amongst all heirs, male and female, even though that contributed to endless division of inherited landholdings.

As for the Native Land Court, under the 1873 Act it remained 'an engine for destruction', though the alienation of Māori land was hindered by the need to get the signatures of all who were listed in the court's memorial of ownership, and, where this was impossible, by the requirement that a subdivision be arranged to cut out the interests of the sellers from those of the non-sellers. Nevertheless, the acquisition of Māori land was accelerated by the return of the Crown to purchasing under the Vogel immigration and public works policy. By 1882, when Fenton retired as chief judge, the court was beginning to intrude into the last bastions of Māori resistance to land alienation: the King Country and the Urewera. Tribes with lands on the fringes of those territories were gradually being drawn into the orbit of the court, as individuals or small groups of sellers negotiated with the Crown or private purchasers and sought the court's endorsement of their claims.[84]

Under the Native Lands Acts from 1865 to 1873 judges of the Native Land Court were required to ascertain Māori rights to land according to native custom but then to transform those rights into certificates of title analogous to English freehold titles. The first Act to attempt that, the Native Lands Act 1862, was not given a proper trial. It was replaced by the Fenton-drafted Native Lands Act of 1865. Because of the misinterpretation of the 'ten owner' rule (section

23), whereby all other right-holders were dispossessed, a change was required. The first attempt, in 1867, specified that all with customary rights were to be listed in the court record, with a recital to this effect on the certificate of title. But Fenton also refused to apply this. Fenton's riposte of 1869 was ineffectual. Finally the Native Lands Act of 1873 required the rights of all owners to be entered on a memorial of title. Fenton and his fellow judges did at least apply this, though the consequences were hardly satisfactory to Māori. It was now easier for the Crown and private purchasers to initiate purchases of Māori land, but more difficult to complete them since they were required to get the assent of all listed owners or, failing that, to get the court to divide the land of the sellers from that of the non-sellers. That too was an enclosure of a kind, at least for the European purchasers if not for the Māori owners of the remaining land.

In ascertaining ownership of Māori land according to Māori custom, the Native Land Court judges behaved like common law judges in England: Māori customary law became judge-made law. As Fenton explained in his Orakei judgment:

> This Court has no common law to direct its steps by; in fact it has by its own operations to make its common law, and then establish 'year books' which may in the course of time afford a code of law to which appeal may be made for guidance in deciding all questions which may come before it.[85]

The hundreds of Native Land Court minute books subsequently kept by the judges did indeed become the equivalent of the English Year Books that recorded common law judgments for several centuries until they were replaced by the law reports. The Native Land Court minute books are an invaluable source for Māori whakapapa and history where there were contending claims. Frequently the judges simply announced their decisions and listed the names of those to go into the certificates of title. But occasionally they put the evidence into narrative form as, for instance, with Fenton's Orakei judgment. The minute books are a mine of valuable but problematic evidence. They also contain what can be described for the purposes of this essay as some occasional pearls of wisdom which, like the quotes from Fenton and Rogan, reveal the sources of their thinking and procedures.

In their making of Māori customary law, Fenton and other judges drew as much from their training in English law and analogies based on that law as they did on original Māori custom. And even that custom did not come to them raw and uncontaminated from the mouths of claimant witnesses in the Native

Land Court. There was already a received body of opinion on Māori customary law that had been built up since the colony was founded and more specifically from official enquiries, such as the 1856 enquiry established by Governor Gore Browne, and from the great debates that erupted with the Waitara purchase and war in 1860. By the time Fenton opened his first Native Land Court there was already an agreed body of opinion on Māori land tenure — and Fenton himself had contributed to that opinion.

Norman Smith, a later judge of the court, maintained that by c. 1895 — following yet another collecting of opinions in association with the Native Land Laws Commission of 1891 — 'claims for *papatipu* [customary] land had become codified to a very great extent by the judgments of the Native Land Court'. By this time the 'inconsistent nature' of earlier decisions had disappeared and 'the rules of Native custom, with proper regard to any exceptions prevalent in different parts of the country, became more or less clearly defined'. Nevertheless Smith admitted that 'what may be termed the generally recognised customs, more or less common to all tribes in New Zealand, were subjected to gradual changes brought about principally by the influence of conditions and demands of advancing civilization and pakeha ideas'.[86]

Although Fenton, like any good black letter lawyer, pretended to follow the intention of the legislature, when he could find it in the relevant Acts, he did not always do so and did not always admit that he had not. The classic cases are his misinterpretation of section 23 of the Native Lands Act 1865 and his refusal to apply the Native Lands Act 1867, designed to correct his failure over the 1865 Act, though in this instance he claimed that the intentions of the legislature were not made clear. Though Fenton could not be blamed for the Act of 1873 that was imposed on him, he was for another nine years to preside over a Native Land Court that was promoting an extreme form of individualisation of land titles and succession to them; a blight that has burdened Māori land to this day.

In the confusion over the native land legislation neither the legislature nor the Native Land Court under Fenton's direction paid proper respect to Māori custom or to the essential requirements of English land law, and a dangerous compound was created. Neither Fenton nor any of his colleagues could see their way out, and it was not until Ngata and others promoted the twin remedies of consolidation (a kind of enclosure) and incorporation of fragmented titles that a solution was found, though even that was not applied everywhere.

It is evident that the procedures of the English enclosures were not followed in New Zealand for Māori land, primarily because the legislators were not interested in enclosing land for Māori *per se* and in helping them to develop it. That would have involved creating consolidated individual holdings on the ground and helping Māori farmers to develop those holdings, as Fenton seemed to envisage in his 1859 'Scheme for the Partition and Enfranchisement of [Maori] Lands', things that were not attempted until Ngata's land reforms of the twentieth century. The trouble was that the framers of the nineteenth-century Native Lands Acts were merely intent on requiring the Native Land Court to create lists of owners — 'transferable paper', as Sewell aptly described it[87] — who could alienate their land to Pākehā settlers or to the Crown. By contrast, consolidation of scattered rights to land was a preliminary and integral part of the enclosure process in England, albeit one that favoured the manorial freeholders and their larger lessees who could afford to pay the costs of surveying and fencing their holdings. In New Zealand it was Māori who had to pay the costs of surveys of land taken to the Native Land Court and of gaining title through often lengthy court proceedings. These costs merely facilitated alienation. Since their interests were simply listed in certificates and not consolidated into individual holdings on the ground, their land remained largely undeveloped and unfenced, often to the annoyance of Pākehā farmers who owned adjoining land.

But there was one similar long-term effect in both countries in that 'enclosure' turned English[88] and Māori 'commoners' into labourers. So long as Māori retained a significant area of land, and the ability to scratch a living from it, they could remain independent of permanent waged labour and opt to be rural dwellers rather than becoming an urbanised working class. They could not do that very long into the twentieth century.

Though Fenton (and others) could see similarities in the customary management of land in England and by Māori in New Zealand, it was naive to assume that the procedures for enclosure in England could be applied to Māori land. Prior to enclosure the English had a sophisticated system for local management of land, one that involved the co-operation of the lord of the manor, tenants and commoners, and local regulations, all modulated by juries. Likewise, Māori had customary rules for the occupation and management of land, operating on a whānau or hapū level. But the one could not easily be transformed into the other, more especially when there was divided and contested authority, with Pākehā officials such as Fenton in control, and transfer of much of the land to Pākehā an ever-present objective. It was Pākehā colonists who became the new lords of the manor through the primitive attempts by Fenton's Native Land Court to enclose the Māori 'commons'.

5

Land Purchase Methods and their Effect on Maori Population, 1865–1901

One of the most regrettable by-products of the first century of European colonisation in New Zealand was a serious decline of Maori population. When Cook visited the country in 1768 the population was probably approximately 240,000.[1] By 1840 it had declined to little more than 100,000 and by 1857 to under 60,000.[2] Even after the wars of the 1860s the decrease continued and was not arrested until the turn of the century. The extent of this post-war decline is shown in the following table based on census returns from 1874. Revised figures by Nancy Pearce are included in parentheses.[3]

```
1874 — 47,330  (49,800)      1891 — 44,177  (44,177)
1878 — 45,542  (47,800)      1896 — 42,113  (42,650)
1881 — 46,141  (46,750)      1901 — 43,101  ——
1886 — 43,927  (43,927)      1906 — 47,731  ——
```

Explaining the decline

Explanations of Maori depopulation have not always been satisfactory. Quite legitimately considerable stress has been placed on the ravages of warfare, particularly in the period of Maori civil wars prior to 1840, and on the effect of European diseases. But not enough stress has been placed on sociological

---

Originally published in *The Journal of the Polynesian Society*, vol. 65, no. 3 (1956), pp. 183–99. I am grateful to Jack Golson who encouraged me to submit this essay, based on my Master's thesis, 'The Purchase of Maori Lands, 1865–1892', Auckland University College, 1955, for publication in the journal.

disturbances, other than warfare, which aggravated the spread of diseases and also prevented Maori from applying satisfactory remedies. This applies particularly to the period after the wars of the 1860s. In explaining this 30-year period of depopulation most writers have relied on vague speculations, usually of a psychological nature, rather than on a detailed examination of Maori social conditions. A favourite theory has attributed post-war depopulation largely to a loss of hope following the defeats in the wars. This view has been expressed most clearly by Ivan Sutherland:

> The effect upon the life and mind of the Maori people of this ten years' struggle ... was profound.... The disastrous consequences of the war were not only a matter of those killed, nor only one of material loss. Its psychological effects were even more important and far-reaching.... They had suffered not only outward, but what was more serious, inner defeat as well. The *mana* Maori was destroyed.... In a fatalistic mood, and in terms of their old magico-religious beliefs the people now felt they could never regain physical, intellectual or spiritual vigour.... This mental attitude had a profound effect on the Maori.... Through subtle interrelations of mind and body in a people of strongly imaginative and suggestive temperament it led to physical deterioration and affected birthrate and numbers.[4]

An examination of Maori conditions after the wars has failed to reveal any substantial evidence to support this theory. Indeed most of the evidence points in a contrary direction. On the basis of Sutherland's reasoning it would be legitimate to expect the decline immediately after the wars to have been greater amongst the defeated Maori — the King party for example — than among the Maori who remained neutral or who fought on the European side. This was not the case. It is suggested here that depopulation was largely a result of the social disorganisation accompanying the continued sale of land.[5] Immediately after the wars land sales were confined to friendly Maori territory in the North Island. These Maori decreased most rapidly in the late 1860s and 1870s. On the other hand the defeated Maori, who refused to sell land immediately after the wars, were spared this rapid decrease until they began to sell land in the late 1880s and 1890s. Admittedly other sociological factors aggravated depopulation, but these were nearly always effective after the land-selling period of each tribe, when small groups of Maori sought to make a living by working on the gumfields, European farms or public works contracts. The unsatisfactory living conditions of these migratory labouring groups meant that depopulation could continue after land-selling had ceased.

Individual Dealing and the 'Detribalisation' of Maori Society

In the late 1840s and early 1850s the Government dealt directly with tribes for land.[6] There was little danger that this form of land purchase would directly disorganise Maori society. But later in the 1850s, when Maori opposition to further sales intensified, the Government sought to hasten purchases by dealing through small tribal groups. This led to tribal disputes with the Government seeking to protect the land-sellers,[7] and finally to the outbreak of war at Waitara in 1860. When the main wars were over the move from tribal to individual dealing was carried one stage further. At the same time a deliberate attempt was made to break down the tribal organisation of Maori society.

With the Native Lands Act 1862 the Government paved the way by abolishing the Crown's right of pre-emption and providing for a new policy of direct purchase by European settlers from individual Maori. The Native Lands Act 1865, passed after the end of the main wars, put this policy on a practical footing. The Native Land Court was required to individualise Maori land tenure before individuals sold land. This policy was maintained practically without interruption until the turn of the century.[8] When the Government returned to purchase in 1871 it applied the same method of dealing with individual Maori, although by this time it was obvious that the policy was having serious effects on the Maori.[9]

The policy was considered not merely a means of promoting land sales, but also the basis of the grandiose scheme of rapid assimilation to be achieved through the 'detribalisation' of Maori society. As Henry Sewell put it:

> The object of the Native Lands Act [1865] was twofold: to bring the great bulk of the lands of the Northern Island which belonged to the natives . . . within the reach of colonisation. The other great object was, the detribalisation of the natives — to destroy if it were possible, the principle of communism which ran through the whole of their institutions, upon which their social system was based, and which stood as a barrier in the way of all attempts to amalgamate the Native race into our own social and political system. It was hoped that by the individualisation of titles to land, giving them the same individual ownership which we ourselves possessed, . . . their social status would become assimilated to our own.[10]

The majority of those who sat in Parliament thought the decline of the Maori could only be arrested by rapid assimilation. As Frederick Whitaker asserted, it was 'absolutely essential, not only for the sake of ourselves, but for the benefit of the Natives, that the Native titles should be extinguished, the Native customs got rid of, and the Natives as far as possible placed in the same position as ourselves'.[11]

It is argued here that individual dealing, legalised by the Native Lands Acts, did provide the way for the breakdown of Maori society. But this promoted rather than arrested the decline of Maori population. Maori had been put on an equal footing with Europeans, and land purchase became the focal point of contact with European society. It was not so much the amount of land purchased — a little over one-third of the North Island in the years 1865–1901 — but the manner of purchase and accompanying social disturbances that were the all-important factors in the decline.

The Mechanism of Purchase

The policy initiated by the Native Lands Acts has frequently been termed 'free trade in Maori lands'. In effect this meant that European dealers were free to exploit the Maori landowners. For the first time Maori lands could become security for debts.[12] This was a fundamental factor that sooner or later coerced even strong opponents of sale into disposing of land.

The beginning of the process was simple. European purchasers could nearly always find one or two individuals of a tribe who were willing to sell land. If they did not make a cash advance they called on the assistance of the local storekeeper or publican, who often acted as 'native land agents' and who offered Maori liberal supplies of goods and liquor on credit.[13] Through debts a hold was obtained on Maori and their land and the next stage was to bring the law to bear on transactions. If Maori debtors were recalcitrant Europeans could always threaten civil lawsuits and imprisonment for non-payment of debts. A sitting of the Native Land Court was arranged and if possible certificates obtained for the land-sellers only. The Europeans could then go ahead and obtain a lease or the freehold. If they failed to obtain a freehold title immediately the credit-debt procedure was applied over again until the final conveyance was obtained.[14]

Once land-selling individuals had taken tribal lands before the Court there was virtually no way that other members of the tribe could save even their own share of the land. The non-sellers had to attend the Court or lose their interests.[15] At Court they usually had to face a lawyer employed by the European dealer to fight the case for the land-sellers, and in employing lawyers themselves as well as paying Court and survey expenses, on top of the cost of living in European towns sometimes for several months, generally lost the land even if they did win the case. If there was competition between several European parties for large single blocks of land the position was worse. After dealing with different groups of Maori owners the Europeans carried their battles into the Court. As the Chief Judge of the Court, J. E. MacDonald, described it: '[The European dealer] . . . will fight his Maori vendor's title to the bitter end. . . . An amount of money has been sunk, and loss is not to be submitted to without a struggle.'[16] These European contests were the main reason for the continuous litigation in the Native Land Court. The Maori concerned were invariably the real losers.[17]

Quite apart from the interference of European interests there were other unsatisfactory aspects of the operation of the Court. Notification of hearings was often defective and legitimate claimants were sometimes unaware that their land had been dealt with.[18] Before the mid-1880s there was no attempt to hold Court sittings in Maori villages and claimants had to travel, sometimes for hundreds of miles, to the European towns. When sittings were arranged all blocks were gazetted together with no indication when each would be heard. Frequently two or three hundred blocks were gazetted and all Maori interested had to arrive on the opening day but many of them had to wait several weeks before their case was heard.[19] Cases were adjourned without being settled; others were advertised but not heard.[20] These circumstances too contributed to the impoverishment of Maori attending the sittings.

It is not surprising that many Maori were embittered by land dealings and the operation of the Native Land Court. They sought redress by appealing to the Supreme Court and Court of Appeal, only to end up on a merry-go-round of debt. The Makauri case, for example, which came before the Native Land Court four times and also before the Supreme Court four times, in fifteen years of litigation, was said to have cost the Maori owners £18,000 in legal expenses.[21] Renata Kawepo, the loyalist Hawke's Bay chief, ran up accounts totalling £7,073 3s 8d with the solicitor W. L. Buller between January 1879 and September 1885.[22] These had to be paid by the sale of land. The same thing happened to another loyalist chief, Major Kemp (Te Rangihiwinui) of Wanganui, with Buller again receiving the bounty.[23] As Mohi Rakuraku, who was aware of the consequences, put it: 'The law has been our ruin. In the time of our ancestors . . . we received no hurt similar to this. Give us back what land is left.'[24]

The Government had provided the opportunity for private purchase with the Native Lands Acts, but after 1871 returned to the market in competition with settlers under the Vogel public works and immigration policy. So long as adequate public and private finance was available and fertile Maori land remained, there was little chance that the Maori could retain their land.

In effect the Native Land Court now served the interests of both the Crown and European purchasers.

The early phases of private purchase were most pronounced in Hawke's Bay, where European squatters had already taken up 'grass money leases' and used the Native Land Court to convert those 'leases' into valid titles. The later phase of competition between private and Crown purchasers was most pronounced around the borders of the King Country. Each of these phases is exemplified by case studies discussed below.

The purchase of the fertile 20,000-acre Heretaunga block, on the edge of Hastings, illustrates much that was typical of land transactions in Hawke's Bay.[25] Here Thomas Tanner, the leader of a group of European squatters and storekeepers who had occupied the land in 1864 and leased it in 1867 after the land had been before the Court, forced ten registered Maori landowners into conveying the freehold by fostering debts, threatening lawsuits and paying secret bribes to the influential chiefs concerned. On the surface these may have appeared legitimate business dealings but behind the scenes there were some unsavoury transactions. Liquor was part of the goods dispensed on credit though the sale of liquor to Maori was prohibited.[26] Some of the debts incurred by one chief — Henare Takamoana — were for goods used in the campaign against Te Kooti. The very night before Henare led a Maori force against Te Kooti, Tanner's associates brought a Court writ against him for unpaid debts. The interpreters, the Hamlin brothers, who were supposed to interpret deeds to the Maori fairly, were in Tanner's pay, being offered £300 'if successful' with their negotiations. The Rev. Samuel Williams, to whom the Maori owners turned for advice, was indirectly associated with Tanner and advised sale. Karaitiana Takamoana, one of the owners, made a special trip to Auckland to seek payment for the war expenses, but Native Minister Donald McLean sent him back to J. D. Ormond, the provincial superintendent. Instead of paying the war expenses, and thus easing the Maori owners' burden of debt, Ormond helped Tanner to bring a further writ against them.[27] Obviously the Maori owners had no chance of retaining their land under these conditions. By the beginning of 1870, three years after he had obtained a lease, Tanner had secured the freehold. And in effect the Maori owners got next to nothing for the land. It was alleged that over £21,000 was paid for the block, but only just over £3,000 of this was paid to the Maori owners in cash; the rest went to the storekeepers who had supplied the clothing, food and liquor.

This was not an isolated example but typical of nearly all transactions under the Native Lands Act 1865 in Hawke's Bay. By 1873, when the Act was repealed, all the valuable grazing land had been secured by squatters. The Ngati Kahungunu tribe concerned were loyal and fought the battles against Te Kooti which made Hawke's Bay safe for European settlers. But they could not fight the battle for land against the European squatters at the same time. Nor were they in a position to prevent the social disruption which accompanied purchase negotiations.

Land transactions on the borders of the King Country were of a somewhat different character. The allegiance of many of the bordering tribes to the King party, with its strong anti-land-selling league, had prevented the successful conclusion of most European negotiations for almost ten years after the end of the wars.[28] But, by 1880, concentrated individual dealings carried out by Government and private agents had broken down much of the opposition. Large blocks of land were being taken before the Court, sitting continuously at Cambridge.[29] As several European parties had acquired interests in single blocks, there was fierce competition to secure favourable decisions in the Court. Storekeepers at Cambridge, working in collaboration with purchase rings, used the Court sittings to 'harvest' the money advanced by purchasers.[30] Then the purchasers were in a good position to finalise transactions. Referring to the Cambridge sitting of the Court the *New Zealand Herald* added:

> The working of the Native Land Court has been a scandal . . . for many years past, but as the chief sufferers were the Maoris, nobody troubled themselves very much. . . . [The] cases went on month after month . . . . All this time the Maoris were living near a European town; to keep them advances were made by land-buyers [and] . . . enormous interest was being charged. The money mostly went for rum . . . and the whole of the time of the sitting . . . was spent . . . in drunkenness and debauchery. The consequence was, that at the conclusion of the Court, they had divested themselves of their land, and had spent the whole of [their] money . . . .[31]

Where the competition was between the Government and private parties the results were just the same. Ten years of competition for the 250,000-acre Patetere block, at the head of the Thames Valley, was only resolved when the Government withdrew its interests in 1882 and virtually handed the block over to a private company.[32] Court sittings for this land were held at Cambridge with the Maori claimants suffering from prolonged sittings and the demoralising atmosphere of the township.[33] At Rotorua, where the Government had proclaimed a large area of land under the Thermal Springs Act 1881 and tried to force the Maori into sale, there were also disturbances. The proclamation prohibited private negotiations but these apparently went on with the usual accompaniment of credit dealings by storekeepers and unrestricted drinking in shanty lakeside hotels.[34]

The Government did not hesitate to apply the same methods of coercion that private agents were using, or, as Daniel Pollen put it, 'were not bound to be stopped ... by any sentimental considerations as to the irregular dealings by other parties with the Natives'.[35]

There was active competition for auriferous land in the lower Thames Valley in the 1870s and James Mackay, the Government purchase agent, fostered Maori debts to secure Government interests.[36] Government agents dealt with land-selling individuals and as far as possible sidestepped those opposing sale:

> By sharp practice and by free bribery of a few natives, the title was obtained in the name of only one native when the land was passed through the Court. This was managed by boldly alleging that there were no dissentients and that all the interested parties had come to a 'voluntary agreement' upon the matter. None of the owners except the wrong-doers were present, and the Court finding no dissentients, confirmed and recorded the so-called agreement. The grantee, a native woman, came to Tauranga a few days after the decision, and concluded her sale to the Government.[37]

J. C. Young, the Government purchase agent at Tauranga, made a regular practice of handing out payments to Maori in want of money and then charging it as purchase money against blocks of land.[38] He worked in league with the local storekeepers, who gave him a personal commission on all Maori orders which they made up by charging the Maori more than they charged Europeans for goods.[39] Young also practised some straight-out forgery. A Government inquiry agent found in his office

> 100 blank vouchers ... purporting to be signed by natives, and not otherwise filled in. They were apparently left to be filled up at pleasure. ... There were cases where accounts had been paid to storekeepers, and the vouchers were signed by the natives beforehand.[40]

Young was dismissed for this forgery — and for pocketing some of the purchase money himself — but otherwise his credit dealings through the storekeepers were not frowned upon. Indeed, credit dealings through storekeepers appeared to be just as pronounced with Government agents as they were with private dealers. One correspondent claimed that:

The Government has fallen into a system of enticing the Natives into debt by freely giving them orders on storekeepers for goods and drink, called 'rations' — *reihana* in Maori phrase. . . . I was told in Auckland that the debt of the Ohinemuri Natives was actually in this way swelled to £26,000.[41]

Purchase transactions enticed Maori away from their own cultivations, led them into dissolute habits and introduced them to all the vices of European civilisation. They became victims of business exploitation: of the purchase agents, storekeepers, publicans and sharp lawyers — the flotsam of the frontier who paved the way for European settlement.

The Social Consequences of Land Dealings

Individual dealing disintegrated tribal unity. The authority of chiefs was undermined as all individuals were awarded full rights to sell their shares of land. Tribal divisions created by individual dealings were solidified as the battles were carried to the new *marae* of the Native Land Court.[42] Once engaged in Court sittings Maori had to ignore their own cultivations and move to the unsavoury atmosphere of the European towns. Here they lived, often for months on end, with unsatisfactory shelter, little wholesome food, and frequently spent long periods intoxicated as they squandered the money advanced by purchase agents. In these conditions European diseases took a greater toll of the population:

> I believe we could not find a more ingenious method of destroying the whole of the Maori race than by these Courts. The Natives come from the villages in the interior, and have to hang about for months in our centres of population. . . . They are brought into contact with the lowest classes of society, and are exposed to temptation, and the result is that a great number contract diseases and die. . . . Some little time ago I was taking a ride through the interior, and I was perfectly astonished at hearing that a subject of conversation at each *hapu* I visited was the number of natives dying in consequence of attendance at the Native Land Court at Wanganui.[43]

It is equally revealing to shift the scene to Ohinemutu, Rotorua, where Government and private parties were competing for interests in land in the early 1880s:

> There has been a sitting of the Lands Court lately and the agents of land buyers have been making advances to the Maoris on their lands. . . . There are three public-houses

in Ohinemutu, around them crowds of Maoris of both sexes have congregated in all stages of intoxication. Women have been lying about the settlement on the roadside, helplessly drunk. The bars have been crowded with these infatuated people; young girls and youths, old men and women, mingling in the noisy, polluted atmosphere, eager for more drink.... There has been an unusual number of deaths ... at Ohinemutu during the past two or three weeks, and in walking through the settlement I saw three persons ... sick beyond recovery.... Unwholesome dwellings and insufficient food are also helping on the sad work.[44]

This emphasises the close connection between land purchase, the drink traffic, and the occurrence of European diseases.

Depopulation of the Land-selling Tribes
Depopulation in land-selling districts is shown in census statistics. Discussing census figures of 1891, the *New Zealand Herald* observed:

In those districts where the natives have sold most of their surplus lands, or at all events where they have not, during the last five years, been subjected to the immoral and destructive influences of land-selling, they have kept up their numbers. In former years it has been noticed that the great decrease took place in those districts in which the natives had been detained from their settlements and their usual occupations in attending Land Courts.[45]

The census returns of the Ngati Kahungunu tribe of Hawke's Bay and the Ngapuhi of North Auckland support this generalisation.[46]

	1874	1878	1881	1886	1891	1896	1901
Ngati Kahungunu	6065	5172	4730	5175	5194	4672	5064
Ngapuhi		5867	5667	5564	5549	6314	5859	6359

The parallel with land purchase is close. Both of these tribes had sold large areas of land before the wars and continued to do so immediately afterwards. But by 1874 in Hawke's Bay, and 1876 in North Auckland, most of the land had been sold and Maori there could adopt more normal habits of living. Hence the steady decline in population of the 1870s was gradually halted and, although recovery was retarded in North Auckland by the poor conditions on the gumfields, there was a positive increase in both tribes by the end of the 1880s.

These figures can be contrasted with those of the tribes who were defeated in the wars but who refused to alienate land until the 1880s or 1890s. The tribes included in the following table[47] were severely affected by defeats in war and subsequent confiscation, and should, according to the theories put forward by Sutherland and others, have shown the greatest decrease immediately after the wars.

	1874	1878	1881	1886	1891	1896	1901
Waikato	4568	4958	5233	4000	3923	3614	4457
Ngati Maniapoto	2210	1390	1528	1685	1531	1263	1570
Urewera	1242	1410	1850	1901	1211	1421	1094
Ngati Ruanui	993	1073	769	1065	835	710	853
Taranaki	557	938	460	947	609	615	639
Ngati Awa	1072	1201	964	947	700	727	719

Some returns were inaccurate, being estimates rather than true enumerations. The 1874 figure for the Ngati Maniapoto tribe was almost certainly too high;[48] the figures for the three Taranaki tribes in 1881 were too low as several hundred Te Whiti supporters were imprisoned in the South Island and omitted from the returns;[49] and the 1896 figures for the Waikato and Ngati Maniapoto were probably too low since these tribes opposed the census fearing the imposition of a tax.[50] Otherwise the inaccuracies are probably not serious enough to alter the general pattern of population changes.

Two generalisations can be made. First, there is nothing to support the theory of associating depopulation with defeats in war; for this theory to be valid there would have to be evidence of a rapid decrease in the 1870s — even more rapid than that of the friendly tribes. Secondly, there are significant correlations between depopulation and the opening of each territory to land purchase and European settlement.

There was apparently an increase in the Waikato in the 1870s while most of the tribe were living under stable conditions in the King Country. The decrease in the 1880s accompanied the gradual move back to small reserves on the Lower Waikato and the dispersal of groups to work on the gumfields, Government contracts and European farms. The Ngati Maniapoto tribe appeared to increase in the late 1870s and again in the 1880s. Although the King Country was opened to the railway and Native Land Court in 1885, the tribe was spared some of the evils associated with land dealing in other districts. The Government had prohibited private purchase in the King

Country in 1884,[51] had concluded an informal agreement to prohibit liquor in 1885,[52] and conducted the Court sittings in the Maori villages rather than in the European towns. By 1890 the Court had individualised most of the titles. The tribe had broken into small groups, earning a precarious living on Government contracts, rabbit-hunting and flax-gathering.[53] The Government had begun to purchase individual interests in land and in the later 1890s broke down remaining resistance and completed the purchase of some large blocks. In the same period there was a certain amount of drunkenness, despite the prohibition.[54] A decrease in population was recorded in both the 1891 and 1896 censuses.

Similar correlations can be drawn for the Urewera tribe. There was a steady increase in the 1870s and probably again in the 1880s — the anti-selling period. In the 1890s the population fluctuated as the district was opened to the road and more European contact. The tribe was almost the only one to register a decrease in the 1901 census. This corresponded with large-scale Government purchase at the turn of the century.

The position of the three Taranaki tribes was more complicated, but population changes were related to social disturbances. Increases were recorded in the 1870s when large numbers of Taranaki Maori were living under stable conditions at Te Whiti's Parihaka settlement. Then in the 1880s there was a marked contrast following Bryce's destruction of the Parihaka settlement, the dispersal of most of the inhabitants and the imprisonment of Te Whiti late in 1881. The high 1886 return was due to the return of the prisoners absent when the 1881 census was taken, and obscured what was almost certainly a continuous decrease throughout the 1880s.

Other evidence on the social conditions of the defeated tribes emphasises that while preventing alienation of land after the wars these tribes could also prevent social disorganisation and a rapid decrease in population.

W. G. Mair, resident magistrate at Alexandra (Pirongia), continually contrasted the favourable conditions of the King party with the disorganised existence of the land-sellers across the border in his reports to the Government between 1872 and 1881.[55] He did, however, consider the population of the King party was slowly decreasing, but at a slower rate than that of the Maori on the European side of the border. In 1877 the *New Zealand Herald* stressed the difference: 'Only the Kingites, who are not gradually selling land and drinking the proceeds, are not rapidly declining in numbers.'[56] A correspondent of the same paper who attended Grey's meeting with the King party at Hikurangi in 1878 made similar observations:

The difference between the Kingites and the Maoris that Europeans are accustomed to see is very marked. The men and women are healthy looking, while the number of children playing about, and of fine stout infants to be seen in the arms of their mothers, is remarkable. It is sad to think that those natives who have least to do with Europeans are in every respect the best of their race; but so it is. It is sad for them, because the separation which at present exists cannot continue for ever.[57]

Reports from Taranaki indicated a similar state of affairs with 'scenes of [Maori] drunkenness and debauchery . . . at those European centres of population on the plains'.[58] On the other hand, at Parihaka there were signs of a well-ordered community, 'vastly superior to any European community of a similar size and existing under similar conditions . . . in any parts of these colonies'.[59] Burdon, in a biographical sketch of Te Whiti, pointed out that:

> For many years Parihaka had been a model of cleanliness among Maori villages, and in health and physical appearance its inhabitants had no equal in New Zealand. Its ruler had set his face sternly against drunkenness and forbidden any kind of alcohol to be brought there.[60]

Dr O'Carroll, after numerous visits to Parihaka, commented on the number of children before Bryce's raid in 1881, and then, on the state of sloth and demoralisation among the few remaining residents after the raid.[61] The rejuvenation of the settlement had to await Te Whiti's return from imprisonment.

Information on the Urewera tribe is also similar. In 1874 S. Locke, resident magistrate for Napier, reported: 'Physically, the Urewera appear to be a fine, healthy people . . . I know of no other place where there are so many children in proportion to the adult population.'[62] Then, with the Urewera example in mind, he went on to make a significant generalisation:

> I consider it a mistaken idea that the Maoris are dying out rapidly: it is the case in certain localities but in others, if they are not on the increase, then that rapid disappearance which seemed probable a small time back, is checked, more especially so in those places where no sudden change in their habits or manner of living has occurred, but where time has been allowed for them to some extent to prepare themselves.[63]

In 1891 a newspaper correspondent who accompanied the Earl of Onslow on the first official visit to the Urewera reported:

Children of all ages appeared to be very numerous, and it is said that the tribe is not by any means dying out. This is no doubt due to their healthy life, and their avoidance of the pakeha. When their silly prejudices against European civilisation get broken down, and they have learnt to appreciate the joys of the whiskey bottle, and have acquired other pakeha vices, they will no doubt diminish as rapidly as other tribes are doing.[64]

Bearing the Standard of Maoritanga

A study of the King movement, Te Whiti's movement and the position of the Urewera tribe after the wars reveals much more than a purely passive resistance against land alienation and European settlement. Myths have been created implying that these groups were disgruntled and hostile renegades living 'within a degenerate exclusiveness'.[65] A more realistic interpretation would point in a completely different direction, regarding the King movement and other similar movements as positive attempts to prevent social disintegration by holding up the onslaught of European colonisation. They could do this partly by preventing the wholesale alienation of land which brought in its train all the disorganising elements of European society. At the same time they had to maintain sufficient elements of their own cultural organisation to assist them in the difficult period of transition to a predominantly European society. The King party achieved both of these ends in the 1870s.

In this period the King party bore the standard of Maoritanga. This was not anti-European or reactionary but was an effective means of maintaining an ordered community. There was hostility towards purchase agents, surveyors and prospectors but not other visitors.[66] W. G. Mair, the Government agent, was well received by King party chiefs throughout the 1870s. Communal cultivations provided for daily wants, and a surplus for the large King party gatherings and for trading across the border.[67] Cash returns were used to purchase European implements to extend the area under cultivation. Large areas of wheat were grown near the border; pigs were sold at the European stockyards across the border. The significant characteristic of King party farming in the 1870s was a progressive adoption of European methods, not a retrogression to outmoded pre-European means of subsistence. The *Tariao* faith,[68] a complex of traditional and Christian religious ideas, with the latter dominant, aided the social and political integration of the movement:

> They invoke God to give Tawhiao strength to preserve peace between themselves and the Europeans; they ask God to assist them in obeying Tawhiao's commands, winding

up each prayer by asking God to watch over Tawhiao and them, and keep them from evil on that day.... There is not a single word of fanaticism in any of [their prayers].[69]

King party chiefs delivered the sermons and quoted freely from the Bible. The annual meetings were attended by representatives from nearly every tribe in the North Island and provided an opportunity to perform traditional cultural activities and at the same time hammer out a policy for the future.[70] Unfortunately they could do little to affect the future. Individual dealing gradually broke down the anti-land-selling league by dividing the unity of the tribes and finally, in 1885, by splitting the Waikato–Maniapoto alliance. The Ngati Maniapoto tribe itself was divided by the subsequent dealing in land. Although there was a reconciliation between the two tribes around the turn of the century much of the land had gone and the King party could no longer maintain its dominating role in the Maoritanga movement.

Te Whiti's movement was similar in many respects to the King movement. It was characterised by an even stricter prohibition of liquor, similar large-scale cultivation,[71] an emphasis on group social activity integrated by Te Whiti's own brand of prophecy and Biblical interpretation, and a desire to provide a haven for traditional cultural activities. After the settlement had been broken up in 1881 and most of the surrounding land occupied by European settlers a slightly changed attitude was necessary. The dominance of the Europeans in Taranaki had been established and it was necessary to conform more closely to European habits of living. When Te Whiti returned to Parihaka in 1883 he made use of European medical aid to treat disease and in the remaining years of his life completely rebuilt the settlement on European lines.[72] European-styled houses were erected together with a public bakery, abattoir and modern water supply. Electricity, surely a luxury in European settlements, was laid on. The Maori at Parihaka ate their meals in public dining rooms where a European chef supervised the cooking. Material benefits of European civilisation had been adopted but inwardly there was still a hard core of Maori cultural sentiment stimulated by the living and worshipping as an organised communal group under the leadership of Te Whiti. But after 1881 the movement was based on limited land resources. Like the King movement it gradually failed to provide more than localised leadership.

After the turn of the century the leadership of the Maoritanga movement passed to the Young Maori Party and the Ngati Porou tribe of the East Coast. Significantly this tribe had been free from the main pressure of European purchase activities and had retained most of its land. Even at this stage the adoption of European material benefits was closely associated with the retention of significant elements of Maori culture. Perhaps the movement initiated by the Young Maori Party was not so much a 'Renaissance' as a continuation of Maori cultural adjustment along similar lines to those followed by the King party in the 1870s.

The survival of the Maori as a distinctive group in New Zealand was due to the gradual elimination of disease and the main social disturbances resulting from European contact. This survival was stimulated wherever Maori retained distinctive elements of their own culture while gradually adjusting themselves to the material aspects of European life. The Maori people have rejected rapid assimilation with its accompanying destruction of their own culture.

6

The Maori King Movement, 1858–1885

> The land does not sin; it is man who sins against the land.
> — *Manuhiri to C. O. Davis, 1870*¹

In June 1858 Potatau Te Wherowhero, aged chief of Ngati Mahuta tribe of the Waikato, was 'elected' Maori King. He had the active support of several powerful inland tribes — Waikato, Ngati Haua, Ngati Maniapoto, Ngati Tuwharetoa — and the sympathy of Maori from a majority of the remaining tribes. The rise of such a confederation in the heart of the North Island at a time when Europeans were flooding into the country, demanding more Maori land and, through their representatives in Parliament, control over Maori affairs, was bound to create apprehension and controversy. Potatau's 'election' symbolised the end of an era in Maori–European relations, the end for at least a time of what many had regarded as a natural trend towards the amalgamation of the two races. A large and the most important section of Maori was going its own way towards separation and this was likely to lead to conflict between the races for supremacy.

Contemporary European observers soon divided into two camps in interpreting the nature and objectives of the King movement. Most of them saw it as a reflection on Government policy — or the lack of it — and used the movement as ammunition for their own political squabbles. They adopted their own political and constitutional terminology to describe the movement and generally regarded it, for differing reasons, as an attempt to emulate European forms

---

Originally published in Robert Chapman and Keith Sinclair, eds, *Studies of a Small Democracy: Essays in Honour of Willis Airey*, Paul's Book Arcade, Hamilton & Auckland, 1963, pp. 33–55.

of government. The official view, suggested first by Native Secretary Donald McLean and adopted by Governor Gore Browne, was that the King movement was a temporary excitement which, if ignored, would soon die out.[2] When the King movement, instead of dying out, showed every sign of increasing its influence Gore Browne asserted that it was a dangerous denial of the Queen's sovereignty which must be suppressed by force.[3]

The opposing view, urged by an assortment of disgruntled officials such as F. D. Fenton, politicians out of power led by William Fox, many of the missionaries, and 'philo-Maori' particularly Sir William Martin, also assumed that the King movement was essentially imitative.[4] As Hugh Carleton, the editor of the Auckland *Southern Cross*, put it in 1857: 'The imitative instinct of the monkey is at work amongst them; they are even now bent upon aping British institutions, and establishing such for themselves — an *imperium in imperio* — with such modifications as please themselves.'[5]

The reasons for the movement, these critics asserted, were plain: Gore Browne's administration had failed to govern the Maori so they were setting up their own government to provide the law and order they required. John Gorst gave classic expression to this view in his celebrated book, *The Maori King*, published in 1864. 'If we had educated the natives in civilisation,' Gorst claimed, 'and fitted them for the enjoyment of those full rights, as British subjects, which the Treaty of Waitangi promised, nothing would have been heard of "land leagues" and "king-movements".'[6]

This has been an influential interpretation, but as Keith Sinclair's recent studies have shown,[7] it is also a misleading one. Gorst underestimated the significance of Maori opposition to selling land, and thought, mistakenly, that they 'were willing to sell their land for civilisation and equality'.[8] The founders of the King movement were in fact opposed to selling their land on any terms whatsoever. Gorst is even more misleading on the issue of government: the King movement was not a result of the administration's failure to govern the Maori — though the charge of failure was substantially correct — but of fear that European government would by its very nature deprive them of their lands. Sinclair's two main points: that the King movement was basically a 'land league', and that more Government interference would only have increased Maori resistance,[9] are essential to an understanding of the movement; but the two points require a further elaboration before their full significance can become apparent. Moreover, these points are intimately related. In the minds of both Maori and Europeans the assertion of 'law and order' or — in the long run — government, meant authority over the land. As the two races were in conflict over the land it was natural that they should set up conflicting authorities to govern the land and the men and women it sustained.

The term nationalist has often been applied to the King movement, though again there has been dispute over how far it was inspired by and attempted to emulate European concepts, institutions and techniques. Hugh Carleton, one of the shrewdest contemporary observers, said that:

> The natives thoroughly understand what they want, and it is not a plaything that they seek. They are resolved upon making an effort to preserve their existence, not only as a race, but as they understand it, a nation, before they shall be overnumbered and therefore out-mastered by the whites.[10]

But Carleton, like Gorst, believed that the King movement was wholly imitative and could have been forestalled or controlled by effective government. Sinclair, however, has pointed out that 'nowhere has good government proved a cure for nationalism'.[11] He has also emphasised that, although European techniques were used to resist the European threat, the imitation of European concepts and institutions was superficial; and that the King movement was essentially a reaction against European society, an attempt to shut out European influence and, with the wars and the subsequent confiscation of Maori land, took an increasingly 'reactionary' turn.[12] These opinions are certainly more convincing, but they need qualification. The King movement, though conservative, was neither reactionary nor a reversion to ancient savagery: it did not adopt the extremist policy of the *Hau Haus*. It was conservative in the sense that it sought to reassert and extend traditional ideals, values and practices in an attempt to resist the disintegration of Maori society resulting from contact with the Europeans. It sought to revive unity within tribes by reasserting the *mana* (authority)[13] of chiefs over individuals, and unity between tribes by asserting the *mana* of a king over chiefs. The Maori nation was to be founded by uniting the tribes against the Europeans and preserving the power of chiefs, subordinate only to the King; not by destroying both as in some other nationalist movements in colonial territories. European techniques were adopted only in so far as they assisted in this objective. Once the tribes had been united, the King party leaders were ready to think in terms of a Maori nation, territorially and politically independent, co-operating with but not submitting to Europeans, and 'in alliance'[14] with the Queen. The constant theme of their speeches, according to one observer, was 'The King on his piece [of land]; the Queen on her piece; God over both; and love binding them to each other.'[15] The majority of the King party leaders did not advocate driving the Europeans out of the country; they merely aimed at stopping their advance inland and, before the wars, adopted the Mangatawhiri river (near Mercer) as the boundary between the King's and the Queen's land. The King movement, bearing the standard of Maori nationalism, was created by the desire of the inland tribes to retain their land. Its survival as a nationalist movement depended on the outcome of the struggle over land.

In the 1850s Government agents, pressed by European demands for more Maori land, adopted underhand methods to secure it where some members of tribes opposed sale.[16] There were numerous attempts to purchase from individuals willing to sell, the opponents of sales being ignored. The result was a series of bitter feuds between the *tuku whenua* (land sellers) and *pupuri whenua* (land holders), with the Government looking on while Maori killed each other, or intervening to assist the land sellers.[17] It was the Government attempt to survey disputed land, 'purchased' from a minority of the Ngati Awa tribe at Waitara, that led to the outbreak of war in 1860. Short of fighting, there was only one effective way Maori could resist Government efforts to buy from individuals. This was to assert chiefly *mana* over tribal land and, as chiefs were likely to offend, to put tribal land under the *mana* of a king. In Taranaki Wiremu Kingi succeeded in asserting his *mana* over the majority of his tribe but attempts to create an inter-tribal land league failed.[18] In Waikato, on the other hand, a land league was formed with the 'election' of Potatau.

On joining the King movement chiefs agreed to put their tribal land under the *mana* of Potatau. As Wiremu Tamihana, the 'King Maker', explained later: 'The reason why I set up Potatau as King for me was [that] he was a man of extended influence and one who was respected by the tribes of this island . . . to put down my troubles, to hold the land of the slave, and to judge the offences of the chief.'[19]

Reports of Maori statements at the various meetings held in June 1858 when Potatau was being 'elected' also emphasise the primary, anti-land-selling objectives of the King movement. At the Ngaruawahia meeting of 2 June, which has been taken as marking Potatau's accession,[20] he was acknowledged as 'King' by a thousand supporters and as *matua* (father) by another thousand. The people were asked if they would 'give all power and land to the King',[21] and they agreed to do so. Tamihana then concluded proceedings by explaining why it was necessary to have a king.

> It is deemed proper that the chiefs should be of one mind, and select a person who shall be entrusted with these treasures for [of?] the earth (that is the protection of our

property, the management of our lands, etc.). We have seen that the wars arise from disputations about land, wherefore we seek out him, that he may be a depository for our lands. He will restrain the father who is badly disposed towards his son, and the elder brother who would take advantage of the younger brother. He will manifest his displeasure in regard to that which is evil; he will do away with the works of confusion or disorder, and he will be a covering for the lands of New Zealand which still remain in our possession.[22]

An even more explicit statement of King party objectives came from a European newspaper correspondent, 'Curiosus', who attended the Ngaruawahia meeting and accompanied the King party up the Waipa valley to Rangiaowhia. He had private discussions with the leaders and claimed to have learnt 'what "The King Movement" really means'. It was, he said:

simply a great Land League formed to prevent the sale of any more land to the Pakehas [Europeans]. Of this league, Potatau has been chosen head, and all who become members of the Union concede to him the veto upon the alienation of any portion of their estates.... The natives simply think that to part with any more land is the road to certain ruin, and to avert such a catastrophe, are adopting the expedient of a Kingi or Land Protector. Every other question is of importance to them only as it affects this.[23]

'Curiosus' was a shrewd observer. He not only recognised the importance of the King party obsession with land but also the relationship of this to other matters arising out of contact with Europeans. Thus the King party attitude to European squatters in their midst, land purchase agents, traders and Government officials (including those sent to administer the law) was governed by their fear that, somehow, any European activities not controlled by the Maori themselves would lead to the loss of their lands. They had good grounds for suspecting the motives of many Europeans who came into their territory.

In the early 1850s, when the Waikato and other Maori tribes were producing a large surplus of agricultural goods for sale and export, a considerable number of Europeans — estimated at 294 in 1855[24] — settled in the Waikato *kainga* (villages). Most of these people were artisans or traders but some were allowed to occupy land. When the agricultural export boom collapsed in 1856, these squatters, like Europeans elsewhere on Crown land, changed over to pastoralism and tried to increase their holdings. Maori, on the other hand, remained agriculturists, and the growth of two different styles of farming proved a fertile field for petty disputes over straying European stock and fossicking Maori pigs.

More serious conflicts emerged when the European squatters tried to legalise their titles. In 1854–55 McLean, unable to purchase any large blocks of Maori land in the Waikato, managed to purchase several of the squatters' homesteads.[25] This enabled the Europeans concerned to obtain Crown titles for their homesteads and, according to one Auckland newspaper, was 'the little edge of the wedge'.[26] But it was a moot question whether the Europeans could drive the wedge home in the face of growing Maori organisation against land sales.

During 1858, when Waikato Maori were busy setting up their King, the settlers in Auckland were calling for the legalisation of direct settler purchase of Maori land, or, as it was euphemistically called, 'the enfranchisement of Maori land'. The agitation received a setback when the Native Territorial Rights Act, passed by the General Assembly to allow a form of direct purchase, was rejected by the Imperial Government in 1859. But this did not deter the agitators. Carleton of the *Southern Cross* and several merchants and farmers including W. C. Daldy and J. C. Firth formed a 'Direct Purchase Association'. This body urged settlers to defy the 1846 Ordinance prohibiting direct negotiations and to emulate the adventurous Hawke's Bay and Wairarapa squatters who had occupied large areas of Maori land in the late 1840s and early 1850s.[27] Late in 1859 an expedition left Auckland to try to obtain 'leases'. It split into two parties: one led by J. C. Firth explored the possibilities in the Waihou valley; the other, led by M. G. Nixon, concentrated on the Waikato. Both were unsuccessful.[28] The King party was opposed to any form of land transaction, public or private. A few months later war broke out in Taranaki and, as Government purchase was discredited by the blunders over Waitara, the direct purchase advocates had little difficulty in passing the Native Lands Act in 1862. This Act, which was approved by the Imperial Government, abolished the Crown's right of pre-emption and allowed settlers to purchase Maori land after a special Court had clarified Maori titles. But by that time it was obvious that the Waikato would have to be invaded before the settlers could buy any land.

The activities of European settlers and Government purchase agents represented the direct side of the threat to the Maori lands of the Waikato. There were also indirect but related dangers. Trade was one of them. Following the collapse of agricultural prices in 1856 many of the Waikato Maori had got into debt with Auckland merchants,[29] largely through purchasing considerable supplies of weapons.[30] Some of the merchants — W. C. Daldy, one of the direct purchase advocates, is an example — were anxious to recover their debts by obtaining Maori land. But the King party was aware of the danger. At the Peria (Matamata) meeting in 1862 it was laid down that no further leases should be accepted, all existing debts repaid and no further credit accepted.[31] This did not mean the King party was attempting to reject trade altogether or to reject 'European society in its economic details';[32] it was only trying to control them as a safeguard against European domination. In fact the King party continued to trade right up to the outbreak of war and it was Europeans, not the King party, who called for a blockade.[33]

Next, there is the important problem associated with the introduction of law, which was also related to the growing conflict over land. Gorst and later historians misunderstood this crucial problem because they interpreted Maori demands for the assertion of law literally — that is as a demand for law *per se* — without recognising the Maori objectives behind the demands. Nor did they realise that Maori objectives were incompatible with those of the Europeans who also demanded the introduction of law. King party Maori like Tamihana wanted law to suppress drunkenness and tribal disputes. Despite urgent Maori pleas[34] no attempt was made to suppress the illegal liquor trade and Europeans were actually granted 'bush licences' for liquor sales in the heart of the Waikato.[35] The liquor trade promoted debt, disorganised Maori social life and helped to pave the way for European purchases of land. In such circumstances it is hardly surprising that the 1846 Sale of Spirits Ordinance remained a dead letter. The tribal disputes which Tamihana and other King party chiefs complained of were caused by European attempts to buy land. Thus when they appealed for law and order, or for 'stopping the flow of blood', they were referring to the tribal fights at Taranaki and elsewhere, and knew that the Government was making no attempt to stop these. As Paora Te Ahuru pointed out: 'The Governor does not stop murders and fights among us. A king will be able to do that.'[36] Tamihana spoke in the same vein: 'I want order and laws. The King can give us these better than the Governor; the Governor has never done anything except when a *Pakeha* is killed. He lets us kill each other and fight.'[37] These charges were substantially correct and the Government, as the Waitara dispute showed, was not willing to refrain from dealing with individuals or to assert the law to punish murderers if they were willing to sell land. And after the war broke out the Government went one stage further and legalised the procedure of dealing with individuals by passing the Native Lands Act of 1862.

When, on the other hand, Europeans called for the introduction of law and order in Maori districts, they were primarily concerned with law that would 'enfranchise' Maori land, permit direct dealing with individuals, and enable them to obtain security for debts and protection for private property. Most European property in the Waikato before the wars had no legal standing, but, pending the introduction of direct purchase, it could be made more secure if ordinary civil courts were set up. How these objectives were meant to work out in practice can be seen from F. D. Fenton's activities during his two brief circuits as travelling magistrate in the Waikato in 1857 and 1858. Fenton not only took active steps to administer the law in favour of European squatters; he also tried to introduce his own scheme of individualising Maori titles before any legislation had been passed to permit it. This was no chance decision. Fenton, with his cousin James Armitage, had started squatting on Maori land at Paetai (near Taupiri) in 1850. Later he claimed that he had obtained a 'long lease' of the land from the Maori.[38] The 370 acres of homestead land which McLean purchased for Armitage in 1854 was probably a portion of Fenton's 'lease'. Although Fenton had left Paetai after a few years and held several other official appointments culminating in the position of travelling magistrate, when he started his circuit in July 1857 Armitage was still on the land. It should also be noted that Fenton and Armitage were in close contact with the direct purchase men in Auckland, particularly Carleton of the *Southern Cross*. Armitage kept the paper informed on King party activities and, under the pseudonym 'A Waikato Settler',[39] wrote letters in praise of Fenton's courts. The ideas expressed in *Southern Cross* editorials[40] on the King movement were identical with Fenton's and were later adopted by Gorst: the King movement was a striving for law and order which the Government had failed to supply; it could be guided into the right channels by Government action — by Fenton's courts, by 'enfranchising' Maori land and allowing direct purchase, by granting the Maori other rights and privileges (like the right to buy liquor and weapons); and, finally, the disastrous withdrawal of Fenton — indicating the abandonment of the only serious attempt to govern the Maori — had encouraged the King party to set up its own government.

Though Fenton's activities while on circuit in the Waikato met with approval from his supporters in Auckland they were hardly likely to appeal to the King party. In his journals he recorded his attitude to his magisterial functions as well as to some of his non-magisterial activities.[41] The first complaint he received was from a Maori, Hohepa, of Taupari,[42] who alleged that a European squatter called Marshall had refused to pay his rent. Fenton declined to hear the complaint on the ground that Hohepa had no legal title to the land; he wanted to show the Maori the evil of their customary title and their need for Crown grants. He was unconcerned about the fact that Marshall was squatting illegally on Maori land.[43] Fenton spent over half of the remaining time of this circuit in the vicinity of Paetai trying to persuade Maori to subdivide their land. At the end of July he noted in his journals that: 'Mr. Armitage ... very much approves of the new [subdivision] movement, and thinks it will greatly benefit the European residents — he approves of the issue of licences to squatters allowed to dwell on native lands.'[44] After holding his final sitting at Paetai, Fenton noted that Maori present offered 'a fine piece of land, to me and my heirs for ever — I sorrowfully declined'.[45] During his second circuit Fenton observed that the squatters were strongly in favour of his system of courts: 'Indeed no one will profit more than they by the establishment of law, especially accompanied, as it must be, by material advancement. . . . The division of land is gaining strong hold on the minds of the natives.'[46] This, however, was where Fenton was wrong.

Fenton did admit that the King party supporters refused to have anything to do with his grasslands and individualisation schemes, but he tried to write off their objections as 'nonsense'.

> The King party said, that they had heard that sheep also were to be given by the Governor, and that such a gift was very bad, and was only meant to make the Maories tame; moreover, that if the wool was sold to repay the money, the bodies of the sheep would not be discharged from the debt. As to the grass-seed, they said that the name of the Queen would stick to all the land covered with grass, and that they would not have the name of the Queen in Waikato; and that Taupiri [a central mountain] would go, with a great deal more nonsense of that sort.[47]

Potatau, the King elect, was also disturbed by Fenton's activities. When McLean saw him at Mangere, just before Fenton's withdrawal, the old chief complained that:

> He had heard a great deal about the subdivision of territory and the distribution of grass-seed and sheep. He intimated that it was an interference with his rights and prerogative to sow the great flat at Taupiri, a property of his own to which he was much attached . . . . and finally declared that he should yield to the solicitations of his people, leave Mangere, and go and live in the Waikato country.[48]

It was not Fenton's withdrawal but the very nature of his activities that stirred up the King Maori, incurred their distrust of any system of courts administered by Europeans and encouraged them to set up a king of their own. Fenton, by choosing the Paetai–Taupiri area for his individualisation schemes, had picked a spot highly valued by Potatau and his supporters. Potatau had a personal interest in it and, as paramount chief of Ngati Mahuta, a major say in its disposal. Taupiri mountain which overlooked the land was the burial place of the Waikato tribal ancestors.[49] It was also precious as the most significant landscape in the Waikato territory, standing as a sentinel at the gateway to the upper Waikato and Waipa valleys. Thus the episode over Taupiri and Paetai symbolised the growing conflict between Europeans and the King party for land and for authority over it. The King party may not have understood the niceties of Fenton's legal procedure, but they were aware of the general implications of the working of his proposed courts.

In 1861 Grey attempted to introduce civil institutions into the Waikato, partly under the direction of Fenton's squatting partner, Armitage. But the King party was even more distrustful of this new attempt to introduce law and order than it had been of Fenton's attempt. By this time the conflicting European and King party attitudes to law and its administration were coming into the open. The King party was imposing its own law on the squatters, charging them rent and fining them for the trespass of stock. The squatters accordingly appealed to the Government for the assertion of law and authority.[50] So far the King party had tolerated the squatters but, now that they were appealing to an outside authority over property disputes, the King party had no alternative but to expel them. The difference had become a question of authority and for both sides it was a question of authority over land which, in the last resort, must be settled by war.

So far only the negative aspects of the King movement have been dealt with: its uncompromising opposition to land sales or leases, the attempts to control debts and boycott courts. To meet direct or indirect European threats to its land the King party often adopted European procedures. Thus the King's *runanga* (council) issued various proclamations or laws, levied fines and taxes, set up a police force and published its own newspaper.[51] But these activities were never conspicuously successful. Something more positive was needed if the King movement was to attain any real unity and prevent the young, the unruly and the thriftless from defecting to the Queen's side. As it was, the Government was always willing to offer salaries or ill-disguised bribes to any important men willing to desert the King or sell land;[52] and this policy had the limited effect of building up a small 'Queen' party in the lower Waikato. The King party gained its cohesion and strength not by imitating European institutions and techniques but by a revival and extension of traditional Maori systems.

Maori scholars have been unanimous in emphasising the traditional rather than 'European' nature of the King movement. Sir Apirana Ngata called it 'one of the organisations evolved by the Maori people for resisting the destruction of their culture and the loss of its foundation, the land'.[53] Pei Jones, biographer of

Potatau, says that, 'The true position as the Maori leaders of the time saw it was that the race was in need of a unifying institution characteristic of its Polynesian ancestry and traditions', and that Potatau accepted the Kingship as a 'means of recapturing the lost prestige of the Maori people'.[54] And the late Dr Maharaia Winiata emphasised that the King movement 'followed the same tendency as in the *runanga*, to graft European procedures, concepts, etc., upon the indigenous foundation of the Maori socio-political system. The *ariki, rangatira, kaumata* and *tohunga* were bound together in their respective positions in the hierarchy of leadership. New titles were borrowed from the European but the old relationships remained.'[55]

The title 'King' was European but the qualifications needed for the office and the way the chiefs went about the selection of a king were Maori. The three essential qualifications were expressed as *mana tangata* (prestige on the human side), *mana whenua* (prestige over land as shown by the possession of significant territory), and *mana kai* (prestige through food resources). According to the traditional story of the selection of the King,[56] a young Otaki chief called Matene Te Whiwhi led a deputation around the North Island asking each major chief to accept the Kingship. The relevant qualifications were named to each one but no chief could be prevailed upon to accept the honour. Finally, five years after Te Whiwhi had set out on his expedition, Potatau was persuaded to accept. He had outstanding qualifications. He was a famous warrior who had led the Tainui tribes in the musket wars of the 1820s. He had genealogical connections with many of the other canoes. He was a *tohunga* (priest, scholar) as well as a famous chief.[57] He was the embodiment of the *mana Maori*,[58] having the prestige to gain the allegiance of chiefs whose traditional *mana* had been declining through the impact of Christianity and European society. The strategic position of Potatau's Waikato tribes was also significant: they barred the gateway to European expansion into the centre of the North Island. This meant that Potatau and not a coastal chief must be King. His qualifications were summed up as: *Ko Potatau te tangata, ko Taupiri te maunga, ko Waikato te moana, he piko he taniwha, he piko he taniwha* — Potatau is the man, Taupiri is the mountain, Waikato river is the sea, in every bend there is a monster. These cryptic phrases summed up a lot that was well known to the Maori audiences concerned. They referred to Potatau's human prestige; to the significance of Taupiri mountain as the burial place of the ancestors, and as sentinel to the whole Waikato–Waipa territory; to the significance of the Waikato river as a line of communication and a source of food; and to the veritable galaxy of important chiefs (the *taniwha*) residing along its banks.

King party meetings were conducted in the traditional style. There were long, seemingly inconclusive *korero* (debates) but no formal resolutions or votes: such European procedures were unnecessary as the majority opinion was usually summed up by the symbolic act of a chief whose prescience and judgement enabled him to gauge the mood of the audience. Potatau was not 'elected' in the European sense of the word. After he agreed to accept the Kingship he was in turn accepted by tribal assemblies — at Ngaruawahia on 2 June 1858 and at subsequent meetings up the Waipa valley. Young mission-educated chiefs took part in King party proceedings and spoke in biblical or European terms, but — Tamihana apart — it was the old chiefs speaking in the traditional manner who were most influential. The greater their *mana* the less they needed to say: many could achieve their effect merely by reciting a traditional poem or song with appropriate contemporary references. At the meetings preceding his accession Potatau seldom uttered more than a few epigrams. It was unnecessary for him to deliver rousing addresses to his 'electors'. At the Rangiriri meeting of June 1857 he recited an epigram about the *kotuku*, the white heron, which in this case meant the *Pakeha*: 'The kotuku sits upon a stump and eats the small fish; when he sees one he stoops down and catches it, lifts up his head and swallows it. That is his constant work.'[59] Potatau followed this epigram with a song and then urged Tamihana to go ahead with his work of forming the King movement.

At a later meeting one old scribe, Wiremu Te Akerautangi, compared the social condition of the Maori with that of a fish once healthful and swimming at ease in its native waters but now looked on as an article of food:

> ... thou art as a fish caught from the sea.
> And placed upon the stalls to dry.

He asked whether the Maori should be satisfied with the systems of foreign people which they were called upon to adopt:

> Are we to feed upon the things that come
> From lands far distant?

He censured those so credulous as to believe that foreigners sought only to benefit Maori by introducing customs so contrary to their sacred ways and concluded that they must maintain their national independence:

> O son, thou gavest this to me
> And caused these lips to be polluted
> Which once were sacred. Lo, I'll lop it off.
> Lest it should lead me to adopt its measures.[60]

Another chief, Te Awarahi, was

> ... pained for thee O wife
> Gone from me to another!

Thus he bitterly regretted that Maori lands (his 'wife') had been sold.[61]

And so the speeches went on. The theme was always the same: the tribes must have a king to protect the land; and in keeping the land they were retaining the human culture it nourished.

The main institutions of the King movement were traditional rather than 'European'. The King's 'Council' was neither a 'Star Chamber' nor a Cabinet but the traditional *runanga* of the King's own tribe, Ngati Mahuta, attended occasionally by other leading chiefs such as Tamihana and Rewi Maniapoto. The elders of this *runanga* were the main counsellors of the King, particularly after Tawhiao's accession following the death of his father in 1860. Young, educated chiefs often represented the King in 'diplomatic' negotiations with the Governor, European ministers or officials, because they had a better grasp of English and European negotiating skills,[62] but it was the elders who were most influential within the King's domain. It was the same with the *runanga* of the other tribes belonging to the movement. Inspired by young chiefs, some *runanga* experimented with codes of law based on a mixture of scriptural and European civil law, but these were largely unsuccessful[63] and the *runanga* reverted to the control of elders who upheld traditional practices.

As a confederation of tribes the King movement was based on the traditional, loosely defined *waka* (canoe) organisation,[64] in this case the group of tribes descending from Hoturoa and the other members of the *Tainui* canoe. The three main tribes of the confederation, Waikato, Ngati Haua and Ngati Maniapoto, had fought together against the Ngapuhi invaders in the 1820s;[65] the confederation was revived with the setting up of the King, this time to resist the potential advance of Europeans. The Tainui tribes formed the solid core of the King movement but, with the development of the conflict over land, the movement assumed a wider, nationalist significance. Kinship affiliations with other tribes were revived, and old vendettas forgiven. Thus, with the outbreak of war in Taranaki in 1860, Wiremu Kingi and the bulk of the Ngati Awa tribe, traditional enemies of the Tainui tribes, joined the King movement.[66] Though the member tribes were seldom unanimous in their allegiance to the King and some tribes did not join at all, the King movement had, by the end of 1860, formed a defensive confederation of tribes stretching right across the North Island — from Ngati Ruanui and Ngati Awa territory on the west coast to Ngai Te Rangi on the east.

Other writers have dealt with the origins of the Taranaki and Waikato wars and with the various campaigns leading to the defeat of the main King party forces at Orakau in 1864.[67] Military defeat and the loss of the best of the Waikato and Waipa lands through confiscation did not break the King movement. Tamihana and the bulk of Ngati Haua defected in 1865, but Tawhiao and most of his Waikato supporters escaped into the fastness of the Ngati Maniapoto domain — which became known as the 'King Country' — where the King movement continued to exercise its role as champion of the Maori cause for over twenty years.[68] This was not a matter of living in 'sullen isolation' or 'within a degenerate exclusiveness', as some writers have imagined.[69] There was prolonged bitterness over the confiscation of land and this was a major stumbling block to the attempts of successive Native Ministers to open the King Country for the main trunk railway and other European enterprises. As Manuhiri, the chief King party spokesman, put it on one occasion: 'If the blood of our people only had been spilled, and the land remained, then this trouble would have been over long ago.'[70] But this was not the only reason for keeping the King Country closed.

The confiscation of almost 2,000,000 acres of Maori land[71] did not satisfy the European appetite. The European population was increasing rapidly, largely through immigration, and the Maori population was decreasing, so there seemed to be good reason to promote further purchases of Maori land. In 1865 another Native Lands Act was passed to put the Native Land Court on a more practical footing and simplify the procedure whereby settlers could purchase land from individual Maori named in the Court's certificates of ownership. This Act represented a dangerous threat to the King party land league. Individuals could now defy their chiefs and sell to Europeans any land the Court awarded them; likewise chiefs could ignore the agreement whereby they had placed tribal land under the King's *mana* and disobey his proclamations against land-selling. The Court was required to base its awards on Maori land custom as it existed in 1840,[72] and this meant that no unit larger than the tribe could be recognised. The land league was an inter-tribal agreement made after 1840 and could not be recognised by the Court. Tawhiao, the Maori King, thus had no more rights to land than any other chief and, as his tribal lands in the Waikato had been confiscated, he was no more than a squatter on the Ngati Maniapoto lands in the King Country.[73]

The King party decided to boycott the Court but this too involved them in a dilemma. Under the Act of 1865 the Court adopted the practice of awarding certificates of ownership to representatives of those who appeared at the sittings. King party non-sellers who boycotted the Court were left out of the awards, even though they might have had a valid claim to the land. Europeans could thus first obtain a valid lease from the sellers and, in time, through buying up the interests of each individual named, gain the freehold. In reply the King party decided to erect an *aukati* (boundary) along the confiscation line and deny Europeans access to any land they had leased across this line. The conflict over the land had been renewed and again it was largely a matter of whether the King's or the Europeans' law would prevail. The Europeans were now in a stronger position as they had the Native Lands Act and the Native Land Court to sanction their proceedings; the King still had his independence and could still issue proclamations against land-selling but it was now much more difficult to enforce them.

At first the Europeans seemed to be gaining the upper hand. Tamihana's defection from the King party enabled Firth to breach the land league and secure a foothold in the Matamata district.[74] Further inland W. T. Buckland claimed to have secured a lease from Ngati Raukawa,[75] and Walker and Douglas leased some more land from a section of Ngati Haua near Cambridge.[76] This was 'the little edge of the wedge' but, before the Europeans could drive it home, a series of skirmishes brought the border almost to a state of war. In 1870 two Europeans were murdered by King party supporters on the King's side of the border. The victims were a gold prospector named Lyons, who ignored the King party ban against prospecting,[77] and a surveyor named Todd, who was surveying disputed land.[78] Then in 1873 there was another murder, this time as a direct result of the land transactions. Timothy Sullivan, an employee of Walker and Douglas, was shot when working on the land they had leased across the border. Porokutu, the alleged murderer, who was a supporter of the King, had a claim to the land but refused to attend the Court sitting or accept the Walker and Douglas lease. He had warned them repeatedly of the consequences of occupation.[79] The irate military settlers of Cambridge and Te Awamutu were anxious to avenge Sullivan's murder by invading the King Country but McLean, now Native Minister, refused to allow the Government to be dragged into more military campaigns or to deviate from his conciliation policy. Once the excitement had died down, purchase transactions were quietly resumed and the King party, anxious to avoid war, made no further resort to violence.

As was the case before the wars, the King party could not rely on purely negative measures to save the land. Tawhiao issued numerous proclamations calling on his supporters to refrain from selling lands, to keep out of the Court, to prohibit surveys and to keep the *aukati* intact.[80] His chief adviser, Manuhiri, appealed to European friends to put an end to land transactions:

> Friend it is well that you should look at the selling and leasing of lands and telegraphs. . . . These matters originate with the white people. I have looked into these things, and they are like the branches of trees which are rubbed together by . . . the wind until they become diseased and broken. While this work is going on we cannot settle down. How could it be otherwise when Covet, and Conceal, and Deceit are at work?[81]

But Tawhiao's proclamations and Manuhiri's appeals were of little avail unless accompanied by positive measures to compensate their flagging supporters for the easily obtained money European purchasers were dispensing. Before long it became apparent that the King party did have some advantages to offer. The land sellers who congregated around the Cambridge Courts soon squandered the proceeds of their bargains. Often they found that the money from sales or leases was all swallowed up by Court fees and the expenses of living in European towns during the prolonged Court sittings; and they had to sell more land to repay advances they had received from European storekeepers, publicans and land agents. They became drunken, demoralised and impoverished. King party supporters who avoided land transactions were spared these social consequences. Newspaper reports were soon pointing out the differences between the two groups. In 1868 the *Southern Cross* emphasised that:

> The European conquests have not weakened the authority of the King . . . nor . . . destroyed the spirit of the Land League. . . . [The King Maori] are prepared to forfeit all profit to themselves to maintain their political and social independence. . . . Shut up in this way . . . the King natives are thriving wonderfully. They are reported to be healthier, and the increase in the number of children is noteworthy. They are cultivating more extensively than formerly. . . . Their men and women . . . live longer than those natives

who frequent our towns ... and they frequently point to that circumstance ... as an argument in favour of King Tawhiao's jurisdiction.[82]

Nine years later the *New Zealand Herald* was making the same contrast:

Before the Maoris could draw upon their lands as upon a bank for money they had a fair prospect of enduring. The last generation have simply been living on the proceeds of their land sales, and killing themselves off with easy got money. Only the Kingites, who are not gradually selling land and drinking the proceeds, are not rapidly decreasing in number.[83]

Despite its attempts to exclude land purchase agents, surveyors and prospectors, the King party did not attempt to shut itself off from European contact altogether. Other European visitors, even the Government agent, W. G. Mair, were allowed in to attend King party meetings.[84] Louis Hettit, a French Huguenot who had married a woman of the Ngati Maniapoto tribe, stayed with the King party during the wars and afterwards acted as its principal trading agent. By 1875 there were said to be seven Europeans living at Te Kuiti, the main settlement.[85] King supporters frequently crossed the border to Alexandra to sell produce, or attend the European race meetings and agricultural shows.[86] An extensive border trade started in 1868 and continued unabated throughout the 1870s. The King party cleared large areas of bush: one clearing was said to be 'miles in extent' in 1868;[87] and on another occasion, in 1875, 600 Maori were seen felling bush.[88] Wheat, potatoes, tobacco and other European crops were sown and the surplus produce sold in Alexandra in return for ploughs, other implements and clothing. Cattle and pigs also were raised for sale in the European markets. The amount of produce sold was considerable: in 1875 Lamb's mill at Ngaruawahia purchased 7000 bushels of wheat and it was said that the total harvest would be 30,000–40,000 bushels.[89] Many more examples could be quoted, but it should already be obvious that, instead of living in 'sullen isolation' or 'degenerate exclusiveness', the King party was making an agricultural and commercial effort comparable to that in the Waikato in the early 1850s, and in much less favourable circumstances.

The general significance of this effort should not be lost sight of. Agriculture and trade, as well as providing useful activity and the necessities of life, kept the King party out of debt and hence out of the clutches of land purchasers. They showed how far the party had managed to incorporate European material benefits into the traditional framework of Maori society. This development was not 'reactionary' but gave to King party society a cohesion and stability that was sadly lacking among the land-selling tribes. Maori visitors from outside districts found this society very impressive. In 1872 the Thames chief, Piniha, reported that the King Maori at Tokangamutu were living 'in great comfort, and [were] supplied with many of the comforts and some of the luxuries of life.... The ancient style of living is adopted here, and I think it very superior to any other that I have seen, and better than Europeans can see in any other native district.'[90] A year later, just after the Sullivan murder, the Auckland chief, Paora Tuhaere, visited the King Country and reported in glowing terms on the scene of industry at Te Kuiti: even the King was to be seen working in the fields with members of his tribe. Tuhaere was impressed with the widespread use of European implements and the abundance of food. King Maori wanted peace and Tawhiao had issued a proclamation stating that no more Europeans were to be killed.[91] Later in the 1870s there was a religious revival which also emphasised the King party's desire for peace. The King party repudiated the extremist *Hau Hau* movement, but it adopted a pacifist form of religion, the *Tariao* (Morning Star) faith, which was a compound of Christian and traditional beliefs, with the former clearly dominant.

> They invoke God to give Tawhiao strength to preserve peace between themselves and the Europeans; they ask God to assist them in obeying Tawhiao's commands, winding up each prayer by asking God to watch over Tawhiao and them, and keep them from evil on that day.... There is not a single word of fanaticism in any of [their prayers].[92]

King party chiefs delivered the sermons and quoted freely from the Bible. The King party had repudiated the European missionaries but not their teachings, though it was now turning these to its own purposes. The practice of the *Tariao* faith, like the large-scale communal agriculture, helped to promote social and political stability.

The pre-war practice of holding large inter-tribal meetings was continued. Hundreds of Maori from outside the King Country, representing virtually every tribe, attended the annual meetings. These were conducted in the traditional style with feasting, songs and *haka* (dances), preceding the inevitable *korero* (debates). The discussions, as before the wars, were mainly about land, though now they emphasised the dangers of European purchase activities and the iniquities of the Native Land Court. The meetings concluded with appeals to uphold the land league and keep the *aukati* intact, reaffirmations of the unity of the movement, pleas for peace and demands for the return of the Waikato.[93]

Yet for all its efforts the King party was losing the struggle to retain the land. After the turn of the 1880s several of the tribes fringing the King Country were prised away from the King's land league. This was a result of the ceaseless activity of European purchase agents. In 1871 the Government, armed with ready cash from the Vogel loans, again began to purchase Maori land. Government purchase agents vied with private agents to secure agreements with any individual Maori willing to sell land and then to force tribal land through the Court. By 1882 the land league was almost broken. Paora Tuhaere warned the King party of its shrinking borders:

> Look at me, a man who knows what it is to suffer. I speak of the 'circular' boundary, that is, the present boundary of the King country, outside of which formerly were included Maungatautari, Wairaka, etc. I speak of the boundary tomorrow, Mokau, Karioi, Pirongia, etc. . . . I suppose some of you have entered into arrangements with Europeans for sale or lease of lands within these boundaries. . . . If surveys be admitted and Crown grants be received within this boundary, you will suffer.[94]

But his warning was of no avail. In the same year a private organisation completed the purchase from Ngati Raukawa of the 250,000-acre Patetere block, along the eastern border of the King Country.[95] Further south the Murimotu block was shared out between the Government and a private organisation,[96] and Joshua Jones secured a lease over the Mokau block on the south-west border.[97] Two years later Ngati Tuwharetoa agreed to have the titles of their Taupo land settled by the Court. Only the Ngati Maniapoto–Waikato alliance remained of the King's once formidable land league and the Government had already taken steps to break this.

In the 1870s McLean and then Grey had made several unsuccessful attempts to obtain Tawhiao's consent for the opening of the King Country. Late in 1883 the Native Minister, John Bryce, decided to abandon formal negotiations and secure the opening of the King Country by what the *New Zealand Herald* called 'the natural way of encouraging and enabling certain natives to put their land through the Court'. It went on to point out that:

> All attempts made to conclude negotiations with Tawhiao and the Kingites *en bloc* have been miserable failures. . . . The Government influence will simply be exerted to enable certain sections of the Kingites to take advantage of the law, and the Land Court will do the rest.[98]

Bryce opened direct negotiations with the Ngati Maniapoto chiefs and ignored Tawhiao and the Waikato chiefs. Rewi and Wahanui, the two leading Ngati Maniapoto chiefs, decided that, to prevent further encroachments, it was necessary to have the Court define tribal boundaries, and they agreed to allow surveyors to mark these off. Surveyors entered the King Country before the end of the year and at the same time 120 members of the Armed Constabulary were sent to watch Tawhiao at Kawhia and prevent him from making more than a verbal protest. In the next two years John Ballance, Bryce's successor, was able to carry the policy to a successful conclusion. The King Country was symbolically opened to European enterprise when the Premier, Sir Robert Stout, turned the first sod of the King Country section of the main trunk railway on 15 April 1885.

It now remained to be seen whether the King party could survive the breaking of the Ngati Maniapoto–Waikato alliance and the opening of its last stronghold to the Europeans. The Ngati Maniapoto tribe was soon mixed up in land transactions as Government agents sought to buy the best of the land along the railway route. Tawhiao and his Waikato supporters moved back to settle on small areas reserved for them in the Waikato. The King party had lost the struggle to retain the land, and with this it lost its political independence. It could no longer assume the mantle of Maori nationalism, but it did live on into the twentieth century as an embodiment of Maori cultural identity, a *Mauri o te Maoritanga* — a bulwark for Maori ideals and values.

7

Polynesian Corpuscles and Pacific Anthropology:
The Home-made Anthropology of Sir Apirana Ngata and Sir Peter Buck

> The Polynesian corpuscles carry us behind the barrier that takes a Pakeha some time to scale.... — *Buck to Ngata, 20 September 1926*[1]

The central theme of this essay is the belief of Ngata and Buck that their Maori ancestry and upbringing gave them a unique advantage over Pakeha in understanding Maori culture. When Buck was about to leave for the Bishop Museum in Hawaii in March 1927, he told Ngata: 'In Polynesian research it is right and fitting that the highest branch of the Polynesian race should be in the forefront and not leave the bulk of the investigations to workers who have not got the inside angle that we have.'[2] Later, in June 1928, Ngata reassured Buck: 'You have the scientific detachment, the analytical ability, and the racial penetration to the "hinengaro" & "ngakau" Maori' — the inner emotions, heart and mind of the Maori.[3] And somewhat later again, in January 1932, Buck returned to the theme: 'Neither you nor I had any special training in ethnology in our university days; yet we both have a field experience that few, if any, ethnologists have been favoured with . . . . Neither the ethnologists of the old school like Peehi

---

This paper was originally delivered as the J. C. Beaglehole lecture to the conference of the New Zealand Historical Association, August 1981. A revised version was subsequently published in *The Journal of the Polynesian Society*, vol. 91, no. 1 (1982), pp. 7–27. That version is reproduced here.

[Best] nor the younger generation like Skinner could tackle the things that you or I know to be of importance.'[4]

As this last quotation indicates, Ngata and Buck were sandwiched between two generations of New Zealand anthropologists; between the amateur ethnologists who founded the Polynesian Society in the 1890s — S. Percy Smith, Edward Tregear and Elsdon Best — and the new generation of New Zealand-born but overseas-trained anthropologists who came to the fore in the 1920s and 1930s — H. D. Skinner, Felix Keesing, Raymond Firth, I. L. G. Sutherland and Ernest Beaglehole. This essay is concerned with Ngata's and Buck's relations with these Pakeha colleagues and, since none of them worked in a vacuum, with the influence of overseas and particularly British and American anthropologists. In their formative years Ngata and Buck were influenced mainly by British anthropologists, but after Buck went to the Bishop Museum and Yale, Americans became more important. However, it is not the formative period that I am primarily concerned with, but the later years, more especially the ten years or so that followed Buck's departure for the Bishop Museum, when, at 50, he became a professional anthropologist. A year later Ngata became Minister of Native Affairs with a long-awaited opportunity to put anthropology into action.

The Schooling of Ngata and Buck

As already noted, Ngata and Buck placed much importance on ancestry and upbringing, though with different emphases. Both had Pakeha ancestry but Ngata's was distant and unimportant to him; he considered himself a Maori. Buck was half and half and felt his Maori and Pakeha ancestry to be equally important. Ngata was brought up in totally Maori surroundings in the Waiapu district of the East Coast and went to Waiomatatini Native School. Buck was born in Taranaki but went to the state Urenui primary school and later worked with his father on a Wairarapa sheep station. Both went to Te Aute and then proceeded to university: Ngata to Canterbury University College, where he completed a BA, an MA in political science, and an LLB; Buck to Otago Medical School where he completed an MB, ChB. Te Aute had an important influence on both men, inspiring them with a burning ambition to ameliorate the condition of the Maori people,[5] but the university influence on them should not be ignored. From their academic records we know that Ngata and Buck were always at or near the top of their classes.[6] In Ngata's lecture notes from Canterbury he recorded, among other things, that in the history of the Roman and British empires 'race intermixture and utter neglect of race distinction led to the disappearance of . . . race morality and the staying power that makes a nation was lost.... The savage civilizations die out before the Western' — a dose of social Darwinism that had for Ngata a much closer to home significance. Buck, like many pioneers of anthropology who had trained in medical schools, gained from Otago an early interest in physical anthropology — no doubt inspired by J. H. Scott, the professor of anatomy, who had published a paper on Maori and Moriori skulls in 1893.[7] Thirty years later Buck expanded on Scott's paper with his essay on 'Maori Somatology' in *The Journal of the Polynesian Society*.[8] Earlier, in 1910, Buck had completed a more substantial exercise in medical history and ethnology, his MD thesis, 'Medicine Amongst the Maoris in Ancient and Modern Times'. He introduced it in characteristic fashion: 'with the priviledge [sic] of the half-breed inheriting the blood and ideas of both races I have been able to detach myself from European thought and look at ... disease from my Maori countryman's viewpoint'.[9]

After university Ngata and Buck turned their professional expertise to the service of the Maori people: Ngata as secretary for the Te Aute College Students' Association and later as organising secretary for Carroll's Maori Councils; Buck as assistant medical officer in Pomare's Maori hygiene division of the Department of Health. But it was not long before they entered politics. Ngata won the Eastern Maori seat in 1905, Buck Northern Maori in 1909. In their years in Parliament before the First World War they came into close contact with Pakeha interested in Maori culture, notably Augustus Hamilton and Best at the Dominion Museum, and Percy Smith of the Polynesian Society. During this period they set their scholarly goals. In 1909 Buck drew up a questionnaire on Maori social organisation and talked of collecting anthropometrical measurements.[10] He started to publish on material culture,[11] and made his first excursions into the Pacific: to Rarotonga in 1910, and Niue in 1912–13. In 1909 Ngata issued a manifesto for the Young Maori Party which stressed the need to preserve Maori language, poetry, traditions, customs, arts and crafts; and to carry out research into anthropology and ethnology.[12]

The First World War scarcely interrupted their scholarly activity. Buck went overseas as Medical Officer to the Maori Pioneer Battalion. He won a DSO at Gallipoli, served in France, and on the way home took the measurements of his men that were used for the essay on Maori somatology. Ngata remained at home, helping the recruitment of the Maori Battalion and, among other things, publishing patriotic haka.[13] After the war Buck was appointed Director of Maori Hygiene but this was increasingly of secondary importance to research and publication, notably of his monographs, *The Evolution of Maori Clothing* (1926), and *The Material Culture of the Cook Islands* (1927). Both were published by the

Board of Maori Ethnological Research which Ngata had been instrumental in establishing in 1923. Buck was also doing the rounds of the academic conferences with his classic lecture 'The Coming of the Maori', given as early as 1908, expanded as the Cawthron Lecture in 1922, repeated at the Melbourne Pan-Pacific conference in 1923, and thereafter in many different places and guises.[14] The Cawthron version was published in 1925 and reprinted by the board in 1929.

In these years Buck and Ngata were meeting some of the big men in British and American anthropology. Most important of all for Buck were the meetings in 1923 in Melbourne and Auckland with Herbert E. Gregory, Director of the Bishop Museum, who nominated Buck to join the museum's expedition to the Cook Islands in 1924; and in turn invited him to join the Bishop Museum staff as ethnologist in 1927. Buck sought Ngata's advice before accepting: 'The past has gradually been training me for it. I think the time is now ripe when I should devote myself entirely to it and keep up our reputation in this branch of scientific work. I know I can more than hold my own with other writers in the Polynesian field.'[15] Ngata approved and Buck was launched on his career as a professional anthropologist; apart from brief visits in 1930, 1935 and 1949, he remained an expatriate for the rest of his life. But Ngata remained firmly rooted in New Zealand, pursuing his political career and his scholarly activities, and only once — a brief trip to the Cooks in 1932 — leaving his native shore. In the correspondence which followed they were so often in agreement that, as Condliffe says, 'their individual contributions cannot be separated'.[16] They were a constant source of encouragement to each other. But their temperaments were very different, for Buck was genial, witty, a superb raconteur and a popular lecturer, urbane and becoming increasingly Americanised; whereas Ngata was ascetic, introspective, formal (even with colleagues of long standing), had a wry sense of humour and a cutting repartee, did not suffer fools, especially Pakeha fools, gladly, and placed his trust in a small circle of confidants like H. R. H. Balneavis (the ever-faithful Bal) and Tai Mitchell. Yet despite their different personalities, there was an intimate bond between Ngata and Buck which survived the different turnings of their careers.

Buck, Ngata and the New Anthropology
As has been suggested, Buck and Ngata were heirs to an older, largely British, school of anthropology which had been introduced into New Zealand by Smith and Best. It was very much concerned with ethnography (descriptive accounts of non-literate peoples) and ethnology (comparative studies and classifications of such peoples on the basis of material culture, language, institutions, and so

on). Though some pioneer anthropologists like E. B. Tylor thought in terms of the independent evolution of cultures, the weight of opinion in British anthropology favoured diffusion from a common centre. New Zealand diffusionists, such as Tregear, Smith and Best were, as I have pointed out elsewhere,[17] determined to trace Maori (and other Polynesians) from a Middle East or Indian homeland. In the first two decades of the twentieth century diffusionism received a considerable boost from the work of Elliot Smith and W. J. Perry at University College, London. American anthropology, on the other hand, was dominated by the culture history school which derived from Germany, and was led by Franz Boas at Columbia.

Both schools came under attack in the 1920s and 1930s from the functionalists, led by Bronislaw Malinowski (who was appointed to the chair of anthropology at the London School of Economics in 1927) and, though he often denied paternity, A. Radcliffe-Brown at Sydney. Buck and Ngata were caught in the crossfire. They came to know many of the combatants, or to read their works; but they were not really converted. In 1933, when he was a visiting professor at Yale, Buck attended the conference of the Anthropological Section of the American Association for the Advancement of Science, accompanied by his student, Ernest Beaglehole. He met Boas — then 75 — and several of his disciples, all carefully jockeying for the succession. Radcliffe-Brown was also there, leading a seminar on fieldwork methods. Buck contributed. He observed that Radcliffe-Brown was busily 'disavowing the fatherhood of the functional school which Malinowski claims as his own creation'. There was, Buck continued, 'somewhat of a controversy about the functional school in America. Malinowski and his followers hold that the American school have been recording the dry complexes of culture in a historical sequence whereas the functional school has as its object the drawing up of a picture as to how various parts of a culture function . . . at the time of writing. The trouble in America is that the Indian culture is about defunct and they have to use the historical method to get anything to write about.'[18] Buck commented again after Malinowski had lectured at Yale later in the year: 'Both methods have their uses and the attempt to create . . . distinctions between various schools are purely academic dodges with no practical uses.'[19] Buck never did have much time for theory.

It is time to turn to some of the more specific points at issue, more particularly as these relate to Buck's and Ngata's work. Since it is impossible to cover the whole range, I shall concentrate on four: the controversy over diffusion; questions relating to social organisation; the role of psychology; and, finally, acculturation, particularly as it related to the use of anthropology in the government of native races. Buck and Ngata were concerned with all topics, though to differing degrees.

First, I look at the controversy over diffusion. Throughout his life Buck clung to the romantic notion that the Polynesians had a Caucasian origin and had come into the Pacific from South-east Asia. So did Ngata. On 24 April 1932, he told Buck he was much attracted by a restatement of the Caucasian theory by Griffith Taylor, Professor of Geography at Sydney. The Mediterranean, Aryan, Mongolian, Arabian, Indian and Malaysian influences, Ngata said, 'gave our forefathers a rich and varied culture whose elements were shed or debased in their enforced speculative wanderings into Oceania'. Ngata and Buck were merely reiterating the older views of Smith and Tregear, but it is worth noting that later in the 1930s they began to express criticism of Smith's scholarship. On 31 May 1936, Buck said he had 'started to read Smith's "Hawaiki" again for I do not believe that it was humanly possible for any people ... to remember accurately a line of ancestry that went back to India in 450 B.C. I believe that genealogies are important in showing common ancestors and ... descent but beyond a certain distance back they cannot be relied on to give accurate dating.' A year later their old friend Herbert Williams — the one Pakeha scholar Buck and Ngata never criticised — published his essay, "The Maruiwi Myth", in *The Journal of the Polynesian Society*,[20] with its trenchant criticism of Smith's use of oral records gathered by Whatahoro Jury, Te Matorohanga and others; criticisms which were reflected in the 1949 revised edition of Buck's *Coming of the Maori*.[21] By this time Ngata was also critical: 'Whatahoro ... rammed many improbable things down old Matorohanga's throat to extract them for the benefit of Percy Smith and Elsdon Best.'[22]

In his studies of material culture in the Pacific Buck became aware of the critics of diffusionism, notably Roland Dixon, Professor of Anthropology at Yale, whose work he was reading and reviewing in the early 1920s.[23] In June 1928 he urged Ngata to read Dixon's new book, *The Building of Culture*, for its criticism of the Elliot Smith/Perry theory of diffusion.[24] Later in the year he complained of students who, lacking information about a particular culture, filled the gap with information from another culture which they thought was similar. Though he expected to 'get into trouble with some of the older ethnologists', Buck was determined to avoid the 'assertive method of the Perry school'. Characteristically he added: 'Fortunately, I have not yet evolved a theory.'[25] Three years later he was still without a theory. Complaining (19 August 1931) of the incorrect labelling of artefacts in the British Museum, he said that only by careful measurements and analysis would it be possible to work out the stratification of culture. 'It is consideration of such details that prevents me from rushing in with generalisations. Much of the writings of Rivers and others will go by the board when their theories and groupings are analysed in detail.'[26] But in December 1933 Buck praised some articles by Gilbert Archey of the Auckland Museum on Maori carving, and declared himself 'rather in favour of his theory of local evolution, especially after seeing the manner in which different developments take place in individual islands of the same group. Diffusion is the refuge of the indoor student and the proximity of similar objects in cases in the same room made diffusion look easy' — as, for instance, in the Pitt-Rivers Museum at Oxford. Buck went on to criticise a diffusionist paper by W. H. R. Rivers and to support a restatement of local evolution by Dixon.[27] He was to maintain this position in his own work.

Buck and Ngata were somewhat at sea on social organisation, but this is not surprising since neither of them pretended to be a social anthropologist. In their earlier work they usually relied on British anthropologists of the old school like Rivers, rather than new men like Malinowski or Radcliffe-Brown. Later, when Buck went to the Bishop Museum, he began to refer to Americans such as Clark Wissler, R. H. Lowie and A. M. Tozzer.[28] His monographs on the ethnology of the different Polynesian groups usually contained brief chapters on social organisation but these were descriptive rather than analytical.

Ngata also did some work on Maori social organisation; he even considered 'writing a tome' on it for a DLitt, but, on Herbert Williams' advice, he decided it would be sufficient to submit *Nga Moteatea*.[29] However, he did complete, though not publish, one substantial exercise in the use of 'the genealogical method as applied to early New Zealand history'.[30] Ngata was not content to use genealogies to create a chronology, in the style of Percy Smith; he also used them to throw light on traditional social organisation. His model was Rivers' paper on 'The Social Organisation of the Torres Straits Islanders', published in *Man* in 1901.[31] Ngata emphasised that the Maori genealogies were much longer and richer than those of the Torres Straits Islanders. From his genealogies Ngata was able to 'cross swords' with Best, who had claimed that Maori did not favour marriages with close relatives. On the contrary, he told Buck (23 June 1928), 'the whakapapa proved that such connections were the rule rather than the exception. The rangatira lines reek with marriages that are almost incestuous.' In addition, genealogies could be used to work out 'the actual growth and development of hapu and tribal organisations and even to determine the actual period and circumstances under which tribal appellations were applied'.[32] Though

Buck responded encouragingly,[33] Ngata did not continue this promising line of research. It was left to Buck himself to take up social organisation. He added a section on it to the 1949 edition of the *Coming of the Maori* but this was based on existing published sources.

Buck and Ngata had little sympathy for the application of psychological theory to anthropology; after all, they considered that they had acquired from their Maori side a unique understanding of Maori psychology. The British functionalists were not much concerned with psychology, but the Americans and French were interested in personality studies and the application of psychoanalysis to social anthropology. Buck merely got impatient with them: 'Freud's Oedipus complex that the psycho-analysts attribute everything to somewhat annoys me as to the importance attached to it.'[34] Ngata was initially uncharacteristically abject. In 1928 he confessed that 'as a Polynesian' he accepted 'without reservation the dictum of students of Maori mentality, that the race had not attained to such a command of ideas and language to express them as ... abstractions and generalizations.... The student of the whakatauki ... will note the poverty in those abstractions which distinguish the wise sayings of the Hebrew, the European, or the Hindu.'[35] The assumption that Maori could not think in the abstract had been promoted by Best and, more recently, by the French anthropologist Lucien Lévy-Bruhl in *How Natives Think*. Ngata read it during a tour of Maori settlements of the South Island in 1929. He described it to Buck as 'a fine example of how the pakeha scientist can go wrong by a wrong conception of the premises on which to theorise. He creates his own type of what a native may be and then deduces what the limits of his range of ideas should be.'[36] By this time, however, I. L. G. Sutherland had put Ngata on to the work of the leading critic of Lévy-Bruhl, the American Paul Radin. After obtaining a PhD at Glasgow, Sutherland had returned to a lectureship in Tommy Hunter's department of philosophy and psychology at Victoria University College in 1924. His paper, 'The Study of the Native Mind', published in *The Journal of the Polynesian Society* in 1929, drew heavily on Radin's *Primitive Man as Philosopher*, which he described as 'an important new book ... of great significance to students of [the] Maori mind and culture ... [and] a striking challenge to accepting assumptions concerning the powers of thought of primitive peoples.'[37] Radin dismissed Lévy-Bruhl's notion that native mentality was 'pre-logical and mystical', and lacked 'individuality in thought and expression'. He spoke of a class of 'savage intellectuals' and found some rich examples of their thought in the lore and poetry of the Maori *whare wananga*. Sutherland used Radin to combat the notion that the Maori lacked the faculty of abstraction, and insisted that there was 'an equality of intelligence between Maori and European'. Any differences of mind and character were of social and cultural, not racial, origin. Here Sutherland was going beyond Radin to Sapir (for the view that individual behaviour was culturally patterned) and to Malinowski (in stressing the 'functional value' of forms of feeling and behaviour). This was probably Sutherland's most important contribution to the study of the Maori, introducing as it did some of the latest in British and American anthropological theory. It also marked the beginning of a close partnership with Ngata — though Sutherland was always to remain a junior partner.

Nevertheless, in 1929, Ngata was treating Sutherland with some caution, admitting to Buck that he had some difficulty dealing with 'psychological jargon' in papers on the mind. Radin's book, he said, would have to be studied from 'Sutherland's angle and then ours'. And now, reversing his view of a year earlier, he said: 'Our whakatauki contain all the wisdom and philosophy of Solomon . . . the songs and chants may be placed . . . beside the philosophic utterances of any race.' But there was, Ngata concluded, much in Sutherland's paper which gave the impression that he had 'not got the key to the Polynesian mind'.[38] That key remained with Ngata and Buck.

Finally, of the topics selected for discussion, there is the question of acculturation. During the inter-war years there was much interest in acculturation in Britain, the Dominions and the colonial empire, and in America. Once again the early inspiration for Buck and Ngata came from Britain. Perhaps the most notable influence was G. H. L.-F. Pitt-Rivers. He had come to New Zealand for the Australasian Association for the Advancement of Science conference in Wellington in 1923. Best took him on a tour of the Maori communities up the Whanganui river. This was reported in *The Journal of the Polynesian Society* in 1924 and reprinted in his influential book, *The Clash of Culture and the Contact of Races*, in 1927. Though this was originally an Oxford DPhil, it was dedicated to Malinowski of the London School of Economics 'to whose work and method I have turned for inspiration'. Pitt-Rivers also thanked Buck for information and comment.[39] Buck recommended the book to Ngata, who read it with 'deep interest'.[40] Indeed, Pitt-Rivers inspired Ngata to a rare personal statement of his own acculturation:

> Such a work as that of Pitt-Rivers opens up a very wide field to chaps like myself; who are perforce immersed in problems of today. . . . One must literally live again the generation and a half that has expired since entering the Waiomatatini school and . . . recover . . . through . . . one's memory . . . the native background of those days. Where one

has so greatly emphasised the period devoted to the acquisition of pakeha knowledge (1881–1899) and its application to the problems of adaptation (1899–1928) what a job it will be now to subordinate all that in the assessment of elements of social organisation that have persisted, though modified in details, to the vaunted days of 'Te Ao Hou' [the New World]. I rather think that you and I, Bal and many others must acknowledge that our hearts are not with this policy of imposing pakeha culture forms on our people. Our recent activities would indicate a contrary determination to preserve the old culture forms as the foundations on which to reconstruct Maori life and hopes.

And Ngata went on to quote Pitt-Rivers on the need 'to distrust all measures aimed at the imposition of innovations and culture forms incompatible with native culture'.[41] Ngata's statement was warmly endorsed by Buck, who added that New Zealand was 'unique in the very powerful assistance she had received from within . . . in what the Maori himself has done to render the assimilation of introduced culture forms possible'.[42]

It was a message, moreover, that Ngata was sedulously promoting through young Pakeha protégés, like the economist J. B. Condliffe, and Felix Keesing, whose revised MA thesis was published in 1928 as *The Changing Maori* — with a warm foreword from Ngata. This explained that those who were now witnessing the fulfilment of the Young Maori Party's aims would be amazed at Keesing's knowledge and penetration, of 'the unfolding of this latter-day experiment in cultural adaptation'.[43] Ngata sent Keesing to the East Coast and published in the Ethnological Board's magazine, *Te Wananga*, his lengthy essay 'Maori Progress on the East Coast of New Zealand'.[44] However, in the privacy of his correspondence with Buck, Ngata was somewhat ambiguous over Keesing, describing his work variously as 'a kind of journalese', as 'a cross between Cowan and Andersen', but also calling him a 'scientific sociologist who will place us in correct perspective'.[45] Nevertheless, Ngata was thankful that he had got Keesing interested 'in the communal and psychological basis of our work here. I was able to direct him here because I have consciously hitched our organisation on to the best elements of the communal system, while constantly seeking to approach intrusive pakeha elements, economical and otherwise through tribal mentality'. And Ngata sent Keesing off to Buck in Hawaii (with money from the Ethnological Board) to launch him on a career in anthropology. But he hoped that Buck, with his analytical ability and racial penetration, would come back to take up the story of acculturation; 'chaps like Keesing . . . cannot get very far in'.[46]

Buck did not come back and it was left to other Pakeha students to take up the task. The most notable was Raymond Firth, an Auckland graduate in economics who was one of Malinowski's first doctoral students at the London School of Economics. Firth published his London thesis as *The Primitive Economics of the New Zealand Maori* in 1929. It drew a rather prickly response from Buck who complained to Ngata that Firth had 'made a display of the little knowledge that he possesses of the Maori tongue and the little fieldwork that he did in his Urewera walking tours'. But Buck was ready for the 'threat' of this new Pakeha expert: 'When you and I get down to tin tacks, we will have to draw upon our own inner feelings and psychology . . . so that our pakeha friends will have to be careful. . . . We have got to meet the pakeha on his own grounds by making the most of any natural assets we may have through our blood.'[47] Later, however, Buck was hoping that a lectureship or a chair could be found for Firth in New Zealand.[48] Ngata thought quite highly of Firth's book and saw his training under Malinowski as 'invaluable'.[49] In his Land Development Report for 1931, Ngata quoted at length from the penultimate chapter of the book, 'The Economic Aspect of Culture Change', in which Firth, with acknowledgement to Pitt-Rivers, had set out four stages of acculturation. But Ngata was not uncritical of Firth, especially of his optimistic final stage of acculturation: Firth had failed to penetrate 'the psychological strata of Maori life and thought'.[50]

Anthropology and the Government of Native Races
Acculturation was an important factor to be considered in the government of native races. Though Pakeha scholars tended to regard acculturation as a measure of the Europeanisation of Maori society, Ngata and Buck saw it as essentially a process of incorporating useful elements of European culture into an enduring Maori culture. Government's role was to facilitate that process, under Maori leadership. In the inter-war years anthropological training was provided for colonial administrators at Oxford, Cambridge and London, and at Cape Town and Sydney. In 1931 Firth, then a lecturer at Sydney, visited New Zealand and urged Ngata to establish a department of anthropological field research which would also train officials in native affairs and islands administration. Ngata supported the proposal and wanted Buck to come back as director but it lapsed for want of funds.[51]

Nevertheless, Ngata and Buck were keenly interested in the uses of anthropology in the government of native races. Ngata's 1928 paper, 'Anthropology and the Government of Native Races in the Pacific', was particularly concerned with 'the method whereby the native mind may be influenced to surrender its concepts and accept new ideas'. Much of the paper was concerned with reviewing the progress of acculturation in New Zealand where the ethnologist could see 'before his own eyes the actual process of the merging of the cultures .... Under no other rule has it been possible to stage such a drama as had been unfolded in New Zealand — the deliberate lifting of a people of lower culture to full equality in politics, social, and moral communion with one of the most advanced races in the world.' And to illustrate the point Ngata went on to discuss the achievements in health and land reform of Carroll and the Young Maori Party. The adaptation of Maori culture had been 'vastly facilitated by the education of the Maori people and the development in them of the facility of seeing from two different angles'.[52]

From New Zealand, Ngata turned to her island territories, to test the view that 'success in New Zealand in administering Native affairs justified the expectation that her administration had thoroughly mastered the art of governing Polynesians'. Ngata complacently assumed that New Zealand had been successful in the Cook Islands, which had been under the control of the Native Department and administrators with an expert knowledge of native affairs in New Zealand, and who had been content to follow a policy of *taihoa* ('procrastination'). But he admitted that New Zealand had failed in Western Samoa, where she had created a special External Affairs department and used officials unfamiliar with native affairs. Moreover, she had failed to consult anthropologists — though Buck was in Samoa for six months in 1927. 'It was not wise,' Ngata said, 'to assume that because we knew the minds of two representative branches [of the Polynesians] we could forthwith effect easy entry into the mind of the Samoan.' New Zealand administrators did not sufficiently appreciate Samoan land tenure, social structure, or the status of hereditary chiefs; and, as a consequence, had provoked the Samoan resistance movement known as the Mau.[53]

Ngata's comments on Samoa were amply supported by Buck during his 1927 visit and in later comments. In March 1928 he wrote: 'New Zealand which holds a world's reputation for the results of the Maori question has come a cropper over this damned Samoa.'[54] Later, he contrasted New Zealand in Samoa with the Australians in Papua, where Hubert Murray had achieved good results because he had employed anthropologists. In January 1931 Buck described meeting the chief Australian anthropologist in Papua, E. W. P. Chinnery, who told Buck of the work he was doing 'to extricate the Australian government from having to answer some awkward questions'. Buck also referred Ngata to a paper by Lord Lugard, doyen of British colonial administrators in Africa, who had urged on delegates at the recent Imperial

Conference the need to employ anthropologists. To Buck this sounded 'very much like what we as empirical anthropologists have been trying to do for many years in our own country.... The training that you and I and others got to better understand our own people and so tide over the difficulties did not come to us from any pakeha school of anthropology. The approach and the double angle of vision came to us through our blood.' It was that double angle of vision that was required in Samoa.[55]

However, there was some change in Ngata's attitudes to the Samoan question once he became a member of the Government. He took over the Cook Islands portfolio but not Western Samoa, which remained under External Affairs and the Prime Minister. Though Ngata had been critical of the use of military men and administrators in Samoa, he accepted the appointment of yet another, the former Brigadier-General H. E. Hart, in 1931. Ngata thought it would be enough if he had 'personality, tact, the knack of balancing Native and pakeha factors, a sense of justice and decency. He may not understand what you mean by "culture", "social organisation", mythological sanctions and so forth, but can in practice appreciate that the Native has evolved his own style of living .... The danger just now is that everybody is having a go at the anthropological approach ....'[56] In Ngata's view administrators were born not made. He also thought that New Zealanders were 'tired of Nelson and the Mau. The Polynesian policy of "Hei aha atu" ['Never mind'] is succeeding well. If less notice had been taken in the past of Samoan incidents and agitations the people would have settled down earlier.'[57] And Buck agreed: 'the political attitude that has been going on is merely a continuation of their normal attitude, which springs from their peculiar social organisation and racial psychology ...'.[58] So far as Samoa was concerned, anthropology justified a policy of salutary neglect.

But there was no possibility of *taihoa* in New Zealand once Ngata became Native Minister at the end of 1928. Frustrated for so long in Opposition, Ngata now embarked on a frantic programme of land development and cultural regeneration, using his senior position in the Cabinet and brooking no interference from tidy-minded bureaucrats. Ngata's activities in office cannot be examined in detail; indeed, it will be necessary to confine comment to Ngata's applied anthropology. Here the main document is Ngata's Native Land Development Report of 1931 — perhaps the most important essay in anthropology that he wrote. As ever, Buck provided valuable commentary from abroad; several extracts from his letters were included in Ngata's report. The report, as already indicated, also quoted from Firth's four phases of acculturation, but with an important qualification of the last. In this Firth had assumed, in the typical manner of the functionalists, that 'the former Maori material culture has been largely replaced by that of the white man, and the old economic structure has given way in corresponding fashion'.⁵⁹ Ngata admitted that traditional material culture

> may completely change its appearance . . . social conditions [may be] profoundly influenced by . . . those of Western culture; while . . . morality must be adjusted to . . . Christian ethics. But beneath the surface Native characteristics may persist and racial influences continue their sway over the mind and spirit of the people to a greater extent than European investigators can appreciate. . . . [C]lose observation reveals the hold of the tribal organization and of Native social custom over the lives of the people . . . . little disturbed by the incursion of Western ideas . . . . [T]he *rangatira* families continue to receive the deference due to their rank . . . . The wise administrator recognizes . . . this element in Maori society and adjusts his policy accordingly.⁶⁰

As Ngata went on to stress, traditional elements in Maori society could be used for land development and industrial progress: 'the Maori workman . . . is cheerful and contented, a philosopher at work. His racial endowment in the possession of a keen eye, a deft touch, and a ready co-ordination of mind and muscle is one that statesmen must build on. . . . [T]he Maori of this generation views with philosophic calm the ever-varying devices of western civilization for achieving the age-old purposes of the human race.' Ngata wanted to work through traditional chiefly organisation and turn old tribal jealousies into friendly rivalries in land development, education, arts and crafts, and sport. '[T]he diffusion of ideas, if it is to succeed, must proceed tribally . . . .' Tribal elders from one district could carry the reforms into other tribal areas. Though Maori were indebted to Europeans, they also owed much to their ability to control assimilation: '[T]he Maori can now select what is suitable in the culture of the Pakeha and retain that which shows a tendency to persist in his own culture.' And he drew on Buck's letter of 24 September 1928 to compare the Maori favourably with other Polynesians:

> Our cousins the Hawaiians are being rapidly absorbed . . . into the Nirvana of American citizenship. Our remote kinsmen, the Samoans, are in the rut of customs so deep that able-bodied men sit around [braiding] coconut sennit and parcelling out governing positions among themselves over a mandated country. Between the two, there should be a balance that moulds the assimilable good of each culture. It seems to me . . . that the Maori race are the only branch that are struggling to maintain their individuality as a race and moulding European culture to suit their requirements.⁶¹

He also quoted Buck on the need to work through the tribes: 'I have always felt, since my Polynesian wanderings, that New Zealand was composed of a number of islands in spirit . . . connected by land.' Buck's qualifications, Ngata concluded, were too well known to be repeated: 'by going away from his homeland he has placed himself as on some far-off peak, where he may get a perspective of the whole picture of Maori life and effort'.[62]

Ngata's paper attracted so much attention that he had to run off an extra 1000 copies. He sent several to Buck for distribution. Buck responded enthusiastically: 'It is a masterly exposition of the greatest thing that has been done for the Maori people.' Buck gave a copy to Robert E. Park, Professor of Sociology at Chicago, then lecturing in Hawaii, who described the report 'as the finest thing he has read. . . . He wants to know the struggles and problems that native people have in adjusting . . . to western culture, and your exposition gives him a clearer picture than any elaborate work on ethnology.'[63] Since Park was one of America's leading authorities on racial interaction, this was handsome recognition. Buck saw a good deal of him in Hawaii and found 'the exchange of ideas very valuable'. He chaired a lecture by Park on 'Marginal Man' — men who belonged to two cultures and mediated between them. 'I recognised you and I,' Buck told Ngata in October 1931.[64]

But the optimism generated by Ngata's land reforms was soon to turn sour. He pushed ahead with his schemes with reckless speed, ignoring in turn the advice of his departmental head, the Public Service Commissioner, the Auditor-General, and Treasury, who uncovered mounting evidence of administrative chaos, accounting deficiencies, and, on the part of some of Ngata's trusted subordinates, fraud. Early in 1934, in the face of widespread public criticism, the Prime Minister, G. W. Forbes, set up a Native Affairs Commission of Inquiry, headed by Mr Justice Smith, to examine Ngata's administration of the Native Department and the land development schemes.

The commission reported in August, upholding many of the complaints of the Auditor-General and roundly condemning Ngata's administration. Among the complaints were his high-handed treatment of Pakeha farm supervisors and his favouritism of Maori tribal leaders, more particularly his own kin. Though Ngata was not accused of fraud, one of his subordinates on the East Coast, Charlie Goldsmith, was successfully prosecuted. The commission recognised Ngata's burning desire to place people on the land but decided there was 'no option' but to place on Ngata himself 'the major responsibility for the breakdown of the financial organisation of the department'.[65] And, as if to emphasise the gap in mental outlook between the Pakeha commissioners and the Maori minister, the report went on to quote Buck on tribal spirit, adding that it was necessary

> to appreciate that the Native Minister [was] himself a Maori. The psychological factors in the situation . . . were the result of tribal habits of thought and feelings to which he was himself subject. These habits involved the care for his own tribe and the support of any other tribes who assisted him . . . . The Minister, although . . . a member of a tribe, was, as a Minister of the Crown, bound to refrain from using state funds, without lawful authority, in the interests of his tribe . . . . We regret to state that the Native Minister failed not infrequently in these matters.[66]

Thus was Ngata hoisted with his own petard of tribalism.

Ngata kept Buck informed on the affair. On 27 November 1933 he complained that 'an administrative system with strong pakeha leanings will not be happy unless the instruments of its will are of its own colour and outlook'. But, he added, 'one has learnt how to eat mud, to endure vilification and to slave under the mana of other men so long as the objectives of one's life are furthered'.[67] Buck replied bitterly:

> New Zealand trots out the Maori people as show case specimens for the outside world to see what they have accomplished . . . but were it not for the Maori people themselves and their leaders, New Zealand would have about as much to show . . . as she has in Samoa. I have come to the conclusion that the Pakeha attitude towards native races is . . . saturated with the deepest hypocrisy. Even in ethnology, I doubt whether a native people is really regarded as other than a project to give the white writer a job and a chance for fame.[68]

And there were similar statements as the commission proceeded with its hearings. When the report was written, Ngata wrote briefly but without rancour to inform Buck of its contents, and of his decision to resign. The commission, he said, had 'adopted a hostile attitude right through, supporting the complaints of the Audit Department'. But the report lacked 'the breadth of vision' he had expected. Ngata's only concern now was to smooth over difficulties with the Maori people and to ensure that the land development schemes continued.[69] Buck's comments were much more pungent, referring to the 'frenzy' of Government officials that Ngata had dared 'to set them aside and break through their taboo restrictions. New Zealand does not come out very well in its dealings with its Polynesian quota. Samoa was bad enough but their persecution of the one leader of the Maori people is a serious blow to the country's reputation. So long as the Pakeha can patronise, he will say nice things about a noble race but when it comes to direct competition, jealousy of race is very evident ... as manifested against you.'[70]

Thus ended the most substantial experiment in applied anthropology, as perceived by its two home-made Maori anthropologists, that New Zealand has seen. Though the commissioner's findings cannot be discussed in detail, it does seem that they revealed an unbending monocultural approach which was hostile to Maori leadership and methods of organisation. If some corruption was revealed (and punished), the rest was probably no worse than the petty pilfering of state property that has been endemic in New Zealand. The charge of tribal favouritism was not convincingly proved. Against the claim of extravagance with state funds, one needed also to remember that Ngata used communal labour, paid lower wages, and made do with cheaper materials. Buck's charge of racial jealousy had some substance.

Ngata's resignation was followed, a year later, by the Labour victory at the polls. Although Labour politicians in Opposition had been Ngata's most vocal opponents, in office they carried on his land development schemes. But Maori staff on the supervision of the schemes and in the Native Department were replaced by Pakeha, and Maori affairs drifted without leadership — at least until Peter Fraser took over the portfolio in 1946. And for Ngata himself these were years of disillusion and despair, marked by the death of close friends like Bal in 1940, defeat at the hands of the Ratana candidate in 1943, and even the virtual ending of his correspondence with Buck. The correspondence had stopped in 1936 after Buck wrote strongly to urge Ngata to support Ernest Beaglehole for a research job in Wellington: 'In view of our deep friendship,' Buck wrote, 'I hope that you may discard any personal prejudice that you may have and look at Beaglehole entirely from the point of view of his academic record and scholastic ability.'[71] Ngata did not reply so Buck wrote again the following year, apologising for anything he had said to offend Ngata and explaining that he was merely acting like an American professor, trying to land a job for a pupil; in any case, Beaglehole had now got a position at Victoria.[72] Ngata did not reply until 15 July 1940, when he accepted responsibility for stopping the correspondence. It was not Beaglehole, not anything Buck had done or said. 'Not even Bal, my daily companion, quite understood the change that had come over one's mind.' And Ngata went on to explain that he had been overcome by a feeling of disillusion brought on by the Labour Government's social security policies which were sapping the will of the Maori people.[73] But although Buck replied at once,[74] there were few more letters after this, though Ngata found time for a considerable correspondence with Sutherland and Eric Ramsden, and for scholarly pursuits like the further volume of *Nga Moteatea* and the revision of the Maori Bible. He received some satisfaction when in 1948 he was awarded a DLitt. It was suggested that it be conferred at Canterbury but Ngata chose to receive it at Victoria, where his youngest son, Henare, was being capped BA — and for the additional satisfaction of having the degree conferred by none other than his old enemy, now Sir David Smith, Chancellor of the University of New Zealand, the erstwhile chairman of the 1934 Commission of Inquiry.

In contrast to Ngata's declining fortunes, Buck's later years were triumphant. In 1933 Buck was selected as Gregory's successor as Director of the Bishop Museum. He took up the position in 1936 when Gregory retired, and with it held the status of a full professor at Yale. Academic honours and prizes followed in quick succession. Buck was awarded DScs by the University of New Zealand in 1937, by Rochester in 1939, by Yale in 1951, and a DLitt by the University of Hawaii in 1948; he was awarded the Hector and Rivers medals in 1936 and the S. Percy Smith medal in 1951. But he had to wait a long time for the honour he most coveted, the KCMG which Fraser awarded him in 1946. Stricken with cancer, he came home in 1949 — the Labour Government paid the expenses of his entourage — to receive the knighthood from his old comrade, Sir Bernard Freyberg, and to make an almost royal pilgrimage round the country, visiting marae, giving lectures to scientific gatherings; above all renewing his old friendship with a frail and failing Ngata. When they parted company at Whenuapai airport both of them knew it would be for the last time. It was Ngata who died first, in 1950. He was buried at Waiomatatini, alongside his first wife, Arihia, on the knoll overlooking Porourangi meeting house, in the distant shadow of Hikurangi. Buck died over a year later but it was nearly two more years before E. B. Corbett, the Maori Affairs Minister in the National Government, arrived back in triumph with Buck's ashes. They were duly interred, after a series of impressive ceremonies, at Okoke, within three miles of Buck's birthplace.

Conclusion

What, then, can one say of Ngata and Buck in conclusion? First, their changing fortunes over the later years can, I think, largely be explained by the different ways in which they were perceived — and received — by Pakeha New Zealand. For Buck was a distinguished anthropologist who had made it overseas; and, as we know, New Zealanders worship their successful expatriates. Ngata, by contrast, failed at home; he had come into conflict with the

Pakeha establishment and he had been brought down. In distinction to Buck, Ngata was a marginal man who tilted too far in the Maori direction; or, as some would say, too far towards tribalism: that 'little black Ngatiporou B---d', as one Maori critic called him.[75] But Buck, whose blood was drawn equally from both sides, remained the perfect specimen of the blending of the two races, that long-unattained Pakeha goal, which he had himself predicted in his 1924 paper 'The Passing of the Maori'.[76] He ended the 1949 edition of *The Coming of the Maori* wishing the two races 'a happy blending'.[77]

Second, it must be admitted that even Buck's anthropology has not pleased all of the professionals. When he died Katherine Luomala noted that the 'principal regret of [the] functionalists' was that Buck's 'conclusions . . . were not always brought out as explicitly as they would have liked'.[78] Maybe, but Buck never really pretended to be a social anthropologist anyway. Material culture was his forte and his work on that still earns respect. As for Ngata's anthropology, that was a series of fragments cast off by a man of affairs always more concerned to apply his anthropology to the task at hand, the regeneration of the Maori people. Where the theoretical and practical came together — in the 1931 Land Development Report — they were, as Park said, better than anything written at the time. Ngata and Buck may not have understood all of the anthropology of their time; but I do not think that mattered very much.

8

Colonial Rule and Local Response: Maori Responses to European Domination in New Zealand since 1860

At first sight it seems strange to include New Zealand in a discussion that is usually confined to tropical colonies. After all, New Zealand became self-governing within twenty years of its foundation as a British colony; thereafter the fate of Maori, already a minority in their own land, rested largely in the hands of the European colonists. But it is one of the themes of this paper that a colonial situation continued to exist long after self-government had been conceded; that New Zealand's 'colonial' rulers were resident white settlers, not expatriate colonial servants. In this respect New Zealand is not unique. The 'colonial' rule of white settlers in southern Africa will spring readily to mind, though the different racial ratios prevents one from pressing the comparison with New Zealand too far; in southern Africa it was white minorities who inhibited the nationalist aspirations of Africans. The Americas and Australia provide closer comparisons with New Zealand. Australians, for instance, have usually assumed that their colonialism was confined to Papua New Guinea. But Professor Rowley recently demonstrated that a species of colonial rule was applied to outback Aborigines.[1] Similarly New Zealanders have assumed that

---

This essay is a revised version of a paper discussed at Professor Sanderson's seminar, 'Colonial Rule and Local Response', at the Institute of Commonwealth Studies, London, in December 1973. It was originally published in *The Journal of Imperial and Commonwealth History*, vol. IV, no. 2 (1976), pp. 127–37.

their colonialism was confined to a mini-empire in the South Pacific. But Dr Alan Ward's study of 'native' policy in later nineteenth-century New Zealand, *A Show of Justice*, has also detected some home-grown colonialism. Ward shows that the resident magistrate system, operating on the New Zealand frontier, had much in common with aspects of British colonial administration in the tropical empire. The RMs were more than mere magistrates; they had many of the responsibilities of district commissioners, though in New Zealand they were instruments of assimilation, not agents for indirect rule. They were, as J. C. Richmond put it in 1869, 'lay missionaries converting the Maoris to civilization'.[2]

Nevertheless, some caution is needed in applying concepts derived from studies of the tropical empire to colonies of settlement like New Zealand. As J. G. A. Pocock reminded us, the political models designed for nationalism in tropical Africa and elsewhere cannot always be fitted to Maori movements in New Zealand.[3] It would be difficult, for example, to follow T. O. Ranger and others who have worked on tropical Africa and find an evolving Maori nationalism, with its roots in 'primary resistance', a secondary stage characterised by the growth of religious independency and welfare societies, and a final victorious phase in which the nationalist masses provide an irresistible surge to independence.[4] Such a nationalism, if not quite strangled at birth, has not developed in New Zealand. The most significant expression of Maori nationalism was the Maori King movement, and this reached the height of its influence during the wars of the 1860s when support for the movement extended well beyond the Tainui tribes which formed the core of the movement to include most of the tribes across the North Island from Taranaki to the Bay of Plenty. Thereafter, as the King movement lost its territorial base and its support contracted to the Tainui tribes, it was often overshadowed by other Maori organisations. The trouble in New Zealand (and it has been evident in other colonies of settlement) was that Maori nationalists were not pitted against a metropolitan imperial authority that would ultimately lose the will to rule, but a tough, relentless settler community, amply reinforced in men and munitions from home, that was determined to assert and maintain supremacy. That supremacy was asserted in the 1860s, thanks initially to 10,000 British regulars and later to a combination of settler militia and Maori auxiliaries. Military supremacy was backed by a rapid influx of colonists at a time when Maori population was still declining:

	1858	1874	1896	1961
European population	59,413	297,654	701,094	2,247,898
Maori population	56,049	47,330	42,113	167,086
Maori % of total NZ population	48.6	13.7	5.7	6.9

Maori nationalists may have done better than the indigenous peoples of North America and Australia, also quickly outnumbered by European immigrants, but their prospect of mounting a successful nationalism has been much slimmer than that of the Africans in southern Africa. At least the Africans can take some comfort in numbers.

Since Maori independence was very quickly ruled out in New Zealand, it is worth asking what else was available. At one extreme there was the possibility of assimilation, implicit in the Treaty of Waitangi of 1840, with its promise to grant Maori the rights and privileges of British subjects, and consistently pursued thereafter by imperial governors and colonial governments. At the opposite pole was the prospect, growing ever more slim, that somehow the Maori could separate themselves and preserve their identity as a people. At Waitangi Lieutenant-Governor Hobson declared: 'We are now one people.'[5] Pakeha New Zealanders have aspired to this goal, since it has always seemed that the Maori population could be subordinated and absorbed. Maori, on the other hand, have usually opted for a qualified separation, summed up in one of the constant themes of early King party meetings: 'The King on his piece; the Queen on her piece; God over both . . . .'.[6] The wars and demographic changes of the 1860s made it evident that New Zealand would remain one nation, under European domination, but by no means certain whether that nation would have one or two peoples. Could the Maori retain an identity, perhaps even a national identity, when they were but a dispersed and subordinate minority?

It is time to look more closely at the situation created by the wars of the 1860s. These wars, it is important to remember, were not a total conflict of the two races. Some tribes, including one or two who had tried their arm against the Europeans in the 1840s, remained neutral or provided auxiliaries for the Europeans. Other tribes were split, with some individuals fighting on the Maori side and others remaining neutral or fighting on the European side; some even changed sides in the course of the wars. In the early stages of the war — in the Taranaki and Waikato campaigns — there were enough outside volunteers to demonstrate that Maori had created more than a tribal, if not quite a national, front. But after the battles of Orakau and Te Ranga the war became a 'fire in the fern', characterised by intermittent but savage guerrilla warfare. New allegiances and divisions arose. With the withdrawal of most of the imperial troops from 1865, the concluding campaigns were carried out by colonial militia and their Kupapa ('friendly') allies. The war had been transformed from a typical imperial campaign, fought largely by British regulars, to a local civil war.

There was no decisive conclusion to the war. From time to time various groups of Maori 'rebels' formally surrendered to British or colonial officers; others simply gave up fighting or retreated into the fastness of the interior, where they remained under arms for ten or twenty years, beyond the pale of colonial authority and law. But this untidy end to the fighting was of some advantage to the Maori since they did not suffer the humiliation of total defeat and unconditional surrender.

There were humiliations enough as it was, and especially in the conditions for peace which were being imposed by the colonial legislature even before the wars had ended — conditions which were little hindered by imperial veto. The most humiliating act was the confiscation. Under the New Zealand Settlements Act 1863, some three million acres of land belonging to the Maori 'rebels' were confiscated (later about half of this was returned or purchased). Moreover, the confiscation was unequally and unfairly applied: some 'rebels' lost all of their land; others little or nothing at all. Probably more important in the long term was the policy of 'free trade' in Maori lands permitted by the Native Lands Acts from 1865, by which European settlers were allowed to buy land directly from individual Maori who had been awarded titles by a Native Land Court. This was part — the most important part — of a larger design which included the Native Rights Act 1865, and the Maori Representation Act 1867, and which was intended to give effect to the promise of the Treaty of Waitangi to grant Maori the rights and privileges of British subjects. The legislation provided the legal basis for assimilation. With this, the New Zealand legislature had set its face firmly against any form of separation and differentiation: there would be no segregation of Maori on reserves; no recognition of Maori authorities, whether chiefs or tribal *runanga* (committees); no codification of Maori law and custom. Thus, in the later nineteenth century New Zealand was to part company with the Australian colonies, where the segregation of Aborigines in remote places was regarded as the only way of saving them, and with South African colonies like Natal.[7]

The New Zealand policy was not pure altruism, designed to promote the civilising mission, though there was an element of this; above all, it was intended to facilitate the settler acquisition of Maori land, under a system of legal equality. This much became evident as soon as the Native Land Court was established and the Native Lands Act of 1865 brought into operation. Wars of the field and the bush now gave way to a war of words as contending European land purchasers and their Maori clients fought their cases through the Native Land Court, and often enough through appeals to the higher courts. The details need not be repeated here; it is sufficient to say that Maori land passed inexorably into European hands often without any real benefit to Maori since much land was taken to pay the costs of litigation.[8] In the next thirty years the greater part of the North Island that had not already been purchased or confiscated by government was acquired by European settlers. By the end of the century only seven million acres of land remained in Maori ownership, and much of this was inaccessible and scarcely habitable. In the twentieth century this estate was to be progressively reduced to about three million acres.

As we turn to look at how Maori reacted to the situation created by the war and the peace, it soon becomes evident that the peace of the Pakeha was more to be feared than his war.

The Maori King Movement

Formed in 1858 with the selection of Potatau Te Wherowhero of the Waikato as King, the movement was essentially an attempt to hold the tribes together in a league against selling land. For a start it had the active support of tribes who traced their descent from the *Tainui* canoe, but with the outbreak of the Taranaki war in 1860, Taranaki tribes, hitherto enemies of Waikato, joined the movement. The resumption of war in Taranaki and the invasion of Waikato in 1863 were designed to break this confederation. This task was achieved with the defeat of the King party forces at Orakau in 1864, and their Ngai Te Rangi allies at Te Ranga in 1865. But after Orakau the King and many of his supporters escaped into Ngati Maniapoto territory — hereafter called the King Country — where they remained for twenty years. It was, to a considerable extent, an independent kingdom in which the King's proclamations prevailed and Europeans, if they were permitted to enter at all, did so on Maori sufferance. So long as this territorial separation lasted, the King movement could act as a focus for Maori nationalism. Indeed, it continued to have the active or passive support of large numbers of Maori who lived outside the King country.[9]

The King's independence could have been ended by force of arms, but by 1872 the Europeans had decided that it would be better to bring the rest of the country under control by peaceful persuasion and due process of law.

Significantly, the King country was opened not by military force but by the operations of the Native Land Court, which gradually prised away the tribes who had committed themselves to the King's anti-land-selling league. When the proprietors of the King country, the Ngati Maniapoto, allowed their land to go before the court, the Waikato King was isolated. The King and his followers had to move back to tattered reserves which were set aside for them within the confiscated block in the Waikato.

Territorial separation had been ended, and the King movement was expected to fade away. But it did survive, though its support now did not extend far beyond its Tainui base. In the 1890s the Kingite leaders tried to promote a form of political separation — Maori home rule — by establishing a Kauhanganui (Great Council) or parliament. Two houses were created as well as a cabinet with a prime minister and, among others, a minister for Pakeha affairs. Needless to say, the activities of this Maori parliament were studiously ignored by the European government — except when some enthusiasts of the King, obeying his laws, transgressed the European law and were promptly apprehended.[10] After some years the Kauhanganui fell into decay, but in the 1920s and 1930s the King movement gained a new lease of life under the inspiration of Princess Te Puea. In 1958 it celebrated its centenary. It remains important, though it has long since ceased to be the main voice of Maoridom.

Pai Marire and Ringatu

The appearance of new religious cults during the war, and the atrocities committed by some of their adherents, added a new bitterness to the war. Pai Marire (good and peaceful), or Hauhauism, was an enigma, since its founder, Te Ua Haumene, obviously had peaceful intentions.[11] But some of his followers used the movement to try to weld the tribes together to continue the fighting. A frenzied form of worship, a revival of ancient practices including cannibalism, a belief that their rites would give adherents immunity from bullets — all these encouraged a renewal of warfare. But the movement also created new divisions within Maori society, and eased the task of the colonial government in recruiting Maori auxiliaries to break up the Hauhau forces.

It was much the same with the Ringatu sect, founded by Te Kooti.[12] He started his career as a guerrilla leader in 1868 with a lightning raid on the European settlers and Kupapa Maori of Poverty Bay, a reprisal for his imprisonment on the Chatham Islands. Thereafter, large forces of colonial militia and Kupapa Maori were organised to pursue Te Kooti through the fastness of the Urewera forests. He managed a few more daring raids, was relentlessly pursued but never captured. He was allowed to take sanctuary in the King country, and ultimately was pardoned. Nevertheless, he was able to found a church which had many adherents on the East Coast and in the Urewera country.

The relationship of Pai Marire and Ringatu to the King movement remains obscure, but there was clearly some connection. Certainly Te Ua, the founder of Pai Marire, regarded himself as a subject of the King; and Tawhiao, the second Maori King, adopted the Pai Marire religion. Te Kooti, too, was to some extent a subject of the King during his long exile in the King country, though his Ringatu church made no progress there. To some extent the guerrilla and religious leaders had forged a common front against the Europeans, but war was no longer a successful instrument of resistance. In the 1870s and 1880s the King movement, Pai Marire and Ringatu were all overshadowed by another movement, led by a prophet of peace.

Te Whiti, the Prophet of Parihaka
Te Whiti o Rongomai remains a significant figure in New Zealand history since he was able to combine millennial Christianity with effective forms of passive resistance to European colonisation.[13] Some of his techniques of passive resistance pre-dated Gandhian satyagraha. For ten years after the conclusion of the war, Te Whiti was able to prevent the European occupation of much of the confiscated lands in southern Taranaki. He sent parties of supporters to obstruct surveys, block roads, plough up settlers' crops. The resisters were arrested in droves, the prisons were filled, and repressive legislation was introduced to short-circuit the legal process. But the peaceful obstruction continued. Eventually in 1881 the Native Minister, John Bryce, resolved to use force, rode to Parihaka at the head of 1500 armed militia, arrested Te Whiti, and dispersed his supporters. The confiscated lands were opened for settlement. Here was a traumatic lesson: passive resistance could be of no avail where in the last resort the Europeans were prepared to use force. It was a lesson that Gandhi's satyagrahas were yet to learn in South Africa.

Rua Kenana, the Prophet of Maungapohatu
The last pockets of Maori resistance were gradually being overcome. Parihaka had been 'invaded' in 1881; the King country opened in 1885. In the 1890s, even the inhospitable Urewera country was opened, at least for surveys and prospecting, if not yet for settlement. It was here that the most colourful of the Maori prophets, Rua Kenana, established himself in the early years of the twentieth century. Proclaiming himself a younger brother of Christ, Rua also

announced that the British King was coming to Gisborne to hand back Maori lands; and, when this failed to come about, he prophesied a great flood that would sweep away all who did not follow him to Maungapohatu.[14] Here he established a thriving settlement with substantial buildings (including a great circular tabernacle). Probably he would have been left alone had he not, during World War I, discouraged Maori from volunteering to fight against the Kaiser. In 1917 armed police were sent to Maungapohatu, and, following a running fight in which two of Rua's men were killed, he was arrested, tried (for sly-grogging), found guilty, and imprisoned. Rua's arrest ended the last pocket of Maori independency; as one historian has suggested, the accompanying gun battle represented the last shots in the Anglo-Maori wars.[15]

The Kupapa

So far the discussion of Maori responses to European domination has been confined to resistance movements. It would be tempting to conclude that this was all, and to see in these resistances, as Ranger and others have done in Africa, a chain connecting primary and secondary forms of resistance. Certainly some New Zealand historians have done something like this, notably in establishing a regular succession of prophets.[16] This obviously has some validity, since several of the prophets, including Ratana (shortly to be discussed), considered that they had been foretold by an earlier prophet. Yet the prophets do not exhaust the range of Maori responses; nor did they, except for some fleeting moments, represent a very large segment of the Maori population.

There remains the important problem of the Kupapa who collaborated with the Europeans in the wars. Collaborators always get a bad press from historians of nationalism, and New Zealand has been no exception. Their motives in fighting on the European side have not been closely investigated.[17] Clearly some of them acted on ancient tribal animosities; others in response to the events of the wars. Nevertheless, it seems likely that a good many, at least of the leaders, acted on a shrewd calculation of self-interest — not so much to indulge in the spoils of war, for these were few, but simply to save their land from confiscation and their people from destruction. It was fairly obvious that the Europeans would win in the end; if the land could be saved, then men could endure.

Indeed, it is possible to suggest that the Kupapa performed a very valuable role. Had all of the Maori fought the British, they would still have been beaten. Even if a hunted remnant had survived, they would probably have been subjected to a humiliating peace. But the Kupapa, by fighting on the British side, could not be totally excluded from the peace; they had earned themselves a stake in the future, however precarious this was to be. As loyalists, they were to be the first to earn the rights and privileges of British subjects: they were the ones who took up the four seats in the House of Representatives and the two in the Legislative Council awarded by the legislation of the later 1860s.

Nevertheless, the loyalty of the Kupapa was soon to be severely tested. Accepting the rule of law, they were the first to bear the brunt of the new land legislation. The Ngati Kahungunu of Hawke's Bay were the most notable case, since they owned a large area of fertile pastoral country, much of it already 'leased' to European squatters. The Ngati Kahungunu sent contingents to fight against Te Kooti, but when the Native Lands Act 1865 came into force they were soon involved in the battle of litigation. This last battle cannot be investigated in detail (though there is some discussion of it in chapter 5, 'Land Purchase Methods'): it is sufficient to say that the squatters, often by highly dubious practices, got legal titles to most of the land.[18]

However, it is important to look at how the Hawke's Bay Kupapa responded. Characteristically, they used European methods of protest, and called on 'friendly' Europeans to help them. They became involved in what was called the Repudiation Movement, seeking to repudiate the agreements by which Europeans had secured the land. The movement began by appealing to government for a commission of inquiry: this was conceded with the Hawke's Bay Native Lands Alienation Commission of 1873, but the two European commissioners turned down the Maori claims (though two Maori assessors on the commission wrote a dissenting report). So the repudiation movement appealed to the courts — to the Supreme Court and the Court of Appeal — again to no avail. Finally, they appealed to Parliament, through the Greyite opposition which launched a bitter denunciation in the House of Representatives of the Hawke's Bay land transactions. The government fell soon afterwards, but when Grey's party took office it did nothing to rectify the Maori grievances.[19] There is little doubt that many of these were justified, but no settler-dominated parliament could seriously support the Maori cause while there was still an insatiable settler appetite for Maori land. There was another lesson: Maori with grievances over land alienation could not rely on European 'allies'. They needed to take the initiative themselves, but as yet they lacked leaders who were skilled in manipulating European institutions. In the meantime, it was necessary for the Kupapa to try another tack.

Kotahitanga
One aspect of the Maori home rule movement has been noted: the King

movement's Kauhanganui. But there was also a rival, more important, movement, Kotahitanga (unity), deriving most of its support from Kupapa districts. Founded at a large meeting at Waitangi in 1892, Kotahitanga also established a Maori parliament.[20] This met in annual session in various Maori centres until 1902. In the 1890s the Kotahitanga leaders, including Hone Heke Rankin, an able young MP for Northern Maori, had tried three times to persuade the European parliament to pass a private member's bill providing for the recognition of the Maori parliament. But his bill was never even considered; there was no chance that the European legislature would grant Maori a substantial degree of home rule.

Nevertheless, a lesser concession was forthcoming which was designed to cut away the support for Kotahitanga. In 1900 James Carroll, the Native Minister (who was half Maori), passed a Maori Councils Act which provided for the establishment of tribal councils with very limited powers of local government. It was the nearest New Zealand ever went towards indirect rule, for the councils were in effect a recognition of traditional Maori tribal committees (*runanga*) which had continued to exist despite the absence of government sanction. Carroll's councils were accepted with considerable enthusiasm; several of the councils eagerly exceeded their meagre powers. In 1906 government clipped their wings and most of the councils went into abeyance. The fate of the councils, and of Kotahitanga, demonstrated once again the impossibility of any effective form of local government, let alone 'home rule'. Maori still had to seek their crumbs from the Pakeha's table.

The Young Maori Party

What they needed above all was skilled, educated leaders, firmly based in the Maori community, yet able to stand on their own in the European world and manipulate the European system to Maori advantage. To some extent Carroll was able to do this. More important, he facilitated the entry of able, young Maori graduates — his 'colts' as he called them — into the Maori seats in Parliament and other positions of influence. The achievements of Apirana Ngata, Maui Pomare and Te Rangi Hiroa (Peter Buck) are too well known to require repetition here. It is sufficient to emphasise their great skill in manipulating the political and parliamentary system to Maori advantage; their ability to publicise a Maori viewpoint and to secure European sympathy; and, above all, their success in stimulating a Maori cultural renaissance — Maoritanga (Maoriness). Pomare and Ngata attained Cabinet rank; Buck became a distinguished expatriate anthropologist. They assumed heroic stature in New

Zealand history in their own lifetimes and received many honours at the hand of a Pakeha New Zealand anxious to symbolise its 'achievements' in race relations. Yet they gradually lost their hold on the political allegiance of the Maori people, who were becoming, in the economically uncertain times after World War I, a dispossessed proletariat in their own land. The 1918 influenza epidemic, which took a disproportionately high toll on the Maori population, reinforced their depressed status, and they looked anxiously for a new saviour.

Ratana

He turned out to be Tahupotiki Wiremu Ratana, an unprepossessing, ill-educated farmer from near Wanganui.[21] In 1918 Ratana had a vision in which the Angel Gabriel called on him to save the *morehu*, the dispossessed ones. Ratana began to display quite remarkable powers of faith healing. His homestead grew into a considerable township, and Ratana established a model farm, a school and other facilities. He institutionalised his religious movement by establishing a regular church, duly registered in 1925, with a stipendiary clergy and a temple. Increasingly he took on a political function. He took up long-standing Maori grievances, like their demand for the ratification of the Treaty of Waitangi, but he soon realised that independency was a dead end. He announced in 1928 that his followers would capture the Four Quarters, the four Maori seats in Parliament. This was steadily achieved, though Ratana did not himself stand: the first in 1932; the second in 1935; the third in 1938; and the last, the great Ngata's seat which he had held for 38 years, in 1943. In 1935 Ratana made an alliance with the victorious Labour Party, and this has endured. Only once between 1943 and 1976 has there been a non-Ratana Maori MP. On two occasions (1946–49, 1957–60) Labour has held office by virtue of its 'Maori mandate', though the Ratana members have usually lacked the political skills to make effective use of this.

Conclusion

Are there any lessons to be derived from this brief survey of Maori responses? Above all, it would seem that there has been no prospect of a successful Maori nationalism, thanks to an unrelenting European domination. The prospect of a territorially based separate Maori nation vanished with the opening of the King country and the Urewera. Religious separatism, combined with passive resistance to European settlement (in the case of Te Whiti) or to military recruitment (Rua), were suppressed by the threat or use of force. Political separatism was equally unattainable since no European parliament was prepared to give official recognition to either the Kauhanganui or Kotahitanga; there could be no effective Maori home rule, or even local government. It became increasingly evident in the twentieth century that there was no alternative to working within the European system; both the Young Maori Party and the Ratana movement concentrated their efforts in this direction.

Even today, with a rapidly rising Maori population, there would appear to be little scope for Maori nationalism. Maori society remains divided and no one movement commands the allegiance of the majority of the Maori population, despite the considerable political influence of the Ratana–Labour alliance (only about 20 per cent of the Maori people belong to the Ratana church). The divisions are not purely a result of Maori factionalism, let alone tribalism; they are very much a consequence of New Zealand's colonial history. Nationalism is a delicate plant that cannot grow in stony soil. Yet, if Maori nationalism has not emerged, it is perhaps true that a latent nationalism exists in the concept of Maoritanga, in the sense of Maori identity which has been preserved. Maori have refused to become assimilated and Pakeha governments have of late given up the impossible task.

9

Maori Representation in Parliament

Introduction
The indigenous inhabitants of New Zealand, who came from eastern Polynesia a thousand years before the first European settlers, had no common name for themselves. But after the arrival of the Europeans they began to use the adjective 'maori' from the phrase 'tangata maori' (ordinary person) to distinguish themselves from the Europeans (Pakeha). It was a sign that the hitherto divided tribes were feeling a common identity. Despite their frequent warfare, Maori tribes did have ways of making peace, carried out at intra-tribal hui and cemented by speechmaking, marriages between important persons, and exchanges of gifts. In Maori society there was a well-established authority structure headed by chiefs who jealously guarded and enhanced their mana (prestige, authority) against rivals. In these respects it could be said that Maori society was highly political. As European visitors soon found, it was necessary to respect the mana of chiefs. Negotiations had to be conducted according to Maori ways.

With the arrival of European explorers, traders and missionaries, Maori quickly took advantage of new commercial opportunities, especially to obtain better weapons. From early in the nineteenth century, the country was racked

---

Commissioned for the 1986 Royal Commission on the Electoral System and published as Appendix B of its report, *Towards a Better Democracy*, in *AJHR*, 1986, H-3. In this somewhat shortened version I have not included the Foreword by the chairman of the Commission, Mr Justice Wallace, my Preface, or the appendices and graphs prepared by Professor Robert Chapman. However, I should like to thank the Hon. Mr Justice Wallace and members of the Commission for their helpful comments and advice on the first draft of the essay; Paul Harris and Lewis Holden, research officers for the Commission, for providing me with material; Spencer Lilley, my research assistant, for cheerfully attending to my many requests; and Julian Sorrenson for assistance with computing.

by vicious warfare as chiefs who first got arms overwhelmed their less fortunate rivals. Hongi Hika and other Ngapuhi chiefs from the Bay of Islands defeated the Ngati Whatua of Kaipara and Waitemata, and raided far to the south: through the Hauraki Gulf to Waikato, the Bay of Plenty and the East Coast, and down the West Coast to Taranaki. Te Wherowhero organised the Tainui tribes of Waikato in resistance to Ngapuhi but in turn followed them into Taranaki. Te Waharoa of Ngati Haua campaigned against Te Arawa of Rotorua. The Ngati Toa chief, Te Rauparaha, led his people from Kawhia, through Taranaki, to the Cook Strait where, from a base on Kapiti Island, he laid waste to the Maori communities of both sides of the Strait, and even as far south as Canterbury. This tribal warfare caused many casualties, led to wide-ranging migrations, complicated land claims, and created long-lasting enmities which influenced later Maori responses to Europeans. By 1830 such tribes as Ngapuhi in the north, Waikato in the central North Island, and Ngati Toa in the south were in a commanding position, and needed to be treated with respect by European negotiators; others, including Ngati Whatua and Taranaki, were greatly weakened, and welcomed Europeans as protectors. At this time the missionaries, who had first settled at the Bay of Islands in 1814, emerged as successful negotiators and peacemakers. It was a role that Henry Williams, the head of the Church Missionary Society in New Zealand, performed effectively when war weariness and an emerging balance of arms encouraged some chiefs to listen to the message of peace, even to accept conversion to Christianity. By 1840 large numbers of Maori had adopted Christianity, often without the aid of European missionaries. Scriptural tracts, made available in large quantities in the Maori language in the 1830s, provided literate Maori with a new source of inspiration and a new political language for negotiations with the Pakeha.

So long as Maori had merely to contend with a few resident missionaries, Pakeha traders, or whalers, there was no great external threat to their authority in New Zealand. But in the 1830s the situation began to change quite dramatically. As European trade and settlement increased, so the British authorities in Sydney and London became concerned with lawlessness of British subjects in New Zealand. Hitherto the British had disclaimed authority in New Zealand. Though James Cook had proclaimed British sovereignty over the country in 1770, no action was taken to make that claim effective. Indeed three British statutes relating to New South Wales and Tasmania in 1817, 1823 and 1828 had specifically described New Zealand as 'not within His Majesty's dominions'.[1] But although the British recognised Maori sovereignty over

New Zealand, they became increasingly aware of the need to protect Maori from the excesses of British subjects in the country. Thus James Busby was appointed British Resident in New Zealand in 1833. Stationed at Waitangi in the Bay of Islands, Busby had no force at his command and therefore no effective authority over Pakeha or Maori. He was often ridiculed or humiliated by chiefs. Yet some of his actions had a rather more enduring significance than has usually been admitted. In 1834 Busby persuaded 25 chiefs at Waitangi to adopt a national flag, so that New Zealand-made ships could be registered for the trans-Tasman trade. That flag was used by later assemblies of Maori leaders as a symbol of a continuing Maori identity.[2] In 1835 Busby embarked on a more ambitious piece of diplomacy. He again assembled northern chiefs at Waitangi, this time to combat an alleged threat that the self-styled Baron de Thierry was about to establish a personal kingdom in New Zealand, and persuaded 35 of them to sign a 'Declaration of Independence'. They asked for British protection. Later several chiefs from the south added their signatures to the document. Busby saw the assembly as the first stage in the creation of a Maori Parliament, modelled on that at Westminster. This too was to have a continuing significance in Maori political history: several later Maori parliamentary assemblies were regarded as direct successors to Busby's pioneer assembly.[3] But for the British Government it was to have a more immediate consequence. Since Britain recognised the 'Declaration of Independence' — yet another acceptance of Maori sovereignty — she was soon to find it necessary to treat with the chiefs of the United Tribes and others for the transfer of that sovereignty. Thus the Treaty of Waitangi was conceived.

In the last years of the 1830s British intervention in New Zealand had become unavoidable. There was an influx of British settlers and speculators from across the Tasman, some of whom claimed to have purchased large areas of land from the Maori. There were rumours of French colonisation and intervention in New Zealand, though these were much exaggerated. Above all, there were the activities of E. G. Wakefield and his New Zealand Association (later the New Zealand Company) which finally forced the hand of the British Government. Wakefield proposed to establish colonies of British settlers in New Zealand and in May 1839 despatched a land-buying expedition, led by his brother William. For some time the Government had been considering a recommendation from Captain William Hobson for a limited form of intervention: the annexation of certain settled ports as 'trading factories' to be controlled by a British consul. But with the despatch of the Wakefield expedition, Hobson's proposals were expanded. Hobson was sent to New Zealand to negotiate with Maori for the cession of the 'whole or any parts' of the country. He soon found that it was indeed necessary to negotiate for the whole of the country.

The Treaty of Waitangi and British Annexation of New Zealand
Before Hobson's departure from Sydney for New Zealand in January 1840, Governor Gipps issued three proclamations. The first extended the boundaries of New South Wales to include territory that Hobson might acquire in New Zealand. The second appointed Hobson Lieutenant-Governor of such territory. And the third stated that titles to land purchased in the future would only be recognised if they were derived from the Crown. Commissioners were to be appointed to investigate previous purchases.[4]

Hobson's instructions made it clear that he was to treat with Maori for the transfer of sovereignty and to respect their rights to land. But he did not arrive in New Zealand with a ready-made treaty. That was hastily drawn up by Hobson, his secretary, J. S. Freeman, and Busby, on Hobson's arrival at the Bay of Islands early in February 1840. It was translated into Maori by the Church Missionary Society leader, Henry Williams, and his son, Edward. Then it was discussed with an assembly of northern chiefs at Waitangi on 5 February and signed by 45 of them the next day. Over the next seven months copies of the treaty were hawked around the country and another 500 signatures were obtained, including 39 signatures on an English language version obtained at Waikato Heads and Manukau.

These are the real Treaties of Waitangi — in that they are the versions signed by various Maori leaders. But it has been the English language version that has usually been regarded by New Zealand Governments, and generally by Pakeha New Zealanders, as the official version — as, for instance, when it was reprinted by Government in 1869[5] and again as recently as 1975, when it was included as a Schedule to the Treaty of Waitangi Act. In one respect it has also been regarded by Maori as providing an important guarantee. The second article of the English language version promised them the 'full exclusive and undisturbed possession of their Lands and Estates Forests Fisheries and other properties', whereas the Maori version merely promised them 'te tino rangatiratanga o o ratou wenua o ratou kainga me a ratou taonga katoa' — the chieftainship of their lands, their villages, and all their property, but not specifically their forests and fisheries. With the reprinting of the English version in 1869, Maori were encouraged to look to this version of the Treaty as a guarantee of their traditional rights to forests and fisheries, both fresh-water and coastal. But otherwise they have looked to the Maori version, as they perceived it, as the guarantee of their rights and status in New Zealand.

The semantic differences between the two versions are the source of a larger difference in interpretation between Maori and Pakeha that has been accumulating ever since the Treaty was signed. As Ruth Ross wrote, 'the Treaty of Waitangi was hastily and inexpertly drawn up, ambiguous and contradictory in content, chaotic in its execution'.[6] It was impossible to translate into the Maori language words such as 'sovereignty' which had a precise constitutional meaning in English but no equivalent in Maori. Moreover, it would have been extremely unwise to have attempted to do so: if the Maori chiefs had been fully informed of the real implications of the transfer of sovereignty, they would not have signed the Treaty. The British, having previously recognised Maori sovereignty over New Zealand, now needed them to sign it away. So sovereignty was translated as 'kawanatanga' — not an indigenous Maori term but a transliteration of 'governorship' which had been in common usage in the 1830s both in relation to temporal rulers like Pontius Pilate and Governors of New South Wales, and in missionary publications of the Scriptures where it was frequently used to emphasise spiritual authority.[7] In explaining Hobson's mission to Maori at Waitangi, Henry Williams stressed the Governor's protective function: Hobson (on behalf of Queen Victoria) was to exercise kawanatanga to impose law and order on, and thus protect Maori from, the horde of Pakeha colonists now pouring into the country. But Williams carefully avoided telling the chiefs that the new Governor's exercise of sovereignty would diminish their own authority, their mana, since they too would be subject to British law in the new colony. As Ross pointed out, the omission of mana from the text of the Treaty, and from the discussions over sovereignty at Waitangi, 'was no accidental oversight'.[8] But to the British, and in due course their settler successors in the Government of New Zealand, the imposition of British law was an essential consequence of annexation and a fundamental, if long delayed, objective of Maori policy. Moreover, the chiefs were reassured by the promise of the second article of the Treaty to guarantee their rangatiratanga — their chieftainship — of their lands, villages and other properties. Some chiefs thought this meant that, although the shadow — the sovereignty — had gone to the Queen, the substance — their chieftainship — had been preserved. It was only later that they discovered that the real position was the reverse, and that British Governors and later settler Governments were using the powers of sovereignty to subject the chiefs and their land to British law. True, Maori were also being accorded the rights and privileges of British subjects, as promised in the third article of the Treaty, but those rights were of little avail when Maori found themselves in a minority in their own country and in Parliament.

In the early years of the colony the Treaty had a precarious existence. It was savagely attacked by the New Zealand Company which resented Hobson's inquiry into its land claims. One spokesman, Joseph Somes, patronisingly dismissed it as a 'device for amusing and pacifying savages'.[9] In 1844 a House of Commons Committee, influenced by Company supporters, recommended that the Treaty guarantee of Maori ownership of land be confined to land under occupation and cultivation. Fortunately the British Government did not implement the recommendation.[10] In the same year Governor FitzRoy abolished the Crown's right of pre-emption, laid down in the second article of the Treaty, and allowed settlers to buy land directly from Maori on payment to the Crown of a fee, initially 10/- per acre but subsequently reduced to 1d. FitzRoy was recalled and his successor, Captain George Grey, restored pre-emption. Grey also made it clear that Maori title to land, based on well-defined tribal or hapu boundaries and effective occupation and usage of cultivations, forests and fisheries, encompassed the whole country. But for the rest of his governorship Grey largely satisfied settler demands for Maori land by establishing an effective system of Crown purchase and buying huge areas of Maori land, especially in the South Island and the southern and eastern North Island, usually at very cheap prices.[11] Moreover, the Crown's monopoly on the purchase of Maori land was written into the 1852 Constitution Act: section 73 laid down that it would not be lawful 'for any Person other than Her Majesty ... to purchase ... from the aboriginal Natives Land ... belonging to or used or occupied by them in common as Tribes or Communities ...'.

So far, apart from the temporary aberration of FitzRoy's abolition of pre-emption, the Treaty guarantee of Maori land rights had been upheld. But the position was not so reassuring in relation to other aspects of the Treaty. In numerous ways the introduction of government regulations and the rule of law began to inhibit the mana of chiefs. In 1842 a Bay of Islands chief, Maketu, was arrested, tried and hanged for the murder of a European woman, her two children and another child — a salutary exhibition of the majesty of British law in New Zealand. But there were other instances where Maori chiefs refused to accept the new laws. The most notable case was Hone Heke's rebellion in the North, since Heke deliberately challenged the sovereignty of the Crown in his repeated assaults on the flagstaff and his sacking of Kororareka. Though Heke was the first to sign the Treaty, he soon became disillusioned over its operation. He resented government regulations which restricted the cutting of timber on

Maori land, and the imposition of customs duties at the Bay of Islands which drove away many of the visiting whalers and thus reduced the profitability of trade. He was persuaded — by republican American whalers — that it was the flag, the symbol of the Queen's authority, that was the cause of his trouble. Heke's revolt can therefore be seen as the first serious Maori challenge to British sovereignty in New Zealand.[12] But his rebellion was quelled by British arms, aided, it should be noted, by a loyalist section of the Ngapuhi tribe from Hokianga under Tamati Waka Nene. It was an earnest of things to come, as other chiefs, singly or in combination, resisted the further assertion and extension of British sovereignty, and once again British and colonial troops, also supported by Maori loyalists, quelled their rebellion. It was also a reminder that Maori were continuing to assert a degree of political independence, outside the constitutional structures erected in New Zealand to accommodate the demands of British colonists for the political and civil privileges they had enjoyed at home.

Since their arrival in New Zealand the colonists had been demanding representative institutions. Although New Zealand had originally been proclaimed a dependency of New South Wales, Letters Patent were issued on 16 November 1840 designating the country a separate colony and Hobson was appointed Governor and Commander-in-Chief. He was responsible to the British Secretary of State for the Colonies but in the colony he was in effect an autocrat. However, he could use the advice of his Executive Council which consisted of himself and his three senior officials, the Colonial Secretary, the Attorney-General and the Colonial Treasurer. He also appointed a Legislative Council which had power to enact laws and ordinances for 'the peace, order, and good government' of New Zealand. This consisted of himself, the same three officials, plus three nominated Justices of the Peace.[13] But the nominees were regarded as the Governor's creatures, the Legislative Council seldom met, and there was soon a widespread settler demand for representative government. This was actively supported by New Zealand Company spokesmen at home. In 1846 Earl Grey, a sympathiser of the Company, passed the New Zealand Constitution Act through the British Parliament. This provided a complicated three-tier system of government with elected municipal corporations at the bottom, two elected provincial Houses of Representatives, and finally, for the whole country, a General Assembly composed of a nominated Legislative Council and an elected House of Representatives. It was an excessively complicated system of government for a mere 13,000 Europeans, let alone the more numerous Maori population. But they were effectively excluded since the franchise was confined to male occupants of a tenement who could read and write English.[14] It was this failure to provide for Maori representation that gave Governor Grey an excuse not to implement the new constitution. He predicted that any attempt to impose it on a reluctant Maori population would lead to a costly war.[15] Governor Grey's views were accepted and Earl Grey suspended the constitution for five years. In that time, according to his own reckoning, Governor Grey brought prosperity and peace to the country, while also setting the two races on the road to amalgamation. Grey also played a significant part in drawing up a new constitution, passed by the British Parliament in 1852.

The New Zealand Constitution Act 1852

The new constitution provided for a two-tier system of government, with six elected Provincial Councils, each presided over by an elected superintendent, and a General Assembly with a nominated Legislative Council and an elected House of Representatives. The franchise for the Provincial Councils and the House of Representatives was granted to all males over 21 who had a freehold estate within the electorate valued at £50, or a leasehold with an annual value of £10, or a tenement with an annual rental of £10 in a town or £5 in the country. This provision did not specifically exclude Maori males from the franchise but, since most of their property was communal and unregistered, few were able to vote. The Provincial Councils had power to legislate, provided their laws were not repugnant to the law of England and legislation of the General Assembly. In addition, thirteen matters were reserved for legislation by the General Assembly, including the sale of Maori land, and laws which imposed disabilities or restrictions on Maori which were not also imposed on Europeans. In addition there were some restrictions on the powers of the General Assembly in relation to Maori matters. The Crown's right of pre-emption over the purchase of Maori land was preserved. The civil list reserved an expenditure of £7,000 per annum for Maori purposes. Section 71 of the Constitution Act provided for the setting apart by Letters Patent of certain districts within New Zealand in which Maori laws, customs and usages, not repugnant to general principles of humanity, were maintained 'for the Government of themselves, in all their Relations to and Dealings with each other'. But this important provision, which would have allowed Maori in proclaimed districts a large measure of self-government, was never implemented. Finally, the constitution was silent on the important matter of responsible government, including responsibility for Maori affairs.

Although Grey arranged for the election of the provincial superintendents and councils before he left the colony in 1853, the General Assembly was not constituted until 1854. The members immediately demanded responsible government. The new Governor, Colonel Thomas Gore Browne, had to await instructions from the Secretary of State. When these arrived in 1856, he conceded responsibility for domestic affairs but not for Maori affairs. E. W. Stafford of Nelson formed the first responsible ministry. It was also the first stable ministry, lasting for five years. But within that time there was a prolonged struggle between the Ministry and the Governor over the control and conduct of Maori affairs. The Ministers and their supporters became increasingly critical of the failure — as they saw it — of Browne and his officials to purchase sufficient Maori land for the rapidly increasing demands of settlement. During the last years of his governorship, Grey had established an efficient system of land purchase under Donald McLean, who remained as Native Secretary and Chief Land Purchase Commissioner under Browne. But Browne lacked Grey's skill in dealing with Maori and became greatly dependent on McLean, much to the chagrin of the Ministry. In the later 1850s McLean and his assistants found it increasingly difficult to purchase Maori land, particularly in Taranaki and Waikato where Maori were co-ordinating their resistance to land sales. In Waikato they created a pan-tribal anti-land-selling league with the selection of a Maori King in 1858. The settlers, resentful of the slowness of the Government to purchase Maori land, campaigned for the abolition of pre-emption. In 1859 the General Assembly passed a Native Territorial Rights Bill which abolished Crown pre-emption and allowed settlers to purchase land directly from individual Maori.[16] It was disallowed by the British Government as an infringement of the Treaty of Waitangi; but it was an earnest of things to come, once the settlers had got responsibility for Maori affairs.

Although access to Maori land was the prime object of settler politicians, it was not their sole concern. They also wanted to extend law and order into Maori districts — to bring Maori, as well as their lands, under British law as rapidly as possible. There was never any support in the General Assembly for applying section 71 of the constitution. Grey had made a start towards extending British law to Maori districts by appointing several resident magistrates. In the later 1850s the Stafford Ministry pressed Browne to expand this system and he appointed F. D. Fenton a travelling magistrate to Waikato. Fenton made two circuits into Waikato in 1857 and 1858. He merely stirred up Maori opposition, provoking the Kingites into finally proclaiming Potatau Te Wherowhero as their King. On McLean's advice, Browne withdrew Fenton. The Ministers claimed that, because Browne had failed to govern the Maori, they were erecting their own Government. It was all part of the guerrilla war that the politicians were waging for control of Maori affairs. In 1858 Browne gave them some ground by allowing one of the Ministers, C. W. Richmond, to be designated Minister of Native Affairs, but Browne himself retained final responsibility. It was an unsatisfactory compromise and was not resolved until, on Colonial Office instructions, responsibility for Maori affairs was transferred to the local Ministry in 1861.[17] But by then war had broken out over the Governor's bungling of the Waitara purchase in Taranaki.

The Maori King Movement, Waitara and the Wars

The outbreak of war at Waitara in 1860 was the culmination of tensions between Pakeha and Maori that had been accumulating in the later 1850s. When the provincial governments gained responsibility for land settlement in 1856, they introduced vigorous policies of colonisation, and immigrants poured into the country. Around 1858 the European population passed that of the Maori, whose numbers were steadily declining. There was growing pressure from settlers and politicians for the Government to increase its purchases of Maori land. Within Maori communities, there was widespread unease; European colonisation was threatening their very existence. Government land purchase activities caused or exacerbated intra-tribal and intra-hapu disputes, which sometimes flared into fighting. The dilemma was discussed at a series of pan-tribal hui which attempted to stop the flow of blood by erecting an anti-land-selling league. At the same time a broader, nationalistic movement to elect a Maori King was in progress.

Although the idea of a Maori King was not new, it was not taken up seriously until the 1850s. In 1852 two young Otaki chiefs, Tamihana Te Rauparaha and Matene Te Whiwhi, led an embassy around the North Island asking one paramount chief after another to accept the kingship. They were not immediately successful, but the idea gained support as pressure for the sale of Maori land mounted. In 1856 at a meeting at Poukawa on the southern shore of Lake Taupo, the Tuwharetoa chief, Te Heu Heu, threw his weight behind the movement, and urged the renowned Waikato chief, Potatau Te Wherowhero, hitherto an ally of the Government, to accept the kingship. Like a true rangatira, Te Wherowhero was reluctant to accept; but pressure on him increased. In 1857 the gifted Ngati Haua chief Wiremu Tamehana took the lead, and prevailed on Te Wherowhero to accept the kingship. At a series of meetings in Waikato, he was proclaimed King. Although support for the King was strongest among Waikato tribes claiming descent from the *Tainui* canoe, there was active or passive support from a wider circle of tribes, more particularly when the outbreak of war over Waitara led to the accession of the main Taranaki tribes.

The King movement was the most important development in the deepening crisis in race relations. It was an effective land league — in that all chiefs who owed allegiance to the King accepted his veto over their sale of land. It was also the most substantial attempt so far by Maori leaders to establish a separate, autonomous political authority; an attempt to restore, indeed to extend, the mana of the chiefs, apparently guaranteed at Waitangi, but which had been gradually eroded by the extension of government authority. The Maori King was thus a Maori answer to Fenton's magistracy and all that it implied. Nevertheless the King's supporters still envisaged a limited form of Maori autonomy, summed up in the statement: 'The King on his piece; the Queen on her piece; God over both; and love binding them to each other.'[18]

The involvement of some Waikato Maori in the Taranaki war meant that sooner or later the war was likely to spread to Waikato. But in 1861 the Kingmaker, Wiremu Tamehana, intervened and brought about a truce. Sir George Grey arrived back in New Zealand for a second term later in the year and formed a 'peace' ministry, headed by Sir William Fox. Although the British Government had agreed to transfer responsibility for Maori affairs to the local ministry, Grey, as Commander-in-Chief of the British forces in New Zealand, had considerable scope to influence policy, and he was no man to lightly give away authority. Between them, Grey and Fox introduced civil institutions into Maori districts — in an attempt to provide Maori with the 'law and order' and good government they were said to be lacking. As Grey told the Kingites, he intended to 'dig around' the King 'till he falls'.[19] He sent John Gorst as a Civil Commissioner to Te Awamutu, right in the heart of the King's domain; and he paid handsome salaries to chiefs who collaborated by becoming assessors to his magistrates. Moreover, despite his protestations of peace, Grey continued preparations for war: as more British regiments arrived, some troops were put to work constructing a military road through the Hunua ranges to the Waikato river. Others were sent to Taranaki where the war was resumed over the disputed Waitara and Tataramaika blocks in 1863. But Taranaki was a sideshow and Grey soon shifted the main front to Waikato. In July he set General Cameron on the invasion, having trumped up a Maori plot to invade Auckland. He threatened the supporters of the King with confiscation of their land, unless they surrendered. Since Grey ordered the invasion before his threat of confiscation was released, the King's supporters had little alternative but resistance. The King's forces, greatly outnumbered by the combined weight of British and colonial troops, were progressively defeated — at Meremere, Rangiriri and Orakau — before the British forces were diverted to Tauranga where, after their reverse at Gate Pa, they overcame the King's Ngai Te Rangi allies at Te Ranga.

Although the British regiments were gradually withdrawn after this, the war was far from over. Encouraged by the Hau Hau faith, many Maori continued the resistance in southern Taranaki, the eastern Bay of Plenty and the East Coast; and in the later 1860s sometimes turned the tables as the guerrilla leaders — Titokowaru on the west coast and Te Kooti on the east — won some stunning victories over colonial troops, until they were finally forced to take refuge in the bush of the interior. In 1872 Te Kooti escaped to the King Country where King Tawhiao, since the defeat at Orakau, had reigned over a still intact kingdom. Tawhiao laid down his arms in 1882, and the King Country was ceremonially opened to the main trunk railway in 1885, but the King movement was to persist as an autonomous Maori political organisation, though it no longer had a separate territory. Nevertheless, the King and his supporters also became involved in the Pakeha political system.

During the wars that system had sought to take advantage of the military victories in the field, achieved largely by British regiments. It is notable that much of the parliamentary legislation of the war years, though intended primarily to serve settler interests, was described as being designed to give better effect to the promises of the Treaty of Waitangi. Even the most outrageous pieces of legislation — the New Zealand Settlements Act 1863, which provided for the confiscation, and the Suppression of Rebellion Act 1863, which allowed the suspension of *habeas corpus* — were regarded as necessary measures to deal with British subjects in rebellion against their Queen. The preamble of the Native Lands Act 1862, which abolished the Crown's right of pre-emption, reiterated in the second article of the Treaty of Waitangi, said that the Act was designed to give better effect to the Treaty. The Act created a Native Land Court to individualise Maori land tenure as a preliminary to sale to European settlers. But individualisation was also necessary to provide Maori landowners with an effective qualification for the franchise, since the Law Officers of the Crown had ruled in 1859 that Maori communal tenure did not qualify them.[20] The Native Rights Act 1865 was also described as a necessary clarification of Maori rights as British subjects which were promised in the third article of the Treaty. Ostensibly, therefore, the colonial politicians, now in control of Maori affairs, were also giving full effect to the Treaty — as they interpreted it. But in granting Maori the rights and privileges of British subjects, the politicians were also requiring them to accept the full responsibilities of citizenship, including a submission to British law — a law that was increasingly being made in New Zealand.

The Maori Representation Act 1867

Whether or not Maori would have a share in the making of the law was a question that was not resolved until 1867. Previously, most discussions in Parliament assumed that elected Europeans could represent Maori who were not yet sufficiently educated to take their place in Parliament. Nevertheless there was one debate which very nearly resulted in Maori being offered fair representation. In August 1862 the Canterbury politician, J. E. Fitzgerald, moved five resolutions in the House dealing with Maori affairs. The first of these laid down that the object of law and policy should be the 'entire amalgamation of all Her Majesty's subjects in New Zealand into one united people'; the second required that the Assembly withhold assent to any law that did not accord each race equal civil and political privileges; and the other three resolutions asked for the Maori to be brought into Government, with fair representation in both Houses, Provincial Councils, juries and the courts. But Fitzgerald's majestic oratory could not persuade the House to accept all of his resolutions. The first two, which emphasised the principle of amalgamation and restated the object of the third article of the Treaty of Waitangi, were accepted. But the third, which required fair political representation, was narrowly defeated, by 20 votes to 17, and Fitzgerald withdrew the remaining resolutions.[21] It was evident that European politicians were reluctant to allow Maori more than a token representation in Parliament, or other institutions of Government, even though the population balance was now running substantially in the European favour, due largely to the gold rushes in the South Island.

When Maori representation was again discussed in Parliament, it was brought up in relation to more insistent demands for representation for the goldfields districts of the South Island. In 1863 a Select Committee on Representation recommended that thirteen new seats be created, ten for the South Island and three for the North, two of which were to be for Europeans elected by Maori voters. But the proposals were not passed into law. There were further discussions in 1865, again prompted by demands for representation for the diggers. This time George Graham, an Auckland member, made the somewhat revolutionary proposal that Maori be granted a universal male franchise — but merely to elect five European members to represent them. However, Fitzgerald, who was now Minister of Native Affairs, preferred to proceed along the lines already foreshadowed when the Native Lands Act was passed in 1862. He repealed that Act and replaced it by a considerably modified and apparently simplified system of individualising Maori land titles, through the agency of a European-styled Native Land Court, which in due course would provide Maori landowners with the necessary property qualifications for the franchise. But it was evident, particularly in view of continuing warfare over much of the North Island, that it would take a long time for the court to individualise Maori land titles. Fitzgerald therefore established a Commission to report on conferring a temporary franchise on Maori, pending the conversion of their titles to Crown grants.[22] Significantly, this Commission was to have a Maori majority: 20 to 35 Maori members as against three to five Europeans. Frederick Weld, the Premier, hoped that it would become a 'kind of constituent assembly' of Maori chiefs, including Wiremu Tamehana and perhaps even the Maori King. Though some loyal chiefs were appointed, Fitzgerald lost office soon afterwards and his successor, Colonel A. H. Russell, failed to proceed with the Commission.[23] Instead he talked of appointing three Maori chiefs to the Legislative Council and six representatives (he expected them to be Europeans) to the Lower House. But that proposal was abandoned when Russell lost office in a Cabinet reshuffle.

It was not the new Ministry, but an old expert in Maori administration, Donald McLean, now superintendent of Hawke's Bay, who brought forward the next proposal for Maori representation in Parliament. Once more Maori representation was considered as a *quid pro quo* for increased representation for the South Island goldfields. McLean's Bill provided for three Maori representatives for the North Island and one for the South, while a Government Bill provided for two General seats for Westland, thus preserving the existing balance between the two islands. McLean introduced his Bill with a brief speech which indicated that he saw Maori representation as essentially a peace measure, though he also reminded the House that Maori owned three-quarters of the North Island and paid a considerable amount of tax.[24] He repeated the last point in moving the second reading of the Bill, noting that some 47,000 Maori were contributing some £47,000 to Government revenue. With South Island demands for goldfields representation satisfied, there was no opposition to the Bill. However, one or two members who supported it feared that Maori members, unable to understand English, would have difficulty following the complicated procedures of the House, but feared that if Europeans were allowed to represent the Maori voters, there would be, as A. S. Atkinson put it, 'a great chance of their getting a very undesirable class of men in that House'.[25] It was this fear that led to an important amendment to the Bill, making it clear that the members were to be chosen 'from amongst and by the votes of the Maoris inhabiting each of the [electoral] districts'. Only two members objected to the Bill on the ground that it constituted what Hugh Carleton described as 'special legislation for the Native race'. He thought it sufficient for the Maori to obtain their franchise through the existing system whereby they obtained Crown titles to their land under the Native Lands Act 1865; but Carleton did not press the point and vote against the Bill.[26] When McLean proposed the third reading of the Bill, W. H. Reynolds raised the point again and moved that the third reading be postponed for six months, but he got no support.[27]

There was rather more opposition to the Bill in the Legislative Council and three of the seventeen members present voted against the second reading. Like Carleton in the House, W. B. D. Mantell expressed opposition to 'special representation'.[28] Colonel G. S. Whitmore hoped that the Bill would be 'the last instance . . . of this exceptional legislation' but he accepted it because it was to be a temporary measure.[29] There was also, as might have been expected, opposition to the proposed manhood suffrage for the Maori electorates. Already in the existing seats there was, as Walter Mantell complained, 'a franchise narrowly approaching it, but he was sorry to see the principle openly adopted'.[30] Other members saw it as objectionable 'class legislation', which, as J. A. Menzies put it, 'even a chartist almost could desire'.[31] J. H. Harris, a fellow Otago member, was even more vitriolic. The franchise, he complained, was being granted to 'a people utterly unable to appreciate it — a people who . . . were, in fact, not amenable to our laws, and who were only nominal subjects of the Crown; who were, in some cases, its open enemies; and who were totally incapable of legislating either for themselves or others'.[32] But there was very little support for such views. Major J. L. C. Richardson, who proposed the second reading, feared that if Harris's views were bruited about they 'would effectively stop any healing process which had been hoped for from the Bill'.[33] Further opposition was voiced when the Bill came back for the third reading, but the opponents did not press for a vote.[34]

'In this way,' Alan Ward has written, 'an important feature of the New Zealand constitution, remaining to this day, stumbled into being.'[35] But no one at the time expected the system of separate representation to endure. The Act was designed to remain in force for a mere five years. It was a temporary expedient, similar to the special representation previously granted to the Pensioner settlements at Auckland and the new seats now being granted to the diggers of Westland. It was a useful way of rewarding Maori loyalists and placating

Maori rebels, while also assuring critics in Britain that the colonists would look after Maori interests. In Britain the Aborigines' Protection Society had been pressing the Colonial Secretary to urge the New Zealand Government to return the confiscated lands, recognise the Maori King, and establish an independent Maori council to control Native Affairs.[36] But the New Zealand Government had no intention of heeding such demands; it was easier to concede four Maori seats in the House. Thus no high principle was involved in Maori representation. But it was still hoped that in due course, when Maori had obtained the necessary property qualifications, they would vote on a common roll and the four Maori seats would disappear. Those who already had such qualifications were eligible to vote for European seats, thereby exercising a double vote since they were also eligible to vote for a Maori seat. This privilege apart, the Maori were considerably under-represented: some 50,000 Maori were given four seats, whereas some 250,000 Europeans had 72. But there was no way that the European members would contemplate allowing Maori to have the fourteen or fifteen seats in the House that were due to them on a population basis, since that would allow them too much power to make and break Governments. In later years there was much concern when a mere four Maori members occasionally held the balance of power.

The 1867 Act was received without enthusiasm by the press, with the *New Zealand Herald* complaining that Maori representation would have been better obtained through the existing system of individualising land titles and thus giving Maori landowners the required property qualification to vote.[37] The *Daily Southern Cross* feared that the Maori members, ignorant of English, would be used by the Government of the day to pass obnoxious measures and 'a great deal of ear-wigging would be done'.[38]

The Maori Representation Act was a short measure of twelve sections. Its preamble explained that, because of the peculiar nature of Maori land tenure, few Maori had so far been able to register and vote for elections to the House of Representatives and the Provincial Councils; therefore it was expedient to make temporary provision for them to do so. The Act defined a Maori as 'a male aboriginal inhabitant of New Zealand of the age of twenty-one years and upwards and shall include half-castes'. It provided for the election of four members to the House of Representatives to represent the Maori race, one each for the electorates of Northern, Eastern, Western and Southern Maori. The boundaries were described in the Schedule. Northern Maori was to comprise all territory northwards of the Tamaki stream which almost connected the Manukau and Waitemata harbours. The remainder of the North Island was given over to

Western and Eastern Maori which were bisected by a line running from the Wairakei stream in the Bay of Plenty along the boundary of Te Arawa territory to Titiraupenga, thence to and through Lake Taupo to the summit of the Ruahine range to Turakirae in Cook Strait. Southern Maori was to comprise the South Island, Stewart Island and adjacent islands. Section 6 of the Act laid down that the representatives were to be chosen by and from the eligible electors in the four seats 'who shall not at any time theretofore have been attained or convicted of any treason felony or infamous offence' — a provision which meant that Maori in rebellion against the Crown could be disenfranchised. Other provisions related to the issuing of writs, the alteration of boundaries, and the conduct of elections (sections 7–10). Section 11 provided for the election of 'one or more' Maori members to Provincial Councils — a provision that was never implemented in the eight years before the provincial system was abolished. Finally, the Act was to remain in force for five years.

Maori Representation in Parliament: The First Phase, 1867–1887

The elections for the four Maori members were carried out in 1868, under the supervision of the Native Department and resident magistrates. There was no general poll since it was feared that this would excite tribal jealousies and swamp the influence of chiefs. William Rolleston, the Under-Secretary of the Native Department, told McLean that he wanted to avoid registration of Maori voters and polling 'all over the country'. Instead, he would have a meeting at one place in the electorate where the

> number of resident natives ... in the event of a poll would turn the election in favour of the local candidate. I would take care that each tribe sent a number of influential men & when they were assembled I would put the case before them — the necessity of their agreeing as a race to send their best men & of sinking their tribal jealousy with this object. I would have a good feast and a good talk and I think there would be little doubt of the thing going off well.[39]

Rolleston's ideas were soon given legal form when the Governor issued a proclamation setting out the regulations for the election of the Maori members. These provided for the appointment of Returning Officers, the notification of polling places, the issuing of writs specifying the time and place of nomination, the calling for a show of hands by voters in the event of there being more than one nomination, and the holding of a poll should this be demanded. Such a poll was to be held a month later at specified polling places and the electors were to vote by declaration, with the Returning Officer writing down the name of the desired candidate and a Maori associate initialling the vote.[40] There was little secrecy about the system, though it remained in force for 70 years. Then another notice was published announcing the polling places: eleven for Northern Maori, fourteen for Western, twelve for Eastern and eleven for Southern Maori.[41]

In the event Rolleston very nearly succeeded in avoiding elections. For Northern Maori the only nomination was F. N. Russell, a half-caste who had the support of Ngapuhi but not of Ngati Whatua. Their leader, Paora Tuhaere, refused to recognise Russell, 'lest we should be twice put into a false position by that nation the Ngapuhi'.[42] For Western Maori the only nominee was Mete Kingi Paetahi, a loyalist chief from lower Waikato who most certainly did not have the support from the Waikato followers of the King. Since Paetahi was an assessor and thus, as a civil servant, technically disqualified from sitting in Parliament, a special Act was necessary to validate his election. In Eastern Maori there was a contest. The nomination of the Ngati Porou candidate, Mokena Kohere, arrived at Napier too late but there was a show of hands for two Ngati Kahungunu candidates in which Tareha Te Moananui defeated Karaitiana Takamoana by 34 votes to 33. For Southern Maori three Kaiapoi men were nominated, a poll was demanded and John Patterson was elected.[43]

In view of the narrow basis of their support and their Kupapa (loyalist) affinities, it would not have been surprising if the Maori members were mere ciphers for the Government. But this did not prove to be the case. On their arrival in Parliament the Maori members were determined to speak and an interpreter had to be brought into the House. Mete Kingi, the former government assessor, angrily refuted suggestions that he or the other Maori members could be 'bought'.[44] They sometimes held the balance of power when European factions in the House were evenly divided; in the 1868 session two of the Maori members supported McLean when he moved a vote of censure against the Government on its Maori and defence policies, and the Government only survived with the Speaker's casting vote. In 1872 Stafford needed Maori votes to form a ministry; and he lost office a month later because he lost that Maori support. In return for their votes two of the Maori members, Wi Katene and Wi Parata, were appointed to the Executive Council.[45]

There was also more Maori interest in the 1871 election. All four Maori seats were contested and two ineffectual members, Russell for Northern Maori and Patterson for Southern Maori, were replaced by Wi Katene and H. K. Taiaroa respectively. We get some idea of the involvement of Maori in the election process from a report by the Deputy Returning Officer at the Bay of Islands, E. M. Williams, of polling day at Waimate North. It was an all-day hui, attended by some 700 men, women and children. Four candidates had been nominated, though one of them withdrew on the day. At Waimate 353 men voted; another 40 to 50 declined to do so. Williams described the meeting as orderly and harmonious: 'Much interest has been manifested by the Natives in this present election, an active canvass has been maintained, and a strong muster brought to the poll.' Although the local candidate, Hone Peti, topped the poll at Waimate, the seat was won by Wi Katene who had the support of Te Rarawa and the Hokianga section of Ngapuhi.[46]

Elections for the Maori seats were still dominated by tribal considerations and it was common for tribes that missed out to press Parliament to increase the number of Maori seats. Rival Pakeha political factions also became involved, sometimes by backing different candidates for the Maori seats. A notable case was the election for Eastern Maori in 1871 when McLean backed Te Moananui and his rival, H. R. Russell, supported Takamoana who won the contest. Takamoana moved three resolutions proposing Maori representation in the Legislative Council and on the Executive Council, and an increase of representation in the House to twelve. Only the first of these resolutions was passed and, as a result, Mokena Kohere and Wiremu Ngatata were appointed to the Legislative Council.[47] Thereafter there were usually two Maori representatives on the Council until its abolition in 1950.

In 1876 Taiaroa introduced a Bill providing for an increase in Maori representation in the House to seven members, but the Bill was not passed.[48] In the same year H. M. Rangitakaiwaho and 394 others of Ngati Kahungunu petitioned Parliament asking for Maori representation to be 'in the same proportion as the representation is of the European race by European members' and for the Maori electorates to be based on tribal boundaries — a plea that was still being reiterated 110 years later.[49]

Sometimes rival European factions recruited Maori with the necessary property qualifications to vote in tightly contested European electorates. The fact that such Maori were exercising a double vote led to some Pakeha criticism.[50] In 1879 most of the Maori votes on the European rolls were eliminated when the householder franchise was abolished. Now Maori could only vote in European electorates if they had a £50 freehold or were ratepayers, whereas the same Act gave Pakeha the adult male franchise. But there was no move to abolish the Maori seats lest the resulting flood of Maori voters onto the European rolls put too many North Island seats in jeopardy. According to

Jackson and Wood, 'any actual move towards amalgamation . . . aroused fears as great in the 1870s and 1880s as in the 1850s'.[51] The 1867 Act was supposed to remain in force for five years; but in 1872 it was extended for another five years; and in 1876 it was extended indefinitely. In time, it was assumed, miscegenation and the steady decline in Maori population, along with the rapid increase in the European population, would mean that it would no longer be dangerous to amalgamate Maori and Pakeha representation. But, so far as Maori were concerned, their special representation came to be seen as their only guarantee that they would be represented at all.

Although the evidence is scanty — neither the Government publications nor the newspapers published the full results in Maori elections prior to 1890, let alone reported electoral proceedings — it seems that Maori were gradually participating more fully in the electoral process. One indication of this is the steady increase in the number of polling places established for each election, no doubt at the insistence of Maori communities. For the 1875 election 13 polling places were established for Northern Maori, 21 for Western, 18 for Eastern and 14 for Southern Maori.[52] By 1887 the numbers had risen to 35 for Northern, 86 for Western, 61 for Eastern and 25 for Southern Maori.[53] Usually a local schoolhouse or courthouse was used, but quite often a chief's house or a runanga house was chosen. Moreover, polling booths were now established in some of the most remote settlements in the North Island, an indication that participation in elections was no longer confined to Kupapa. For the 1886 by-election for Western Maori five polling places were established in the King Country. In the event the King party tribes split their votes, with Ngati Maniapoto supporting the Ngati Raukawa candidate, Hoani Taipua, and the King and his Waikato tribes supporting Major Wiremu Te Wheoro, a former Kupapa who had also previously held the seat. Taipua polled a total of 1158 votes to Te Wheoro's 516, a result that gave the Government agent some smug satisfaction as 'showing how small now is Tawhiao's following within the Western Maori electoral district'.[54] By 1887 polling places were established at Ruatahuna, Fort Galatea and Lake Waikaremoana on the fringes of the Urewera country.[55] Three years later a polling place was established at Hetaraka Te Whakaunua's house at Maungapohatu, in the heart of the Urewera, and the hapless Deputy Returning Officer, J. T. Large, was sent off on a fifteen-day trek from Lake Waikaremoana to record the votes. But he found on arrival that Te Whakaunua and his people had gone off to Whakatane and that those who remained 'expressed indignation at a polling place being established under their sacred mountain'. He was told to count the trees for votes but eventually persuaded a few of the men to cast their votes. And, despite getting lost and injured, he concluded that it was all worthwhile: 'it has undoubtedly the effect of maintaining friendly relations between the government and this isolated tribe'.[56] With this effort it could be said that all of the Maori tribes, if not all of their eligible voters, had been brought into the electoral process.

Although there is insufficient electoral data to present a full analysis of Maori voting behaviour in this period, there seems little doubt that tribal considerations were uppermost in the selection and support for candidates. They were sufficient, according to Ward, to 'render invalid an analysis of Maori elections according to the normal criteria of psephology'.[57] There were enough rivalries to ensure that elections seldom went uncontested, with the Government being put to considerable expense and bother to collect what was often a mere handful of votes from remote polling places. Election to Parliament had become a matter of considerable personal and tribal mana.

But in Parliament the Maori voice was often ineffectual on matters of vital importance to them. Their members invariably opposed the Native Lands Acts that were designed to facilitate settler purchase of Maori land; but their protests were ignored.[58] Although all four Maori members sat on the Native Affairs Committee, set up in 1872 to handle the flood of Maori petitions that poured into the House, they were invariably outvoted on large issues — like the return of the confiscated lands — but sometimes won favourable decisions on lesser matters. According to Ward, the committee 'was one institution which helped . . . to prevent the Maori from quite despairing of the parliamentary system'.[59] Yet for the Maori members, despair and despondency must have been common for much of the time. Usually unable to speak English and therefore unable to follow the normal cut and thrust of parliamentary debates, and very often ignored or ridiculed when they did speak on important Maori matters, the Maori members were little more than a token representation that enabled the Pakeha members to salve their consciences while also relieving Maori of much of their remaining land and autonomy.

Since Maori members were largely powerless in Parliament, it seemed to many Maori that they would better protect their interests by remaining outside the European system. Indeed some Maori groups had remained outside the system for some time after the last shots in the New Zealand wars. After the battle of Orakau the Maori King and his Waikato supporters had taken refuge south of the confiscation line along the Puniu river in Ngati Maniapoto territory, henceforth known as the King Country. Here, for more than 20 years, Tawhiao resisted all Government overtures for the opening of the King

Country to land sales and the law, and the approaching main trunk railway, always insisting on a complete return of the confiscated Waikato lands. As was the case before the war, the Kingites were trying to preserve local autonomy. In 1884 Tawhiao came out of the King Country and led a Maori delegation to England to present a petition to the Queen asking her to 'grant a government to your Maori subjects ... that they may have power to make laws regarding their own lands, and race, lest they perish by the ills which have come upon them'.[60] Once more the Kingites were hoping that section 71 of the Constitution Act would be applied to them. The British had long been sympathetic to this plea — Newcastle, as Secretary of State for the Colonies, had recommended it to the New Zealand Government in 1861, but that plea could be ignored since Newcastle had also agreed to the transfer of responsibility for Maori affairs. In 1884 Tawhiao and his deputation were politely referred back to the Government in Wellington, and that Government had no intention of applying section 71 to the King Country or any other Maori district. In any case by 1884 the due processes of law — more especially the operations of the Native Land Court — were effectively eroding the King's independence. By that time, the leading Ngati Maniapoto chiefs, anxious not to let Tawhiao and his Waikato followers establish a title by occupation to land in the King Country, had agreed to allow the Native Land Court to adjudicate the external boundaries. They were duly rewarded when the court in the Rohepotae judgment of 1888 upheld their titles. In 1885 Ngati Maniapoto allowed the main trunk railway to enter the King Country — thus ceremonially opening it to European enterprise — and Tawhiao and his Waikato supporters withdrew, thereafter to follow a peripatetic existence, moving from one reserve to another within the confiscated block. Although territorial autonomy was no longer possible for the King movement, it still attempted to maintain political autonomy while also participating in the election of members for Western Maori. In the last years of his life Tawhiao continued to resist Government offers of a pension and a seat in the Legislative Council; and he continued to issue proclamations warning Europeans that they too were subject to 'the laws of the Government of the kingdom of Aotearoa.'[61]

Though the King's independent stand earned him much Maori sympathy, if little practical support, there were other centres of independency. The Urewera, home of Tuhoe and Te Kooti's Ringatu supporters, also remained beyond the pale of Pakeha law, though Te Kooti himself lived in the King Country until he was pardoned in 1883. There was yet another centre of independency: that of the prophet Te Whiti who organised passive resistance to the European occupation of the Taranaki confiscated lands from his settlement at Parihaka. For a while in the late 1870s and early 1880s Te Whiti commanded more support than the Maori King. He caused a succession of Pakeha politicians to over-react. Passive resisters were arrested and imprisoned in droves. *Habeas corpus* was suspended. Then in 1881 the Native Minister, John Bryce, led 1500 heavily armed militia on Parihaka, and Te Whiti, along with his chief lieutenant, Tohu Kakahi, were arrested, and held without trial for fifteen months in the South Island. It was a heavy-handed demonstration of the Pakeha determination to bring all Maori within the reach of the law.

But even within those Maori districts ostensibly under the law there remained some degree of autonomy. Maori communities, particularly at the level of hapu and whanau, remained very much to themselves, guided, for most domestic matters, by acknowledged chiefs, and local runanga (committees). Maori matters continued to be regulated by tribal law and custom, though this was considerably modified by Christian codes. It was only when they had to deal with local Pakeha, whether settlers or officials, that Maori had to abide by Pakeha law. There was also a huge amount of intra-tribal activity, perhaps most conspicuously the annual hui held by the King movement and by Te Whiti, but also in other tribal districts. These gatherings were intensely political: though tribal rivalries and animosities remained, Kingites rubbed shoulders with Kupapa, and policies were thrashed out to combat the insistent Pakeha demand for land, the operations of the Native Land Court, and legislation emanating from Wellington. There was an important attempt to institutionalise these proceedings when the Ngati Whatua chief, Paora Tuhaere, a man with an impeccable loyalist record, tried to reconvene the Kohimarama conference, first held in 1860, in 1869. Ten years later he summoned a Maori Parliament at Orakei. The movement gathered force in the 1880s with a series of hui culminating with a meeting at Waitangi in 1889 at which a Maori Union of Waitangi was formed.[62] Significantly, this meeting looked back to that earlier assembly at Waitangi, some 50 years ago, at which Maori chiefs thought that they had preserved their power and authority. Now the chiefs would attempt to regain that authority, hopefully from the Parliament in Wellington, but if not from a Parliament of their own. And they looked to their representatives in Wellington, particularly the member for Northern Maori, Hirini Taiwhanga, to assist them with this new endeavour.

Maori Representation in Parliament: The Second Phase, 1887–1935

In 1887 two talented English-speaking Maori won seats in the House: Hirini Taiwhanga for Northern Maori and James Carroll for Eastern Maori.

Taiwhanga was educated at St John's College in Auckland, and then worked as a surveyor and government assessor. He was no stranger to politics, having contested every election for Northern Maori since 1871. According to Ward, he was 'too excitable and radical' for Ngapuhi in the 1870s but he gradually won their trust in the next decade through involvement in the Maori Parliament and Treaty of Waitangi movement.[63] However, Taiwhanga was much distrusted by Europeans, mainly because of his organisation of Tawhiao's visit to England in 1884. Taiwhanga quickly made his mark in the House and in 1888 was involved in a famous 'stonewall' when he attempted to delay the passing of a Native Land Bill designed to facilitate settler purchase of Maori land.[64] But Taiwhanga's one-man filibuster was soon put down and the Bill was passed. His colourful contribution to Parliament ended with his death on the eve of his probable re-election in 1890. In 1893 the equally gifted and rather more stable Hone Heke, a nephew of the leader of the 1845 rebellion, won Northern Maori and represented the electorate until his death in 1909.

James Carroll, the new member for Eastern Maori, was to play a more substantial role in Parliament than either of the members for Northern Maori. Carroll was part Irish, part Maori. Though he had only two years of formal schooling, Carroll was employed as a clerk in the Lands Department and then as Native Interpreter to the House of Representatives. It was here, no doubt, that Carroll began to acquire his knowledge of parliamentary procedure and debate that made him one of the finest speakers in the House. He stood unsuccessfully against Wi Pere for Eastern Maori in 1884 but defeated him in 1887. Carroll held the seat until 1893 when he switched to the European seat of Waiapu until 1908 and then to Gisborne which he held until 1919. To hold these seats he had to tend the interests of Pakeha electors while also trying to protect the welfare of Maori. As a staunch supporter of the Liberal Party, Carroll was soon appointed to Cabinet: as Member of the Executive Council Representing the Native Race in 1892, Minister for Stamp Duties in 1896, and Minister of Native Affairs in 1899, holding that office until the Liberals were defeated in 1912.

As Minister of Native Affairs, Carroll gained an unprecedented degree of Maori support for his policy and legislation.[65] His Maori Councils Act of 1900 provided for the establishment of eleven tribal councils and below these numerous village committees. The councils were given authority to impose sanitation, control liquor, and promote health reform and education — belated recognition of the long-standing Maori demand for local government by tribal runanga. It was also a shrewdly conceived means of cutting Maori support for a larger form of autonomy, then being powerfully advocated by the Kotahitanga or Maori Parliament movement. In 1900 Carroll passed another important piece of legislation, the Maori Lands Administration Act, which established Maori-controlled land boards to develop Maori land and lease any surplus. The Act had the signal effect of greatly reducing alienation of Maori land — only 6773 acres of land had been leased to Europeans by 1905. There was a hue and cry from the press and Parliament, and Carroll was forced to amend the Act, placing the land boards under European control and giving them power compulsorily to lease Maori land. Then in 1907 the Stout-Ngata Commission was appointed to determine how much land should be retained for Maori use and how much could be made available for European settlement. The Commission examined some 3,000,000 acres of Maori land, and recommended that some 600,000 acres be made available for European settlement, mainly by leasehold. Threatened by a seepage of backblocks farmer support to the rising Reform Party, Carroll and the Liberals were having to meet the incessant European demand for Maori land in the North Island.

Although Carroll was personally opposed to separate Maori representation in Parliament,[66] he was party to several legislative changes that helped to perpetuate that system. In 1893 the Liberal Government extended the franchise to women, including Maori women who voted for the Maori seats. At the same time the Liberals ended the dual Maori vote whereby Maori registered on the European rolls by virtue of property qualifications could also vote in a European constituency. When property qualifications were abolished in 1896, it was laid down that Maori could vote only in Maori electorates. Only half-castes, hitherto required to vote for the Maori seats, were now given a choice. Thus the electoral systems were segregated and any hope of a single amalgamated system, originally envisaged when the 1852 Constitution Act came into force, was left to the piecemeal process of miscegenation. The four Maori seats were more firmly established than ever.

Ironically, Carroll was to ensure that those seats were more effectively occupied than ever before — by bringing his 'young colts',[67] the gifted men of the Young Maori Party, into Parliament. The first was Apirana Ngata, who defeated Wi Pere for Eastern Maori in 1905. Born at Waiomatatini in 1874, educated at the local native school, Te Aute College in Hawke's Bay, and Canterbury and Auckland University Colleges, where he took degrees in arts and law, Ngata was the most gifted Maori of his generation. He was destined to become one of the great parliamentarians of the twentieth century. He held Eastern Maori for 38 years, in that time becoming 'Father' of the House. In 1909, following the sudden death of Hone Heke, Carroll managed to facilitate the election of another Te Aute graduate, Pita Te Rangi Hiroa, better known as Peter Buck.[68] Then in 1911 the third of the Te Aute College old boys, Maui Pomare, like Buck a trained doctor, entered Parliament as member for Western Maori. Buck had graduated from Otago Medical School but Pomare had attended the Seventh-day Adventist Medical College at Battle Creek, Chicago. It was possibly this American experience that led Pomare to differ from Buck and Ngata in his approach to the place of Maori in New Zealand society. Pomare was an outspoken assimilationist, and wanted Maori to become Pakeha as rapidly as possible, whereas Buck and Ngata were more cautious, more sympathetic to Carroll's taihoa (by and by) policy. Though all three were members of the Young Maori Party, this was never a political party in the European sense. While Ngata and Buck remained loyal to the Liberals, Pomare supported Massey's Reform Party.

In contrast to Carroll and the Te Aute trio, the members for Southern Maori were undistinguished. Southern Maori had become a family fief, held by Tame Parata from 1885 to 1911, by his son Taare until 1918, then by J. H. W. Uru until 1921 and his son Henare until 1928. The Paratas and the Urus seldom intervened in debates, except on the long-standing grievance of the Ngai Tahu — the failure of successive Governments to set aside adequate reserves or make sufficient compensation following the original purchase of the Canterbury block. But their persistence was eventually rewarded when a Commission was established to investigate the grievance in 1925.

The contribution of the three giants of the Young Maori Party to Parliament cannot be adequately summarised in a few paragraphs.[69] Buck can be discussed first since he spent only five years in Parliament. As would be expected, Buck was mainly interested in medical matters; indeed in 1913 he took leave from Parliament to carry out inoculations against a smallpox outbreak in his constituency. He was not as strict a party man as Ngata and at times spoke out sharply against Liberal legislation which he saw as facilitating European acquisition of Maori land. On one occasion he lamented that soon the only soil left to the Maori 'will be what they have under their finger nails'.[70] However, his commitment to politics was gradually giving way to a consuming passion for anthropology. Buck took advantage of parliamentary recesses to visit the Cook Islands in 1911 and Niue in 1913. Even in the House, he had the habit of poring over anthropology books instead of contributing to Hansard.[71] Buck was also well aware of what he called the 'absolute impotency' of Maori members, 'when a policy measure is going through that is inimical to them'.[72] But Buck, like Carroll, was not committed to separate representation and in the 1914 election stood for the European seat of the Bay of Islands. He very nearly won it, failing by only 108 votes. He soon went off to the war — as Medical Officer to the Maori Pioneer Battalion — and never again returned to politics.

Pomare, by contrast, remained in Parliament from his election to Western Maori in 1911 until his death in 1930. His assimilationist views and support for Reform gave him a rapid entry into Massey's Cabinet, if not to high office. He was appointed as Member of the Executive Council Representing the Native Race in 1912, but not to the portfolio of Native Affairs which was handed first to W. H. Herries and then to Gordon Coates. However, Pomare did become Minister for the Cook Islands in 1916, Minister of Health in 1923, and Minister of Internal Affairs in 1928. Pomare's 'desertion' of his Young Maori Party colleagues earned him their bitter enmity. Their differences were sharply revealed in the debate over the Native Land Amendment Bill — designed to facilitate European freeholding of leases of Maori land — in 1913. Ngata and Buck attacked the Bill with Buck saying that 'under the cloak of enabling the Maori to individualize his land . . . the Government is only taking a step in denuding him of his land'.[73] But Pomare replied that individualisation of titles was 'one of the chief essentials to the solution of the Native land problem. . . . Communism has been the death-trap of the Native race.' Ngata interjected that this was just 'pakeha clap-trap'. But Pomare continued:

> No amount of communism will save any race. . . . If the Maori tomorrow were dispossessed of all his land, and began to go on his own initiative and commenced to work, he would be a better citizen than continuing to be a spoon-fed Native . . . the only way to salvation of the Maori is by individual effort. . . . I say there should be one law for the Pakeha and for the Maori. . . . We have one King, one country and we should have one law.[74]

And so the interchange proceeded with what one historian has called 'some of the bitterest remarks ever made by one Maori to another on the floor of the House of Representatives'.[75]

But in later years there was some reconciliation between Pomare and Ngata. They worked together to recruit Maori volunteers during the war. After the war, when Pomare had more mana in Cabinet and the sympathetic Coates was Minister of Native Affairs, Pomare and Ngata persuaded the Government to investigate a number of long-standing Maori land grievances, including the confiscations carried out during the wars of the 1860s. A Royal Commission recommended compensation. It was Pomare's finest achievement. Just before his death Pomare persuaded his Taranaki people to accept an annual payment of £5,000, and Ngata, now Minister of Native Affairs, persuaded his Cabinet to approve. As Ngata explained to Buck, 'My honour was involved in the Parliamentary affirmation of the settlement . . . but the financial situation was most difficult and [Prime Minister] Forbes on the eve of departure for London. A fortnight before the arrival of [Pomare's] ashes I wrapped my resignation round the kaupapa [proposal] and handed both to Forbes. At 5 p.m. of the day he left . . . the settlement received his formal approval and that of Cabinet.'[76] Despite their earlier antagonism, Ngata and Buck were generous in their summation of Pomare's contribution to Maori politics. Ngata said that

> he had made it possible to weld the Tai-hauauru peoples together for the most important developments ahead of them. He talked in parables, indulged in 'whakatauki' and so on, because probably greater definiteness would have disappointed his people. To some extent he filled the role of Carroll who propounded general ideas in terms indefinite and elastic enough to cover practical schemes of more prosaic minds. As with Carroll he was able to hold the interest and support of many of the elders of the Western tribes up to the last.

Buck, in reply, referred to Pomare's

> oracular method of speech based on the methods of Te Whiti. . . . Carroll found it useful for, like the Delphic oracle, the utterances were left to the people to interpret in the way that suited them best. If it did not come off, it was the interpretation that was wrong and not the original utterance.[77]

Ngata's achievements in Parliament tower over those of his fellow Maori members. He entered Parliament as Carroll's protégé and in his early years loyally served his chief on Commissions of Inquiry, on the Native Affairs Committee, and in drafting legislation and steering it through the House. He was assiduous and hard-working, and, unlike Carroll and Buck, steered clear of Bellamy's and the social whirl of Wellington. Tom Seddon, who sat on the Native Affairs Committee with Buck and Ngata, gives us an inside view of the Committee at work. He described it as 'the friendliest in the House'. It was presided over by Carroll, 'always smiling indulgently at the three of us', with Ngata 'all the while most vigilant and prompting his chief'.[78]

Perhaps Ngata's greatest achievement at this stage of his parliamentary career was his part in drafting the 1909 Native Land Bill with the Solicitor-General,

Sir John Salmond. The Bill consolidated some 50 years of Maori land legislation and 'laid the foundations of modern Maori land law'.[79] Although the Bill freed up existing restrictions on European purchase of Maori land, it also imposed new controls by giving the land boards authority to approve alienations and, in the case of land owned by ten or more individuals, requiring the approval of a meeting of assembled owners. But the Bill also provided for the development of Maori land by encouraging assembled owners to form incorporations or consolidate their individual interests, thus giving legal sanction to the land reforms that Ngata was already carrying out with his Ngati Porou people. Ngata and Carroll cleverly slipped the massive Bill through the House in the dying stages of the 1909 session. On 15 December at 11.30 p.m. Carroll suddenly proposed the second reading; Massey tried to stonewall with a speech lasting an hour and a half; but the 441 clauses of the Bill were pushed through before a few uninterested members. The Bill received its third reading the following day.[80] It was left to Ngata to bring the Act into operation. Between them Carroll, Ngata and Salmond had gone a long way to satisfying Maori owners on the one hand and European purchasers on the other, although the emphasis on leasing rather than outright purchase was to give the Opposition, with their demand for freehold and condemnation of Maori 'landlordism', a rallying cry that would contribute to their election victory in 1912.

Ngata's star was still rising. He was taking over more responsibilities from Carroll, having attained Cabinet rank with his appointment in 1909 as Member of the Executive Council Representing the Native Race. He was set to succeed Carroll as Minister of Native Affairs but that succession was long delayed since the Liberals lost office in 1912 and did not regain it, in the guise of the United Party, until 1928.

In the meantime Ngata had remained loyal to the Liberal Opposition. But this did not stop him from working very closely with Coates who said in 1925, 'Mr Ngata was not a party man. . . . We form a little Parliament of five, myself as Native Minister and the four Maori members. It is all done in private but we appreciate Mr Ngata's help very much indeed.'[81] In this way Ngata was able to persuade Coates and his Reform Government to back his land development schemes and a variety of other measures for Maori welfare. Coates twice offered Ngata the portfolio of Native Affairs, but he remained loyal to the Liberal Party.[82] Then, to Ngata's great surprise,[83] the erstwhile Liberals, now renamed United, won enough seats in the 1928 election to form a government — with Labour's tacit support. Ngata was suddenly propelled into office as Native Minister.

Ngata was now 54 but he entered upon his long-awaited responsibilities with the verve and energy of a man of half his age. Although he had begun land consolidation and development schemes among his own tribe before the First World War and these reforms spread gradually to other tribes after the war, it was not until he got into office that Ngata had the opportunity to push rapidly ahead. Ngata took personal responsibility for many of the schemes, making decisions on all manner of things with a network of tribal leaders on the ground. The departmental officers and accountants in Wellington were unable to keep up with the paperwork. Ngata was critical of bureaucratic red tape[84] and looked on land development, not so much from a clinical commercial viewpoint, but also as a way of regenerating Maori culture through local tribal leadership. He preferred to use local Maori leaders with mana, like Te Puea Herangi in Waikato, than trained European farm supervisors. Above all, Ngata was determined to increase expenditure and get as many land development schemes under way as rapidly as possible. This was ultimately to be his undoing, since he was increasing expenditure on Maori land development at the very time that an acute depression was forcing the Government (with his approval) to cut expenditure in other fields. As a result of pressure from the National Expenditure Commission, Ngata's powers over the Native Land Court and the Maori Land Boards were curtailed in 1932. But the critics were still not satisfied. The following year the Auditor-General refused to endorse the accounts for the Maori land development schemes and was supported by the Public Accounts Committee. In the face of mounting public criticism, much of it barely disguised racism, Prime Minister Forbes decided in 1934 to appoint a Commission of Inquiry. Headed by Mr Justice Smith, the Commission took a very hard line: the land development schemes were closely scrutinised, along with all items of expenditure; some of Ngata's subordinates were found to have been involved in corrupt practices — one was subsequently prosecuted — and Ngata himself was criticised for high-handed administrative actions, as well as having used his position to favour his tribe and his family. The Commission said that

> it was necessary to appreciate that the Native Minister was himself a Maori. The psychological factors in the situation . . . were the result of tribal habits of thought and feelings to which he was himself subject. These habits involved the care of his own tribe and the support of any other tribes who assisted him. . . . The Minister, although . . . a member of a tribe, was, as a Minister of the Crown, bound to refrain from using state funds, without lawful authority, in the interests of his tribe. . . . We regret to state that the Native Minister failed not infrequently in these matters.[85]

During the course of the inquiry Ngata said little, except when called to give evidence, but he did say privately to Buck that 'an administrative system with strong pakeha leanings will not be happy unless the instruments of its will are of its own colour and outlook', adding, with uncharacteristic rancour, 'one has learnt how to eat mud, to endure vilification and to slave under the mana of other men so long as the objectives of one's life are furthered'.[86] When the report came out Ngata merely noted that the Commission had 'adopted a hostile attitude right through, supporting the complaints of the Audit Department' and that the report lacked the 'breadth of vision' that he had expected.[87] Ngata loyally took responsibility for the criticisms and tendered his resignation. But Buck, writing from the Bishop Museum in Hawaii, was much more outspoken on the 'frenzy' of government officials when Ngata had dared 'to set them aside and break through their taboo restrictions. . . . So long as the pakeha can patronise, he will say nice things about a noble [Maori] race but when it comes to direct competition, jealousy of race is very evident . . . as manifested against you.'[88] On the Pakeha side Ngata had few supporters — the most notable was Professor I. L. G. Sutherland[89] — but numerous critics. The *New Zealand Herald* bluntly proclaimed that after what the Commission had found, no Maori should ever be put in charge of Maori Affairs again.[90]

The affair cannot be examined at greater length, but it is worth noting that it revealed more sharply than anything before or afterwards the inability of the Pakeha establishment — Parliament, the bureaucracy, the judiciary and the press — to bend procedures to allow a Maori Minister to do things in a Maori way. But the Commission and its report provided the Labour Opposition with a golden opportunity to lambast the beleaguered Coalition Government. Labour were soon to be rewarded in the 1935 election and Ngata spent his remaining years in Parliament in the Opposition — until he was himself defeated in 1943.

Ngata's parliamentary career demonstrated more clearly than those of any of his colleagues both the opportunities but also the ultimate limitations of the existing system of Maori representation in Parliament. A trained lawyer with a brilliant mind and an unrivalled command of English, Ngata was able to foot it with any of his Pakeha colleagues or rivals in Parliament. He was also a loyal party man who frequently put party before his personal interests and often compromised the larger interest of the Maori people. Before the First World War he could only hinder, not stop, the alienation of Maori land; and even after the war, when there was a more sympathetic Pakeha attitude to Maori needs, it was a long time before he got Government to fund Maori land development. Even then, Ngata sometimes accepted lower standards for Maori than were being applied to Pakeha — for instance, lower unemployment benefits. But, as the Commission of Inquiry demonstrated, there was a limit to how far a Maori Minister of Native Affairs could go before setting off a Pakeha backlash.

Yet it was in the period considered here, from 1887–1935, which spans the high points of the careers of Carroll and his Young Maori Party protégés, that the system of Maori representation in Parliament became firmly fixed in the New Zealand political system. For Carroll and his young colts brilliantly demonstrated that Maori members could operate the system as well as any of the European members. Their success allowed Europeans a little reflected glory, since the Young Maori Party, helping to foster a Maori renaissance, were also giving Pakeha New Zealanders an opportunity to claim success in race relations, if not yet in amalgamating the races. All provided, of course, that those Maori members did not overstep the limits, as Ngata unfortunately did.

The abolition of the Maori seats was occasionally discussed. Carroll sometimes spoke in favour of it, saying in 1905 that the Maori would be better off without special representation and would receive more attention if they voted on the General roll.[91] In that debate several European members spoke to the same effect, but significantly Hone Heke defended special Maori representation by referring to the Cape Colony where a common roll was in existence and there was a widespread European fear that the more numerous non-Europeans would eventually control the Parliament.[92] Europeans in New Zealand held no such fears, despite a recent upturn in Maori numbers, since Maori constituted a mere 5.6 per cent of the population.

Although European members saw the abolition of the Maori seats as ultimately desirable in the interests of assimilation, any such abolition meant that Maori voters would have to be registered on the common roll. For many years no Government was prepared to grasp that nettle. An Act of 1914, providing for the preparation of Maori rolls, remained a dead letter for 35 years. In 1919 the Electoral Department made a halfhearted attempt to prepare a roll, based on the declaration votes recorded in 1914. Posters calling on them to enrol and enrolment forms were sent to post offices and other places where Maori were likely to congregate. A mere 796 enrolled. The Chief Electoral Officer considered that the task was hopeless, unless the Government made registration compulsory.[93] Since the Government was unwilling to pass such legislation, there was a stalemate. Each time there was a request for the preparation of rolls, the Chief Electoral Officer, in typical 'Yes Minister' fashion, raised numerous difficulties or said that 'it was very doubtful whether the time was opportune'.[94] Although the United Party election manifesto for 1928 promised that Maori rolls would be prepared, the inaction continued. Eventually, in response to several requests from the member for Southern Maori and Maori electors, the Chief Electoral Officer reiterated his opinion that the 'time was not opportune'. Forbes referred the advice to Ngata who agreed that the preparation of Maori rolls was 'not practicable'[95] — and there the matter rested until the Labour Government grasped the nettle in time for the 1949 election.

Since Maori elections were conducted without a roll of registered voters and as semi-public affairs lacking an effective guarantee of secrecy, there was bound to be criticism from time to time. In 1908 one of the judges presiding at the hearing of an election petition over the Northern Maori seat roundly condemned the existing practice, which allowed a vote by a show of hands if a poll was not demanded. As a result, the Legislative Amendment Act of 1910 abolished this system and required voting by declaration for all Maori elections. Each Maori voter had to declare for one of the candidates before a Returning Officer and a Maori associate who could, if necessary, act as an interpreter. At the time the Prime Minister, Sir Joseph Ward, said that 'more time should be given to the Maoris before we compel them to adopt the European system of elections'.[96] In the debate the Leader of the Opposition, W. F. Massey, had spoken of the need to abolish the Maori seats and complained that the Southern Maori seat represented no more than 2000 Maori people, compared with the average European seat in the South Island which represented some 12,000 persons.[97] But he did not attempt to abolish the seats when he came to power. Nor did the Liberals when they returned to office as the United Party in 1928, though they could scarcely do so with Ngata number three in Cabinet.

The success of the Young Maori Party leaders in Parliament contributed to the gradual demise of autonomous, extra-parliamentary Maori political movements. The most notable of these was the Kotahitanga movement which at its height at the end of the nineteenth century claimed, with some exaggeration, to have the support of 37,000 Maori.[98] The ideal of Kotahitanga, or Maori unity with autonomy, had a long but tenuous history. It began with Busby's confederation of northern chiefs, continued through the King movement, the Kohimarama conference of 1860, took more tangible form with Paora Tuhaere's Parliament at Orakei in 1879, and culminated in the formation of a 'Maori Union of Waitangi' in 1899. Over the next two years, hui at Waiomatatini, Omahu and Wanganui supported the proposal. In 1891 Te Arawa petitioned the Queen for a separate Maori Parliament, 'as your Majesty has already concluded with us the glorious bond of union in the Treaty of Waitangi'.[99] The petition was bound to fail since the Queen would not intervene in New Zealand politics; it was necessary for the Maori leaders to take their project to the New Zealand Parliament in Wellington. Meeting at Waitangi in April 1892, they agreed to form a Maori Parliament. This was to be composed of a lower house of 96 elected members, and an upper house of 50 members, chosen by the lower house. It was thus similar to the European Parliament in Wellington, although the electoral districts were based on tribal boundaries. The Maori Parliament held its first session at Waipatu in Hawke's Bay later in the year. It continued to meet annually in different Maori settlements for the next eleven years.

The Maori Parliament had a very considerable measure of support, more particularly from the loyalist or Kupapa tribes, the very people who had long been involved in electing members for the four Maori seats. But it failed to gain the adherence of Te Whiti's supporters at Parihaka or the King movement. In 1894 the Kingites decided to set up their own Parliament, or Kauhanganui, at Maungakawa near Cambridge. However, it soon became evident that the Pakeha Parliament in Wellington would brook no rival. Although that Government did not interfere with meetings of either the Kingite Kauhanganui or the Kotahitanga Parliament, any attempt by the Maori Parliaments to exercise authority which resulted in a breach of the law was suppressed. When Kerei Kaihau, a follower of the Maori King, decided to destroy survey pegs for a government road in Waikato — because 'he recognised no laws but King Tawhiao's'[100] — he and his supporters were promptly arrested and jailed at Mount Eden.

As befitted their loyalist reputation, the supporters of the Kotahitanga Parliament had a more law-abiding approach. They sought recognition of their Parliament from the Pakeha Parliament, and worked through their elected representatives in the four Maori seats. At the second meeting of the Maori Parliament in 1893, a Federated Maori Assembly Empowering Bill was drafted and was sent with a petition to the Native Minister, A. J. Cadman, for passage through the General Assembly in Wellington. Cadman did not deign to put it before the House. So in 1894 the Maori Parliament prepared a draft Native Rights Bill which left the constitutional details of the Maori Parliament to be worked out later. This time the member for Northern Maori, Hone Heke, presented the measure as a Private Member's Bill. But most of the European members present walked out of the House so that there was no longer a quorum to debate the Bill. Heke presented it again during the 1896 session but it was defeated on a vote.[101]

Clearly, the European members were unwilling to recognise any form of Maori autonomy, just as they had always been unwilling to set aside Maori districts under section 71 of the Constitution Act. The most that they were prepared to concede was Carroll's Maori Councils Act of 1900, with its very limited powers of local government. Although Carroll had been initially sympathetic to the Maori Parliament movement, he had decided by the end of the century that Maori must rely on the European Parliament. The young Ngata agreed with him. It was their opposition and their Maori Councils Act that effectively destroyed the Maori Parliament, although it continued to meet for several more years. So did the Kingite Kauhanganui, although as early as 1886 the Kingites had thrown their support behind Major Te Wheoro in the Western Maori by-election. Later they supported Henare Kaihau and, when he let them down, transferred their allegiance to Pomare in 1911. Moreover, the third Maori King, Mahuta, was inveigled into taking a seat in the Legislative Council in 1903 and was for three years a Member of the Executive Council, though his was essentially a token membership. Maori autonomy was a lost cause but with the appearance of the Young Maori Party at least there was the compensation that Maori were now being very effectively represented in Parliament. Thereafter, with the exception of the prophet Rua Kenana in the Urewera, Maori leaders invariably attempted to prosecute their causes in the Wellington Parliament.

The most notable case was that of Tahupotiki Wiremu Ratana.[102] He first gained prominence as a faith healer from 1918 and then as the founder of the church which still bears his name. But Ratana soon took on a political function, although he never stood for Parliament. In 1922 his son Tokouru stood for Western Maori and came within 800 votes of unseating Pomare. Ratana's supporters lodged a petition against Pomare's election, alleging corruption and partisanship on the part of the Returning Officers, but the petition was dismissed.[103] T. W. Ratana took up and popularised various Maori causes, including a demand for the ratification of the Treaty of Waitangi. Like Tawhiao and Te Rata before him, he led a delegation to England to seek a resolution of Maori grievances from the Crown. He began to promote the interests of the morehu — the landless and unemployed Maori who were now rapidly increasing in number, despite Ngata's land development schemes. In 1928 Ratana announced that he intended to capture the 'Four Quarters' — the four Maori electorates. Although Ratana candidates were unsuccessful in the 1928 election, they ran second in the four electorates and Eruera Tirikatene failed only by the casting vote of the Returning Officer to win Southern Maori. Ngata somewhat misread the result by informing Buck that 'the wave of Ratanaism which has been steadily receding since 1922, will have its backward pace accelerated'.[104] In 1931 the Ratana candidates again came second in all four electorates, but Tirikatene did take Southern Maori in a by-election in 1932. Then in 1935 Ratana gained his second seat when his son Tokouru won Western Maori, and Ratana candidates came second in the other two electorates. Moreover, the two Ratana members now joined the Labour Party and supported the new Government in the House.[105]

Though few realised it at the time, Ratana victories in 1935 marked the beginning of a fundamental realignment in Maori politics from the old tribally based alliances, astutely managed by a prestigious parliamentary leader like Carroll and later Ngata, to a class-based grassroots movement, organised by a network of Ratana branches and in due course firmly aligned to the Labour Party.[106] The influence of the Ratana/Labour alliance will be discussed in the next section, but it is worthwhile in concluding this section to make further reference to the continuing influence of traditional tribal factors in Maori politics, so far mentioned only in passing. In Parliament the Maori members had to behave according to the long-established British traditions — and there is no doubting the ability of Carroll and the Young Maori Party representatives to do that — but out in the electorates they had to practise their Maoritanga. That term was invented by Carroll at a hui at Te Kuiti in 1920. But he refused to define it and, in his usual enigmatic way, said it was up to others 'to give it hands and feet'.[107] The others most certainly included Ngata who eventually did define it as including emphasis on Maori culture, 'pride in Maori history and traditions... retention of old-time ceremonial, the continuous attempt to interpret the Maori point of view to the pakeha in power'.[108]

All of those things needed to be cultivated by Maori aspirants for Parliament. Buck was unusual amongst candidates of the period in that he was not a 'native speaker' of Maori. In his youth he lost the Maori he had picked up as a small child and, after graduation from Otago, had to learn again the language of his Maori kin. Although he was well known in the North from his work there as a Medical Officer, Buck had no lineal connections with the northern tribes and owed his selection as a candidate for the electorate in 1909 to Carroll. When the previous member, Hone Heke, died in Wellington, Carroll and Buck accompanied the funeral cortège to Kaikohe for the tangi. At the ceremony Carroll announced that Heke's mother wanted to repay the debt for bringing her son's body back from Wellington by 'marrying their son's widow to a chief from the south'. He asked the assembly to accept a somewhat startled Buck as the 'husband' for the widow.[109] Buck was duly elected despite competition from several disgruntled local candidates. And he was by no means the last to be launched into a political career during a tangi for a deceased member.

Pomare's successor for Western Maori, Taite Te Tomo, was selected on the marae at Waitara in 1930 in the same way. He got the backing of Pomare's tribal supporters ahead of the Young Maori Party candidate, Pei Te Hurinui Jones, a young man very much in the mould of Ngata. Though Jones had the support of important Kingite leaders like Te Puea and some of his own Ngati Maniapoto tribe, he failed to get the backing of the King, Te Rata, and the bulk of the Kingites. They had given their support to Pomare in 1928 and preferred to back his chosen successor, Te Tomo, who had been Pomare's secretary and electorate organiser. But Jones, with the politician's habitual optimism, thought that he could win.

His letters to Ngata during the campaign provide a rare and revealing insight into the conduct of a Maori election at this time. On the eve of his campaign he wrote: 'I have seen all my kaumatuas and I leave knowing their hearts are with me.... as far as the younger people are concerned they should come with me.... Summed up, Api, I think my chances are not too bad.'[110] He took up the slogan of the Young Maori Party — 'Ka pu te ruha, ka hao te rangatahi' (when the old net is cast aside, the new net is used for fishing) and issued a printed party manifesto. Five days later he wrote

> the slogan 'Te Ao Hou' has caught on. Yesterday was a very strenuous day. We addressed meetings at Meremere, Waiokura, Manaia and finished up at Parihaka. Our intention was to return to Hawera late last night, but the response to our appeal was so exuberant that we stayed up all last night. We had three Taite supporters ... to contend with. We disposed of all their points and questions to the entire satisfaction of our audience with the result that they retired in dismay shortly after mid-night and left us to enjoy the rest of the night with pois and paos.... So far I have been doing extremely well.[111]

And so the campaign continued, with Jones forever hopeful, apparently getting a warm response in south Taranaki — 'the more progressive they were, the surer we were of getting ... support'.[112] He was even allowed to address a meeting at Ratana Pa, despite the fact that Tokouru Ratana was standing — and got a solitary vote for his pains. Jones was enthusiastically supported by the local Pakeha press. As the *Hawera Star* put it, Jones was 'the outstanding candidate' because of his 'training and experience and progressive outlook'.[113] But he did not win. Indeed he came a poor third to Taite Te Tomo and Tokouru Ratana. Taite's tribal alliance of the Waikato Kingites and Pomare's north Taranaki tribes had prevailed by some 800 votes over Tokouru's burgeoning support from the morehu of the Ratana movement. Although Taite retained his seat in the 1931 general election, Tokouru narrowly ousted him in 1935. The politics of tribe were giving way to those of class.

Maori Representation in Parliament: The Third Phase, 1935–1985

Ratana cemented the alliance with the Labour Party by leading a deputation to the Prime Minister, M. J. Savage, at Parliament House in April 1936, leaving with him various gifts 'as a mark of unity in politics'.[114] In the same year Ratana's cousin Rangi Mawhete, who had done much to forge the Ratana/Labour alliance, was nominated to the Legislative Council. Ratana's quest for the Four Quarters was soon to be achieved. In the 1938 election the Ratana/Labour candidate, T. P. Paikea, won Northern Maori but Ngata retained Eastern Maori, though on a minority vote. The opposition vote was divided between the Labour-endorsed candidate, R. T. Kohere, and the Ratana candidate, Tiaki Omana. Labour did not make the same mistake in 1943 and endorsed Omana who just beat Ngata for the seat he had held for 38 years.

In view of their growing influence in the Labour Government, the Ratana members were well placed to achieve their original objectives. They had entered Parliament on a platform of ratification of the Treaty of Waitangi, the resolution of long-standing land grievances, the equalisation of welfare benefits, and electoral reform, including an increase in the number of Maori seats to six to allow for growth in Maori population. They attempted to promote this policy through the Maori Organising Committee (later the Maori Advisory Council) of the Labour Party, in caucus, and on the floor of the House. But neither of the Maori members was admitted to Cabinet — the Prime Minister, M. J. Savage, took on the portfolio of Native Affairs — and they had only limited success in other respects. In the matter of electoral reform, their main demand for increased representation was ignored, although in 1937 the Government applied the secret ballot, which Europeans had had since 1870, to the Maori electorates, by allowing Maori voters to mark their ballot papers in the normal way without the advice of Maori associates. But, despite a promise from Walter Nash to Tirikatene that electoral rolls would be prepared for Maori seats for the 1938 election, they were not in fact ready until the 1949 election.[115] The Electoral Office had continued to exaggerate the difficulties of compiling a roll until Fraser decided to use the Welfare Officers of the Maori Affairs Department to flush out Maori enrolments in time for the 1949 election.[116]

But in the welfare field the Labour Government was quicker to attend to Maori needs. Maori were placed on an equal footing with Europeans for unemployment pay in 1936, though it was some time before they were brought onto the same rates as Europeans for old age and widows' pensions.[117] With the passage of the Social Security Act in 1938 Maori were eligible for the child benefit on the same basis as Europeans. But Labour was slow to act on long-standing Maori land grievances; for instance the Waikato and Ngai Tahu compensation claims, in abeyance since Commissions of Inquiry in the 1920s, were not finally resolved until the late 1940s. And Tirikatene's frequently reiterated demand for ratification of the Treaty of Waitangi was ignored. Altogether Labour's record in Maori affairs prior to the war was decidedly uneven; as Claudia Orange put it, the Government 'just muddled along'.[118] There was little leadership from the top with the portfolio of Native Affairs nominally in the hands of the ailing Savage but most of the responsibility devolving to the insensitive Acting Minister, F. Langstone, who formally took over the post on Savage's death in 1940. Moreover, the Ratana movement became divided with the death of T. W. Ratana in 1939 when the presidency of the church was conferred on his son, Tokouru, but leadership of the movement in Parliament remained for the time being with Tirikatene. The Ratana members 'seem to have remained peripheral to policy decisions on Maori matters'.[119] Nevertheless the Ratana/Labour alliance remained firm since Labour's social welfare and economic policies were bringing many benefits to Maori — as well as to Pakeha.

The outbreak of war in Europe and later the Pacific was to divert attention from domestic concerns. A Maori Battalion was recruited and sent overseas in May 1940. At home a Maori War Effort Organisation was formed under the chairmanship of Paikea who had been appointed to the Executive Council as Representative of the Native Race.[120] The Organisation was primarily concerned with recruitment and support for the Maori Battalion, but it also began planning for rehabilitation of returned servicemen after the war.[121] It worked through a network of tribal committees, was outside the control of the Native Department, and soon began to develop larger ambitions; indeed some of those involved saw it as a way of reviving that long-unachieved will-o'-the-wisp, Maori autonomy. Paikea once described it as fulfilling a recommendation made by Sir George Grey 80 years before that Maori could best be governed through their tribal leaders.[122] But the Organisation did not survive the war, although the tribal committees were kept in existence under the Maori Social and Economic Advancement Act of 1945. As Ngatata Love puts it, 'the government effectively destroyed the incentive and initiative of a large measure of self-determination which had been the motivating factor behind the Tribal Committees during the time of the Maori War Effort Organisation'.[123] But, much to the dismay of the Maori members, the committees were no longer part of an independent structure; they were made responsible to a newly constituted welfare section of the Native Department.[124] Later, however, two important Maori organisations grew out of the remains of the War Effort Organisation: first the Maori Women's Welfare League, formed in 1951, and then the New Zealand Maori Council, a male-dominated confederation of tribal committees, formed in 1962. But neither of these gender-oriented organisations possessed great independence; they could attend to purely Maori social and cultural matters within their particular spheres, but otherwise their powers were only advisory.

The 1946 election was a close-fought contest. There was some dissatisfaction with the Ratana/Labour members and in the Northern and Eastern electorates there were unsuccessful attempts to field other candidates bearing the Labour banner. The National Party, under the vigorous leadership of S. G. Holland, ran Ngata again in Eastern Maori and made much use of officers from the Maori Battalion, including J. C. Henare, son of the former member, who stood for Northern Maori. But in a high poll in which more than 85 per cent of Maori adults cast their vote,[125] the four Ratana/Labour candidates came home with increased majorities — and with 63.9 per cent of the total valid votes.[126] In Eastern Maori, where 2521 more votes were recorded than in 1943, there were allegations of plural voting, but they were not sustained.[127] Since the Maori election was held a day before the general election, Fraser was able to capitalise on Labour's victory in the Maori seats. But when the general election was held, Labour and National won 38 seats each and Labour clung to office by virtue of the Maori seats.

The Maori members had a golden opportunity to extract the maximum advantage. Unwilling to hand over the portfolio of Native Affairs to one of the Maori members, Peter Fraser reluctantly took it on himself — and became the most successful Pakeha holder of the office since Coates. Tirikatene was eventually given a minor portfolio: Minister in Charge of the Government Printing Works and Stationery Supplies. But he had little influence in Government since Fraser could not 'swallow him'.[128] The other Maori members were even less influential. Matiu Ratana, who had succeeded his brother in a 1945 by-election, was not fluent in English; and neither Omana in Eastern Maori nor T. P. Paikea, who had succeeded his father in Northern Maori, was at all forceful.[129] So the initiative remained with Fraser, a shrewd and astute politician, and his Ministerial Secretary, M. R. (Mick) Jones. It was he who persuaded Fraser to have the term 'Native' replaced by 'Maori' in all official documents and communications. Commissions were set up to examine outstanding land grievances in Taranaki, Northland and elsewhere. Fraser personally settled the Waikato,

Whakatohea and Ngai Tahu claims. When G. P. Shepherd retired Fraser appointed Tipi Ropiha as Under-Secretary to the Maori Affairs Department, the first Maori to hold the position, thus outflanking Ratana critics who complained that the Department was run by Pakeha. But despite further initiatives from Fraser in housing and welfare, little else was achieved. The undeveloped state of some Maori land, exacerbated by rapid urbanisation, provided the Opposition with an opportunity to attack the Government.

As the 1949 election loomed, it became increasingly risky for the Maori members to exploit their mandate. This was ceaselessly panned in the pro-National press, as, for instance, in Gordon Minhinnick's cartoons in the *New Zealand Herald* which showed Fraser forever pandering to a grass-skirted Maori 'mandate'.[130] It seems likely that Labour's dependence on the so-called Maori 'mandate' was a significant factor in their defeat in the 1949 election.[131] After the election Walter Nash ruefully admitted that 'Fraser laid too much stress on the Maori side of his campaign to the detriment of his pakeha voters. The Tory press . . . played it up for all it was worth and with the winning of the four Maori seats in the first day of the election, I think a lot of pakeha voters changed overnight.'[132] Separate representation did guarantee the Labour Party four seats, thanks to the strength of the Ratana movement and the increasing proletarianisation of the Maori population. But there was no effective way those Maori Labour members could demand of their Government the affirmative action that was needed to lift their people in the social and economic scale to the level of the Pakeha population, without causing a Pakeha backlash at the polls. Nor was anything to be gained by crossing the floor and bringing down the Labour Government since National offered a worse alternative. The four Maori members considered but rejected this strategy.[133]

Without any Maori in his party, the National leader S. G. Holland appointed E. B. Corbett, a Taranaki farmer, as Minister for Maori Affairs. Ngata feared that the National Government, drawing much of its support from Pakeha farmers, would make a last raid on Maori land, 'at what remains of Naboth's vineyard'.[134] But the elder statesman was able to give Corbett some salutary advice and the land development schemes which Ngata himself had initiated were continued under the National Government, as were the urban housing and trade training schemes initiated by Labour. Yet, although National won the snap 1951 election with ease, and the 1954 election, it could not capture any of the Maori seats, despite Holland's advice to the Maori voters to back the winning horse.[135] In fact the National percentage of Maori votes in this period steadily declined and, as a consequence, the four Ratana/

Labour members, despite lacklustre performances in the House, continued to increase their majorities.[136]

Though National was philosophically inclined towards assimilation, it did nothing to abolish the Maori seats. Just before his death in 1950, Ngata told Corbett that 'the Maoris themselves will demand the abolition in the course of a few years'.[137] But Maori leaders made no such demand. National, unwilling to eliminate the Maori voice from Parliament, continued to hope that it would win back at least one of the Maori seats. In the meantime, it was content to tinker with the existing system. Thus in 1950 and 1951 legislation was passed to schedule Maori elections on the same day and same hours as the general election; and in 1954 there were changes to the electoral boundaries, mainly to increase the Southern Maori electorate by bringing it into the southern North Island. There was some concern over the state of the Maori rolls, but Corbett adamantly refused requests from the Electoral Office to use Maori Welfare Officers to recruit Maori voters. In September 1954 he told the Minister of Justice, J. R. Marshall, that 'it would be unwise to have officers of my department engaged in matters related to the enrolment on the Electoral Roll. . . . It was previously reported to me that when Welfare Officers were engaged in this work that their enthusiasm went further than the business of enrolling electors and took the form of political propoganda [sic].'[138] Evidently Corbett regarded the Welfare Officers as recruiting agents for the Labour Party. To get round the problem Maori enrolment was made compulsory in 1956, in line with European enrolment which had been compulsory since 1927. But now a new problem arose because the old rolls were destroyed and all Maori voters were required to re-enrol. Though the Electoral Office sent out re-enrolment cards to all Maori on the previous roll, only about half replied within the required two months and the Office once more requested the aid of the Welfare Officers, only to be turned down again by Corbett.[139]

In the longer term, Corbett was looking for a way of eliminating the Maori seats. He told Marshall in July 1957 that 'the time has arrived when consideration should be given to amendments being made to the Electoral Act whereby Maori electors are given the option of enrolling on European Rolls if they so desire'. He claimed that there was a feeling among Maori 'that their interests could be best served by local European members of Parliament, and that the time has arrived when the Maori electorates should be abolished'. But 'rather than place the responsibility on the Government to arbitrarily abolish the electorates, it would be better for the Maori people themselves to decide the issue by going on the European Rolls if they so desire and if the numbers on the Maori

Electoral Rolls fall below a fixed minimum, then the time will have arrived for doing away with the electorates'.[140] But the Government did not introduce amending legislation before the November election. Ironically, there was also talk among Pakeha members of the Labour caucus of abolishing the Maori seats — in the hope that Labour would pick up more than four urban seats — but the Maori Advisory Council of the Party, headed by Tirikatene, came out firmly against the idea. Instead, the Council demanded that Maori representation be increased in line with the increase in population. It was now evident that in terms of total population, if not registered electors or valid votes, Maori were considerably under-represented in comparison with Europeans.[141] This was to be a constant refrain of Labour's Maori members for 30 years.

In the 1957 election Labour was narrowly returned to office — with 41 seats to National's 39 — and was once more dependent on the four Maori seats. The four Ratana/Labour members had been returned, though two with decreased majorities as a result of the intervention of Social Credit candidates. Nevertheless Labour's share of the qualified Maori vote increased to 56.4 per cent while that of National decreased to a mere 14.4 per cent.[142] But once again high hopes of the Maori members were soon dashed. Walter Nash took the Maori Affairs portfolio, though Tirikatene was named as the Associate Minister and was also given the comparatively minor portfolio of Minister of Forests. Moreover, Nash refused to allow Tirikatene to play any effective role in the formulation of Maori Affairs policies, keeping these, as indeed many other aspects of government, under his sole control. The Maori Policy Committee of the Party was also ignored. Though Tirikatene frequently represented Nash at Maori gatherings, he was unable to give firm answers on problems that were raised; everything had to be referred back to Nash in Wellington, and Government became paralysed by the bottleneck in the Prime Minister's office.[143]

Unable to take decisions himself, Nash brought in J. K. Hunn from the Justice Department, made him Acting Head of Maori Affairs, and instructed him to carry out an 'accounting of Maori assets to find a way of using them for the good of the Maori people as a whole'.[144] Although the Hunn Report was ready by June of 1960, Nash refused to consider it before the November election. Nash and Tirikatene were also publicly at loggerheads over the 1960 All Black tour of South Africa. Tirikatene had forthrightly condemned the decision of the Rugby Union to send a team without Maori, but Nash refused to intervene, carefully avoiding a commitment for or against the tour.[145] There was continued criticism of the Government by the Maori Policy Committee, but, as the election approached, the Maori members decided that loyalty to the party was more important than threatening its defeat. Once again, the Maori 'mandate' had proved of little value, though a more skilled and energetic leader than Tirikatene might have gained more in Cabinet. Even Love, who is very sympathetic to Tirikatene, admits that he was not popular in Cabinet, overstressed his points, and built up resistance from colleagues to Maori issues.[146] Love concludes that, 'as in the 1947–1949 period, the Ratana members lost their chance to take a more forceful role in securing their objectives'.[147]

National, now led by K. J. Holyoake, won the 1960 election with a majority of twelve seats. But Labour retained the four Maori seats though with diminished majorities in all except Tirikatene's seat. There was some recovery of the National vote and a strong challenge from Social Credit, whose candidate for Eastern Maori beat the National candidate into second place.[148] The portfolio of Maori Affairs was handed to J. R. Hanan, a Southland lawyer on the liberal wing of the party. One of Hanan's first tasks was to consider the Hunn Report. Hunn had not been content with the simple 'accounting' of Maori assets but had spoken out boldly on broad matters of policy. He recommended that the policy of assimilation, promoted by New Zealand Governments for more than a century, should be replaced by integration. This he defined as an attempt to 'combine (not fuse) the Maori and pakeha elements to form one nation wherein Maori culture remains distinct'.[149] Hanan and the National Government accepted integration as the basic objective of their Maori policy, but it was regarded with great suspicion by Maori leaders, many of whom saw it as a new euphemism for the old assimilation policy.[150] The rest of Hunn's Report was concerned with land, housing, education, employment, health, crime, and legal differentiation. It provided the National Government with clear guidelines for future action. To their credit, Hanan and the Holyoake Government accepted many of the recommendations. Some, like the proposal to set up a Maori Education Foundation, met with Maori approval; others, such as the attempt to eliminate uneconomic fragments of land (later reiterated by the Pritchard-Waetford Report and incorporated in the 1967 Maori Affairs Amendment Act), provoked bitter Maori resistance.

The Hunn Report made only passing reference to Maori representation in Parliament — under the heading 'Legal Differentiation'. Hunn's research team had compiled a list of 264 instances of differentiation in New Zealand legislation. Of these, 58 were said to have conferred a Maori privilege, 35 a Maori disability, 69 a Maori protection, and 102 merely set out a different procedure. The electoral provisions were described as conferring a Maori privilege, a disability, and a different procedure. Hunn did not make recommendations on the items of differentiation, but merely suggested that they should not 'endure indefinitely by default'.[151] But he did go on to include the electoral provisions as one of nine items meriting 'sceptical scrutiny'.[152]

Since the National Government was without Maori representation in Parliament, and now committed itself to the integration of the races, it is surprising that it did not take advantage of Hunn's recommendation for a 'sceptical scrutiny' of separate Maori representation. Hanan himself was against separate representation, saying on one occasion that he did not think that in the electoral field there should be special privileges for anyone.[153] But he was unwilling even to take up Corbett's plan to allow Maori voters to register on the European rolls.[154] However, from time to time National members spoke mildly in favour of integration of the seats. In 1965, during a debate on an Electoral Amendment Bill to peg the General seats in the South Island at 25 and increase those in the North Island, Tirikatene made yet another plea for an increase in the number of Maori seats in line with increased Maori population. But Holyoake replied that:

> Maori representation had never been regarded as being on a population basis. . . . Over the years, whether the population justified it or not — and mostly it did not — the Maoris have been represented by four members in this House, and in all the years I have been here the general understanding in the House has been that the next step in Maori representation should be complete integration; that we should join together and be on the same roll.[155]

The Labour Opposition defended separate Maori representation but, as the debate became increasingly acrimonious, Holyoake charged that such representation was 'a form of apartheid'.[156]

Nevertheless Holyoake did not take the next step to integration. However, in 1967 an Electoral Amendment Act was passed which removed the disqualification preventing Maori, other than half-castes, from standing for European electorates, and allowed Pakeha to stand for Maori seats. The Act did not confer the same rights on voters, although this had been recommended by Corbett in 1957. But, in an odd reversal of party attitudes, the new Leader of the Labour Opposition, Norman Kirk, said, 'it might have been a much wiser step to have moved towards integration by leaving the Maori an area of choice to enrol either as a European or as a Maori elector, thus automatically giving him the right to contest a seat either as a European or as a Maori'.[157] The amendment, and Labour's new stance, were to be significant in the future. In the meantime, however, National had to soldier on without Maori representatives in Parliament. In the 1969 election, which National won with a slightly reduced majority, the party failed to put up Maori candidates for winnable General seats and the four Maori seats, now all fielding Ratana-aligned candidates, were won by Labour, all with enhanced majorities.[158] The Maori Affairs portfolio was now in the hands of Duncan McIntyre, a Hawke's Bay farmer who developed a warm rapport with Maori in some rural areas. He began to shift policy pronouncements from integration towards biculturalism, or rather, in recognition of the growing number of island Polynesians residing in New Zealand, towards multiculturalism.[159]

Although such statements were usually politely received by Maori gatherings, important new divisions were appearing in Maori society though these were not fully reflected in Maori representation in Parliament. National Governments did have a measure of Maori support — albeit not nearly enough to win Maori seats — which was expressed through the tribally organised and rurally oriented New Zealand Maori Council. The three chairmen of the Council — Sir Turi Carroll, Pei Te Hurinui Jones and Sir Graham Latimer — were at one time or another unsuccessful National candidates for Maori seats. While such leaders controlled the Council there was little danger that it would claim more than advisory powers and set out for the long-lost goal of autonomy, as some of the urban radicals who had captured the Auckland District Council would have wished. The Maori Women's Welfare League represented yet another but more progressive strand of Maori opinion, although the women confined their attention largely to social issues. The Ratana/Labour alliance held the middle ground, with Maori trade unionists like Matiu Rata (who won Northern Maori in 1963), Steve Watene (a Mormon who won Eastern Maori in 1963) and Paroane Reweti (who replaced Watene in 1967) beginning to occupy prominent positions, thus reflecting the massive shift since the war of the Maori population into urban areas and unskilled occupations. Then, on the left, there appeared from the late 1960s several radical groups, coming partly from the trade unions, the universities, including Nga Tamatoa (a student group at Auckland University), and the Wellington-based Maori Organisation for Human Rights. Inspired by the Civil Rights movement in the United States and the nationalist movements which had secured independence from European colonial rule in tropical Africa, the Caribbean, and the Pacific, these Maori movements attacked expressions of racism they detected at home, and the 'internal colonialism' which they saw as suppressing Maori rights, aspirations and culture.

In 1968 there was an attempt to revive the Kotahitanga movement, some

80 years after the movement was founded, this time at a meeting on Otiria marae at Kawakawa. Proposals were advanced for Maori self-determination, the ratification of the Treaty of Waitangi, and a symbolic unity under the Maori Queen. Matiu Rata, the member for Northern Maori, attended the meeting and reported that the Kotahitanga movement was a 'long-standing one and occasionally comes to the fore at apparent dissatisfaction', as in this case over the recent Maori Affairs Amendment Act. Rata admitted that many people expressed concern at Maori demands for self-rule, but he thought, from his discussions with them, that they were more interested in getting recognition of the right of Maori to have a greater say in their affairs. He saw the demand for the ratification of the Treaty in the same light: 'as a symbolic recognition of Maoris within New Zealand society in a broad context, although they do not seem to realise that the ratification does not or cannot bestow on individual Maoris what they want from life'.[160] Rata's comments here are a useful demonstration of the role of Maori MPs in Maori community affairs at this time. They tended to follow and even to moderate the demands coming from Maori organisations. But they had also to lend their weight to the growing cultural renaissance and more particularly the revival of Maori language that Nga Tamatoa had called for. It was no longer sufficient for Maori members to be competent in English; they had to embody and promote Maoritanga in their constituencies.

The radicals also became involved in the campaign against sporting contacts with South Africa which raged unabated from 1960, and divided Maori as much as it divided Pakeha. Inevitably the Maori members of Parliament and the political parties were dragged into these controversies. Tirikatene had opposed the visit of the All Blacks to South Africa without Maori; Rata was one of the first to say that it was no better for Maori to go to South Africa as 'honorary whites', as happened in 1970.[161] The National Governments under Holyoake and Marshall were content to 'build bridges' with South Africa, once Maori could be included; Labour, pressed by radical and trade union groups, was forced to oppose any further sporting contacts.

In 1972 a reinvigorated Labour Party, led by Norman Kirk, had a landslide victory with a majority of 23 seats. Labour's Maori members again came home with increased majorities and accumulated 82.4 per cent of the valid votes in the four constituencies, compared with a mere 12.8 per cent for National.[162] Kirk, having failed to persuade, then told the Rugby Union not to proceed with the planned Springbok tour of New Zealand for the winter of 1973. The following summer Christchurch triumphantly hosted the Commonwealth Games, attended by athletes from black African Commonwealth nations.

Later in the year Tanzania's president, Julius Nyerere, made a state visit to New Zealand. Kirk was a dominant figure at the Montreal Commonwealth Conference.

He also quickly developed considerable empathy with Maori and made Waitangi Day a national holiday — the closest a Labour Government came to the long-espoused Ratana demand for the ratification of the Treaty — taking full advantage of the Waitangi ceremonies to bring the races together. This third Labour Government gave its Maori members a full part in Cabinet. Rata and Whetu Tirikatene-Sullivan were elected to Cabinet, and Rata was given Maori Affairs, the first Maori to hold the portfolio since Ngata. There was also an important electoral change, already foreshadowed by Kirk in 1967. In the Maori Affairs Amendment Act of 1974 the definition of a Maori had been broadened to include any person descended from a Maori, and in the 1975 Electoral Amendment Act Maori as so defined were given the option of registering on the Maori or the General roll. Hitherto this option had been confined to half-castes. The option was to be exercised at the next census. Then the number of Maori seats was to be calculated on the same basis as General seats.[163] The Maori electoral population was to be made up of all Maori who opted for the Maori roll, plus their children under eighteen, and each Maori electorate was to have a similar electoral population to General electorates. This left open the possibility of an increase — or a decrease — in the number of Maori seats.

In 1974 the Labour Government began to founder. Kirk's deterioration in health and death left it rudderless; his successor, W. L. Rowling, lacking Kirk's charisma, was unable to establish himself before the election. The economy was hit by a rapid escalation in oil prices and ensuing inflation. Some of the Cabinet, including the two Maori Ministers, were not on top of their portfolios, and were ruthlessly targeted by an invigorated National Opposition, led by R. D. Muldoon. There was racial tension in the suburbs where many new immigrants resented being unable to obtain houses. There were smouldering resentments over the cancelled Springbok tour. All of these opportunities were exploited by Muldoon during the 1975 election campaign and this time National won handsomely, exactly reversing Labour's majority. But once more the four Maori electorates remained faithful to Labour, withstanding the landslide in the General seats, though it was notable that the two Maori Ministers had diminished majorities while the two non-Ministers increased their majorities.[164]

Yet National also got some Maori representation for the first time since 1943. Two candidates of Maori descent won General seats: Ben Couch in Wairarapa and Rex Austin in Awarua. As new members of Parliament they could not expect immediate promotion to Cabinet and McIntyre was again made Minister of Maori Affairs. Having got some Maori members, the National Government was content to retain the existing system and those members began to defend it. In 1976 Couch said that it was National Party policy to retain the four Maori seats, and Austin added that the seats would not be abolished until the Maori people said that they did not want them.[165] Minor changes were introduced by the Electoral Amendment Act of 1976. Although Maori electors retained their right to choose between the Maori and the General rolls, the number of Maori seats was pegged to four, irrespective of the results of the Maori exercise of their option during the 1976 census. According to Elizabeth McLeay, the result was not made public, and Muldoon simply announced that the four Maori seats would remain 'until such time as the Maori people indicate their desire to be on a common roll with no special Maori seats'.[166] But the result was eventually published in *The New Zealand Census of Population and Dwellings*, showing that 145,087 Maori electors and their children had opted for the Maori roll, just over 40 per cent of the total Maori population.

There was much bickering over the state of the rolls for the 1978 election which National won comfortably, though losing some seats. Couch was made Minister of Maori Affairs. He lacked the guile of more sophisticated politicians, and was much criticised for supporting sporting contacts with South Africa, but was well regarded by some rural Maori. In 1979 National gained a third member of Maori descent when Winston Peters was awarded the Hunua seat after a judicial recount and inquiry. In 1980 there was a split in Labour's Maori ranks when Matiu Rata, complaining that the party machine was giving insufficient attention to Maori matters, resigned his seat, formed the Mana Motuhake Party, and contested the ensuing by-election for Northern Maori. He lost by less than a thousand votes to Labour's official candidate, Dr Bruce Gregory.

The 1981 election was one of the most bitterly fought in New Zealand's recent political history. Held in the wake of the 1981 Springbok tour, which had torn the country into warring camps, it was much influenced by that traumatic event. Muldoon, who tacitly encouraged the tour and used the full force of the state to enable it to proceed, held on to the rural seats, where support for the tour had been strongest, but he lost seats in the cities and in the end scraped home by a single seat. The Maori were equally divided over the tour but their decisions at the hustings were probably influenced more by the vigorous intervention of Mana Motuhake in all four seats. The new party plugged a more nationalist line than any before it — more so than even the Ratana candidates in their heyday — but it failed to win any of the seats from Labour. However, the Mana Motuhake candidates did come second in all four electorates.[167]

In the 1984 election Mana Motuhake made a bigger effort, fielding four candidates in General seats as well as four in the Maori seats. This time they conceded second place to National in two of the Maori seats and their total vote was considerably lower than in 1981.[168] Once more the four Labour candidates won handsomely — as did the new-look Labour Party under the leadership of David Lange. Labour's Maori candidates had obtained 77.6 per cent of the total valid vote, compared with 9.6 per cent for Mana Motuhake and 7.1 per cent for National candidates.[169] Now membership of Ratana church was only incidental — only two of the four Maori members were of the Ratana faith. Labour's Maori support was based on class — working class — rather than religious lines, even if most of its Maori representatives, like most of its other members, were now from the professional middle class. Once more two of the four Maori were elected to Cabinet: Koro Wetere, who was given the Maori Affairs and Lands portfolios, and Peter Tapsell who became Minister for Internal Affairs.

The 1984 election result was but another phase in the remorseless accumulation of Maori support for the Labour Party which characterised the whole of the period considered in this section. The loss of Maori support by National was even more dramatic, since National was not picking up Maori voters occasionally disillusioned with Labour. Instead, they voted for minor parties like Social Credit and, more recently, Mana Motuhake. A good many did not vote at all. National hopes that Maori voters would eventually support candidates for the party in Government, as usually happened (with the notable exception of Ngata) before 1935, were dashed. The growing Maori support for Labour since 1935 exactly paralleled the shift in their socio-economic position from a rurally based people, with sadly depleted and underdeveloped land resources in the inter-war period, to a largely urban proletariat after the Second World War. Ngata's land development schemes, continued by the first Labour Government and by National, could not arrest that process. The great bulk of a now rapidly increasing Maori workforce had to turn to unskilled jobs on the wharves, in the freezing works, on public works projects, and in the factories. They became unionised and supported Labour, the party of the unions. In Government that party first gave Maori full unemployment benefits — in due course full employment — child benefits, and a full range of other welfare benefits and services. As Ngata ruefully put it in 1940, 'the Labour policy of increased social benefits, higher wages for less work, and equality of pakeha and Maori was striking a severe blow at the things I had come to regard as fundamental to the maintenance of the individuality of the Maori people'.¹⁷⁰ But Maori voters knew where their material interests lay and remained loyal to Labour.

That loyalty was an expression of the growing significance of class in Maori politics. As Paul Potiki put it in 1971: 'I see most of our problems as being identical with the mass of the working class — made a little more difficult and intensified perhaps by the fact that our skin pigmentation is different.'¹⁷¹ There was an accompanying diminution of tribal if not yet of family considerations. Candidates were still selected on a marae, with the tangata whenua having an advantage over carpet-bagging manuhiri (visitors), but traditional tribal factors were now usually outweighed by family or party considerations. The former were particularly important when a sitting member retired or died in office. In Southern Maori Whetu Tirikatene-Sullivan succeeded her late father, Sir Eruera, in 1967. In Western Maori Matiu Ratana succeeded his late brother, Tokouru, in 1945 and on his death in 1949 was replaced by his wife, Iriaka. In Northern Maori Tipi Paikea succeeded his father in 1943. But it is notable that Steve Watene's son, Apanui, failed in a bid to secure the Eastern Maori nomination on his father's death in 1967. It went instead to the Ratana nominee, Paraone Reweti, a Tauranga waterside worker. The Arawa hosts, who had never had a member of their tribe in the seat, failed to get their candidate nominated. However, they eventually succeeded when Reweti retired in 1981 and Dr Peter Tapsell was selected.¹⁷² Nevertheless, National could not work miracles with prestigious family candidates. Neither Turi Carroll, nephew of Sir James, nor Henare Ngata, the distinguished youngest son of Sir Apirana, could win back Eastern Maori. Nor could J. C. Henare, whose father Tau held Northern Maori from 1914 until 1938, win it back for National. Yet they were opposing sitting Ratana/Labour members whose parliamentary performances had been undistinguished.

Nevertheless their performances in debate and on holding ministerial office were probably on a par with the average Pakeha MP or Minister. Like other members, the Maori MPs had the usual array of duties to constituents but these were exacerbated by numerous social problems facing a rapidly growing and urbanising Maori population. According to David Tabacoff's sampling of Matiu Rata's correspondence from constituents from 1968 to 1972, 149 out of 221 letters were concerned with housing, land, education and social services.¹⁷³ But Maori members had a number of additional problems which did not affect Pakeha members. Maori constituencies, especially Southern Maori, were very much larger than any of the European electorates, and impossible to service properly. Maori members were expected to attend numerous important, though time-consuming, Maori functions, like annual hui of the Ratana and King movements, or tangihanga, and when there to perform political functions. It is notable that all of the Maori MPs whose constituent activities were surveyed by Tabacoff in 1972, except Mrs Tirikatene-Sullivan, regarded attendance at tangi as a necessary obligation.[174] Popular members like Matiu Rata were in much demand as speakers who would provide a Maori viewpoint at student or civil rights meetings. He seldom turned down invitations.[175]

Although the concerns of Maori politics were responding to changes in the socio-economic condition of the Maori people and the internationalisation of race issues, the practice of Maori politics did not change very much after 1935. Having followed Pei Jones on the campaign trail in the 1930 by-election, it is worth accompanying another Maori MP at a later date — this time Paraone Reweti for Eastern Maori in 1967. Thanks to S. K. Jackson's MA thesis on the Eastern Maori electorate, it is possible to present an intimate, though necessarily much abridged, account of that campaign.[176] Reweti set himself a punishing schedule of 46 meetings — in fact he held several more — with two or three per day in different settlements of his wide-flung electorate. Most of the meetings were held on marae; and even when they were not the protocol was distinctly Maori. Reweti's political speeches were always preceded by a ceremonial welcome in which he was aided by several of his kaumatua who travelled with him. The length of these ceremonies meant that Reweti could be late for his next scheduled meeting, but he accepted the fact that he could not abide by 'Pakeha time'. Meetings were also prolonged by religious services and, although Reweti was a member of the Ratana church, he readily accepted services by spokesmen for other denominations as part of the kawa of different marae. This illustrates how a candidate had to know the customs, traditions, psychology and religious affiliations of his hosts; or, if not, to take some kaumatua who could act correctly for him. Reweti's National opponent, Henare Ngata, did this too, as his famous father had done before him — a reminder that no matter what mana a Maori MP might gain from his membership of Parliament, he must always accede to the greater mana and wisdom of local elders on a particular marae. For the most part Reweti's meetings were conducted in Maori, with Reweti only using English when a questioner had done so. By contrast Rata, who accompanied Reweti at several of the meetings, preferred to speak in English to get across the finer points of Labour policy. On the marae Maori voters were quite open about their party allegiance. Even when they opposed Reweti, as was usually the case in the Ngati Porou territory of the East Coast, they politely told him: 'We vote for Henare because he is ours. . . . We like your policies but Henare is our man.'¹⁷⁷ This was a quaint reminder of tribal loyalty to the Ngata family, but of course it was no longer sufficient to put a Ngata back into Parliament, given the support for Labour elsewhere in the electorate. It is also a reminder of the gentlemanly conduct of Maori elections. There was no heckling of candidates — at least in rural areas and small towns not yet touched by the rise of urban Maori radicalism. There was not a great deal of detailed discussion of policy, though Reweti carried with him a Maori version of the party manifesto, and took the opportunity to conjure up memories of the first Labour Government's efforts for Maori welfare. There was much more concern in the electorate about the intentions of the current National Government, especially in view of its recently passed Maori Affairs Amendment Act, with its powers of compulsory purchase of uneconomic fragments of land; and National's apparent intention to abolish the Maori seats. On this last point Reweti promised that Labour would give electors a choice of registering on the Maori or the European rolls and would, if necessary, increase the number of Maori seats. After two years in Parliament, in which he had maintained a fairly low profile, Rewiti was no longer a novice, but he was generally held by his electors to have acquitted himself well. He had a decisive victory, increasing his vote by just over 12 per cent to 60 per cent.

So far as Maori constituents were concerned, performances in Parliament had still to be accounted for and matched by performance on the marae. To Pakeha separate Maori representation was a constitutional oddity, a hangover from the nineteenth century, but Maori had made it something of their own. It had been indigenised.

Conclusion

Separate Maori representation in Parliament, introduced in 1867 as a temporary expedient for a five-year period, has endured in the New Zealand constitution for 119 years. It is not an entrenched clause and could be abolished by legislation passed by a simple majority in the House. Yet, although European opinion in the country has been solidly in favour of abolition[178] and politicians of various hues have often spoken of it, no one has seriously attempted to abolish the seats. And the political parties — other than the New Zealand Party during the 1984 election — have been remarkably coy in committing themselves to abolition. This does not mean that the parties have become philosophically committed to the idea of separate racial representation, but merely that they have seen no sufficient political advantage in abolishing the seats in the face of what was bound to be considerable Maori opposition. That potential opposition has effectively stopped the abolition of the seats.

In the early decades of Maori representation it seemed more important to bring Maori fully into the political process, especially those tribes still disaffected by the wars, than to attempt to abolish the seats. That process was complete by the 1890s when Maori in the remote King Country and Urewera were recording votes and the franchise was granted to Maori women. Thereafter aspiring Maori politicians competed vigorously for representation in Parliament. Indeed between 1890 and 1985 there have been only two uncontested elections: in 1911 and 1919 when Ngata was re-elected unopposed for Eastern Maori. Very often there were numerous candidates, most of whom lost their deposits.[179] During the long reign of the Liberal Party, the first modern party in New Zealand political history, Maori representation was securely established under the aegis of Carroll — though he personally favoured abolition — and the leaders of the Young Maori Party. Even though Reform was inclined towards abolition, it failed to take up the idea and during Coates's premiership relied considerably on the co-operation of the Maori members — even of Ngata who remained in the Opposition. And United could not move on abolition at all since Ngata was a powerful force in their Cabinet.

With the advent of the first Labour Government an enduring alliance was forged between the Ratana movement, which had captured two of the seats by 1935, and Labour. By 1946 Labour was beholden to its Maori 'mandate' and there was little chance that it could abolish the seats without endangering its hold on office — or at least of losing four safe seats. Hitherto the Maori members, with one or two notable exceptions, had supported the party in power. But after 1949 they stuck with Labour through long periods in Opposition — a recognition of the proletarian status of the bulk of the Maori electorate. For more than 40 years Labour's Maori members pleaded for the retention of the seats, and frequently requested more on the ground of increasing Maori population. They won the battle for retention and gained at least the possibility of an increase in seats with the Electoral Amendment Act of 1975. But that possibility was negated when National pegged the seats at four in 1976. The position in 1986 remained unchanged, though Labour was committed to a return to the 1975 situation. The party believed that 'Maori people [were] entitled, as of right, to representation in Parliament in proportion to the number of people who elect[ed] to put themselves on the Maori roll', and that the number of Maori seats should be determined on the same basis as General seats. In this way Maori representation would be retained 'as long as the Maori people so wish because as the original tangata whenua they have a special place in the New Zealand political system'. Since Maori people comprised a disproportionate number of the unemployed, the prison population, under-achievers in education and of those with health problems, separate representation allowed such matters to be more effectively represented and articulated.[180]

In contrast to Labour, National was not beholden to Maori members, having been without a Maori seat since 1943. Moreover, it had been in office most of the time since 1949 and thus had ample opportunity to abolish the seats. But National Governments were extremely cautious in moving towards abolition. In the 1950s Corbett was thinking of a gradual erosion of the Maori electorate through allowing Maori to register on the European rolls and the eventual abolition of the Maori seats. But that policy was not followed through by National Governments in the 1960s, since National still hoped to win at least one Maori seat, but possibly also because the party hierarchy deferred to the plea of its Maori Advisory Committee, led by Mat Te Hau, not to abolish the seats.[181] But in 1967, in a final admission of its inability to win back even one of the Maori seats, National altered the electoral law to allow Maori to stand for European seats. Little advantage was taken of this opportunity[182] and it was not until 1975 that National put up Maori candidates in winnable General seats. Couch and Austin were elected. With this National decided to peg the Maori seats at four, hoping that in due course the seats would be whittled away by transfer of Maori voters to the General rolls. In 1986 the party was in favour of a 'phased abolition' to be carried out over the next two or three elections.[183]

Critics have charged that separate representation amounts to apartheid. This is a considerable distortion since in South Africa blacks were never allowed parliamentary representation, whereas in New Zealand Maori have been represented in the national Parliament on conditions similar to those applying to Europeans. On the other hand, supporters of separate representation for Maori say that it has been the only guarantee that Maori would be represented in Parliament at all. This was largely true for the 1870s and 1880s, but less so afterwards, as Carroll and much later Couch, Austin and Peters demonstrated. Had the Maori seats been abolished, then it would have been necessary for Maori candidates to secure the nomination of one or other of the main parties. In the twentieth century independents and representatives of small parties found it well-nigh impossible to get elected, given the first past the post electoral system. However, it is likely that the main parties would have felt morally obliged to put up more Maori candidates for winnable seats, as National, unable to win Maori seats, ultimately decided to do. But whether Maori would have got more than four seats, as they deserved to get on the basis of their total population, remains a moot point; probably not, since Pakeha New Zealanders have never been able to take their tokenism very far, as can be seen from their apprehension whenever the Maori representatives in Parliament have held the balance of power, the disparaged 'Maori mandate'.

In fact the advantages to Maori of occasionally holding the balance of power in Parliament have been more apparent than real, since taking too much advantage would have brought a Pakeha backlash and the Opposition to power. There was more to be gained by getting powerful positions in Cabinet, especially the portfolio of Maori Affairs, as Ngata above all demonstrated. But, as his fall showed, a vigorous Maori Minister could go too far for the Pakeha bureaucracy and electorate to stomach. There were some signs of a similar reaction to the Maori Ministers and policies of the third Labour Government. In short, Maori representation in Parliament and in Cabinet has been acceptable to Pakeha New Zealand so long as it has not gone too far. It has remained a comfortable form of tokenism to be tolerated until Maori became assimilated or integrated into the dominant community. This was long assumed to be the inevitable destiny of the Maori people, but it has not come about. They have retained a distinct identity, if not a political autonomy, and jealously guard separate representation as an expression of that identity. But separate representation has never really been seen by Pakeha New Zealanders as a proper expression of biculturalism. If it were to be so recognised, there could be a demand from other ethnic communities, like the various Island Polynesian groups, now integrated into the General seats, for their own representatives in Parliament.

But, so far as Maori are concerned, the four seats have become a last guarantee of their tangata whenua status and their rights as a minority in their own country. Progressively, since the Treaty of Waitangi was signed and New Zealand was annexed as a British colony, Maori autonomy has been whittled away. Once the colonists got self-government under the 1852 Constitution Act and subsequently gained responsibility for domestic, including native, affairs they gradually asserted their control over the Maori population and brought them within the realm of law and order, much of it locally made by the settler-controlled Parliament. Maori resisted the complete fulfilment of this process for many years, particularly by creating extra-parliamentary organisations of their own, like the King movement and later the Kotahitanga Parliament. These were condoned by Europeans so long as they remained innocuous, but were never officially recognised, let alone permitted to exercise legal powers. At best the European Governments were prepared to recognise lower-level tribal committees with strictly confined powers of local government, as happened with Carroll's Maori Councils Act of 1900. Every Maori effort to create a national organisation with effective and autonomous powers was fenced off, as happened with the Maori War Effort Organisation which Tirikatene wanted to vest with real and enduring power. Instead, the New Zealand Maori Council was created in 1962, but it was no more than an advisory body whose advice could be and was ignored.

So, in the last resort, Maori organisations had to come back to Maori representation in Parliament as their last vestige of a lost autonomy. The King movement, hitherto ostentatiously aloof and haplessly trying to erect their own Parliament, did so when they backed Major Te Wheoro, a former Kupapa, for the Western Maori seat in 1886. The Kotahitanga leaders, fruitlessly manoeuvring between their own Parliament and the real Parliament in Wellington, ultimately had to come behind Carroll and the Young Maori Party. Ratana was shrewd enough not to go his own political way, but merely sought to capture the Four Quarters; so too the latest to attempt to construct a new nationalist party, Matiu Rata, though his Mana Motuhake failed to capture any of the Maori seats.

In the meantime some Maori radicals, frustrated at the powerlessness of Maori in the parliamentary machine, have been trying to reclaim their lost autonomy, or 'Maori sovereignty' as they now call it. According to Dr Ranginui Walker, Maori sovereignty has been perpetuated all along in the 'rangatiratanga (chieftainships) over their lands, homes and treasured possessions' guaranteed to the Maori in the second article of the Treaty of Waitangi. If only 3 million acres of that Maori land remain today, the 'turangawaewae (nurturing ground) of Maori sovereignty consists of the 600–700 marae reserves throughout New Zealand, and the hearts and minds of the people who know that they are the tangata whenua'.[184] An English constitutional lawyer would hardly agree, and would point to Article 1 of the Treaty whereby Maori sovereignty, equated with kawanatanga (governorship), was transferred to the British Queen. The differences are irreconcilable, with each side interpreting the different articles of the Treaty according to different linguistic and cultural traditions, but they are an earnest of the gulf which still divides the races in New Zealand. That gulf has not been bridged constitutionally — except by that long-standing 'temporary' expedient, the four Maori seats.

However, the Maori dilemma remains: the four seats were the maximum concession they could extract from the Pakeha parties; frequent Maori requests for additional seats, on the strength of the increasing Maori population, were always turned down, often on the ground that in terms of votes cast Maori were considerably over-represented by four seats.[185] By operating within the system Maori leaders were not able to gain very great benefits, even when they were in

Government, without attracting a Pakeha backlash. All that can be said is that they did considerably better in the twentieth century than in the nineteenth, thanks to a fall-off in the European demand for Maori land and a willingness of twentieth-century Governments to allow Maori a share of development and welfare expenditures. But such Governments seldom went far in providing the affirmative action necessary to lift the Maori population in the socio-economic scale to the level of the European population.

Although most articulate Maori opinion favours the retention, indeed the increase, of the Maori seats, a few prominent Maori recently spoke out in favour of abolition. Robert Mahuta, Director of Waikato University's Centre for Maori Studies, supported abolition on the ground that an influx of Maori voters onto the General rolls would force members for those constituencies to 'become more knowledgeable about, and pay more attention to, Maori voters and interests'.[186] Hiwi Tauroa, the Race Relations Conciliator, wrote a series of pamphlets under the general title of *Let's Work Together*, taking a similar approach. But neither attracted much support. The attitude of the rank and file is harder to estimate, although a poll conducted in 1976 showed that 56 per cent of Maori respondents favoured the continuation of the separate seats.[187]

Yet, despite the continuing Maori plea for separate representation, there was no corresponding grassroots support for the Maori seats in terms of registration and voting on the Maori roll. Since the introduction of a Maori roll in 1949 there was a persistent, if sometimes slightly fluctuating, fall-off in the percentage of eligible Maori registering on the Maori roll, despite the introduction of compulsory registration in 1956. In 1949 77.7 per cent of the eligible Maori population were registered, but by 1975, when the basis of registration was changed from half or more to anyone descended from a Maori, the percentage had fallen to 58.3. There was an even larger fall-off in valid votes as a percentage of the total eligible population — from 84.8 per cent in 1949 to 27.7 per cent in 1975. Though the change in 1975 increased the potential Maori electorate very considerably — from some 118,180 persons of half or more Maori descent in 1975 to some 154,400 who were descended from a Maori — there was no corresponding increase in the number of registrations on the Maori rolls.[188] The increases in total enrolments since 1975 were more or less in line with the natural increase in population, plus the additional numbers resulting from the lowering of the voting age from 20 to 18 in that year. At the time of the July 1984 election only 77,564 Maori, out of an estimated 209,600 who were eligible, were registered on the Maori electoral rolls. Some 132,000 were registered on the General rolls or not registered at all.[189] This suggests that nearly two-thirds of Maori voters did not care about maintaining the Maori seats — or that they had chosen to vote in marginal General electorates where their vote could be more useful, something that party organisers were only too willing to encourage. There was probably an advantage for the Labour Party here: with four safe seats from the Maori electorates, there was much to be gained by getting as many 'Maori' voters as possible onto the rolls in marginal General electorates.[190] According to one recent analysis, there would have been a slight gain for National in the 1981 election if the four Maori seats had been abolished and the votes redistributed among the existing General seats.[191] However, any future abolition and redistribution would also require a redrawing of electoral boundaries and that would not necessarily confer advantage on one party or the other.

Another feature of Maori electoral behaviour over recent years was the high and increasing percentage of Maori who did not vote or who cast invalid votes. Maori voting was always been hampered by insufficient polling booths over their wide-flung electorates, although this was less so in recent years when improved transport and urbanisation meant that it was easier for the bulk of Maori voters to reach polling booths. Yet, as Professor Chapman's graphs clearly indicated, there was a steady rise in non-voting from the 1950s. Since 1966 Non-Vote has been the second largest 'party' after Labour.[192] 'Special Votes Disallowed' also rose alarmingly, especially in the 1981 and 1984 elections, due largely to failure to register or to technical errors in the exercise of the Maori option.[193] Here is yet another indication that separate Maori representation, though desperately defended on principle by most articulate Maori, had become so complicated in electoral terms that it was increasingly failing to involve the rank and file of the Maori population. And for a long time both major parties tended to accept the status quo while awaiting a clear statement from the Maori people for abolition. That was not forthcoming.[194]

Nevertheless the system does provide those persons descended from a Maori with a free choice to vote on the Maori or the General roll; and an opportunity to change from one roll to another after each census. The Maori option exercised in 1982 resulted in a net loss of 4544 voters from the Maori roll, although there was a net gain to the Maori roll of 973 from the 1986 Maori option. The total Maori electoral population in 1984 — made up of those Maori opting for the Maori roll, plus their children — was 140,421, giving an average electoral population of 35,105 per Maori seat, some 2500 more than the average for the 91 General seats. This was not enough to justify the creation of another Maori seat. On the other hand the average valid votes per seat in the Maori electorates in 1984 was 14,783, compared with an average of 20,550 for the General seats; as ever, the Maori members have been elected by fewer voters than the Pakeha representatives.

Such cold statistics mask a more complex human situation, including the fact that the Maori people, depressed economically, frequently changing addresses, and not yet fully literate in an alien European culture, were notoriously reluctant to fill in and return registration forms. Many eligible Maori voters — perhaps as high as one-third — are unregistered on either roll, and thus take no part in the political process. Many are young Maori who are unschooled in their rights as citizens, let alone in the niceties of the constitution. They have not been politicised by the Maori members of Parliament, or by the political parties. Nor have they been recruited to the slim ranks of the urban radicals. Politics, particularly that distinctly Maori variety waged mainly on the marae, is very much an activity of the middle-aged and the elderly. For them separate Maori representation remains as the best that they could secure: the crumbs that have fallen from the Pakeha table.

10

Towards a Radical Reinterpretation of New Zealand History:
The Role of the Waitangi Tribunal

Until recently, most commentators have relied on the English language text of the Treaty of Waitangi. According to this the Māori chiefs transferred their sovereignty to the Queen of England, were guaranteed the possession of their lands, forests, fisheries, and other properties, yielded a right of pre-emption to the Crown to purchase their land, and were granted royal protection and the rights and privileges of British subjects. New Zealanders have generally assumed that these provisions of the Treaty have been upheld. The Treaty has been seen as a fundamental instrument of a broader policy — of bringing Māori and their lands within the compass of British (and in due course colonial-made) law; a policy of assimilating the Māori, thereby making one people, according to Hobson's well-known dictum, 'he iwi tahi tatou'. That saga has formed a central theme of most Pākehā versions of New Zealand history.

But, we need to remember that the Treaty of Waitangi was written in two languages, English and Māori. With the exception of the English language text signed by 39 Māori at Manukau and at Waikato Heads — often subsequently regarded as the 'official' version — all of the copies signed by Māori were in their language. Māori people have usually regarded this as the real and binding version of the Treaty. Its meaning to them has been very different from the

---

Reprinted from I. H. Kawharu, ed., *Waitangi: Maori and Pakeha Perspectives of the Treaty of Waitangi*, Oxford University Press, Auckland, 1989, pp. 158–178. That essay, in turn, was a revised and updated version of an essay originally published in *The New Zealand Journal of History*, vol. 21, no. 1 (1987), pp. 173–188.

meaning Pākehā have taken from the English version. Some of the key concepts in the English text, like sovereignty, could not easily be rendered into Māori. The translators fell back on transliteration, with sovereignty rendered as 'kāwanatanga', or governorship. That concept was not unknown to Māori since it had been used in translations of the scriptures and in reference to the British governor of New South Wales. Under the Treaty, kāwanatanga was to be exercised by a new governor in New Zealand. According to the preamble, he was to protect the Māori and their property from Europeans now colonising the country. However, the power and autonomy of the chiefs — their 'rangatiratanga o o ratou wenua o ratou kainga me o ratou taonga' (their chieftainship over their lands, their homes and other treasures) — was expressly preserved in the second article of the Treaty. To the Māori chiefs who signed the Treaty, that rangatiratanga was far more than a guarantee of their possession of land and other properties; it was also a guarantee of their autonomy and authority, above all their mana, as chiefs; even, in some recent interpretations,[1] a guarantee of Māori sovereignty. Such Māori views of the Treaty have been frequently voiced at Māori gatherings since 1840, have sometimes found their way into the written record, and have been increasingly noticed by historians and lawyers over recent years.

The fact that there are two histories of the Treaty of Waitangi, stemming from the English and Māori texts, is a sure reminder that Hobson's hope that the Treaty would facilitate the formation of one people has not been realised. Because of the determined efforts of the Māori people to resist assimilation and preserve their identity, the Treaty has become the basis, rather, for the coexistence of two peoples within one nation.

The recent attention of historians and lawyers to the Māori text of the Treaty has provided an academic background to attempts by successive Governments to give better recognition to the promises of the Treaty. Ruth Ross's seminal essay, 'The Treaty of Waitangi: Texts and Interpretations', published in 1972,[2] was the first significant analysis of the two texts of the Treaty, and of the role of Henry Williams in devising a Māori text and persuading the Māori chiefs assembled at Waitangi to accept it. D. F. McKenzie has taken the process of textual analysis much further.[3] Claudia Orange's published doctoral thesis[4] also considerably elaborates the textual studies, while making the fullest examination yet of the signings of the Treaty, at Waitangi and elsewhere, and of its continuing significance for both races in subsequent New Zealand history. She has done more than any other historian to recover that submerged Māori history of the Treaty which has hitherto existed largely in oral tradition.

Such work of historians has been paralleled by that of lawyers. Until recently it was common for academic lawyers to reiterate court judgments on the Treaty, stemming from that of Chief Justice Prendergast in 1877 to the effect that it was a nullity. In 1934 H. F. von Haast summed up the prevailing view by arguing that the Treaty was not cognisable in international law and was only applicable in domestic law in so far as certain provisions had been adopted in local statutes.[5] Von Haast's views were generally accepted by lawyers — and by historians like James Rutherford[6] — until the late 1960s. Then a new generation of academic lawyers, including F. M. Auburn,[7] W. A. McKean,[8] P. G. McHugh[9] and D. V. Williams,[10] inspired by changing interpretations of international law and important decisions in the courts, especially in North America, began to chip away at the established doctrine. In consequence, the Treaty has been resuscitated: it has been deemed cognisable in the colonial law of the time, like similar treaties in other British territories. Like the historians, the lawyers have not been content to rely on the English language text. They have drawn attention to recent judgments in North American courts where assenting parties of treaties have been required to pay attention to the indigenous language texts, and the promises made by the British Crown when the treaties were negotiated. Accordingly, the way has been paved for radical new interpretations of the Treaty of Waitangi and its role in New Zealand history.

The Waitangi Tribunal, as constituted by The Treaty of Waitangi Act 1975 and its amendment of 1985, has been given a vital role in that reinterpretation. Both pieces of legislation, it should be noted, were passed by Labour Governments and sponsored by Māori Ministers of Māori Affairs: the first Act by Matiu Rata and the amendment by Koro Wetere. The preamble of the 1975 Act noted that the English and Māori texts of the Treaty differed from one another, and section 5 required the Tribunal to have regard to both texts. Moreover, for the purposes of the Act, the Tribunal was to have 'exclusive authority' to determine the meaning and effect of the Treaty as embodied in the two texts, and to decide issues raised by the differences between them. Section 6 of the Act allowed 'any Maori' to submit a claim to the Tribunal on the grounds that he [sic] was 'prejudicially affected' by any Act, regulations, or Order in Council, or any policy or practice of the Crown, currently in force or proposed, which were inconsistent with the principles of the Treaty. This section had some important limitations. No Pākehā could submit a claim. Although subsection 1 did allow Māori claims against any legislation, policy, or practice currently in force, subsection 6 specifically excluded from the Tribunal's jurisdiction 'anything done or omitted before the commencement of this Act'. Moreover, the Tribunal itself had no power of remedy; if it considered a claim to be well founded it could merely recommend that the Crown compensate for or remove the prejudice. Section 7 allowed the Tribunal to refuse to investigate any claim that was deemed trivial, frivolous, or vexatious, or for which there was an adequate remedy elsewhere. Section 8 required the Tribunal to ascertain whether any draft legislation referred to it was contrary to the principles of the Treaty.

In interpreting the meaning, principles and effect of the Treaty, the Tribunal could hardly confine itself to the two texts. It had to examine the contemporary intellectual climate to assess what was in the minds of the men who made, negotiated and signed the Treaty. That in turn required an investigation of the historical traditions of both sides: on the British side some centuries of jurisprudence and colonial policy; on the Māori side orally recorded traditions of lore and custom. There was no way of avoiding such historical analysis, despite the limitation in the Act excluding actions or omissions of the Crown before 1975.

The Tribunal was to consist of three persons: the Chief Judge of the Māori Land Court, who was to be chairman, and two others appointed by the Governor-General, one on the recommendation of the Minister of Justice, the other (who was to be a Māori) on the recommendation of the Minister of Māori Affairs. The original appointees were Chief Judge Kenneth Gillanders Scott, L. H. Southwick, an Auckland QC, and as Māori representative, Sir Graham Latimer, chairman of the New Zealand Māori Council. Their first full hearing concerned the claim of Joseph Hawke and others of the Ngāti Whātua tribe of Orakei to fishing rights in the Waitemata Harbour.[11] Ironically, the tangata whenua of Tamaki Makaurau, whose tribal territory was now reduced to a tiny fragment of the metropolitan area of greater Auckland, were obliged to meet the Tribunal in the unfamiliar surroundings of the ballroom of Auckland's plush Intercontinental Hotel. Hawke lost the claim, though he subsequently lodged a new one that concentrated on the loss of land at Bastion Point. In 1980, on the retirement of Judge Scott, E.T. J. Durie was appointed Chief Judge of the Māori Land Court — the first Māori to hold that position — and became chairman of the Tribunal. In 1984 Paul Temm, another Auckland QC, replaced Southwick. Judge Durie transformed the Tribunal, both in procedure — henceforth it met on the marae of the claimants, and observed their kawa in its hearings — and in its philosophical approach to the issues.

It is not possible in a short essay to review all the findings of the Tribunal in the ten years of its existence under the 1975 Act. In any case several claims were either dismissed or withdrawn before the Tribunal completed its hearing, and need no further discussion. I shall examine six claims — Motunui, Kaituna,

Manukau, Te Reo Māori, Orakei and Muriwhenua fishing — all of them presided over by Judge Durie. And I shall use the Tribunal's findings to illustrate its role in interpreting — and reinterpreting — the Treaty and its place in New Zealand history.

The Motunui claim was lodged by Aila Taylor on behalf of Te Atiawa of Taranaki, who held that they were or would be prejudicially affected by the discharge of sewage and industrial waste (coming mainly from the proposed Motunui Syngas plant) on to their traditional fishing grounds and reefs at Waitara. Such pollution was said to be inconsistent with the principles of the Treaty of Waitangi. The Tribunal reported its findings in March 1983, upholding the claimants' case.[12]

Before setting out its findings on the specifics of the Motunui claim, the Tribunal made some important statements on the interpretation of the Treaty, based largely on a memorandum submitted by the Department of Māori Affairs. On the question of a possible conflict between the two texts, the memorandum quoted Lord McNair's text, *The Law of Treaties*, to the effect that 'in the absence of a provision to the contrary neither text is superior to the other', but that it was permissible to interpret one text by reference to the other. However, the memorandum went on to argue that 'should any question arise of which text should prevail, the Māori text should be treated as the prime reference' since this was the text signed by most of the chiefs. The Tribunal made no comment. Nevertheless, it did decide that it was not obliged by statute, nor the precedents of international law, nor Māori tradition, to confine itself to a literal interpretation of the texts of the Treaty. It cited from the Māori Affairs memorandum a paper by I. M. Sinclair, who argued that if the language of treaties was ambiguous or obscure (which was certainly the case with the Treaty of Waitangi) recourse could be had to 'extraneous means of interpretation such as consideration of surrounding circumstances'. Furthermore, treaties were to be interpreted 'with reference to their declared or apparent objects and purposes'; and even 'the subsequent conduct and practice of the parties in relation to the treaty'.[13] Finally, the Māori Affairs memorandum cited decisions of the United States Supreme Court to the effect that treaties made with Indian tribes were to be construed 'in the sense which they would naturally be understood by the Indians'.[14]

All of this argument was relevant to the interpretation of the two texts of the Treaty of Waitangi. It was accepted by the Tribunal 'from the standpoint of European legal concepts', and as being consistent with a Māori approach to the Treaty, which 'would imply that its wairua or spirit is something more than a literal construction of the actual words used can provide. The spirit of the Treaty transcends the sum total of its component written words and puts narrow or literal interpretations out of place.'[15]

The Treaty was not to be regarded as simply a tract for its time, a 'Maori Magna Carta'. 'It was not intended to merely fossilise a status quo, but to provide direction for future growth and development.' It was to be 'the foundation for a developing social contract'. That contract was not what Hobson had hoped, the formation of one people, but rather the coexistence of two peoples within a single nation. 'The Treaty was an acknowledgement of Maori existence, of their prior occupation of the land and of an intent that the Maori presence would remain and be respected. . . . It established the regime not for uni-culturalism, but for bi-culturalism.' The Tribunal concluded that the Treaty was 'capable of a measure of adaptation to meet new and changing circumstances provided there is a measure of consent and an adherence to its broad principles'.[16]

Although these findings of the Tribunal represent the collective view of its members, there is little doubt that the new chairman, Judge Durie, had a powerful influence in the formulation of that view. In two later lectures on the work of the Tribunal he made similar points. He told a Wellington District Law Society Seminar in September 1986 that 'we can read into the Treaty what we might modernly call the heads of agreement for a bi-cultural development in partnership'.[17] He went on to discuss the novel procedures — particularly respect for marae protocol — that the Tribunal had adopted, and added that the Tribunal had 'regard not only to civil law, but to Maori customary or ancestral law as well'.[18] Overseas this interplay of civil and customary law was common, and customary law held status within the legal systems, in contrast to New Zealand where there had been a steady determination of Governments to apply one law to Māori and Pākehā alike. Lecturing to a race relations class at Auckland University, Judge Durie said that 'as a constitutional document it [the Treaty] must be always speaking. To speak in our time it must be stripped of its old law clothing, and . . . its essential body exposed to view.'[19]

With such general comments in mind, it is useful to examine the Tribunal's interpretation of specific guarantees in the Treaty in relation to the Motunui claim. Like most of the other claims before the Tribunal, Motunui was more concerned with fishing rights than land; as Judge Durie put it later, 'the first Maori claims to the Tribunal came from the sea as though the land was no longer theirs'.[20]

Māori fisheries were specifically protected in the English but not the Māori text of the Treaty. The few Māori who signed the English text at Manukau and Waikato Heads should have been informed of the guarantee, but with the official publication of this text in 1869 and on numerous subsequent occasions, Māori people generally became aware of it. They made many unsuccessful petitions to Parliament and appeals to the courts for the guarantee to be upheld. It is therefore not surprising that they also appealed to the Waitangi Tribunal, more especially as their traditional fishing resources were threatened by recent economic developments.

In looking at Te Atiawa's claim to the Waitara fishing grounds, the Tribunal accepted their view that these were indeed part of their tribal taonga, their tribal 'treasure troves'.[21] Moreover, the Tribunal argued that the Māori people had retained control over their fisheries by virtue of 'te tino rangatiratanga' in the second article of the Māori text of the Treaty. In the English version of this article 'rangatiratanga' had been interpreted as possession, but the Tribunal argued that 'te tino rangatiratanga' could be taken to mean 'the highest chieftainship' or, indeed, 'the sovereignty [sic] of their lands', and that the 'Maori text of the Treaty would have conveyed to the Maori people that . . . they were to be protected not only in the possession of their fishing grounds but in the mana to control them . . . in accordance with their own customs'.[22]

The Tribunal's interpretation of the guarantees in the second article of the Treaty had radical implications, since it struck at the very heart of the long-standing Pākehā doctrine that the transfer of sovereignty in Article 1 provided the foundation for one system of law, British law. Nevertheless, the Tribunal's final recommendations on the Motunui case were mild and conciliatory. It drew attention to the long title and preamble of the 1975 Act, which referred to its responsibility to make recommendations for the 'practical application of the Treaty'. Indeed the Tribunal concluded that it was 'not inconsistent with the spirit and intention of the Treaty . . . that the Crown and the Maori people affected should . . . agree to alter the incidence of the strict terms of the Treaty in order to seek acceptable practical solutions'.[23] In this respect Te Atiawa had agreed to seek a workable compromise. The immediate result was the suspension of the proposed effluent outfall off Motunui, but more than five years later a compromise solution that involved land-based treatment and a new outfall at Waitara had only just emerged. It was likely to take four years to complete.[24]

The Kaituna claim was lodged by Sir Charles Bennett and others of the Ngāti Pikiao tribe against the proposal of the Rotorua City Corporation to divert treated sewage from Lake Rotorua into the Kaituna river. Once again the Tribunal's findings included a lengthy discussion on the Treaty. Much of this was based on memoranda submitted by two academics: by Professor Hugh Kawharu, then Head of Māori Studies and Anthropology at Auckland

University, who discussed the Māori understanding of the meaning of the Treaty; and by P. G. McHugh, Fellow of Sidney Sussex College, Cambridge, who dealt with the legal aspects of the Treaty in relation to customary and colonial law.

Kawharu argued that, since the Māori had an oral culture, the chiefs at Waitangi had placed their faith in the spoken words of the missionary translator, Henry Williams, who was more successful than newcomers like Hobson could have been in persuading them to sign the Treaty. Although the British regarded the transfer of sovereignty as providing them with the authority to establish all the paraphernalia of a Crown Colony, the chiefs saw themselves as surrendering only a part of their rangatiratanga — that which had hitherto 'enabled them to make war, exact retribution, consume or enslave their vanquished enemies and generally exercise power over life and death. . . . [T]hey would [not] wittingly have divested themselves of all their spiritually sanctioned powers. . . . They would have believed they were retaining . . . their customary rights and duties as trustees for their tribal groups.'[25]

Drawing on McHugh's paper, the Tribunal noted that for more than a hundred years it had been assumed in the courts that the provisions of the Treaty had 'no place in New Zealand law', except where they had been incorporated in municipal law.[26] The Tribunal went on to summarise McHugh's attack on this doctrine. McHugh had argued that the 'Colonial policy of the British Crown included punctilious recognition of the rights of indigenous peoples wherever the British flag was raised'. He cited evidence for this from British policy in North America from the beginning of the seventeenth century, including a Crown right of pre-emption to purchase land. And he concluded that by 1840 it was 'a settled principle of colonial law that the land rights of aboriginal people were protected by the Crown', citing Lord Normanby's Instructions to Hobson to this effect. McHugh maintained that the rights guaranteed in the Treaty were respected by New Zealand courts until the Prendergast judgment of 1877, which argued that the Treaty 'could not transform the natives' right of occupation into one of legal character since, so far as it purported to cede the sovereignty of New Zealand, it was a "simple nullity" for no body politic existed capable of making such a cession of sovereignty'. McHugh argued that Prendergast's proposition was wrong since it was based on a concept of international law and not on established principles of colonial law. All subsequent judgments that applied the Prendergast argument were wrong for the same reason.[27]

The Tribunal concluded that there was 'much force in Mr McHugh's argument',[28] but it did not attempt to make a ruling, preferring to leave that to the courts in the event of the matter being raised there. Since the Tribunal was not a court it could not issue judgments, but it could, and did, speak out boldly on matters within its statutory jurisdiction. The Tribunal did have such authority to make a finding on whether any act or omission of the Crown under any statute, regulation, or Order in Council that had remained in force since 1975 was inconsistent with the *principles* of the Treaty: 'any Act on the statute books that prejudicially affects a Maori may give rise to a claim no matter when it was passed by Parliament'.[29] It added that this 'wide power enables us to look beyond strict legalities so that we can in a proper case identify where the spirit of the Treaty is not being given due recognition'.[30] Likewise, the Tribunal's Act required that any future legislation or policy of the Crown 'must be measured against the principles of the Treaty'.[31] And the Tribunal concluded:

> This is a remarkable result. From being a 'simple nullity' the Treaty of Waitangi has become a document of importance approaching the status of a constitutional instrument so far as Maoris are concerned. . . . But it does expose the Crown to the risk of a claim that the statute in question is in conflict with the Treaty and . . . it would seem prudent for those responsible for legislation to recognise the danger inherent in drafting statutes or regulations without measuring such instruments against the principles in the Treaty.[32]

So far as the Kaituna claim was concerned, the Tribunal concluded that the proposed pipeline to discharge effluent into the Kaituna river was likely to prejudice the claimants' spiritual or cultural values and reduce the quality of their fisheries in the river. It also found that Ngāti Pikiao had retained uninterrupted ownership of the river since 1840, and with that the right to fish the river, its estuary and the adjacent sea, and to use the flora along its banks. These were taonga that were guaranteed to them by the Treaty. Finally, the Tribunal recommended that the Rotorua City Corporation investigate alternative land-based sites for disposing of the effluent that would avoid Lake Rotorua and the Kaituna. The corporation subsequently adopted a scheme to spray treated effluent on to the Whakarewarewa State Forest.

By contrast to Kaituna, the Manukau claim was large and complex; the most wide-ranging that the Tribunal had so far considered. It was lodged by Nganeko Minhinnick and Te Puaha ki Manuka, a section of the Waikato-Tainui tribal group, who claimed that their use and enjoyment of their land and traditional fishing groups had been or would be prejudiced by a variety of private and public works on or adjacent to the Manukau Harbour. A major concern was the proposal by New Zealand Steel Ltd to take water from the Waikato river for a slurry pipeline and to discharge the effluent into the Manukau. Such works were said to be in contravention of the promise of the Treaty of Waitangi to full, exclusive, and undisturbed possession of Māori lands, homes and fisheries.

To provide a context for the events since 1975, which were within its jurisdiction, the Tribunal embarked on a lengthy history of the sufferings of the Tainui and Ngāti Whātua peoples of the Manukau, 'because consequences have followed that still have their effects today'.[33] The Tribunal examined what it called 'The Land Wars: Te Riri Pākehā or "the White Man's Anger"'; that is, the attacks on the homes and property of the Māori people of Manukau on the eve of the invasion of Waikato in 1863, and the subsequent confiscation of much of their land under the New Zealand Settlements Act 1863. This survey was based mainly on the Report of the 1927 Royal Commission on Confiscated Lands which in turn had relied largely on the contemporary observations of J. E. Gorst in his book *The Maori King* (1864). But the Tribunal also referred to the work of more recent historians and quoted at length from Keith Sinclair's *The Origins of the Maori Wars* (1957). The Tribunal concluded: 'all sources agree that the Tainui people of Waikato never rebelled but were attacked by British troops in direct violation of Article II of the Treaty of Waitangi'.[34] Altogether 58,877 hectares of land were confiscated, although small portions of this were subsequently returned, including some land around the marae at Ihumatao where the Tribunal held its sittings.

From the confiscations during the wars of the 1860s, the Tribunal went on to investigate 'Te Riri Ture, the Anger of the Law', whereby private purchasers and public authorities used a variety of legal means to acquire much of the Māori land that had remained after the confiscations. The loss of land had left an enduring mark on the Māori people of Manukau: 'For them it is as though the confiscations and dealings occurred yesterday.' But there could be no 'happier base' for the coexistence of the races 'that was once the hope implicit in the Treaty of Waitangi' unless 'we . . . lay bare the truth of history for he who does not know the past will never understand the present'.[35] Of course the Tribunal could not right the wrongs of the past — at least those prior to 1975 — so it fell back on an impassioned plea to Government to do so: 'We are frankly appalled by the events of the past and by the effect that they have had on the Manukau tribes. Unlike our jurisdiction, that of the Government is not constrained. . . . It may be practicable to provide a measure of relief at this stage. . . . [W]e would urge that steps be taken now, for they are long overdue.'[36] No such relief has been provided.

The Manukau claim was not confined to the land; the claim to the harbour and its food resources was equally important. As the Tribunal put it: 'The harbour was as much owned and apportioned to the care and use of different tribes as the land was. To the local tribes the Manukau was their garden of the sea. Accordingly, to them any loss of the use of the harbour is as much a loss as the loss of the land.'[37] With the harbour the Tribunal had an opportunity to take up and develop issues already investigated in the Motunui and Kaituna claims.

For a start the Tribunal dealt with what it called the 'comprehensive claim' — to ownership of the Manukau Harbour. The Tribunal acknowledged that under English common law the Crown owned harbours and foreshores, and that this had been consistently maintained in legislation and in court decisions in New Zealand, although in the case of the Manukau the tidal lands had been vested in the Auckland Harbour Board by the Manukau Harbour Control Act of 1911. On the other hand the Manukau tribes maintained that the harbour was theirs under customary law and that the Treaty promised them that Māori customary law would prevail: 'It is on the Treaty that they pin their hopes, the hope that the Treaty will be upheld as the supreme law.'[38] In the end the Tribunal did not support the claim of the Manukau tribes to ownership of the harbour; it merely suggested that they should have a share, as kaitiaki or guardians, in the control of it.

The Tribunal then proceeded to examine the vexed issue of fishing rights, noting that section 88(2) of the Fisheries Act 1983 specified that 'nothing in this Act shall affect any Maori fishing rights'. However, the question remained of whether there were any such rights, since the courts had persistently denied that the fishing rights guaranteed by the Treaty had any legal standing. Although legislation had allowed Māori fishing grounds to be set aside, this had not been done — except in the case of some oyster beds set aside on the Manukau at the turn of the twentieth century. Only one of these, known as the Needles Reserve, was still in existence, but the oysters there had died. As the Tribunal put it: 'For the Manukau people the law is as empty as the oyster shells on the Needles Reserves . . . .'[39] Although the Fisheries Act of 1983 allowed special reserves to be established, past experience of the Ministry of Agriculture and Fisheries suggested that Māori fishing grounds would not be reserved. The Tribunal admitted that the reservation of Māori fishing grounds had been destroyed by pollution, public works and reclamations.[40]

Yet the Tribunal was not content to confine its findings to traditional fishing and held that the Manukau tribes should have a share in commercial fishing in the harbour. It noted that some countries, more particularly Canada and the

United States, had gone much further than New Zealand in expanding customary rights 'not just to fish, but to husband and harvest fishing for domestic and commercial purposes'.[41] Yet the Ministry of Agriculture and Fisheries, though it had the power under the Fisheries Act of 1983 to confer 'special rights' on 'special communities', had not even considered granting such rights to the Manukau tribes; nor had the Ministry considered 'compensating Māori interests for the depletion of their fisheries',[42] though it had admitted that the harbour was seriously over-fished. The Ministry, the Tribunal concluded, 'has not discharged its responsibilities in respect of the Manukau harbour'.[43]

But, despite such criticism, the Tribunal's recommendation was mild and compromising. It would be 'unfortunate', the Tribunal maintained, 'if Maori fishing rights fell to be determined solely on a literal interpretation of the Treaty which guarantees as *exclusive* use of *all* Maori fisheries, for Maori fisheries are extensive and indeed, the whole of the Manukau could be described as a traditional Maori fishery'.[44] It was necessary to make compromises, to minimise the conflict between Māori, private and commercial fishing interests, and to begin a search for options available for the recognition and protection of Māori fishing grounds and securing compensation for Māori fishing losses. It was necessary to identify 'particularly important tribal fishing grounds'[45] and, in the meantime, to reserve the Whatapaka and Pukaki inlets as the claimants had requested. This was a far cry from concluding that the Manukau tribes should be given an exclusive right to the kai moana of the whole harbour.

So far as New Zealand Steel's slurry pipeline was concerned, the Tribunal concluded that there was no great danger to the environment or the fisheries in the transfer of water from the Waikato river to the Manukau. But it did not accept the claimants' view that the transfer was culturally offensive: that the 'mauri of the two water bodies is incompatible'. The Tribunal went on to observe that: 'In our multicultural society the values of minorities must sometimes give way to those of the predominant culture, but in New Zealand, the Treaty of Waitangi gives Maori values an equal place with British values, and a priority when the Maori interest in their taonga is adversely affected.'[46] Although the Tribunal recommended a change in the laws to admit Maori values, it accepted that New Zealand Steel had been granted a water right to discharge the water from the pipeline into the Manukau but hoped that it would be able to work out an acceptable compromise with the claimants.

In its general findings the Tribunal concluded that: 'In the Manukau the tribal enjoyment of the lands and fisheries has been and continues to be severely prejudiced by compulsory acquisitions, land development, industrial developments, reclamations, waste discharges, zonings, commercial fishing and the denial of traditional harbour access.'[47] The failure of the Crown to provide a protection against these things was contrary to the principles of the Treaty of Waitangi. Admittedly, such omission had begun last century with the policies that led to war and confiscation of tribal territories, but it had continued into the twentieth century, even beyond 1975 with 'an omission to recognise or give appropriate priority to Maori interests in laws and policies and in planning'.[48]

The Tribunal wanted such omissions to be rectified in future legislation and policy. The Ministers concerned were asked to consider amending a great deal of legislation to ensure that Māori sensibilities, rights and interests were taken into account in planning and development relating to the Manukau and its environs. The Ministry of Agriculture and Fisheries was called on to carry out urgent and comprehensive research into Māori traditional fishing activity 'for the recognition, protection or compensation of Maori fishing interests'[49] and on the effects of commercial fishing in the Manukau and the lower Waikato river. The Tribunal called for the formulation of a Manukau Harbour Action Plan to take positive measures for the cleaning up of the harbour, and for the appointment of guardians representing Māori and environmental interests. Pending the formulation of the Action Plan, the Minister of Transport was asked to suspend further reclamations of the harbour — as it turned out, the only one of the Tribunal's recommendations that the Government set aside for further study late in 1986. But acceptance of the other recommendations did not mean action; three years later, most of them are still not implemented.[50]

In contrast with the complicated Manukau claim, the Te Reo Māori claim was singular and straightforward. It was lodged by Huirangi Waikerepuru on behalf of Nga Kaiwhakapumau i te Reo Inc. (the Wellington Board of Māori Language), which asked that Māori be recognised as an official language throughout New Zealand for all purposes. Despite this apparent simplicity, the claim was regarded by the Tribunal as potentially the 'most difficult' so far, in view of its political, social and financial ramifications.[51] The four weeks' sitting was the longest the Tribunal had held. But those who spoke did so with a rare degree of unanimity. 'They "came from the four winds" and they spoke with one voice.'[52]

The Tribunal concluded from the evidence and argument presented that 'by the Treaty the Crown did promise to recognise and protect the language and that promise has not been kept. The "guarantee" in the Treaty requires affirmative action to protect and sustain the language, not a passive obligation to tolerate its existence and certainly not a right to deny its use in any place.'[53] These bold assertions were argued at greater length later in the report. Although the Māori language was not specifically listed in the Māori possessions guaranteed in the second article of the English text of the Treaty, it came under the heading of 'o ratou taonga katoa' in the Māori text, variously translated 'as all their valued customs and possessions', or 'all things highly prized'. In the Manukau finding, the Tribunal had decided that taonga in the context of the Treaty meant more than objects of tangible value and included intangibles. So in the Te Reo Māori finding, the Tribunal simply concluded that 'the language is an essential part of the culture and must be regarded as "a valued possession"'.[54] The version of the Treaty signed by most of the Māori chiefs was in their language and 'the right to use the Maori language would have been one of the rights expected to be covered by the Royal guarantee by those chiefs who signed the Treaty'.[55] It was unlikely that many of the chiefs would have signed had Hobson denied that the guarantee covered their language.

Having established these points of principle, the Tribunal went on to consider the teaching of Māori in the education system, praising recent developments such as the kohanga reo — the language nests for pre-school instruction in Māori — yet also lamenting the fact that too many Māori children were not reaching a sufficient level of attainment in their formal schooling. 'The promises of the Treaty of Waitangi of equality in education as in all other human rights are undeniable.[56] Judged by the system's own standards Maori children are not being successfully taught, and for this reason alone, quite apart from the duty to protect the Maori language, the education system is being operated in breach of the Treaty.'[57] Nevertheless, the Tribunal did not attempt to determine what was wrong with the system, and was content to call for an urgent inquiry into the way Māori language and culture were taught in the schools.

The other major area discussed was broadcasting, but, since a Royal Commission was currently investigating the broadcasting system, including the role of Māori language and culture, the Tribunal thought it inappropriate to make any specific recommendations. It was content with a broad generalisation: 'It is consistent with the principles of the Treaty that the language and matters of Maori interest should have a secure place in broadcasting.'[58]

Finally, on the large question of the official recognition of the Māori language, the Tribunal was equally restrained. There was no opposition to the proposition that the language should be officially recognised — not one of the Government departments consulted by the Tribunal had opposed the idea — but the Tribunal was not prepared to go very far in terms of practical measures. For instance, it turned down a demand that all public documents, notices and newspapers should be printed in both Māori and English, largely on the ground of expense. On the other hand the Tribunal did recommend that Māori ought to be allowed to use their language in the courts and in dealing with Government departments or local authorities. But once again the Tribunal was cautious in applying this proposal: it was unwilling to require fluency in Māori as a condition of appointment to all positions in the civil service, and merely suggested that this should be a requirement in some positions and a qualification to be encouraged in others. The Minister of Internal Affairs was asked to establish a statutory body to supervise and foster the use of the Māori language.

Thus, in the Te Reo Māori claim, as in the earlier ones, the Tribunal's findings were potentially radical, but its recommendations were mild and accommodating, and could be achieved without much pain or expense to the predominant Pākehā community. Whether this will always be so is a moot point, more especially under the new regime created by the Treaty of Waitangi Amendment Act 1985. That amendment enlarged the Tribunal to seven and gave it a built-in Māori majority by requiring at least four of the members to be Māori. The Tribunal was allowed to observe 'te kawa o te marae' as it thought appropriate for a particular case, provided that it did not deny any person the right to speak on grounds of sex — a provision that was clearly intended to overcome the custom which prevented women from speaking on some marae. But the biggest change of all was the extension of the Tribunal's jurisdiction back from 1975 to 6 February 1840, when the Treaty was signed by northern chiefs at Waitangi. The change had enormous potential since every act or omission of the Crown in some way related to the principles of the Treaty since 1840 came within the purview of the Tribunal. But despite this greatly enlarged jurisdiction, the Tribunal still could not do more than make recommendations. Since it was clear that there would be a great increase in the Tribunal's work, the amendment also provided for extra assistance. The Tribunal was allowed to sit with a quorum of three people (one of whom had to be a Māori), each of the members was to have a deputy, counsel could be appointed to assist the Tribunal and/or the claimants, and extra staff could be appointed to assist with administration and research. Finally, the errors in the Māori text of the Treaty printed as a schedule to the 1975 Act were corrected.

It is hardly surprising that the amendment encouraged a veritable flood of claims; within two years, more than 160 had been submitted. These represent merely the tip of the iceberg, since there is not a Māori community in the country that does not have grievances over the loss of land or other resources, tangible or intangible. Many grievances have already been the subject of inquiry by official commissions, though the Māori claimants were often dissatisfied by the results, and are likely to try again before the reconstituted Tribunal. A notable case is the raupatu — the confiscation of Māori land carried out under the New Zealand Settlements Act 1863 during the New Zealand wars — which was the subject of a Royal Commission in 1926. Although that Commission's recommendations were eventually given effect by the Government, the Māori tribes involved have long been dissatisfied with the scope of the Commission's findings and the amount of compensation awarded. Some submitted claims to the Tribunal. Other old land grievances had already appeared in claims now before the Tribunal. In the Taipa claim, for instance, Crown purchases of the 1840s in the Mangonui district were called in question; so too the Crown's handling of the pre-1840 land claims, including the retention of the 'surplus land' not awarded to the European claimants, which was retained by the Crown and was the subject of a Royal Commission in 1948.

In the revived Orakei claim the Crown's role in the purchase of 283 hectares of prime waterfront land near the centre of Auckland city was examined by the Tribunal under its 1985 amendment. Since any act or omission of the Crown in relation to the block since 1840 could now be in breach of the principles of the Treaty, the Tribunal was obliged to prepare a detailed history of the Crown's acquisition of the block. The Tribunal made an exhaustive examination of the documentary record — reports of previous inquiries, departmental files, Native Land Court records, newspapers, historical dissertations and essays — and took written submissions from interested parties and members of the public. It also recorded the oral testimony of Ngāti Whātua kaumātua and kuia; this provided a traditional perspective on Ngāti Whātua history and vivid testimony of the more recent, harrowing events in the long-running Orakei saga. This material was compressed into a narrative history of the Crown's acquisition of the Orakei block which ran to more than 100 pages, over half of the final report issued in November 1987.[59]

The narrative provided a platform for an analysis of the scope of the Treaty and breaches of its principles. In the Tribunal's view the 'critical damage' was done by the Native Lands Acts of 1865 and 1867 and an 1869 Order of the Native Land Court

> vesting the whole of the land then in communal ownership in thirteen members only of the tribe as legal and beneficial owners, to the complete exclusion of the great majority. This necessarily destroyed the mana or authority of the tribe in and over their land. Subsequent breaches of the Treaty built upon and reinforced these ... critically

destructive violations.... Nor, in many cases, did the Crown comply either with its statutory or Treaty obligations to ensure that Ngati Whatua owners would not be rendered landless. That Ngati Whatua were powerless to prevent the consummation of the Crown's objective of obtaining the whole of their land was finally demonstrated by the Public Works Act taking of the 10 acre exchange block and the papakainga accompanied by the ejection of all those living on there and, shortly thereafter, by the physical destruction of... the marae, leaving only the Church and urupa intact.[60]

Since large areas of Māori land in other parts of the country were acquired in a similar manner, the Tribunal's findings in the Orakei claim were likely to have considerable influence when it considered other claims.

Nevertheless, in keeping with the attitude of the old Tribunal, the recommendations of the new Tribunal in the Orakei claim were restrained and achievable.[61] The Tribunal accepted the fact that the bulk of the land acquired by the Crown had already passed into private ownership; some of it was occupied by high-value houses, the remainder by State houses, many of which had also passed into private ownership. However, the Tribunal did recommend that Ngāti Whātua people be given preference in the allocation of remaining State houses in the block. Most of the land still in Crown ownership was in public reserves and used for active or passive recreation. These included the 15-hectare Okahu Park sports grounds and the 38.5-hectare Bastion Point headland which the Tribunal recommended should be transferred to a Ngāti Whātua of Orakei Reserves Board, composed of equal numbers of Ngāti Whātua and City Council representatives. But they were to remain as public reserves. The Ngāti Whātua Trust Board was to retain the former State houses of Kitemoana Street, to gain ownership of a 1.79-hectare block which the Housing Corporation had proposed to sell for private housing, several other small sites, and regain control of the marae, church and urupā. Finally, the Tribunal recommended that a $200,000 debt be cancelled and that Ngāti Whātua of Orakei be awarded a general payment of $3,000,000, as a tribal endowment for housing and other purposes.

In this last recommendation the Tribunal had shied away from attempting to quantify Ngāti Whātua's loss in terms of the capital value of the land within the Orakei block, a sum which would have run into many millions of dollars. Instead, the Tribunal tried to calculate the minimum sum that would be needed to provide an economic base — or at least adequate housing — for those members of the tribe who wished to return to Orakei. Since the bulk of the land to be returned to Ngāti Whātua was to remain in public reserves, there was little left over for other tribal economic activities. In relation to the true market value of the land, the $3,000,000 payment was cheap. It was accepted with some relief by Treasury[62] and Government, along with nearly all of the Tribunal's other recommendations. The settlement, with its emphasis on the cheaper alternative of a tribal endowment, set a precedent for the settlement of other land claims.

The other major claim reported on by the new Tribunal — the Muriwhenua fishing claim — could not be so easily resolved, though the Tribunal's report[63] was no less significant than that on Orakei. Part of a broader claim that included land and spiritual concerns, the Muriwhenua claim was lodged by the Hon. Matiu Rata, the Te Hapua 42 Incorporation, and the five northern tribes: Ngāti Kurī, Te Aupōuri, Te Rārawa, Ngāi Takoto and Ngāti Kahu. But the hearing of those other claims was set aside to enable the Tribunal to report on the fishing claim. During the first hearing at Te Hapua in December 1986 it was disclosed that the Ministry of Agriculture and Fisheries was about to issue further fish quota which the claimants held contravened their rights under the Fisheries Act and the Treaty of Waitangi. The Tribunal's plea for the quota to be withheld was not accepted by the Minister. The Tribunal's hearings continued but in September 1987, when the Ministry was preparing to issue yet more quota, the chairman of the Tribunal issued a statement that the issue of quota 'would be contrary to the principles of the Treaty'[64] and called on the Crown to negotiate with the Muriwhenua claimants before taking further action. At the same time counsel for the claimants began an action in the High Court where Mr Justice Greig issued an injunction restraining the issue of further quota in the Muriwhenua district. In November a separate action in the Court resulted in a further injunction over the issue of fish quota for the remainder of the country. The Government then set up a Joint Committee, with four of its own nominees and four representatives of the New Zealand Māori Council, to try to negotiate a settlement on the allocation of fishing quota. While those negotiations proceeded the Tribunal came under considerable pressure to complete its hearings and report on the Muriwhenua fishing claim. The findings of the Tribunal on the extent of Muriwhenua fisheries, the nature of the Treaty guarantee on Māori fishing rights, and possible breaches of these by the Crown were likely to be of crucial importance in the Joint Committee's negotiations. Meanwhile, the Tribunal had been proceeding with its hearings of the claim: it held sittings at Ahipara in March, Kaitaia and Auckland in April, and at Wellington in September 1987 and in March and April 1988. The report was issued in June.

Although it referred only to the fishing claim, the report was no mean document; indeed at 371 pages it was considerably longer than the Orakei

Report. And, although Māori fishing rights had been an important component of earlier Tribunal inquiries, the Muriwhenua Fishing Report was by far the most comprehensive examination of traditional Māori fisheries and their progressive diminution since 1840 that had yet been published. At its hearings in the North the kaumātua provided the Tribunal with a wealth of oral evidence on the nature of fishing practices, their fishing grounds and the species caught. This was taken into account alongside the extensive documentary evidence assembled by the Tribunal's consultant, Dr George Habib, from the journals of early European navigators, the accounts of ethnographers, and the findings of archaeologists.

From this material the Tribunal concluded that the Muriwhenua tribes had made 'full and extensive fishing use' all round the year of their fresh water and coastal fisheries (out to about 3 miles), 'intensive and regular but mainly seasonal' use of the balance of the continental shelf (to about 12 miles), and occasional use of selected fishing grounds beyond (even, in one case, a fishing ground 48 miles off shore).[65] The fishing technology was in some respects superior to that being used by Europeans at the time. For instance, James Cook discovered in 1769 that Māori nets were considerably larger than the ones he had on board the *Endeavour*; such nets were still being used a century later. Moreover, the Tribunal found (and during the hearing counsel for the Crown conceded the point) that traditional Māori fishing had a 'commercial' component in that coastal tribes habitually traded fish for other products with inland tribes. That 'commerce' expanded with the arrival of Europeans, so that by the 1840s Māori were the main suppliers of fresh fish to the burgeoning markets in the new settlements. Although the tribes of the Far North gained little of this new commerce, they continued to fish commercially, if on an intermittent basis, as they did for domestic consumption. Nevertheless, as the Tribunal's report went on to demonstrate, Māori were progressively eliminated from the commercial fishery from the later nineteenth century. Although fisheries legislation provided some protection for Māori fishing rights, it was assumed that these were confined to the gathering of fish or shellfish for domestic consumption and that it was unnecessary to provide specific protection or assistance for Māori in the commercial fishing industry. The Tribunal found that the failure of Government to provide for such protection or development was contrary to the Crown's obligations under the Treaty. In its interpretation of the Treaty, the Tribunal concluded that the guarantee to Māori of 'the full exclusive and undisturbed possession of their ... fisheries' (in Article 2 of the English text) meant precisely what it said. The 'only difficulty with the words', the Tribunal added, 'is the inconvenience they present. The meaning is altogether too clear. "Exclusive" means "exclusive" . . . .'[66] It added that there was nothing inconsistent in the Māori text (which did not specify fisheries, although these were by implication included in taonga, or valued possessions). Moreover, the Māori text guaranteed Māori the rangatiratanga (not merely possession but chiefly control) over their taonga. They were guaranteed possession and control over their fisheries so long as it was their wish to retain them. Unlike the situation over land, there was no specific provision for alienation of fisheries — and nowhere in the historical record was there any evidence that Māori, in Muriwhenua or elsewhere, had alienated their fisheries or willingly surrendered their control over them. On the contrary, there was a massive array of evidence, much of it documented by the Tribunal, of Māori protest, by petitions and otherwise, of their loss of fisheries since 1840.

This loss has been most pronounced in the last few years, although some Māori, including a number of Muriwhenua fishermen, had participated as individuals or in joint ventures in the commercial fishery over the years, most notably in the years of unrestricted licensing between 1963 and 1983. But that lack of restriction, especially with the opening up of export markets, encouraged gross overfishing of the inshore fisheries. By 1980 the Ministry of Agriculture and Fisheries recognised the need to reduce the total allowable catch. In 1983 a moratorium was placed over the issue of new licences and those not in use were cancelled. When new licences were issued, in the form of individual transferable quotas (ITQs), these were based on a pro rata reduction of a fisherman's average catch over the previous three years. As a result many small or part-time fishermen, if they got quota at all, received so little that it was uneconomic, and they sold out to the larger holders. The Ministry had clearly embarked on a policy of removing small fishermen from the industry; in 1964–65 nearly 300 were eliminated in Northland alone and these included at least 29 Māori fishermen, nearly all of those involved in commercial fishing in the Muriwhenua area.[67] Moreover, the Ministry persisted with this policy in the face of the Fairgray Report of September 1988 which warned of the grave economic and social consequences of the policy for Northland communities. Unless there was a major reversal of the policy, the Tribunal concluded, 'the traditional association of the Muriwhenua people with their ancestral seas will be non-existent, and their communities will be in disrepair'.[68]

It was evident that the Muriwhenua Fishing Report had important implications for the rest of the country. What had been said of Māori fishing in Muriwhenua clearly applied, to a greater or lesser extent, to the fisheries of other tribes, not least the Ngāi Tahu of the South Island whose claim, which included rights to fisheries right around the island, was also being heard by the Tribunal. Clearly the Muriwhenua Fishing Report added considerable substance to the claims of the New Zealand Māori Council negotiators on the Joint Committee. Indeed much more could be claimed than the Government could readily concede, and it is not surprising that negotiations became acrimonious and inconclusive.

What of the future? Since the Waitangi Tribunal is a creation of the legislature, it has always had an uncertain future, one that is subject to the whims of the politicians and ultimately the electorate. Legislation now, in 1987, before the House to increase the membership of the Tribunal will hopefully improve its chances of reducing the backlog of claims. But one thing is certain: so long as the Tribunal retains its retrospective jurisdiction to 1840, it will continue to recover a hitherto largely submerged Māori history of the loss of resources and mana, supposedly protected by the Treaty. The Tribunal's findings are not always going to be palatable to many New Zealanders, but it would be perilous to ignore them.

11

Giving Better Effect to the Treaty:
Some Thoughts for 1990

These days, any discussion of the Treaty of Waitangi must begin with the acknowledgement that there are in fact two treaties: one written in English, the other in Maori. Neither is a copy or translation of the other and at times they say rather different things. The differences are important since they are the source of alternative Pakeha and Maori historical traditions that lie at the heart of our race relations. Until recently the English text was regarded as the official text, but now it is commonly said that the Maori text is the valid one since it was the one that was agreed to by all but 39 of the Maori signatories. This argument has some force: what was said in Maori clearly had more meaning to Maori signatories than the English text with all its tortuous legalisms. But of course there are always at least two parties to a treaty and, although William Hobson, as representative of the British Crown, signed both texts, it was the English text that had meaning for him. That was why he regarded it as the official text and the Maori text as merely a translation.

Since 1975, when the Waitangi Tribunal was established under the Treaty of Waitangi Act, both texts have been regarded as valid. Under section 5 of that Act the Tribunal has an exclusive authority, for the purposes of the Act,

---

This essay is a revision of the lecture, 'Waitangi: The Treaty and the Tribunal', delivered in the Auckland Institute and Museum's Winter Lecture Series, 19 June 1989, and subsequently published in *The New Zealand Journal of History*, vol. 24, no. 2 (1990), pp. 135–49. Although I am a member of the Waitangi Tribunal and discuss some of its findings, my comments here are not to be regarded as having the endorsement of the Tribunal.

to determine the meaning and effect of the Treaty as embodied in the two texts, and to decide issues raised by the differences between them. That task has not been undertaken lightly; Tribunal reports contain lengthy discussions about the meaning of the texts and the principles behind them. Quite often, however, the Tribunal has given greater weight to the Maori text. There are good precedents in international law for doing so. For instance, in its Motunui–Waitara Report the Tribunal referred with approval to the accepted principle, expressed as long ago as 1899 (in the US Supreme Court case, *Jones v Meehan*),[1] that a treaty with an Indian tribe must 'be construed, not according to the technical meaning of its words to learned lawyers, but in the sense in which they would naturally be understood by Indians'.[2] The application of that to Maori and the Treaty of Waitangi was obvious. And to ascertain how such a treaty was understood by Indians, or Maori, it was necessary to consider what was said at the time of the signing — how the words were translated and explained, what additional promises might have been made — not just the words that were written in the texts of the treaty. What was said at Waitangi and elsewhere by Henry Williams and other interpreters was particularly important. As D. F. McKenzie recently reminded us, Maori culture was still essentially oral. Despite the efforts of the missionaries, few Maori were literate. Only 72 of some 530–40 who 'signed' the Treaty were able to write their names; the rest used a cross or moko.[3] Moreover, as commentators on the texts of the Treaty from Ruth Ross (1972) to Bruce Biggs (1989) pointed out, much of the Maori text of the Treaty was missionary Maori and some Maori words were made to bear new burdens.[4] Henry Williams, in devising a Maori text, always had his eye on the need to negotiate it with proud and suspicious chiefs. The Treaty negotiations were as much an exercise in diplomacy as semantics. All of which is to say that it is no easy task today to discover what the Treaty may have meant to Maori 'signatories' in 1840.[5] Moreover, it is not sufficient to confine our attention to Waitangi, the best reported of the signing ceremonies. We need to know what was said to, and understood by, Maori at other signings, some of which, such as Hokianga and Kaitaia, were comparable in size and ceremony to Waitangi. These are particularly important when the Tribunal is considering claims that come from those districts. For instance, the Tribunal's consideration of the Muriwhenua claim, not yet completed, could well take the Kaitaia meeting of 28 April 1840, where 61 chiefs adhered to the Treaty, into account. It was here that Nopera Panakareao made his famous declaration: 'the shadow of the land is to the Queen, but the substance remains to us'.[6] The fact that he very soon reversed that statement is an eloquent comment on Maori disillusion at the way government had begun to operate the Treaty. Similarly, in the Ngai Tahu claim, currently before the Tribunal, it will be necessary to take into account Maori understandings of the Treaty as it was explained to them at various South Island signings.

From time to time a good deal has been made of the fact that important inland tribes and chiefs did not accept the Treaty. So far as the British were concerned, that hardly mattered; indeed Hobson declared British sovereignty over the North Island on the basis of Maori acceptance of the Treaty on 21 May 1840 even before all of the signed copies of the Treaty came back, and over the South Island — this time on the basis of Cook's 'discovery' — before any had come back. But with over 530 'signatures' the Treaty must be one of the most fully signed international treaties in existence. So far as the non-signatory tribes are concerned, some, like the Waikato supporters of Te Wherowhero, the first Maori King, claimed that they were not bound by the Treaty. This has not stopped later generations from claiming the benefits of the Treaty, even to the extent of lodging claims with the Waitangi Tribunal. Other tribes who did not sign, like Arawa, have a long tradition of loyalty to the Crown and the Treaty. So, in one way or another, most Maori tribes have adhered to the Treaty; it binds both parties. In 1840 and for nearly 40 years afterwards the Treaty was regarded as a valid treaty of cession. It is now so regarded by lawyers, despite mistaken views to the contrary stemming from Chief Justice Prendergast's judgment of 1877 — which described the Treaty as a 'nullity'.[7]

But of course the Treaty was far more than a treaty of cession. It was also a charter for the future: meant to protect Maori rights and resources while also setting the guidelines for British colonisation of New Zealand. I shall now consider that rather more difficult aspect of the topic, including the different histories stemming from the two texts of the Treaty.

Until recently, the Maori history of the Treaty, like the Maori text, has been submerged, though it has been carefully preserved and often reiterated in tribal traditions. But to a considerable extent Claudia Orange's recent book has restored the balance.[8]

The Pakeha version, based on the English text, is more familiar, simply because it has been part of the public and historical record for so long. In considering the relationship of history to text, we should remember what Bruce Biggs has called the 'Humpty-Dumpty principle' — 'when I use a word it means exactly what I choose it to mean'[9] — not just in interpreting the meaning of words in the Treaty, but also in tracing how the words and promises of the Treaty were carried forward into government policy and legislation. The Treaty as a whole has never been embodied in New Zealand municipal law, but certain aspects of it have been from the beginning. Moreover, some parts of the Treaty have received greater emphasis than others. Article 1, which provides for the transfer of sovereignty from the Maori to the British has been, in the Pakeha view, the vital part from which all else follows, including the protection of land and other resources in Article 2 and the grant to Maori of the rights and privileges of British subjects in Article 3. British sovereignty was seen as one and indivisible. In theory, if not for many years in practice, it covered the whole country and subjected Maori, as British subjects, to the civil and criminal law of England as well as to locally made statutes. (I have said England, because the Scots remained apart, a precedent that does not seem to have been seriously considered for the Maori.) There were one or two exceptions in the early years which allowed Maori runanga to operate, making by-laws of local concern. But these were regarded as temporary expedients until all Maori were brought within the realm of the ordinary institutions of government. Section 71 of the 1852 Constitution Act allowed districts to be proclaimed where Maori law and custom could prevail. Though no such districts were ever proclaimed, relations between Maori *inter se* were in fact governed by traditional law and custom, except in the case of warfare or major crimes, for a good many years. On the other hand there was always a steady and fixed determination by governments in New Zealand to bring relations between Pakeha and Maori, especially over property, under the ordinary domestic law. And that was part of a larger objective: to amalgamate the races by assimilating the Maori, thereby creating one people, 'he iwi tahi tatou', which Hobson had promised at Waitangi. The objective was steadily pursued through war and peace. Indeed, it was the legislation passed during the war years of the 1860s, when the colonists had got responsible government and thus freedom to deal with the Maori unfettered by imperial control, that set in place an assimilation policy that lasted for a hundred years.

The sovereign authority exercised by the New Zealand legislature under Article 1 was brought to bear on Article 2 of the Treaty. This was longer and more specific in the English text than in the Maori. It guaranteed Maori the 'undisturbed possession of their Lands and Estates Forests Fisheries and other properties' (whereas the Maori text did not specify forests or fisheries) and it yielded to the Crown a right of pre-emption to purchase such land as the Maori were willing to sell. From the beginning, there was strong pressure from the colonists to reduce or remove these guarantees. They tried repeatedly to get rid of the pre-emptive clause so that they could purchase land directly from the Maori. It was abolished by FitzRoy in 1844, restored by Grey in 1846, abolished by the Native Territorial Rights Bill in 1859 (though this was disallowed by the imperial government), and abolished again by the Native Lands Act 1862. This did receive royal assent since the imperial government had surrendered control over Native Affairs. Pre-emption was never comprehensively resumed, though from time to time the Crown did resume it by proclamation or special legislation for specific blocks of land. The preamble of the 1862 Act recited the second article from the English text of the Treaty and claimed that 'it would greatly promote the peaceful settlement of the Colony and the advancement and civilization of the Natives if their rights to land were ... assimilated as nearly as possible to the ownership of land according to British law'. It was the beginning of a long-continued attempt to use statutes to transform Maori customary land tenure into individual Crown-granted certificates of title.

The Native Lands Act was also justified by reference to the third article of the Treaty, granting Maori the rights and privileges of British subjects. In 1859 the Law Officers of the Crown had held that the communal nature of Maori land tenure disqualified individuals from exercising the franchise which was then dependent on a property qualification. It was assumed that Maori who were issued with certificates of title would therefore be eligible to vote. In fact, the legislature did not wait for the Native Land Court to produce a significant body of Maori voters, and in 1867 created four Maori seats for the lower house, with an adult male franchise, some time before this was available to Pakeha men. There were several other Acts in the 1860s which were deemed to be giving effect to the third article. Perhaps the most notable was the Native Rights Act 1865 which affirmed that Maori were indeed British subjects and clarified their right to appeal to the higher courts, a dubious blessing considering that they were soon involved in costly land litigation and that their attempts to plead the Treaty were invariably dismissed. Moreover, any Maori British subjects who were in rebellion against the Crown could be punished with the loss of their land and liberties under the New Zealand Settlements and Suppression of Rebellion Acts of 1863 and the Outlying Districts Police Act 1865.

Under cover of the English text of the Treaty a settler-dominated New Zealand Parliament was relentlessly pursuing a dual aim: the promotion of colonisation through the acquisition, by one means or another, of Maori land; and the extension of substantive sovereignty by bringing all Maori within the compass of civil and criminal law. But what of the fiduciary duty that was spelled out in the preamble of the Treaty: that Her Majesty was 'anxious to protect' the 'just rights' of the chiefs and tribes and 'to secure them the enjoyment of Peace and Good Order'? And the guarantee of 'full exclusive and undisturbed possession' of lands and other properties? Those promises look a little hollow when we come to look in detail at land purchases and the great pressures that were exerted on chiefs like Wiremu Kingi at Waitara, or organisations such as the King movement in Waikato, who resisted sales. Indeed, if we examine the whole field of Maori land acquisition by the Crown and by individuals under licence from the Crown for the remainder of the nineteenth century, as I did many years ago[10] and as the Tribunal is now beginning to do, then I think we must conclude that the fiduciary duty imposed on the Crown by the Treaty was largely, if not wholly, neglected. There were a few exceptions: some piecemeal attempts were made to stop the worst abuses through Frauds Prevention Acts, and occasionally committees or commissions of inquiry looked into specific Maori grievances. There have been some improvements in this century with a slowing down in the acquisition of Maori land, assistance to develop remaining land, attempts to settle land grievances, the introduction of social welfare benefits, and a gradual abandonment of the old assimilation policy. However, as the Tribunal has pointed out on several occasions,[11] the Crown's fiduciary duty was not confined merely to the protection of Maori resources guaranteed by the second article of the Treaty: it included an obligation to ensure that Maori received a fair share in the development of new resources, including those not contemplated in the Treaty. This was a benefit Maori hoped to receive from accepting a significant measure of British colonisation.

So much for the English text and Pakeha use of it. What of the Maori text and the rather different Maori history deriving from it? I think we can also say that Maori, in their ways, have applied Biggs' Humpty-Dumpty principle to their text. They have tended to downplay the first article, as Henry Williams encouraged them to do, by suggesting that the kawanatanga, the governorship or governance that they surrendered, was essentially a right to govern the Pakeha. The word kawanatanga was a fairly recent invention, having been used by the missionaries in translations of the scriptures into Maori, and in relation to secular governors like Pontius Pilate and the British governors of Australian colonies. But it was not clear how far the new Governor's powers were to extend over Maori, an issue that was perhaps deliberately fudged by Williams. It does seem that some Maori were willing to surrender some of their authority, 'part of their mana and rangatiratanga', as Hugh Kawharu has put it, including the right to make war on other tribes.[12] But there were instances of inter-tribal fighting at Tauranga and in the Far North in the 1840s when the chiefs involved were unwilling to allow the Governor to intervene. Although Maori at this time were becoming concerned about the influx of British colonists, it seems that most of them wanted colonisation to continue, provided the colonists were properly controlled as the Treaty seemed to promise. Yet it is unlikely that the Maori signatories had any idea of the extent of the colonisation that would follow, or of the all-embracing ways that kawanatanga would be applied to their land and their lives.

But, whatever their misunderstanding of the real purport of Article 1, they were reassured by Article 2, even though the Maori version was somewhat more vague than the English text. Though the Maori text did not specify forests and fisheries, such valuable possessions were covered by the term taonga which probably also included intangibles, such as language. Even more important, Maori were assured of their rangatiratanga or chieftainship over these treasures: not merely ownership of, but control over them — and the people they sustained. Indeed, if we look back to the Busby-inspired Declaration of Independence of 1835, the term rangatiratanga was used for independence and the phrase 'ko kingitanga ko te mana' for sovereign power and authority. Williams replaced this with the single word kawanatanga in the Treaty, knowing full well that the chiefs would not sign away their mana. Twenty-six of the chiefs who had signed that Declaration at Waitangi in 1835 also signed the Treaty there in 1840. At that second signing those chiefs at least must have felt assured that they had retained their rangatiratanga and their mana — their independence, and their authority to control their land and their people. And they were also assured, by Hobson's verbal promise (the so-called fourth article), that their tikanga, their religion and customs, would be preserved as well.

But they had been misled, as they soon discovered. That was why Nopera, having found that the Governor and his men were indeed interfering with the way he conducted his land transactions and conflicts with his rivals, said it was only the shadow that now remained and that the substance had gone to the Queen. That was what soon began to agitate Hone Heke, the first to come forward to sign at Waitangi, when he found the Governor's magistrate interfering with him at Kororareka. He was soon persuaded that the Union Jack flying on Maiki hill was the symbol of his diminished rangatiratanga. And in subsequent years chiefs in many parts of the country refused to accept that the British magistrates and their laws should prevail over them. Their independence was demonstrated most conspicuously in Waikato before the war, when they set up one of their number, the distinguished warrior Te Wherowhero, as a King to protect their land and administer their law through their own runanga. The Kingites wanted 'the King on his piece; the Queen on her piece;

God over both; and love binding them to each other".[13] But Governor Gore Browne saw it as an *imperium in imperio*, a rival sovereignty that needed to be put down.

Though the Kingites, who had for the most part refused to sign the Treaty, could hardly base their independence on it, other loyalist chiefs were soon to do so. With the outbreak of the Waitara war, Browne summoned some 200 still loyal chiefs to a conference at Kohimarama, hoping to get them to declare themselves against Kingi and the Waikato King movement. He assured them that the Treaty had been and would be upheld. They endorsed the Treaty as a solemn covenant, and Browne accepted a request from the conference that it be made an annual affair, a kind of Maori parliament. Although this promise was not kept, the Maori chiefs did not give up the idea. Paora Tuhaere, the Ngati Whatua chief, summoned a parliament to Orakei in 1879. In later years there were numerous hui in the North and elsewhere to promote a Maori parliament that would give effect to the rangatiratanga originally promised in the Treaty. A Maori Parliament was formally constituted in 1892 and went on meeting annually in different Maori settlements until 1902. But it was never legally recognised by the Pakeha-dominated Parliament in Wellington, despite frequent requests. So the rangatiratanga of the Treaty was denied, and Maori had to look to other ways to preserve the fragments.

There was a shift in Maori strategies in the early twentieth century as the old loyalist or Kupapa leaders of the Maori Parliament or Kotahitanga movement were eclipsed by the new men of the Young Maori Party. They looked to parliamentary representation in Wellington to safeguard the remnants of rangatiratanga. Even Ratana, who formed the largest independent Maori church, looked to Parliament to further the Maori cause — and to ratify the Treaty. By turning to the Pakeha-controlled Parliament, Maori leaders were of course exercising their rights and privileges as British subjects — not, however, to become British, as the assimilationist doctrine expected, but to remain Maori, which in their view the Treaty allowed.

It follows from much that I have said that there has been a vital conflict between Pakeha and Maori in New Zealand over the interpretation of the Treaty. At the heart of this conflict are the differing interpretations of kawanatanga and rangatiratanga. As I have emphasised, the Pakeha used the legislature to impose their view of kawanatanga, a sovereignty that was one and indivisible, on the Maori, whose rangatiratanga — chiefly independence — was progressively diminished. Any suggestion that sovereignty might be divided, as happened in the United States with the recognition of Indians as domestic dependent nations, was quickly dismissed in New Zealand. For instance, the suggestion of the first Attorney-General, William Swainson, that Maori tribes that had not signed the Treaty retained their own sovereignty, was dismissed by the Colonial Office, which took the view that British sovereignty covered the whole country.[14] A similar claim by the Kingite tribes was also adamantly rejected. And section 71 of the 1852 Constitution Act, which would have allowed a limited exercise of Maori sovereignty in proclaimed districts, was never implemented and was finally repealed by the Constitution Act 1986.

Has anything changed? In the last 20 or so years there have been considerable changes in government policy. Assimilation, after a brief interregnum of 'integration' in the 1960s, has given way to biculturalism. Our education system, our government departments, are required to develop the taha Maori, the Maori side. The Treaty, particularly the Maori version, is acquiring a new significance, quite apart from the annual pilgrimages to Waitangi. Cabinet and government departments — even the Treasury — are required to take it into account in their planning. Several recent Acts have required the Crown to abide by the principles of the Treaty. Geoffrey Palmer proposed to make the Treaty part of the fundamental law of the country by putting it into the Bill of Rights. The Waitangi Tribunal has been created and has told us that the Treaty is a 'constitutional instrument',[15] the basis for a 'developing social contract',[16] views that were reiterated by Sir Robin Cooke and other judges in the Court of Appeal judgment in the 1987 *New Zealand Maori Council* case.[17] And F. M. Brookfield, in his inaugural lecture at Auckland University's Law Faculty, tried to find in the Treaty a basis for the legitimacy of our constitution.

These are heady developments. But I do not think that all that has been promised will be achieved. It will be difficult to get far with taha Maori in the face of Pakeha intransigence and electoral backlash. The Treaties in full are unlikely ever to become part of our statute law. How could they when they say different things? In its most recent legislation, Parliament has either dropped all reference to the Treaty, or merely stressed 'a duty to consider the Treaty', to quote section 6 of the Resource Management Bill currently before the House. That is a far cry from requiring the Crown to observe the principles of the Treaty. Palmer has dropped the reference to the Treaty as fundamental law from the latest draft of the proposed Bill of Rights. He has also forthrightly rejected Moana Jackson's proposals for a separate system of criminal justice on the ground, constantly reiterated by his predecessors, that there can be only one system of law in New Zealand.[18] Rangatiratanga, in so far as it exists at all, has been largely reduced to a measure of Maori control over Maori things.

Existing national Maori bodies, such as the New Zealand Maori Council and the Maori Women's Welfare League, hardly constitute a Maori parliament, though they have been legitimised by legislation. Sometimes they are consulted by government over proposed legislation and other Maori matters; more often they have to fight government over the neglect of Maori interests. It has been said recently by the Tribunal and the Court of Appeal that the Treaty was a partnership between the Crown and the Maori, and that both parties have an obligation to behave towards one another reasonably and with the utmost good faith. But historically there has not been much partnership between Maori and the Crown, let alone treatment of Maori as equal partners.

How, we might ask, has the Crown performed? It is a question that is frequently asked of the Tribunal. Clearly, no final judgement can be presented here on what is a very large question, although it will be evident from some of my general comments that in my opinion the Crown has not done very well. Of course it is easy to be wise after the event, and we must be careful not to apply too many of today's standards to the past. As I have been emphasising, our view of the Crown's obligations under the Treaty has been expanding very rapidly of late, especially with the consideration now being given to the Maori text by the Waitangi Tribunal and the courts. Since its Act was amended in 1985, the Tribunal has had quite staggering powers of jurisdiction to inquire into breaches by the Crown of the principles of the Treaty. Indeed, any Act, regulation, Order in Council, or any policy or practice of the Crown since 6 February 1840 could be held to be in breach of the principles of the Treaty and thus prejudicially to affect a Maori claimant. But the fact that the Tribunal can only recommend a remedy leaves the solution of grievance with the Crown. The Tribunal has reported on only a small number of the claims so far submitted. The old Tribunal reported on six; the enlarged Tribunal, created by the 1985 amendment, has reported on one full claim and parts of two others, and completed one arbitration. Several other reports are in preparation. There are nearly 200 claims on the register, though a good many of these are likely to be amalgamated or withdrawn.

I have summarised the main reports elsewhere[19] (and they are discussed in the two chapters that follow), so there is no need to comment on them in detail here. They contain lengthy discussions on the history of the particular claims and on principles of the Treaty as they relate to each claim. Professor Gordon Orr recently prepared an analysis of principles, which he sees as emerging from the Tribunal reports and recent court decisions.[20] He has discovered seven, plus another which has not clearly emerged. These can be summarised as follows:

- the gift to the Crown of the right to govern (kawanatanga) was in exchange for the protection by the Crown of Maori rangatiratanga;
- there were limits on the authority of the Crown to govern — Crown sovereignty was not absolute;
- there was a tribal right of self-regulation — tino rangatiratanga;
- the Crown, in exercising its right of pre-emption, had a reciprocal duty to ensure that Maori who sold land retained a sufficient endowment for their own uses;
- the Crown had an obligation actively to protect Maori Treaty rights;
- the Treaty signified a partnership and required the Pakeha and Maori partners to act towards each other reasonably and with the utmost good faith;
- the Crown has a duty to remedy past breaches of the Treaty; and, probably,
- the Crown is under a duty to consult its Treaty partner.

Orr pointed out that this list was far from exhaustive: it had merely arisen from the claims that had been considered by the Tribunal and the courts; and that more principles would be discerned from time to time.

There is no need to spell out the breaches by the Crown of these principles in relation to claims considered by the Tribunal; these have been detailed in the various Tribunal reports. In each case the Tribunal has gone on to recommend remedies, and a large number of these have been accepted by government, or are still under consideration. Government has been accommodating because the Tribunal's recommendations have been extremely moderate, despite the magnitude of Maori losses that was revealed in several of the claims. Perhaps the most notable case of this is the Muriwhenua Fishing Report, which aroused great controversy, provided elaborate documentation of frequent and continuing breaches of the Treaty by the Crown, but simply recommended that the two parties — the Crown and the representatives of the New Zealand Maori Council — continue their negotiations for a settlement of Maori fishing rights. It is evident that this claim, and all the other Maori fishing claims that are tied up with it, are not likely to be easily and fully settled, since they involve the return to Maori of large and valuable resources in fish, which the Tribunal's report holds were wrongly alienated as private property rights. And this could be true for many of the other claims on the Tribunal's register. Remedying the Crown's excessive alienation of Maori resources is bound to be costly and controversial.

It is with this problem in mind that I want to make some final, but far from comprehensive, comments on the future of the Treaty and what will be needed to make it more effective. It will of course have a future, of a kind; just as we cannot obliterate the Treaty from our history, so we cannot eliminate it from the future. It stands as a foundation of our nation and at the fulcrum of Maori–Pakeha relations. We can expect the Treaty to remain a source of debate, as each side appeals to the different texts for justification of its causes. Because of their differences, contradictions even, the treaties are unlikely ever to be wholly incorporated in our statute law, or in a Bill of Rights. In any case the legislature, the Tribunal and the courts have recently been saying that it is not the strict text that has to be considered, but the principles, the spirit. As the Orakei Report put it, the Treaty is to be regarded as more than an affirmation of existing rights. It was not intended as a finite contract but as the foundation for a developing social contract.[21] It is in this broad, general sense that the Treaty should be seen as providing a guide, more especially to the settlement of grievances, to the making, administration and interpretation of our laws, the allocation of our resources, and to our social welfare and cultural and intellectual life. I cannot touch on all of these topics and shall merely discuss the settlement of grievances, the law and the allocation of resources.

It seems that the Waitangi Tribunal, if unhindered by politicking or a change of government, is the best, though not the only, means of resolving grievances, often by conciliation or arbitration. I doubt whether it needs any substantial increases in membership, staffing, or finances. Nor does it need any significant increase in jurisdiction: it should remain essentially a recommendatory rather than a judicial body. Nevertheless, there is one respect in which the Tribunal's authority could be usefully extended. At present, under section 8 of its Act, the Tribunal has authority to report on whether any proposed legislation referred to it by the legislature is contrary to the principles of the Treaty. The section has been inoperative. I think it should be amended so that the legislature is obliged to refer such legislation to the Tribunal for an opinion. This would require a small increase in staff, particularly in the legal division of the Tribunal.

I have examined the Tribunal's overall performance in my previous chapter and the two that follow and believe that it has had more influence than any other body in our history in giving 'better effect to the Treaty'. Given further goodwill and a generous response from government to its recommendations, it will continue to perform that function. And it is likely that the courts, as they continue to hear cases that in some way arise from the Tribunal's activities, will also treat its findings and recommendations with the same respect that was seen in the recent Court of Appeal judgment. Nevertheless, not all Maori grievances arising from breaches of the Treaty will be solved easily and rapidly, more especially if the present adverse balance of resources remains.

Second, there is the question of law. In my discussion on kawanatanga versus rangatiratanga, I suggested that the former had been exerted to the disadvantage of the latter. We must find some ways of reducing that tendency; in other words, ways of restraining or dividing the sovereignty of the Crown to allow a greater expression of rangatiratanga. It is significant that some authorities have admitted, as Orr has put it, that 'Crown sovereignty is not absolute'. To illustrate the point he went on to quote the then Attorney-General, Geoffrey Palmer's statement, 'that our system of Government and indeed our very existence here stems from the signing of the Treaty in 1840'.[22] That point was taken up by Brookfield, who said in his inaugural lecture that, with the 1986 Constitution Act, our constitution has finally been domesticated, it has 'become autochthonous, its roots, its legitimacy are now here in New Zealand'.[23] But, if I understand them rightly, neither the Attorney-General nor the Professor said how the Treaty was linked in law to the constitution. Moreover, as I have said, section 71 of the old 1852 constitution, which would have allowed a measure of rangatiratanga, was repealed by the Attorney-General's new 1986 constitution. Brookfield, who noted this, went on to suggest that we find a modern substitute for section 71 by 'an imaginative use of a modified concept of Maori Districts'.[24] Unfortunately, he did not explain what he had in mind. I think it is probably too late to contemplate separate Maori districts, a territorial division of sovereignty like that which the King movement sought to achieve in New Zealand and American Indian nations did largely achieve. But perhaps there are other ways of restraining or dividing sovereignty.

There is the notion of political, as distinct from legal, sovereignty which Paul McHugh has been advancing.[25] It is based on the idea that much of the British, and likewise the New Zealand, constitution is based on convention — long-standing practice — rather than written law. For some odd reason McHugh uses Maori representation in the New Zealand Parliament as an example of this, though that representation is based on statute, albeit one that was meant to have a temporary, five-year life. Perhaps the fact that it is still with us is a kind of convention. It can also be seen as a very limited recognition of rangatiratanga in our constitution; one, incidentally, that has been jealously guarded by Maori as the best that they could get. Should it be retained and, if so, expanded? I think it should be retained — so long as Maori electors demonstrate that they want to retain it. And they can do this quite simply by registering and voting in the Maori electorates, which could be adjusted upwards or downwards to equate the numbers on their electoral rolls with those for the general electorates. On a population basis, Maori are entitled to more than four seats, but on a basis of registered voters to slightly less than four.²⁶ The same principles should be applied to local government. This would restore a greater degree of rangatiratanga to the existing institutions of government. But it hardly makes Maori equal partners, which has been described as one of the principles of the Treaty. Some say that this requires allowing Maori equal representation, but I do not think that we should infringe the democratic principle of one person one vote to that extent. It is necessary to find other ways of enhancing rangatiratanga.

One way would be to increase the authority and responsibilities of the two statutory national Maori bodies that we already have, the New Zealand Maori Council and the Maori Women's Welfare League. (We must remember that the rangatiratanga of Maori women, if I can use that word in relation to them, has not been very well regarded either in the negotiation of the Treaty — only five signed — or since.) Both should be consulted as of right at an early stage and during the passing of legislation of general concern to Maori. Both bodies have stood the test of time and, despite occasional criticism from more radical groups, have represented Maori concerns with dignity — in true rangatira style. Nevertheless, the New Zealand Maori Council, as a creature of the Pakeha legislature, has never had widespread Maori support. It might well be supplanted by an organisation with fuller flax-roots support like the new iwi-based National Maori Congress, which, as a result of the current devolution policy, might well supersede the New Zealand Maori Council. Some of the iwi authorities, such as the Ngai Tahu, Taranaki, Arawa, and Tuwharetoa Trust Boards, are more than 50 years old and well used to administering tribal funds. These and other iwi authorities should gain increased resources and authority under the devolution policy. But other iwi, so far without trust boards, need to get them, and the many Maori who have lost their tribal affiliation need to be able to enter the fold, or to have their interests safeguarded by other organisations such as the Maori Council or Women's Welfare League, as has been recently proposed. Of course, rangatiratanga is a matter of allowing Maori the tribal right of self-regulation, to own but also to manage their resources, and to preserve their taonga. But it is also more than that, since Maori, though a minority in their own land, must have a real share in the government of the country as a whole and the allocation of resources on a national scale. The Treaty of Waitangi does not just apply to what has been left to Maori from 150 years of Pakeha colonisation, to the bits of dirt under their fingernails, if I may reapply a comment of Peter Buck's on the loss of Maori land.²⁷

So we come back to the exercise of kawanatanga, of sovereignty. In a democracy such as ours, with a very considerable Pakeha majority, recognition of the rights of the Maori minority, of what they are entitled to under the Treaty, is very largely a matter of restraint by consenting (Pakeha) adults. In other words, that the legislature imposes some restraints on the Crown — as it has done with the legislation relating to the Tribunal and several other recent Acts which require the Crown to abide by the principles of the Treaty. Such legislation needs to become commonplace rather than merely occasional. Is there any way of ensuring this? I believe so. The Treaty, it will be recalled, was signed by Hobson, on behalf of Queen Victoria. Maori have always made much of their personal relationship with the British monarch that derives from the Treaty. This did them precious little good in the later nineteenth and early twentieth centuries when they tried to petition or send deputations to Buckingham Palace pleading for the Treaty to be upheld. Since responsibility for Maori affairs had been transferred to the New Zealand government, they were referred back to the Pakeha government in Wellington. At least this has been the public response. I have not searched the unpublished archives, though I doubt whether the British monarchs have ever stopped advising their Governors-General in private. The present Queen has sometimes ignored the advice of New Zealand Prime Ministers: for instance, she insisted on an unscheduled call on the Maori King at Ngaruawahia in 1953. I sometimes wonder whether Queen Elizabeth, as Queen of New Zealand, regards herself as having a residual responsibility for upholding the Treaty that was signed in the name of her great-great-grandmother. After all, at this year's Waitangi Day ceremony the Queen's speech, which can hardly have been written by her New Zealand Prime Minister, differed markedly from his speech — most notably in her statement that the Treaty had been 'imperfectly observed'.[28]

Then there is the related point that the Governor-General, on behalf of the Queen in New Zealand, gives the final assent to a parliamentary Bill. This has been refused in the past. Perhaps the most relevant case is the Territorial Rights Bill of 1859, on the ground that it infringed the Treaty. Could it not be argued that a modern Governor-General retains some residual responsibility for upholding the Crown's side of the Treaty and might therefore withhold assent to a Bill that s/he regarded as infringing the Treaty? I think so, and I am strengthened in my view by McHugh's suggestion that the Governor-General's assent might well have been withheld from the proposed Fisheries Bill (which was revised and passed after McHugh's essay was written).[29] But I am in no position to advise a Governor-General; I am merely raising a hypothetical point that needs to be debated. It is, after all, a rather murky area that appears to have been little discussed in New Zealand, or elsewhere in the Commonwealth.

Governors-General do have some rather significant residual powers — as we saw a few years ago when Sir John Kerr dismissed Gough Whitlam in Australia. But who advises them when they are in dispute with their 'responsible advisers'? And who, for that matter, trains them in their constitutional responsibilities, something of considerable concern now that so many of them have no constitutional law in their background? I am not suggesting that a Governor-General would lightly or frequently withhold assent to Bills — the essence of a veto is that it is there, to be used as a last resort, and that is usually enough to ensure that legislators do not provoke its use. But there are one or two occasions when assent might be withheld, in addition to that suggested by McHugh: for instance, if the legislature ignored a recommendation of the Waitangi Tribunal on a draft Bill (as I have suggested above); or a similar recommendation by the New Zealand Maori Council and Maori Women's Welfare League, indicating very widespread Maori resistance to a particular measure. This at least would allow a rather more significant expression of rangatiratanga than exists at present. Withholding of assent would allow the parties to talk, the public to express views, and Parliament to think again, something that is important in a unicameral legislature. But if, after all that, the government was determined to press ahead, the Governor-General would have to give way — or invite dismissal.

I have not investigated the constitutional role of the courts and am scarcely competent to do so, but it is worth noting two points that have been further developed by two legal academics and which could perhaps help to restrain the exercise of sovereignty by the legislature. First, as McHugh has argued on numerous occasions, there is probably scope for a further development of the common law — and more particularly a New Zealand common law that incorporates surviving Maori 'aboriginal' law. We have seen what might be called a first win for the McHugh view in Mr Justice Williamson's judgement in *Te Weehi v Regional Fisheries Officer* (1986), though that decision was possible because the aboriginal fishing right had been protected by legislation, rather than taken away, as has happened with Maori land.[30] The second area of restraint lies in international law, more especially in United Nations conventions which New Zealand has adopted and which, as Benedict Kingsbury has argued, might be used for claims against the Crown for the non-fulfilment of obligations under the Treaty.[31]

Finally, there is the allocation of resources. Some of the constitutional measures I have suggested are essentially negative; they could help to prevent the Maori from being despoiled by the Pakeha majority. But what can be done about the despoliation that has already occurred? The relentless acquisition of Maori land by the Crown and by settlers has reduced the Maori estate to about one million hectares, some 2 per cent of the country, plus a small but indeterminate area under general titles. Moreover, the land in Maori ownership is unevenly distributed, with some tribes having a considerable amount and others very little. It has been too long assumed in New Zealand that the reservoir of Crown land acquired from the Maori was to be available solely for Pakeha colonisation. Maori could make a living from their own land or in the Pakeha economy. It is, in my view, a matter of some urgency to start returning Crown resources — not just land and most certainly including fish quota — to the Maori, more especially to those iwi that have ended up with very little. I am not suggesting that resources should be simply given back, but that the prices should be to some extent concessionary, as was the case when much Crown land and other resources were allocated to Pakeha over the years. Maori iwi should also be given a preferential right to bargain for Crown resources before these are privatised, so that they are not faced with having to try to claw them back through appeals to the Waitangi Tribunal under the present State-Owned Enterprises legislation. In addition, the Crown should facilitate the purchase for Maori of land and other resources in private ownership by setting up and financing a Commission like that which was recently in existence in Australia, to buy land for Aborigines. I am not suggesting compulsory purchase, but merely purchase on the open market on a willing buyer, willing seller basis. If the Australian experience is any guide, no great area of land would become available, but a Commission could be used to acquire strategic assets for under-resourced iwi, or land of spiritual or historic significance. A little of this has already been done: recently the Minister of Maori Affairs helped Ngati Porou to purchase a Pakeha farm around the base of their sacred Mount Hikurangi. It should also be possible to return areas that have a similar significance in National Parks and other Crown reserves so that they are under iwi management but still available as public reserves. The government acceptance of Tribunal recommendations for parts of the Orakei block — to be returned to Ngati Whatua ownership on condition that they remain public reserves or parks — and the proposals of the Tribunal's mediator for the Waitomo caves, are encouraging illustrations of what can be achieved.

Such measures help to restore the balance between the two parties to the Treaty. They are necessary if the Crown is belatedly to fulfil its fiduciary obligation to its Maori partner — to ensure that, in the acquisition and allocation of resources, Maori rights were properly safeguarded. It is the burden of this essay that these rights were not properly safeguarded in the past, but that they must be in the future. And not just in the areas I have discussed. Indeed there remains a range of social questions relating to welfare, health, education and the criminal justice system that I have not touched on. How has the Treaty been applied and how should it be applied to them? Those are very large questions. But some of the principles I have discussed above will be relevant, more especially the need always to temper the harsh application of Pakeha kawanatanga by a proper recognition of Maori rangatiratanga.

12

The Waitangi Tribunal and the Resolution of Maori Grievances

This essay rests on the proposition that Maori grievances, founded on the loss of land, other taonga, and rangatiratanga since the beginnings of European colonisation, are unlikely to be fully resolved on our lifetime. Like fleas on a dog's back, if I might rework a statement by a former Minister of Maori Affairs in reference to protesters, it is likely that Maori grievances will always be with us in some shape or form.[1] So long as Maori remain a disadvantaged minority in their own land, they are likely to seek a resolution of the causes of that disadvantage. Moreover, it is simply unrealistic to assume, as politicians have done recently, that all of the claims on the Waitangi Tribunal's register, or even the major historical claims, can be resolved by the year 2000. Even if we were to assume that the Tribunal could get through the claims — and it would need a major increase in funding to do so — there is no way the Pakeha majority in the country would agree to return the resources, mostly in private ownership, or alternatively to pay reparation. There would be very strong resistance to the idea that this generation alone should bear the whole cost. In addition, as Professor Alan Ward recently argued, we need a measured, cautious approach that would allow the claims to be properly researched and heard rather than subjected to pressure-cooker treatment.[2] And even then we should not assume that we will necessarily get it right in our generation. After all, some of the major historical

---

This essay is based on a paper presented to the New Zealand Present and Future Conference in Edinburgh, May 1994. It was subsequently published in *The British Review of New Zealand Studies*, no. 8 (1995), pp. 21–36. That version is reproduced here.

claims, including the South Island Ngai Tahu claim and the North Island confiscation claims, have been the subject of previous inquiries, followed by 'full and final settlements'. They are before the Waitangi Tribunal, but are far from resolution.

The Pre-1985 Waitangi Tribunal

The Waitangi Tribunal was established by the Treaty of Waitangi Act 1975, passed in the last year of the Third Labour Government. Under the Act 'any Maori' could submit a claim to the Tribunal that 'he' was 'prejudicially affected' by any Act, regulations, order in council, or any policy or practice of the Crown, currently in force or proposed, which was inconsistent with the principles of the Treaty of Waitangi. However, 'anything done or omitted' before the commencement of the Act was excluded from the jurisdiction of the Tribunal. This meant that the Tribunal had to confine its attention to claims founded on developments since the passage of the Act. If the Tribunal found that the claim was valid, it could recommend that the Crown provide an appropriate remedy.

There was little Maori interest in the Tribunal at first, but with the quickening pace of economic development in the early 1980s, a number of essentially environmental claims came before the Tribunal.[3] The first significant claim to be reported was Motunui, which arose from a proposal by the Syngas plant in Taranaki to discharge effluent through an offshore pipeline. This claim was discussed in chapter 10, 'Towards a Radical Reinterpretation of New Zealand History: The Role of the Waitangi Tribunal', where I noted that the Tribunal's Report recommended an onshore treatment of all waste before the residue was discharged through an offshore pipeline. Government reluctantly accepted the recommendation. The Tribunal adopted a similar approach to the Kaituna claim, relating to the discharge of partly treated sewage from the city of Rotorua into the Kaituna river, this time recommending land-based treatment and discharge. Likewise with the wide-ranging Manukau claim, which was also concerned in part with the discharge of industrial waste into the Manukau harbour to the detriment of traditional fishing grounds. Again the Tribunal found most of the claims justified and recommended appropriate action by Government. Some of these Recommendations have still not been implemented, ten years later.[4]

The Tribunal's Recommendations on these claims, though laying stress on Maori values, were also in keeping with environmental standards and opinion. Yet each of these Reports was greeted with alarm and controversy. Why? If we look closely at the Reports we find, as I pointed out in chapter 10, that the Tribunal's Findings were much more radical than its Recommendations; its bark was worse than its bite.[5] Findings usually related to breaches of the principles of the Treaty by the Crown. In considering these the Tribunal was required to have regard to both the Maori and English texts of the Treaty. Previously, the English text of the Treaty, though signed by only a handful of Maori, was always regarded as the official text; and the Maori text, which most Maori had signed, as a mere translation. In fact, as academic commentators were beginning to point out in the 1970s, there were important, even unreconcilable, differences between the two texts. That was recognised by the Treaty of Waitangi Act 1975 which required the Tribunal to consider breaches of the principles rather than the provisions of the Treaty.

Needless to say, that has been no easy task which is in many respects still incomplete; every claim that is heard can involve the Tribunal in a new examination of the principles and provisions of the Treaty. If we judge by their response to those early essays in Treaty interpretation in the Motunui, Kaituna and Manukau Reports, Pakeha New Zealand was much disturbed by the Findings of the Tribunal. But the Findings were not especially radical either in terms of treaty interpretation in international law, or in terms of New Zealand history in general and Maori history in particular. Thus in the Motunui–Waitara Report the Tribunal noted that the Maori text should be treated as the 'prime reference', since this was the text signed by most of the chiefs. According to the well-known *contra proferentem* rule, enunciated by the US Supreme Court in *Jones v Meehan* (1899),[6] treaties made with Indian tribes were to be construed 'in the sense which they would naturally be understood by the Indians'.[7] For Indians we can read Maori. Moreover, the Tribunal was unwilling to leave the Treaty buried in the past since its foundation statute required it to apply the Treaty to the present. The Treaty, the Report continued, 'established the regime not for uni-culturalism, but for bi-culturalism', and 'was not intended to merely fossilise a status quo, but to provide direction for future growth and development', 'the foundation for a developing social contract'.[8]

If this expansive interpretation of the Treaty and its principles was most disturbing to Pakeha opinion, it had no need to be, more especially when we look to the Tribunal's Recommendations. Here the Tribunal was constrained by the preamble and long title of the Treaty of Waitangi Act 1975 which required it to make recommendations for the 'practical application of the Treaty'. The Tribunal interpreted that as meaning what was practical in the circumstances prevailing at the time; in other words since 1975. Indeed in its

Motunui–Waitara Report the Tribunal went so far as to conclude that it was 'not inconsistent with the spirit and intention of the Treaty . . . that the Crown and the Maori people affected should . . . agree to alter the incidence of the strict terms of the treaty in order to seek acceptable practical solutions'.[9] This meant that the claimants were expected to seek a workable compromise with private interests, local bodies and the Crown, even if this meant compromising some of the protection they had sought: in the Motunui case, continued discharge of effluent, albeit in treated form, offshore; in the Kaituna case, discharge of effluent, again in treated form, though this time on forest rather than the waterways; and in the Manukau case, to take just one example, discharge of water taken from the Waikato river for a steel slurry pipeline into the Manukau harbour, though the Tribunal found that this was spiritually offensive to Maori.[10] In each case the Tribunal was compromising Findings on principle in favour of 'acceptable practical solutions'. Pakeha interests had little to worry about. Some notice would have to be taken of the Treaty in the future, but the failure to apply it in the past could be ignored.

The Post-1985 Waitangi Tribunal

This situation changed dramatically when the Labour Government amended the Treaty of Waitangi Act in 1985 to give the Tribunal retrospective jurisdiction right back to the signing of the Treaty in 1840. The amendment opened up a veritable Pandora's box[11] of historical claims, some, as indicated, relating to large-scale acquisitions of Maori land, but many other comparatively small claims which had long rankled with local Maori communities. Moreover, each claim that was submitted tended to beget others when research and hearings revealed additional, perhaps long-forgotten grievances, and the Tribunal found it necessary to allow the claimants to amend their Statements of Claim. Rather more ominous were the urgent claims provoked by the Government's hiking-off of publicly owned resources to State-Owned Enterprises (SOEs) or into private ownership. Although there was nothing in the Tribunal's legislation to prevent it recommending that the Crown acquire private property to satisfy a claim, it was generally presumed that only public resources would be used. This applied particularly to the considerable area of unalienated Crown land — about a sixth of the total area of the country — then about to be transferred to SOEs, and notably to Landcorp. But there were also many other resources under Crown ownership or control, including large areas of exotic forests, sub-surface minerals, hydro- and geothermal energy, offshore fisheries, and even the airwaves. Fisheries were being surreptitiously privatised by the issue to commercial fishermen and companies of individual transferable quotas (ITQs) — in effect private property rights — in blatant disregard of the protection of Maori fisheries in the Treaty and in fisheries legislation. The Tribunal was soon overwhelmed by claims. Whereas there were only 25 claims on the register by the end of 1985, the number rose to 87 by the end of 1987 and 209 by the end of 1990. Urgent claims, provoked by Government policies and sometimes by Maori litigation in the courts, had to take precedence over historical claims.

A notable example was the Muriwhenua fisheries claim, which has been discussed in more detail in chapter 10, 'Towards a Radical Reinterpretation of New Zealand History'. There it was noted that because of the impending issue of ITQs, the Tribunal had to set aside all but the fishing aspects of the claim and that the Government refused the Tribunal's request to withhold the issue of further ITQs, pending the completion of the Tribunal's Report. The claimants went to the High Court and got an injunction requiring Government to suspend the issue of quotas, initially in the Far North but subsequently for the whole of the country. The Court also required the Crown to negotiate in good faith with Maori to safeguard their Treaty rights and to allocate them a fair proportion of the commercial fisheries.[12] The Tribunal's Report, with its detailed account of the neglect of Maori Treaty rights in the past, gave added weight to the High Court's requirement.[13]

This is no place to narrate the long and sometimes acrimonious negotiations that led to an imposed interim 'solution' by the Labour Government with its Maori Fisheries Act of 1989, promising to buy back for Maori 10 per cent of commercial fisheries quota, and the subsequent 'final solution' negotiated by the National Government late in 1992, which included the purchase by the Crown for Maori of a half-share of the largest commercial fishing company in the country, Sealord, for $150 million.[14] This provided Maori with another 13 per cent of existing quota and promised them 20 per cent of quota for new species. In the negotiations Maori had set their sights on 50 per cent of the quota; they got 23 per cent. But a notable if controversial feature of the agreement, accepted with some reluctance by most Maori iwi, was that it removed the Maori Treaty right to commercial fisheries and therefore removed these from the jurisdiction of the Waitangi Tribunal — and the courts. The agreement was validated by the Treaty of Waitangi (Fisheries Claims) Settlement Act, passed at the end of 1992. According to its preamble, this constituted a 'full and final settlement of all Maori claims to commercial fishing rights'. All Maori commercial fisheries claims before the courts were extinguished and neither the courts nor the Waitangi Tribunal were permitted to hear such claims in the future. It was a classic example of the exercise of sovereignty: the Treaty was at the mercy of Parliament, as it had always been. Parliament could give effect to parts of the Treaty, or it could nullify them, and there was nothing the courts could do about it. The Waitangi Tribunal protested in vain.[15]

What of other resources threatened by the Labour Government's SOE and privatisation policies which were continued by the National Government? It is not possible to discuss all of these, though it should be noted that recently the Tribunal began preliminary hearings of claims to hydro- and geothermal resources, usually under urgency.[16] Initially, the Labour Government, especially under its Minister of Justice (and subsequent Prime Minister) Geoffrey Palmer, did make some significant moves to protect Maori rights under the Treaty. Palmer was responsible for an amendment suggested by the Waitangi Tribunal and inserted during the final stages of the State-Owned Enterprises Bill in 1986. Section 9 of the Act prevented the Crown from doing anything under the Act which was inconsistent with the principles of the Treaty. Several other Acts passed at this time, such as the Environment Act 1986 and the Conservation Act 1987, also required the Crown to uphold the principles of the Treaty. Indeed section 4 of the latter said that it was to be 'interpreted and administered to give effect to the principles of the Treaty of Waitangi'. Palmer proposed to include the Treaty as part of the supreme law of the country in a Bill of Rights. But in his earnest endeavours to uphold the Treaty Palmer was fashioning a stick to beat his back. This first became evident when the New Zealand Maori Council went to the Court of Appeal to prevent the Crown from transferring assets to nine of the SOEs. All five judges of the Court came to the conclusion that section 9 was the overriding provision and that other powers in the SOE Act were subject to it. The Court required the Crown and Maori to work out safeguards for Maori interests and submit them to the Court for approval.[17] This was done with the Treaty of Waitangi (State Enterprises) Act 1988 which provided for the mandatory return of SOE land to Maori on the order of the Waitangi Tribunal — incidentally, the only judicial authority so far granted to the Tribunal. Where SOE land was on-sold to a third party, a memorial was to be placed on the title to the effect that the Crown would reacquire the land in the event of the Tribunal upholding a Maori claim to it.

Thereafter there was a gradual retreat from commitments to uphold the Treaty. In the last years of the Labour Government weaker formulae were used in legislation, which now required the Crown to 'take into account the principles of the Treaty', the phrase used in section 6 of the Resource Management Act, introduced by Palmer but finally passed by the National Government in

1991. That change was criticised by the Tribunal in its Ngawha Geothermal Resource Report, 1993, which concluded that 'the Crown in promoting this legislation has been at pains to ensure that decision-makers are not required to act in conformity with, and apply, relevant Treaty principles. They may do so, but they are not obliged to do so. In this respect the legislation is fatally flawed.' The Tribunal recommended that the Act be amended to ensure that all persons acting under it 'shall act in a manner that is consistent with the principles of the Treaty of Waitangi.' That Recommendation was reiterated in the Tribunal's Preliminary Report on the Te Arawa Representative Geothermal Resource Claims, later in the year, but it has been ignored by the Government.[18] Alternatively, the obligation to apply the principles of the Treaty was dropped altogether from legislation. This happened when all reference to the Treaty was dropped from the Bill of Rights that was finally passed in 1990; and it has happened with increasing regularity ever since. Another tactic has been for Government to sidestep the Treaty of Waitangi (State Enterprises) Act by not on-selling Crown land, but, for instance, by merely selling cutting rights over exotic forests while retaining the land beneath in Crown ownership. Or it removed resources from the jurisdiction of the Act by legislation, as happened with Petrocorp, and power board assets under the Energy Companies Act 1992.[19] In the case of surplus railways land, Government chose to negotiate a settlement of Maori claims prior to putting the land on the market — in this case through a Joint Working Party from the Crown and the National Maori Congress — thus diverting claims from the Waitangi Tribunal. Yet another tactic has been to encourage claimants who were being heard by the Tribunal to abandon the Tribunal and go into direct negotiations with the Crown. I shall return to these points later.

Thus in one way or another Government, and particularly the current National Government, has been clipping the wings of the Waitangi Tribunal. As already indicated, fisheries have been removed from Tribunal jurisdiction. Following a row over the Te Roroa Report which recommended that the Crown 'take all steps' to acquire some Northland farms in private ownership for the Maori claimants,[20] the Government passed the Treaty of Waitangi Amendment Act 1993 to prevent the Tribunal from making such recommendations. There was also constraint on Tribunal funding. Although membership of the Tribunal has been increased progressively from three to seventeen (thus allowing several Tribunal panels to sit concurrently) and there has been some increase in staffing, these have not been commensurate with the increased workload of the Tribunal since 1985. Until very recently Tribunal funds have been pegged while Government has increased funding for other branches of the Justice Department involved in the claims resolution process — for instance TOWPU (the Treaty of Waitangi Policy Unit) which has had an annual grant of $4.6 million compared with the Tribunal's $2.5 million.[21] Hitherto TOWPU was mainly concerned with advising the Minister on Tribunal Recommendations, but increasingly it became involved in the direct negotiations with claimants that the Minister encouraged as an alternative to the Tribunal process.

Yet, despite Government attempts to reduce the role of the Tribunal in the claims resolution process, Maori still look to it as the main avenue for a resolution of their grievances. Claims continue to pour into the Tribunal office from all over the country. Once again, with the quickening pace of economic recovery and further threats of privatisation of public resources, many of these were urgent claims which displaced the larger historical claims in the hearing process. By 19 January 1994 there were 414 claims on the register, although many of these have been wholly or partly dealt with. According to a report prepared for the incoming Minister after the 1993 election, the standing of the 396 claims then on the register was as follows:

Claims reported	44
No further inquiry	26
Deferred	7
In mediation	3
In negotiation	13
Under Tribunal research	48
Under claimant research	90
In hearing/proceedings	72
Research completed awaiting hearing	15
Referred to Maori Appellate Court	1
Referred to Maori Land Court	2
No action	75
TOTAL	396 [22]

As this table indicates, the Tribunal had reported on or otherwise dismissed about a fifth of the claims on its register; another three-fifths were under research, hearing, or some other form of investigation; and the remaining fifth were not yet actioned. No doubt some of the larger claims under investigation will take a long time to complete, but others could be and were being reported very quickly. For instance Wai-413, Hare Puke's claim on the Maori Electoral

Option, was lodged on 19 January 1994, heard at two Tribunal sittings on 27-28 January and 2 February, and Recommendations were delivered to the Minister in a 44-page Report on 11 February; probably a record for the Tribunal. Since the Prime Minister promised in his Waitangi Day speech in 1994 to increase the Tribunal's $2.5 million budget by $1.9 million, it should be able to speed up its hearing of claims.

But speeding up the Tribunal's reporting on claims will not necessarily hasten their resolution. It remains with the Crown to deal with Tribunal Recommendations. The record here is far from clear. Although the Crown has not outrightly rejected many Recommendations until recently, it has usually been slow to give effect to the remainder. But it is difficult to be precise on this since the Tribunal itself keeps no record of the fate of its Recommendations. However, the Parliamentary Commissioner for the Environment, Helen Hughes, prepared a report on the Crown's response to Tribunal Recommendations in 1988, and Professor W. H. Oliver included an appendix on implementation in his *Claims to the Waitangi Tribunal*, published for the Tribunal in October 1991.[23] Oliver noted that the Tribunal had made Recommendations in respect to 10 of the 12 claims reported between 1983 and 1991. It had made a total of 86 Recommendations of which 24 had been fully implemented, 21 were embodied in legislation, another 9 were partly implemented, 5 had been rejected by Government, and another 21 had not yet been considered.

But neither Hughes' nor Oliver's report has been updated. TOWPU supplied the material for Oliver's report but has lost the original and has not created an updated replacement. Information on specific claims is buried in its computer. However, the Chief Historian of the Unit gave me some information from the computer on 35 Tribunal claims in various stages of consideration.[24] These can be tabulated as follows:

Reports Under Consideration by Crown	3
Pre-negotiation & Negotiation	15
Part Settlements	6
Settlements	11
Total	35

The Part Settlements included what was described as a 'land bank', which included three Wakatipu pastoral leases for Ngai Tahu and the Hopuhopu military camp for Tainui, pending a final settlement with those iwi, along with unspecified 'monetary advances' for other claims. However, there was some overlap with the different categories: some of the claims listed under Pre-negotiation & Negotiation were also in the Part Settlements category. Moreover, several of the claims, including Manukau, listed under Settlements, do not appear to have been fully settled anyway since they were described as 'under implementation'.

It is evident that there is a state of utter confusion in the claim settlement process. This is being exacerbated as claimants, with some encouragement from the Minister for Treaty Settlements, switch from the Tribunal to direct negotiation and sometimes back again to the Tribunal; and as Tribunal Recommendations do the rounds between departments and their Ministers. Though the Tribunal reports in the first instance to the Minister of Maori Affairs, its Recommendations are frequently directed to other Ministers. The Minister of Maori Affairs appoints members of the Tribunal, but Tribunal staff are employed by the Department of Justice where the Tribunal's office is located. The Minister of Maori Affairs has in his department a unit which advises him on Treaty and Tribunal matters. But it is the Minister of Justice, not the Minister of Maori Affairs, who is responsible for the settlement of Treaty claims and he is advised by his unit, TOWPU. It is a bureaucratic nightmare that is beyond anyone's comprehension, let alone resolution. Perhaps it is only the historians who get any comfort out of the situation since they know that much of this has happened before. The confiscation claims, which the Tribunal is now hearing, were the subject of a Royal Commission in 1927, but the so-called 'full and final settlement' based on its recommendations was not completed for 20 years. We must be excused a feeling of *déjà vu*.

To be fair, there are reasonable explanations for many of the delays. As Professor Oliver noted, the longest delays were usually where Tribunal Recommendations required legislation. He instanced the case of Orakei, where the Report was lodged with the Government in November 1987 but the required legislation was not passed until 1992. He also noted how some of the major pieces of legislation in the period, such as the State-Owned Enterprises Act 1986, the Treaty of Waitangi (State Enterprises) Act 1988, the Maori Fisheries Act 1989 and the Resource Management Act 1991, 'reflected to some extent the recommendations of the Tribunal'.[25] Another cause of delay was that some Tribunal Recommendations required large public works — for instance the sewerage works recommended in the Motunui–Waitara and Kaituna Reports took just on eight years to complete. In its early Reports the Tribunal usually made quite detailed Recommendations, often requiring legislation. But in its more recent Reports, starting with the Muriwhenua Fishing Report of May 1988, the Tribunal usually examined the grievances in relation to their historical setting, spelled out the extent of prejudice in terms of breaches of the principles of the Treaty, but merely recommended that the claimants and the Crown negotiate a settlement. This approach was also followed in the Tribunal's massive 1991 Report on the Ngai Tahu land claim, covering much of the South Island, and its accompanying Report on the Ngai Tahu fishing claim. Although the latter has been settled as part of the general fishing settlement already discussed, the land claim is still under negotiation.

This last example illustrates that negotiations over large claims, whether following from Tribunal Reports or undertaken directly with claimants, are not easily or quickly completed. A fortuitous occurrence, such as the availability of fishing quota when the Sealord company came on the market, or when surplus military or railway land becomes available, might allow some claims to be quickly settled. But, since the Minister of Justice has indicated that the cost of these settlements has to be included in the global cost of all settlements — the so-called 'fiscal envelope' — the money available for settlements yet to be negotiated is correspondingly reduced.[26] Maori claimants at the end of the line — well down on the Tribunal's register of claims — are worried that they will lose out altogether.

Direct Negotiations: The Crown-Congress Joint Working Party
It is worth asking whether claimants are better off if they go into direct negotiation with the Crown. Here the record is no better than that of Crown representatives in dealing with Tribunal Recommendations. Take, for instance, the Crown-Congress Joint Working Party (CCJWP). This was set up by the Minister of Justice late in 1991 on the assumption that Maori claims to surplus railway land could be more rapidly and cheaply researched than was happening under the Tribunal, and then quickly settled by negotiation. A team of researchers under Professor Alan Ward was engaged and duly completed their task. Whether the research and accompanying legal costs were lower than comparable Tribunal costs is a moot question — the figures are not available. No doubt the research has been of similar calibre to that done for the Tribunal, but it has never been made public or subjected to cross examination as happens with the Tribunal. The research team has been disbanded and, ironically, most of the researchers have been employed by the Tribunal. Although the Crown and Congress have been in negotiation for some time, very little has been concluded. Some tentative agreements have been made over Auckland railway land,

including a monetary payment of $4 million, and Wellington railway land, with a payment of $3 million; but that is all.[27] Moreover, iwi claimants for land in question have sometimes been fearful that a deal will be done over their heads by the Crown and the National Maori Congress, and they have sought urgent hearings by the Tribunal to establish their rights. For instance, the Tribunal was called on to report on various claims to South Auckland railway lands and concluded that 'the disposal of railway assets without a prior arrangement or agreement with local Maori would be contrary to the principles of the Treaty of Waitangi'. It then listed the iwi organisations which needed to be considered.[28] But it is not clear whether they are in fact being considered.

Though the Tainui raupatu or confiscation claim is outside the CCJWP process, it seems also to have run into limbo. It was submitted originally to the Tribunal by the Tainui Trust Board but the Board was unwilling to wait for the Tribunal to complete its hearing of Taranaki's raupatu claim and went into direct negotiation with the Minister. Those negotiations have produced little agreement. An army camp near Ngaruawahia, formerly a mission station gifted to the Crown for a school, has been returned, but nothing has been concluded on the confiscated land, now almost entirely in private ownership, let alone the coal below, which Tainui have also claimed.[29] It is rumoured that negotiations have been abandoned — not as a result of the intransigence of the Crown but because of disagreements between claimants. This is a reminder that settlements, particularly of larger claims, are sometimes inhibited by disputes between claimant groups, and even when a settlement is clinched, as in the fishing deal, there can be considerable wrangling over the division of the spoils.

So whether we are considering negotiations over claims reported on by the Tribunal, or other claims where the Tribunal has been bypassed, very little has been concluded, apart from the fisheries settlement. Understandably, the National Government was unwilling to court Pakeha voter disapproval by concluding large and expensive settlements before the 1993 election. There was talk of a big deal, being promoted by Sir Graham Latimer, chairman of the New Zealand Maori Council and a former Maori Vice-President of the National Party, which would have involved handing over a large part of the Landcorp estate in full and final settlement of the Maori land claims. Quite apart from its cost and the likely unpopularity with Pakeha, such a deal is not very practicable since most of the Landcorp estate is not in the same places as the major Maori land claims. There is little Landcorp land in Waikato and Taranaki, for instance, the two main districts where the largest areas of Maori land were confiscated. Ever since the Royal Commission on Confiscated Lands reported in 1927, it has been admitted that these confiscations were unjust, even by the current Minister of Justice,[30] It seems that any overall settlement — the Minister's 'fiscal envelope' — will involve a combination of two things:

1. a cut-off date, probably 1996–97, for the lodgement of historical claims to the Tribunal which would, in turn, be given a cut-off date for hearing of these claims, probably 2010 rather than 2000; and
2. settlement of these and other claims by returning Crown land and other resources where possible, or monetary compensation, probably spread over some ten years. A figure of $1 billion has been suggested, though this would include fisheries and other payments already made.

But, if the fisheries deal is any guide, the price for Maori of all this will be an end to claims under the Treaty before the Tribunal and the courts. The Tribunal, like the Indian Claims Commission in the US, will have a finite life. However, one wonders whether any government or any legislation can stop litigation forever; or, for that matter, stop the Treaty of Waitangi from operating in the future. Governments have not been wholly successful in ignoring it in the past.

Unresolved Dilemmas: Taonga and Rangatiratanga

So far, I have been discussing Maori grievances in terms of the loss of resources; and I have not discussed all of these — for instance, claims to hydro- and geo-thermal resources, some of which have been reported by the Tribunal, and to minerals and petroleum, yet to be examined. I have also ignored less tangible things, or taonga. This in the Maori text of the Treaty meant more than its translation as 'other properties' in the English text. As the Tribunal pointed out in its Te Reo or Maori language Report, it certainly included the taonga of language which the Crown was obliged to protect, though it had failed to do so.[31] Te Reo was the first of a clutch of claims that have been considered by the Tribunal and have sometimes gone on to the courts, even the Privy Council, as Maori have tried to preserve their language and culture through access to radio and television and, as these have been privatised, by gaining a measure of ownership. There is no space to summarise the contest or the outcome; but it must be said that Maori have gained very little in comparison with private operators, often foreign: a little more time (in off-peak hours) on public radio and TV, and some funding for private radio stations. As the communications revolution gathers pace and our airwaves are flooded with cheap foreign imports, Maori language and culture will have great difficulty in surviving, especially with the young — despite impressive progress in recent years in teaching Maori language from kindergarten through to university.

A notable if unusual feature of Te Reo and the other language and broadcasting claims was that they were made on behalf of all Maori, whereas most other claims were made on behalf of iwi, hapu, or even individuals. Another nationally supported claim was Harry Puke's claim on the Electoral Option, lodged on behalf of the New Zealand Maori Council, the National Maori Congress and the New Zealand Maori Women's Welfare League. The claim had to be hurriedly reported since it was a request for funding to publicise an option for Maori to enrol on either the Maori or General roll which had to be exercised between 15 February and 14 April 1994. The number of enrolments on the Maori roll would determine the number of Maori constituency seats under the new MMP system. It was thus a matter of great importance for Maori — the first time since the four Maori seats were established in 1867 that they would have an opportunity to increase their representation. But they could also lose seats if the number on the Maori roll decreased. The claim had an even broader significance, a Treaty dilemma which has never been resolved: the extent to which in constitutional terms the Maori kawanatanga (sovereignty), transferred to the Crown in the first article, was to be tempered by respect for tino rangatiratanga (chiefly authority) which was guaranteed in the second article.[32] Since 1840 Maori have persistently tried to maintain independent authority, usually on a tribal basis, sometimes through supra-tribal organisations like the Kingitanga and the Kotahitanga Parliament. Some Maori autonomy could have been recognised under section 71 of the 1852 Constitution Act which allowed separate districts to be set aside where Maori law and custom would prevail. But no such districts were ever established and section 71 was finally repealed by the New Zealand Constitution Act of 1986. Pakeha, on the other hand, have always held that the sovereignty obtained under the first article was one and indivisible and was properly exercised by elected national, provincial and local governments. Maori could be represented in those governments on the same basis as other citizens. But because they did not have the necessary property qualifications they were granted four seats in the lower house as a temporary expedient in 1867. The seats have remained by default ever since, though Maori have been considerably under-represented most of the time, and largely in recent years because more people of Maori descent have chosen to enrol on the General roll or have failed to enrol on either.[33] As Maori see it, the four seats are a last vestige of their rangatiratanga. Maori leaders, if not all their apolitical rank and file, have persistently demanded the retention, indeed increase, in the number of seats, usually on the basis of total Maori population. Since 1943 (at least until the last election) the four seats have been in the keeping of the Labour Party, and National Governments have often contemplated but not quite had the nerve to abolish them. The present National Government chose to include them in the constituency seats in the event of the country voting for MMP in the referendum held in conjunction with the 1993 election. The price was that the number of Maori seats would rise or fall according to the number of Maori who opted for the Maori roll. The country did vote for MMP so it has been necessary to run the Maori option to determine the number of Maori seats before working out the remainder of the constituency seats for voters on the General roll.

After 127 years the Maori seats are assured as part of the New Zealand electoral system; the number of seats rests with Maori themselves. But that is not a very significant measure of rangatiratanga. Maori will remain a minority in Parliament, as they will in the country at large, perhaps, under MMP with enhanced opportunities to wheel and deal with the major parties. But if their lack of success when holding the balance of power — the so-called 'Maori mandate' — in previous Parliaments is any guide, they will not do very well.

Other constitutional developments are also likely to bring dilemmas for Maori and, in the end, little satisfaction. It is likely that Maori will oppose the abolition of the monarchy which, even for New Zealand, now seems a distinct possibility, once Australia has led the way. The Prime Minister has talked of holding a referendum to decide whether New Zealand should become a republic in the year 2000. It is no coincidence that he also sees this as the year 'for clearing up all outstanding Treaty of Waitangi claims'.[34] The move towards a republic will probably start with abolition of appeals to the Privy Council which has sometimes given a little comfort if few tangible gains to Maori litigants, since New Zealand Governments have usually applied a legislative remedy to any defeats before the Privy Council.[35] The royal honours system will be next, which Maori may regret since royal honours and particularly knighthoods have always been appreciated as a recognition of rangatiratanga; but they might be satisfied if they get plenty of spoils from a local honours system. As for abolishing the monarchy itself, there will be considerable Maori resistance since they have a strong personal attachment to the incumbent monarch as a direct descendant of Victoria in whose name the Treaty was signed. But that personal attachment has often obscured the hard realities of their constitutional position when, after the transfer of responsible government to a local settler regime, Maori could no longer get direct access to or redress of their grievances from the reigning monarch, no matter how often they sent petitions or deputations to London. They were always referred back to the hard-hearted politicians in Wellington.[36] Even in this century royals and their representatives in New Zealand have encouraged Maori to hope for some of that royal protection promised by the Treaty. The present Queen is no exception. She started her reign by visiting the Maori King at Ngaruawahia, much to the dismay of her New Zealand Prime Minister. In her Waitangi address in 1963 she said that 'it remains the sacred duty of the Crown today as in 1840 to stand by the Treaty of Waitangi'.[37] During her last visit, when she spoke at the sesquicentennial celebrations at Waitangi, she said the Treaty of Waitangi had been 'imperfectly observed' — somewhat to the dismay of the then Prime Minister who tried to give a more glowing impression.[38] But a few sympathetic words from the Queen cannot obscure the fact that the Treaty is and has long been observed only in so far as the New Zealand Parliament has prescribed. It is doubtful therefore whether the preservation of the monarchy is a necessary means to secure the Treaty. Perhaps we should look to America where, more than 200 years ago, the British monarchy was thrown out but Americans preserved in their new republican constitution the treaties that British monarchs had made with the Indian nations. If we lost the chance to incorporate the Treaty in our recent Bill of Rights, we might be able to preserve it, or at least some of its guarantees, in new republican arrangements.

This leads to a final dilemma: how will Maori — and New Zealand — fare in the continuing internationalisation of human rights?[39] Since the Second World War and the creation of the United Nations and associated organisations, Maori activists have often looked abroad for support for their causes at home, and they have been critical of New Zealand diplomats who claimed that our 'success' in Maori–Pakeha relations at home was an object lesson for the rest of the world. If New Zealand was quick to decolonise in the Pacific, she was slow and reluctant to withdraw from contacts, especially sporting contests, with apartheid South Africa, and this also called into doubt our commitment to racial equality at home. Nevertheless New Zealand adopted various UN human rights conventions, such as the International Convention on the Elimination of All Forms of Racial Discrimination 1966. To give proper effect to this convention, New Zealand passed the Race Relations Act in 1971.[40] This provided for the appointment of a Race Relations Conciliator who has sometimes been a Maori. The Conciliator's work in the early years was largely concerned with Maori complaints of discrimination, but recently the complaints have been coming mainly from other minorities.

Other conventions or declarations have dealt with the rights of indigenous peoples to development — a right taken up by the Tribunal in its Muriwhenua Fishing Report.[41] There is also a developing body of international law and convention relating to the protection of indigenous culture, including traditions, religion, sacred sites and artefacts.[42] Yet the most controversial issue is yet to come: the draft UN Declaration on the Rights of Indigenous Peoples. This, with its stress on autonomy and the right to self-government of indigenous peoples, could raise long-forlorn hopes of Maori for a proper expression of tino rangatiratanga and therefore some very sticky constitutional issues for New Zealand. According to Maori lawyer, Joe Williams, New Zealand's performance so far in relation to Treaty and developing international standards has not been very impressive. 'New Zealand,' he said, 'has done reasonably well in some areas and appallingly badly in others. We have honoured the Treaty in some respects but not in others. There has been insufficient protection of Maori culture; tribal land tenure has been destroyed, resulting in the "decimation" of the tribal land base; the right to autonomy [he meant tribal autonomy] has been ignored.'[43] But, if the past is any guide, Pakeha New Zealand will not easily surrender to Maori any real autonomy.

Conclusion

Perhaps in the end we can only conclude that there will be no conclusion. The most striking aspect of our history, particularly the history of relations between Maori and Pakeha since 1840, is that the Treaty, despite long periods of official non-recognition and neglect, will not go away. To Pakeha it is something of an albatross around their necks, but to Maori it is a guarantee of their right to a fair share of resources and of their identity; their Magna Carta. So long as there is an unequal distribution of resources, Maori claims, founded on the Treaty, will continue, long beyond any artificial limits imposed by politicians. And Maori claims will not rest on resources alone, since Maori will continue their struggle to maintain their culture and identity, their Maoritanga, within the nation and society. Moreover, there will be new claims, prompted by developments from abroad as well as within, that cannot be conceived by us.

But I do not want to end on a negative note. I see nothing wrong in an indefinite continuation of the claims process, so long as there is reasonable restraint on costs. For the process itself has a therapeutic effect, especially on the Maori and Pakeha who attend Tribunal hearings. The claims resolutions are an essential part of the continuing adjustments that Maori and Pakeha must make as they continue to live in New Zealand and share its resources.

13

Waitangi:
Ka Whawhai Tonu Matou

Eight years ago New Zealand celebrated its sesquicentennial; it was 150 years since the Treaty of Waitangi had been negotiated between a representative of Queen Victoria and Maori chiefs at the pleasant Bay of Islands resort of Waitangi. 'Waitangi' means in English 'waters of lamentation'; one might say that New Zealanders, both Maori and Pakeha, have been crying over the Waitangi treaty ever since. That view is too extreme, but it is true that New Zealanders' attitudes to the Treaty have usually been ambiguous, and sometimes bitterly divided. The divisions have been mainly, but not exclusively, between Maori on one side and Pakeha on the other. Divisions that tend to be exacerbated each Waitangi Day, when Maori in particular are inclined to look back over those 150-odd years and ask: 'What have we to celebrate, when the Treaty, as we understand it, has not been honoured?'

To illustrate that point, let me return to the 1990 Waitangi celebration. Not surprisingly, there was a bigger celebration at Waitangi than the usual annual gathering, with Her Majesty, Queen Elizabeth, great-great-granddaughter of Victoria, present. There was a crowd of some 30,000 people, including numerous Maori protesters waving banners saying 'Honour the Treaty'. As if to meet their challenge, the official speeches referred in varying

---

'Our enduring struggle'. The lecture reprinted here was delivered at the Australia-New Zealand Studies Center of the Pennsylvania State University, which also published it. It was reprinted in Patty O'Brien and Bruce Vaughn, eds, *Amongst Friends: Australian and New Zealand Voices from America*, University of Otago Press, Dunedin, 2005, pp. 172–88. The text and endnotes that follow are from the Penn State version of the lecture.

ways to how the Treaty had been honoured. The Prime Minister, Geoffrey Palmer, explained how his Labour Government had been attempting to resolve Maori Treaty-based grievances and, although there were two parties to the Treaty, there was only one land, and that it was necessary to complete the task of nation building. But his speech was so interrupted by the protesters that Palmer left his prepared notes and expounded on the virtues of democracy and the rule of law which allowed the protesters to voice their opinions. Her Majesty's speech said, among other things, that the Treaty of Waitangi had been 'imperfectly observed'. And she reminded her New Zealand ministers that the Court of Appeal had recently told both Treaty partners 'to show each other the utmost good faith'; coded language that the Treaty, which was not part of New Zealand domestic law, needed to be upheld.

Then there were two Maori speakers, the chairman of the New Zealand Maori Council, Sir Graham Latimer, who made a conciliatory speech, and the Maori Bishop of Aotearoa, Whakahuihui Vercoe, who said that since the signing of the Treaty, 'you, our Treaty partners, have marginalised us. You have not honoured the Treaty. We have not honoured each other in the promises we made on this sacred ground. Since 1840 the partner that has been marginalised is me — the language of this land is yours, the custom is yours, the media by which we tell the world who we are is yours.' He detailed other examples of marginalisation and concluded that he had come to Waitangi 'to weep for what could have been a unique document in the history of indigenous peoples'. He pleaded with Maori and Pakeha to sit and listen to one another. Vercoe's speech received a huge cheer from the protesters, captured the headlines in the media, and was remembered long after the other speeches were forgotten.[1]

I have spent some time on the 1990 celebration, not because it was unique, but because it was in many ways typical of what happened at Waitangi in 1840 and from time to time since. It was a situation in which everyone was talking and no one, or at least hardly anyone, was listening; a situation where Maori and Pakeha were talking past one another. But while that may be usually true, there have been since 1840 occasions when Maori and Pakeha have comprehended one another. Bishop Vercoe's speech was one such moment, because, in saying that Maori had been marginalised, he was saying something that everyone knew was true, though few liked to admit. Since 1840, despite the promise of the Treaty to protect Maori, their land, and other resources, they had lost all but some 5 per cent of their land and most other resources. Despite enjoying the rights and privileges of British subjects, which the Treaty also promised, they had become marginalised in the lower socio-economic rungs of New Zealand society.

As I discovered when I attended a Minnesota conference on promoting racial economic equality two years ago, statistics on socio-economic conditions for African Americans and Native Americans are very similar to those for Maori.

But in New Zealand, the problems are not confined to improving Maori socio-economic conditions. We are still grappling with the problem of how to incorporate Maori, now a minority of some 12 per cent of the total population, in the politico-constitutional structures of the country, and with the problem of how to recognise their tino rangatiratanga (chiefly authority), as they call it, also guaranteed in the Treaty, and which has been variously interpreted as Maori sovereignty, autonomy and self-determination. That is why I have called Waitangi our enduring struggle. It is not a unique situation, but common to all indigenous groups, sometimes called 'entrapped nations', who have been overwhelmed and outnumbered by colonists. The similarity with Native Americans is evident.

Since 1990, Waitangi Day celebrations have remained acrimonious, and two years ago the official ceremony was moved to Government House in Wellington. Behind a closed fence, the Governor-General and the Prime Minister mingle with the diplomatic corps and invited New Zealand guests, and polite speeches are made. But the unofficial celebrations at Waitangi continue, much as before, with the Deputy Prime Minister (and this year, for part of the day, the Prime Minister) representing the Government, and the Leader of the Opposition also present, taking the opportunity to enjoy the discomfort of the Government. Protesters have been less vociferous.

Since we often quarrel over the Treaty and its annual commemoration, you might well wonder whether we are a nation at all. A good question. Perhaps Americans have no such problem; after all, 4 July is a pretty clear-cut celebration of independence, even though that was proclaimed some years before the British were expelled and some years again before the former colonies became the United States of America. And perhaps you might wonder why we celebrate our becoming a British colony, not our independence from Britain. Well, that would be a problem because if you asked, most New Zealanders would not be able to tell you what day or year that independence occurred; and if you ask me, I would have to take longer than I have got to explain it. In any case we are hardly wholly independent now, since we owe allegiance to a member of the House of Windsor, née Hanover, though she is now 'Queen in right of New Zealand'. If the opinion polls are right, we are less likely than Australia to become a republic. In any case, finding a Fourth of July, an independence day for New Zealand, would not solve our national day dilemma: Maori would say,

'We might be independent of Britain, but when are we going to be independent of those descendants of the British, the New Zealand Pakeha, who control us?' Oddly enough, many Maori support retention of the last vestige of British rule — the monarchy — and are strongly opposed to becoming a republic, because they hope, usually in vain, that the descendant of Victoria will protect them, as Victoria herself promised to do in the Treaty of Waitangi.

As for celebration of other great events, they too are equally problematical. You recently celebrated 500 years since America was discovered (if not quite for the first time). As I remember it, Native Americans objected to the celebration of the arrival of Columbus. My guidebook says that, though Columbus Day is a federal holiday, 'many Native Americans do not consider this event to be cause for celebration'.[2] Australian Aborigines either protested about or ignored the celebration of the bicentenary of Cook's arrival. And I doubt whether they are enthusiastic in celebrating Australia Day. I did not see any Aborigines at the recent Australia Day dinner in Washington, or hear any reference to them in the speeches. Though there was little Maori protest over the celebration of the Cook bicentenary in New Zealand, the celebration was largely a Pakeha affair.

We cannot be surprised, then, if Maori are ambivalent, and sometimes antagonistic, towards the celebration of 'their' national day. Like Bishop Vercoe, they look to 150 years of non-fulfilment of the Treaty (as they interpret it), 150 years of Pakeha colonisation, and find that they have been marginalised. That notion might be equally applied to Native Americans, who had many treaties, and Australian Aborigines, who had none.

The Two Texts of the Treaty

Americans might well be surprised that we make so much fuss over our single treaty, whereas the 367 or so treaties that were negotiated with their Native Americans are largely forgotten. I shall give details of the Treaty of Waitangi in a minute, but note here that Waitangi differed from most North American Indian treaties in that it applied to the whole of New Zealand. It was signed by more than 530 chiefs (including five women), representing most, if not all, of the tribes of the country, and was therefore more thoroughly approved than any of the North American treaties. Under the English text of the Treaty of Waitangi, Maori ceded sovereignty. The American Indians did not do this; they remained, in Mr Justice Marshall's long-remembered phrase, 'domestic dependent nations',[3] and were allowed to retain, at least where they also retained reservations, a degree of autonomy. Maori have not been allowed to retain even that limited autonomy in New Zealand. For better or worse, New

Zealand authorities have insisted on imposing the Austinian notion that sovereignty within the nation was one and indivisible,[4] and that the New Zealand Parliament, so long as its legislation was not incompatible with the law of the imperial Parliament, had the sole authority to exercise that sovereignty. Though legal pluralism remained alive in other parts of the Empire (especially the tropical parts and to some extent in America), there was every attempt, until recently, to stamp it out in New Zealand, by bringing Maori and their land within the scope of imported English- and New Zealand-made law. We have had what a fairly recent Attorney-General described as 'the best of British law'. I shall return to this point later.

Our treaty differed from American Indian treaties in that it did not cede land; indeed Maori were promised the full and undisturbed possession of their lands, forests, fisheries and other properties; and the rights and privileges of British subjects. Because of this it has often been referred to as a 'Maori Magna Carta' and as providing a charter for the nation that was founded at Waitangi in 1840.

Having pointed out some differences between the Treaty of Waitangi and North American treaties, I must be careful not to lapse into that habit of too many of our academic historians, of claiming that the Treaty of Waitangi and the race relations that flowed from it were unique; not only were the Maori better treated under the Treaty than other colonised peoples, but race relations in New Zealand have been better than in 'South Australia, South Dakota and South Africa', to borrow a title from an essay by a colleague who was knighted for his services to New Zealand history. The Treaty of Waitangi, at least in its English text, is virtually identical to several treaties signed by Britain with various west African dignitaries at the same time, though it has been more enduring. And race relations thereafter were not noticeably better than in other jurisdictions; after all, we had our frontier Maori Wars, as they were called, when Americans were having their Indian wars in the West. The treatment of Maori after those wars has been no better (and maybe no worse) than the treatment of Native Americans, though for a long time both tended to be written out of the history books.

Another important difference was that, although American Indian treaties were always written in English, the Treaty of Waitangi had two texts, English and Maori. Moreover, the Maori text was not a straightforward translation of the English text. I want to talk briefly about both texts, beginning with the English one since this was regarded as the official text for more than 100 years and in that time was the principal vehicle for Government Maori policies.[5]

The English Text of the Treaty

The Treaty of Waitangi is a very brief document which, in addition to a preamble and brief conclusion, consists of three articles.

- In Article 1, Maori ceded sovereignty to Queen Victoria.
- In Article 2, they were guaranteed the 'full, exclusive and undisturbed possession of their lands, forests, fisheries and other properties' and yielded an exclusive right of pre-emption to the Crown to buy such land as they wished to sell.
- In Article 3, they were granted the rights and privileges of British subjects and offered royal protection.

There is no need for a lengthy dissertation on implementation of this version of the Treaty; that is well covered in Claudia Orange's *Treaty of Waitangi* (1987). But it is sufficient to say that the early imperial governors and the later colonist governments used the sovereign authority that was conceded in the first article to bring Maori, their land and other resources within the scope of colonisation. The Crown's right of pre-emption was vigorously exercised, and in the first 20 years the whole of the South Island and much of the North Island were purchased, often at purely nominal prices. Some of these transactions resembled what were called treaties in the US — for instance the Ngai Tahu or Canterbury purchase, whereby some 34 million acres of the South Island were purchased for £8,750, or 0.06 pence per acre, and a promise of reserves (which turned out to be minuscule in American terms), schools and hospitals (which did not eventuate). Ngai Tahu grievances over that have been prosecuted for over 100 years, have been the subject of numerous inquiries, including one by the Waitangi Tribunal, and have recently been settled by the Government. In the North Island, where the bulk of the Maori population were situated, Crown pre-emptive purchase ran into Maori opposition, and the attempt to enforce a disputed purchase at Waitara in Taranaki provoked the outbreak of the first of the wars of the 1860s. One result was that the Government, then controlled by settler politicians, abolished the Crown's right of pre-emption, supposedly guaranteed by the Treaty, and under the Native Lands Acts from 1862 allowed colonists to purchase land directly from Maori once a Native Land Court had adjudicated and individualised customary titles. Under that legislation further large areas of Maori land were purchased, but the Crown returned to the scene from 1870, in competition with private buyers, and sometimes to get the better of them restored pre-emption by proclamation to enable Crown purchase of specific blocks. In one way or another, the greater part of remaining Maori land was purchased in the later nineteenth century and the first two decades of the twentieth.

Ironically, the native lands legislation was justified as giving better effect to the Treaty — in the sense that Maori were now being given the opportunity to exchange their customary titles for the security of individual Crown-granted titles, which at that time were needed for the franchise. And that was part of the broader policy of granting Maori the rights and privileges of British subjects, guaranteed in the third article of the Treaty. Other legislation of this period, including a Native Rights Act and a Maori Representation Act (giving them four seats in Parliament), was also regarded as fulfilling that third article. Though I must note also, yet other legislation that passed during the height of the war, including a New Zealand Settlements Act, to provide for the confiscation of land, and a Suppression of Rebellion Act, which suspended *habeas corpus* for those Maori who were deemed to be in rebellion. The legislation was taken from Ireland, not the US. Under the confiscation legislation some three million acres of Maori land was seized, though about half was returned; and that confiscation, or raupatu as Maori call it, has long been a festering grievance. It has also been the subject of numerous inquiries, one of which (in 1927) resulted in the payment of an annuity form of compensation, which, being fixed, soon became inadequate. Once again the raupatu claims have come before the Waitangi Tribunal and one — that of Tainui in Waikato — has been settled, though by direct negotiation with the Crown rather than Tribunal inquiry.

There was yet a broader aim to the legislation: the first and third articles of the Treaty were being used to bring Maori and their resources within the scope of English- and New Zealand-made law, both civil and criminal, as part of a broader policy of assimilation. This was to be complemented by educational policy — originally promoted by the missions, later by native and secular state schools. All of this will be familiar to Americans, since assimilation policies were applied to Native Americans in what remained of their reservations. Though the terminology used in New Zealand was sometimes different, the intentions were the same: for our Native Lands Acts, read your Allotment Act (1887), whereby reservations in the West were carved up into 160-acre allotments, allocated to heads of families, and often sold off later to white settlers. The New Zealand reserves (we did not call them reservations) were invariably smaller, deliberately so because the American system was condemned in New Zealand, for instance by the founder of the New Zealand Company, E. G. Wakefield, for shutting the Indians away from assimilation into European society. Since Maori reserves in New Zealand were seldom regarded as inalienable, few have remained in Maori ownership, and dispossessed Maori were put under greater pressure to assimilate; a situation that parallels that of Native Americans east of the Mississippi (though Maori were spared the pain of removal treaties).

In promoting the assimilation policy under the first and third articles of the English text of the Treaty, New Zealand governments have seen that as the proper means of implementing the Treaty. They have seen it as a way of amalgamating the races, Maori and Pakeha, into a single society (something that has been facilitated by a high and increasing degree of intermarriage); of forming a 'One New Zealand'. At Waitangi in 1840, as Lieutenant Governor Hobson, the Queen's representative, got each Maori signature on the Treaty, he uttered the only Maori words he knew: 'He iwi tahi tatou' — 'We are now one people'. That injunction has been uttered many times since and by successive governors at Waitangi anniversary ceremonies who could still get away with it in the middle years of this century. But not any more. To explain why, I have to look at the Maori text of the Treaty, and what, over the years, Maori have hoped to get from it.

The Maori Text of the Treaty

Although the Treaty was originally drafted in English by Hobson and his officials, this was given to the head of the Church Missionary Society at the Bay of Islands, Henry Williams, who, with his son Edward, rendered it into Maori. I say 'rendered' into Maori because Williams did not do a straight translation of the English text, but creatively reworked it into a Maori version that he believed Maori chiefs would accept.[6] Sometimes, Williams was able to use Maori words as a direct translation of English, but at other times he made them bear new meanings. At yet other times, when there was no Maori word remotely suitable, he used transliterations of some English words which were at least partly familiar to Maori. For instance, there was no Maori equivalent of 'sovereignty', so Williams used 'kawanatanga'. 'Kawana' is a transliteration of 'governor' and was familiar to Maori who had been told about the Roman governor, Pontius Pilate, and some had been to Sydney or Hobart, where they had seen real British governors. Hobson was clearly one of them. Williams added the causative suffix 'tanga', making kawanatanga, intended to signify 'governorship' or 'governance', which Maori were to cede in the first article of the Treaty. But during the negotiations at Waitangi, the significance of that was played down by Williams and Hobson, who gave Maori the impression that the powers of governance would be exercised largely to keep the whites in order, not to interfere with the authority of chiefs; though it was suggested that the new governor, like Williams and other missionaries beforehand, would use his authority to prevent Maori fighting one another.

The second major change that Williams made was to use the phrase 'tino rangatiratanga' for what had been written as 'full possession' (of lands and other properties) in the second article of the Treaty. The other properties were described as 'taonga', a word that to Maori means much more than mere tangible things and includes intangibles of a cultural and spiritual nature. Now tino rangatiratanga means much more than mere possession; it means 'full chieftainship', which includes control over, as well as ownership and possession, of land. Assured of that full chieftainship, the leading chiefs, after vigorously debating the Treaty (as it was read out in Maori to them), assented to it at Waitangi on 6 February 1840 and thereafter at many other places around the country. They believed that whatever vague powers they might have conceded to the kawana or governor, they retained their traditional chiefly authority. Moreover, since all but some 30 of the 530-odd who signed the Treaty signed the Maori text, they had every right to expect it to be fulfilled. In international law, subsequently expressed in the US case *Jones v Meehan* (1899),[7] they had every right to that expectation.

Needless to say, when the governor and his officials tried to exercise the sovereign authority they thought they had acquired in the English text of the Treaty, bringing Maori and their possessions under English law, there was trouble. Indeed in the Northern War that broke out in 1844, the Maori 'rebels' were led by Hone Heke, the first Maori to sign the Treaty, who repeatedly cut down the British flag since he saw it as a symbol of British authority being asserted, in the actions of various petty officials, over his tino rangatiratanga. This was also an issue in many later disputes, perhaps most notably in Waikato, where a Maori King was established in 1858. (He had much in common with those other Polynesian monarchs, the Kamehamehas of Hawaii.) A Maori King was needed to reassert the authority of the chiefs who put themselves under his allegiance in order to resist land sales and the imposition of British law. His territory was invaded by British and colonial troops in 1863, so that Waikato land could be confiscated and this rival sovereign could be put down. The land was confiscated, but the King and his supporters escaped south into what is still known today as the King Country. His law, rather than colonial law, prevailed there for 20 years. The 1852 Constitution Act — the basis of New Zealand's constitution until 1986 — had a provision whereby native districts could be set aside where Maori law and custom would prevail (and these could have given

Maori groups the status of domestic dependent nations). However, the provision was never implemented, though Maori supporters of the King repeatedly appealed for this status to be allowed to them. As I have said, New Zealand governments have persistently insisted that the sovereignty they exercised was one and indivisible.

Nevertheless, in later years, Maori did not give up their quest for separate autonomy, which they believed was guaranteed by their text of the Treaty. The Maori King movement remains to this day, though its support is now confined mainly to the Tainui tribes of Waikato. However, the present Maori Queen, the fifth in succession, is tacitly recognised, both by the New Zealand Government and by Queen Elizabeth (who has been able to accept monarchs in other parts of the Commonwealth). There have been other Maori 'nationalist' movements, such as the Kotahitanga ('unity') movement in the late nineteenth century, which established a Maori Parliament, modelled on the New Zealand Parliament in Wellington. But although it went on meeting annually for eleven years, it was never recognised; the Wellington Parliament was not going to allow its sovereignty to be divided. In this century several other national Maori organisations have been formed, including the Maori Women's Welfare League, the New Zealand Maori Council and, most recently, the National Maori Congress. However, their powers are limited; they can advise and at times negotiate on behalf of Maori with Government; but they do not rule over Maori. As such, they are very limited expressions of tino rangatiratanga; they do not give Maori autonomy, let alone the 'status of independent governments' which I note that Native Americans claim for their reservation authorities.[8]

Having failed to get any autonomous authority outside the New Zealand Parliament, Maori leaders have had to make the best of what they have been allowed, as representatives of a minority, within it.[9] They were granted four seats in the House of Representatives as a temporary measure in 1867, with the members elected from a separate roll and for separate constituencies that divided the country into four. It was usual to add one or two nominated Maori representatives to the upper house, the Legislative Council, until this was abolished in 1950. When Pakeha women got the vote in 1893, Maori women were also enfranchised. People of mixed ancestry have usually had the choice of voting on either the Maori or the General roll. As a somewhat under-represented minority in a house of some 90 members, Maori members were frequently overridden, particularly on matters relating to the alienation of their land. But over the years they have had some outstanding representatives, including Sir James Carroll and Sir Apirana Ngata, who both held important ministerial portfolios, including Maori Affairs. That portfolio has usually been held by a Maori member in recent years, as it is at present. The present Deputy Prime Minister, Winston Peters, is Maori.

The system of separate Maori representation has often been criticised by Pakeha New Zealanders as separatist, even as amounting to apartheid. This is scarcely correct since voters can only register on one roll, but it is true that voters of Maori descent have a choice of either (and in fact in recent years about half of the Maori who have registered have done so on the General roll). Over the years there have been many proposals to integrate the two systems, but none has been implemented. In the end, Pakeha members of Parliament, of both major parties, have respected the plea of Maori members to retain their separate representation.

In 1986 a Royal Commission on the electoral system recommended that our first past the post system be replaced by a mixed member proportional system, with half the 120 members elected for constituencies and the remainder chosen from party lists according to the proportion of votes received by each party. The Commission believed that this system would enable Maori to gain sufficient representation, since it was assumed that the parties would put Maori representatives high enough on their lists to be elected. But, when Maori objected, the Minister of Justice, Douglas Graham, agreed to retain the Maori constituency seats, and indeed to allow them to rise or fall according to enrolments on the Maori roll. Sufficient Maori voters shifted to the Maori roll to allow a fifth seat for the 1996 election and since then a further increase has allowed for a seventh seat. Since all of the major parties placed Maori high on their party lists several others were also elected to Parliament in 1996, giving Maori some fifteen members. This approximates to their proportion of the population; for the first time, one could say, Maori have been fairly represented in Parliament. In terms of majoritarian democracy, this could be regarded as equitable. But it is hardly an adequate expression of the tino rangatiratanga that Maori thought they had been given in the Treaty. I shall return to this point later.

Finally, I should note, so far as the Maori text of the Treaty is concerned, that Maori have always resisted the assimilation policies promoted by New Zealand governments and, as I noted, supposedly justified by the first and third articles of the English text of the Treaty. They have seen, in the second article of the Maori text especially, the guarantee of tino rangatiratanga over their land and other resources, including taonga, which includes intangibles such as language and culture. They also argue that in the third article the Queen also offered her protection of that culture. Moreover, at Waitangi in 1840, Governor Hobson, in response to a plea from the French Catholic bishop for freedom of religion, not only promised that, but also included a guarantee for Maori religion, expressed as 'ritenga' or 'culture'; sometimes referred to by Maori as the 'fourth article' of the Treaty.[10] Under the *contra proferentem* principle, enunciated in *Jones v Meehan*, promises made during the negotiation of a treaty are to be taken into consideration in interpreting that treaty.

Although, as I have said, governments in New Zealand promoted assimilation policies for many years, indeed until the 1960s, since then, it has been admitted that Maori should be entitled, even encouraged and assisted, to retain their own culture and identity, seen most notably in attempts to revive the nearly defunct Maori language, now taught at all levels of the educational system, and used more frequently in ceremonial occasions on marae. Associated with this cultural renaissance has been a reconsideration of the Maori text of the Treaty.

The Treaty of Waitangi Act of 1975 and the Waitangi Tribunal

Until the 1970s the English text of the Treaty was regarded as the official text. If the Maori text was considered at all, it was regarded merely as a translation of the English text. However, as I have indicated, Maori had long considered the Maori text gave them different (and greater) rights. The changed appreciation of the Maori text was, in my view, due largely to a superb essay by the historian Ruth Ross, titled 'Te Tiriti o Waitangi: Texts and Translations', published in *The New Zealand Journal of History* in October 1972. By translating and analysing the Maori text, Ross demonstrated convincingly that it said different things from the English text; and she reminded us that it was, after all, this text that nearly all Maori signed. Subsequent analyses by other scholars, most notably the 1989 essay 'Humpty-Dumpty and the Treaty of Waitangi' by our pre-eminent Maori language scholar, Professor Bruce Biggs, have validated and elaborated Ross's findings.[11]

Three years after the publication of Ross's essay, the Treaty of Waitangi Act 1975, which established the Waitangi Tribunal, gave the Maori and English texts equal status and printed both (though not without mistakes in the Maori text) in a schedule to the Act. The preamble of the Act noted the English and Maori texts of the Treaty differed from one another and that it was desirable that the Tribunal, in making recommendations 'on claims relating to the practical application of the principles of the Treaty . . . determine its meaning and effect'. Section 5 of the Act elaborated by stating that in exercising its functions the Tribunal was to 'have regard to the 2 texts of the Treaty' and to have 'exclusive authority to determine the meaning and effect of the Treaty as embodied in the 2 texts and to decide issues raised by the differences between them'. That gave the Tribunal an important authority in the interpretation of the two texts of the Treaty — at least in Maori claims submitted to it. We must note, however, that Maori claims submitted to the Tribunal for consideration were, under section 6 of the Act, to be confined to breaches by the Crown of the *principles*, not the *provisions*, of the Treaty. Probably, because the provisions of the two texts differed, it was considered advisable for the Tribunal to find some central principles that were common to both. That was to be no easy task, especially as the Act gave no definition whatsoever of the principles; they were to be worked out on a claim-by-claim basis as the Tribunal proceeded, and as the courts were sometimes called on to hear Maori cases, more especially as the Tribunal itself at this stage was given no judicial authority. It could merely recommend that the Crown act to remove any breach of principle that the Tribunal found was prejudicial to the claimants. Moreover, the Tribunal was limited at this stage to hearing claims of breaches of the principles from the date that the Act was passed (10 October 1975).

Because of this limitation, and because the incoming National Government of Robert Muldoon delayed for several years appointing members to the Tribunal, it was not until the early 1980s that the Tribunal came out with some effective reports on the few claims submitted to it. These coincided with the appointment of Edward Taihakurei Durie as Chief Judge of the Maori Land Court, the first Maori appointed to that position, whereby he also became chairman of the Waitangi Tribunal. Durie was joined on the Tribunal by Sir Graham Latimer, chairman of the New Zealand Maori Council, and Paul Temm, a prominent Auckland barrister. Between them they brought out reports, mainly on environmental issues relating to peri-urban developments that were damaging Maori resources (kaimoana) that stunned New Zealanders and forced a reluctant Muldoon Government to take note of the Tribunal's recommendations. As I have already observed, the Tribunal's seemingly radical reports were nothing of the kind.[12] It was saying what historians had long said about the rape of Maori resources, and what lawyers elsewhere, perhaps most notably in Canada and the US, had also been saying for some time about aboriginal rights and treaties. But compared with the apparently radical findings on breaches of the principles of the Treaty, the Tribunal came out with remarkably mild recommendations to the Crown on how to repair those breaches. It merely asked the Crown, or local bodies acting as agencies for the Crown, to impose more stringent conditions for the treatment and disposal of sewage or industrial effluent and so on, in order to protect Maori estuarine resources from pollution and destruction; conditions that the environmental movements wanted to be imposed anyway. Most recommendations were eventually implemented.

In 1985 the Waitangi Tribunal was given a massive increase in jurisdiction when, under the Treaty of Waitangi Amendment Act, passed by the Lange Labour Government, it was authorised to investigate claims by Maori that the Crown had been in breach of the principles of the Treaty at any time since it was negotiated in 1840. This opened a Pandora's box of historical claims, many of which had been the subject of previous inquiries and sometimes had resulted in compensation payments as 'full and final settlements', such as the Ngai Tahu claims over South Island Crown purchases, and various tribal claims relating to the confiscation of land during the wars which I have previously mentioned. There was a considerable escalation in the number of claims submitted to the Tribunal: from a mere 25 on the register at the end of 1985 (when the amendment was passed) to 87 by the end of 1987 and 209 by the end of 1990 (the number registered is by now over 650). It was necessary to expand the Tribunal — from the original three members to sixteen by 1988 — and increase staffing and funds, so that several Tribunals could sit concurrently. However, although more claims were reported over the next few years, the backlog of unheard claims has continued to increase. As with the Indian Claims Commission, it was assumed that the Waitangi Tribunal would have a limited lifespan, and politicians have sometimes talked about cutting it off at a certain date, such as 2000, but so far no one has dared to make a firm commitment. New Zealand is too committed to upholding the Treaty for that.

However, it would be misleading to blame the escalation of claims on the Tribunal's retrospective jurisdiction; many of the claims lodged after the Act was amended were contemporary claims relating to current or contemplated Crown actions. The most notable of these were a consequence of the Labour Government's corporatisation or privatisation of state assets; known in New Zealand as 'Rogernomics', after the then Minister of Finance, Roger Douglas,[13] who tried to exceed both President Reagan and Prime Minister Thatcher. The trouble with this policy, so far as Maori were concerned, was that the Crown was proposing to sell into private ownership the very resources that were needed to settle long-standing historical grievances. Already, since 1840, the greater part of Maori land and other resources had fallen into Pakeha private ownership and there was no way the Tribunal or the Crown could recover it; but there were considerable areas of farmable land still held by the Crown (and about to be transferred to Landcorp) and exotic forests (about to be transferred to Forestcorp). Other resources including coal, hydro- and geothermal power, telecommunications, radio and television were either being transferred or fattened up for the market. The Government even privatised the fisheries by introducing individual transferable quotas (ITQs) — sellable property rights — with scant regard for Maori fisheries guaranteed by the Treaty and which had never been willingly alienated.

It was these developments which provoked a series of Maori claims to the Tribunal, and, if they were being frustrated there, to the ordinary courts. By skilfully shifting from one to the other, and back again, Maori and their legal advisers caught the Government in a cleft stick. It began when we in the Tribunal were hearing the Muriwhenua fishing claim, late in 1987, and we heard that the Government was about to issue more fishing quota before we had reported on the fishing claims of these northern tribes. We made an urgent plea to the Minister to withhold the quota, but he refused and so the Muriwhenua claimants went to the High Court, which issued an injunction. Then the New Zealand Maori Council went to the Court and got the injunction applied to the whole of the country. That, of course, was only the beginning of the struggle, but I cannot recount details of the remainder. It is sufficient to say that after tortuous negotiations, further litigation, and eventually legislation, Maori got access to some 22 per cent of the fishing quota for the country, a solution made possible partly by the coming onto the market of a half share of the Sealord company, which had about 24 per cent of the quota. The half-share was purchased by the Crown for $150 million, and went to the Maori Fisheries Commission (for later allocation to Maori interests). Since then, the Commission has purchased or been allocated more quota, and now holds 50 per cent of all commercial fishing quota in the country. In this respect, at least, the Crown has adequately fulfilled its Treaty obligation to Maori. Legislation passed to confirm the fisheries agreement laid down stated that there were to be no more claims to the Tribunal over commercial fishing rights.

Meanwhile, other resources were also being corporatised or privatised. Tainui in Waikato were able to stop the sale of Coalcorp by getting a Court of Appeal injunction against sale while their raupatu claim was still under consideration; that claim has been settled, but Coalcorp has not been privatised — yet. There was a bigger danger that Landcorp's farmable land would be sold. This time the New Zealand Maori Council, with the backing of the Tribunal, made a last-minute bid to amend the draft legislation to set up the State-Owned Enterprises (SOE) Act. Section 9 of that Act required the Crown to uphold the principles of the Treaty and section 27 laid down that, in the event of the Tribunal upholding a Maori claim to SOE or former SOE land, the Crown would recover it for the claimants. Nevertheless, Maori were dissatisfied with the way in which the Act was implemented, and the Maori Council went to the Court of Appeal in 1987. In a stunning decision, in which all five judges wrote separate judgments, cogently reviewing the SOE policy in relation to the principles of the Treaty, all concluded that the Crown had failed to abide by sections 9 and 27 of the SOE Act.[14] The Court required the Government and the Maori Council to negotiate an agreement to protect Maori interests during the transfer of Crown property to SOEs. The outcome was more legislation: the Treaty of Waitangi (State Enterprises) Act 1988, which provided detailed instructions on how the Crown was to recover SOE or former SOE land if the Tribunal upheld Maori claims to it; in effect giving the Tribunal a substantial judicial authority (which, incidentally, it has not used to enforce recovery).

But after this there was a subtle retreat by the Government from further commitments to uphold the Treaty. There were no more section 9s, requiring the Government to uphold the principles of the Treaty in subsequent legislation; the phrase was either weakened or deleted altogether. Some state-owned properties, such as Petrocorp, were not brought under the SOE Act. As far as Forestcorp was concerned, the Government decided to sell the trees but not the land, though it agreed with the Maori Council to set aside a proportion of the rental money for a Crown Forestry Rental Trust, which was to research claims to the land for hearing by the Tribunal. So far the Tribunal has not required the Crown to hand back any of the forest land, though several claims are in hearing.

In the meantime, in the last ten years, the Tribunal has been steadily producing reports, sometimes on relatively small but urgent claims, sometimes on large historical claims, including the Ngai Tahu land and fishing claims, and the Taranaki Report, the first of the raupatu claims reports. These reports have usually produced a considerable outcry, usually because of the Tribunal's uncovering of long-hidden historical maltreatment of Maori at the hand of settler governments, sometimes because the Tribunal's expression of this has been excessively extreme (for example in the recent Taranaki Report). But, having revealed the extent of the grievance and Crown breaches of the principles of the Treaty, the Tribunal has usually stopped short of recommendation, other than saying that the Crown and Maori claimants should negotiate a settlement of the grievance. As I have said, a settlement has finally been reached over the Ngai Tahu land claim, six years after the report was completed, and several smaller settlements have been reached over other reported claims. Finally — this will be my last discussion of Treaty claims — settlement has been reached, or nearly reached, in several claims which have bypassed the Tribunal.

Douglas Graham and the Direct Negotiation of Claims

The final stage I want to discuss owes much to the current Minister for Treaty Settlements (and Minister of Justice), Douglas Graham. The scion of a pioneer Auckland settler (who meddled in Maori land and affairs), Graham has done more than any conservative minister to resolve Maori grievances since Gordon Coates grappled with them in the 1920s. Graham has been ably supported by the former Prime Minister, Jim Bolger. I have no time to detail all of Graham's settlements, and have already mentioned the Tainui raupatu settlement, but I urge you to read the moving description of them in his recent book, *Trick or Treaty?*[15]

The settlements go back a little further than those described in Graham's book and include particularly those negotiated for surplus railways land by what was known as the Crown-Congress Joint Working Party. This time, instead of working with the Maori Council, the Government decided to work with another, more recently established, Maori body, the National Maori Congress, a grouping of tribes initiated by the paramount chief of Ngati Tuwharetoa, the late Sir Hepi Te Heu Heu. Instead of using the Tribunal to research Maori claims to the railway land, the Working Party appointed a team of historians, headed by Professor Alan Ward. It was largely on the basis of their reports, though the Tribunal was sometimes called in to assess them, that surplus railway land, some of it valuable urban property, was returned to Maori tribes that formerly owned it, not always without payment. Some other surplus Crown land, including school sites, has also been returned by direct negotiation, sometimes at concessionary prices.

Nevertheless the National Government had a much bigger deal in mind, as Graham's book admits: the settlement by about 2000 of all the major historical claims, whether the Tribunal had reported them or not. The proposal was dubbed the 'fiscal envelope' since all historical claims were to be settled with a total payment of $1 billion, paid over ten years. Impatient with the slow, meticulous research and lengthy reports of the Tribunal, Graham was prepared to accept the major historical grievances as proven, so that he could get on and settle them. That's fair enough (though I must say that most Tribunal inquiries reveal even more Maori grievances than he, or I, are aware of). However, the proposal was greeted by widespread Maori opposition; at hui after hui around the country, it was rejected by the tribes. Graham accepted this response with equanimity — but, although quietly dropping the $1 billion ceiling, steadily proceeded with the settlement of claims. To date, in addition to the $150 million fisheries settlement, the Government has settled most of the Tainui claim, for land and cash to the value of $170 million, and the Ngai Tahu claim, with land and cash also worth $170 million. It has also agreed in principle to a settlement of the Whakatohea raupatu claim for $40 million. Each time a settlement is reached, the claimants are required to renounce further claims to the Tribunal. These settlements alone have taken over half of the so-called fiscal envelope, and other Maori claimants, especially those whose claims have not yet been heard by the Tribunal, are concerned that there is likely to be little left for them, even though the $1 billion ceiling has been abandoned.

Compared with previous settlements, Doug Graham's settlements appear generous, though we need to remember that the payments are to a considerable extent an exercise in bookkeeping, with much of the cash payments coming from savings in the much-reduced Maori Affairs/Te Puni Kokiri budget. The amount of Crown land transferred — paid for out of the cash settlement — amounts to only a tiny portion of the area lost originally; in the case of Tainui, a mere 40,000 acres out of the 800,000 originally confiscated. That 40,000 acres took $100 million of their $170 million package. Though much of the remaining money is being used to purchase further private land on the open market, there is no way Tainui will ever recover a substantial portion of their confiscated land, now some of the most valuable farming land in the country. Likewise Ngai Tahu, though getting a couple of high-country pastoral runs as part of their settlement, and a considerable cash payment, have the opportunity to buy land in Canterbury, and are steadily doing so (though urban rather than rural property). But they too have little chance of recovering more than a small portion of the original 34-million-acre Canterbury block.

Conclusion

It is obvious, of course, that Maori cannot hope to recover all the land and other resources they lost, mainly in the later nineteenth century, no matter how inequitable the processes whereby they lost that land; and no matter how often the Crown was in breach of the principles of the Treaty in its involvement in those losses. The Tribunal has repeatedly admitted that a complete restoration is neither possible, nor even desirable. Well over half the country is in private ownership and successive governments have usually taken a strong line against compulsory acquisition of private land for the settlement of Treaty claims (apart from the exception of SOE or former SOE land already mentioned). Indeed in 1993 when Te Roroa Tribunal recommended that the Government take 'all possible steps' to acquire some farms in private ownership to settle that claim,[16] Minister Graham hastily amended the Tribunal's Act to prevent it from making such recommendations. Much of the remaining land in Crown ownership in New Zealand is set aside as National Parks and there is fierce opposition to handing over any of that to settle Maori claims. Although there is a considerable area of Crown land controlled by Landcorp and Forestcorp, Maori claims to most of this have not yet been dealt with by the Tribunal. The land is likely to become available for part-settlement of claims, as happened on a limited scale with the Tainui settlement. Recently they had returned to them land with a small exotic forest plantation on it.

The remainder of the settlements will have to be paid in cash, as has already happened with the ones I have described. But how much will be needed, and how long will it take? Some authorities such as Professor Alan Ward have argued that the Government would be better advised to spread the settlement payments over a longer period, since there is no good reason why this generation alone should meet the full cost.[17] That's a sensible suggestion which the Government may well follow.

But many New Zealanders, especially Pakeha New Zealanders, are asking: 'When will the claims process ever end?' Many would like a finite date to be put on the Tribunal's proceedings, though 2000, which has been suggested previously, is now too soon. No doubt, if more New Zealanders were aware of the history of the Indian Claims Commission, they would regard its fate as an admirable precedent; for the Commission, having been appointed for a five-year term in 1946, had that term repeatedly renewed, until Congress abolished it in 1978.

Abolishing the Waitangi Tribunal, however, probably would not solve the Treaty claims problem in New Zealand, and could make it worse since the Tribunal over the years has acted as a safety valve against Maori protests over disputed land. The trouble is that New Zealanders over the years have made so much of the Treaty as our founding document, as a charter for relations between Maori and Pakeha, that it cannot readily be forgotten or abandoned. It might well be an albatross around the Pakeha neck, but for Maori it is their Magna Carta, their guarantee of their place in a country that has come to be controlled by Pakeha, not all of them residents. It is beholden on them to respect that Maori place by giving better effect to both texts of the Treaty.

Epilogue

I have not called these final words a conclusion since many of the matters discussed in the previous chapters have not concluded but are continuing, perhaps in directions that we cannot anticipate. An epilogue gives me an opportunity to make further comment.

In my introduction I noted the circumstances and sketched the intellectual environment in which the chapters were created, often as public lectures or seminar papers, and subsequently published. I also noted that the texts have been reproduced here substantially as they were published. Since the essays were published up to 57 years ago, much has happened to Maori and Maori–Pakeha relations in the intervals, and in the interpretation of these matters by historians and other scholars. Here, I provide a brief summary of those developments.

To start at my first chapter, I note that the search for 'The Whence of the Maori' has continued unabated. Scholars have generally concluded that Maori came to Aotearoa from their central Pacific Hawaiki in the thirteenth century — though some awkwardly puzzling evidence has been unearthed suggesting a much earlier human arrival on this last to be colonised land mass. It is now considered that Maori and other Polynesians assumed their characteristic linguistic and cultural identity in the Pacific, though their ethnic origins have been traced back to Taiwan. The possibility of an American origin, once vigorously argued by Thor Heyerdahl, has been dismissed. Though I have not followed up the question of origins beyond my 'Whence of the Maori' essay and subsequent book *Maori Origins and Migrations*,[1] fellow historian Kerry Howe has done so in a wider context in *The Quest for Origins: Who First Discovered and Settled New Zealand and the Pacific Islands?*[2] It can safely be assumed that the scholarly quest for Maori origins will continue.

My 1991 essay 'Treaties in British Colonial Policy', chapter 2, was an attempt to set the Waitangi Treaty into the context of British colonial policy. This background had been recently neglected amidst a good deal of nationalistic praise-singing which portrayed the Treaty as a unique explanation for our apparently amicable race relations. Though I was raised in the old tradition of imperial history, the subject has gained a new lease of life in recent years, particularly with the publication of John Darwin's *After Tamerlane: The Global History of Empire since 1405*,[3] and James Belich's *Replenishing the Earth: The Settler Revolution and the Rise of the Anglo-World, 1783–1939*.[4]

The issue of race relations is picked up again in chapter 3, 'How to Civilise Savages'. This looked at prevailing nineteenth-century racial theories and how Maori were fitted into them — as suitable objects for amalgamation (assimilation) and civilisation — always on the assumption that these objects could be achieved while Maori were being steadily relieved of their lands. Assimilation has long been abandoned and was, from 1960, briefly replaced by 'integration', as defined by J. K. Hunn, the Secretary for Maori Affairs, in his controversial *Report on Department of Maori Affairs*. Hunn defined integration as to 'combine (not fuse) the Maori and pakeha elements to form one nation wherein Maori culture remains distinct'.[5] But Hunn's integration was vigorously opposed by Maori and some Pakeha as merely a euphemism for assimilation.[6] It was quietly dropped from official definitions of Maori policy and replaced by 'biculturalism' which envisaged Maori identity and culture as enduring indefinitely. Maori do not accept the notion, increasingly promoted by some of the new immigrant groups, that we are a multicultural nation, but insist that we are a bicultural nation composed of Maori, the tangata whenua, and Pakeha, who include all others.[7]

Chapter 4, 'Folkland to Bookland', deals with the origins of the attempt to turn Maori communal land tenure into individual titles. Though the Native Lands Acts from 1862, which gave effect to this policy, were mainly designed to make Maori land available for acquisition by Pakeha, they were usually dressed up as part of the civilising mission. The essay explores this mission through the role of F. D. Fenton, the first Chief Judge of the Native Land Court, who helped to draft the legislation. Like other early jurists, including the first Chief Justice, Sir William Martin, Fenton did not come empty-headed to his tasks in New Zealand, but found his precedents in the long evolution of English customary law. That habit of seeking legal precedents from abroad has not ceased: as I note below, it has been followed in legal submissions to and in the reports by the Waitangi Tribunal.

I briefly explore the early development and application of the native land laws in chapter 5, 'Land Purchase Methods', but as a preliminary to an examination of the social and demographic effects on Maori of land transactions and the operations of the Native Land Court. Those operations successively enveloped Maori communities in the later nineteenth century while Maori population was still declining. I argue that purchase activities and the operations of the Court aggravated the depopulation. That thesis has not been disputed (so far as I know). It has been supported by the demographer Ian Pool,[8] and a good many reports prepared for the Waitangi Tribunal. However, it was never meant to be a substitute for medical explanations of depopulation, especially the continuing toll of new infectious diseases such as tuberculosis and influenza on a population that had not developed immunity to them. Since my essay was written, much work has been published on the decline and recovery of Maori population, including Ian Pool's *Te Iwi Maori: A New Zealand Population, Past Present & Projected*,[9] and Raeburn Lange's *May the People Live: A History of Maori Health Development 1900–1920*.[10]

I do not examine the tortuous history of the native land legislation, with its long-running attempt to individualise titles (not ended until the passage of Te Ture Whenua Maori Act in 1993), nor the continuing purchases of Maori land, privately and by the Crown, though others have done so, including my long-standing friend and colleague Alan Ward.[11] Overall the area of land remaining in Maori title (usually called Maori freehold land) has been reduced to some 1,214,083 hectares, from the surface area of New Zealand of 26,709,834 hectares. However, these global figures need to be qualified. About half of the total area of the country is public domain, usually under the control of the Department of Conservation, not in private Pakeha ownership. Maori also own an undefined but probably small area of land under general title, mainly in the form of urban sections. And Maori tribal authorities who have achieved settlements through the Waitangi Tribunal process or direct negotiation with the Crown have been buying land in general title, though mainly urban rather than rural land. Nor do I examine here the attempts, led by Sir Apirana Ngata, to deal with the problem of fractionation of titles by consolidations and incorporations, and his land development schemes on remaining Maori land during the inter-war years, though I have done so elsewhere.[12] Also, my edition of Ngata's correspondence with Peter Buck has a great deal of discussion on these matters, particularly on Ngata's involvement in Maori land development.[13]

However, Ngata's land development schemes, though carried on by the first Labour government, did not save the greater portion of Maori from poverty. Most had to seek their livelihood away from their land, often in unskilled jobs in country districts, such as freezing works, forestry, and building hydro dams, but increasingly also in urban manufacturing. Though Maori urbanisation increased from 11.2 per cent in 1936 to 22.9 per cent in 1951 and to 78.2 per cent in 1981, they continued to languish on the lower rungs of New Zealand society. They were merely being transformed from a rural to an urban proletariat. Hunn's 1960 report revealed a considerable gap between the living conditions of Maori and Pakeha.[14] Though the incoming National government adopted and tried to apply most of Hunn's recommendations, there has been little, if any, progress in closing the gap. Indeed in 1998 Te Puni Kokiri (formerly the Maori Affairs Department) published a report called 'Closing the Gaps'.[15] According to Richard Hill, this actually 'confirmed that some socio-economic disparities between Maori and pakeha had widened since the introduction of free-market economics' (by Roger Douglas, Minister of Finance in the Lange Labour government).[16] During periods of recession, and particularly since 2010, Maori have suffered a considerably higher rate of unemployment than Pakeha. Though Maori, like Pakeha, have enjoyed some improvements in their standard of living, particularly in periods of prosperity, their health, life expectancy, housing, educational achievements, employment and general participation in the economy are not yet on a level with Pakeha: as if to say, Maori have been standing on the escalator but Pakeha have been walking past them.

Three of the essays discuss Maori politics. These were conducted on two levels: among themselves at tribal or intra-tribal hui, and between Maori and Pakeha, especially through Maori representation in Parliament. Intra-tribal relations were greatly complicated by the pre-1840 warfare that followed the introduction of muskets. Maori who acquired muskets first embarked on deadly warfare that resulted in considerable relocation and long-standing enmities that complicated claims to land. After 1840 the conflicts often resurfaced, when new conflicts over land arose between Maori and Pakeha. Maori needed to overcome their old tribal animosities and unite against land-selling. The King movement or Kingitanga was the most significant Maori attempt to stem the sale of land and to unite all tribes into a Maori nation. That endeavour and the wars that followed in the 1860s have been intensively examined, particularly by James Cowan, Keith Sinclair and James Belich.[17] My contribution to the questions was the 1963 essay on the Maori King movement (chapter 6), written a few years after the movement had celebrated its centenary. Nevertheless, the movement did not get active support beyond Tainui of Waikato, Tuwharetoa of Taupo, and Ngai Te Rangi and Tuhoe of the Bay of Plenty. When the King's forces were finally defeated at Orakau in 1864, he and his Tainui supporters withdrew into Ngati Maniapoto territory in what is known to this day as the King Country. The 'opening' of the King Country to European settlement in 1885 is described in my essay. But I do not examine the subsequent history of the Kingitanga. Nor has any other historian in any comprehensive way, though Michael King's biography of 'Princess' Te Puea[18] throws much light on the movement. The Kingitanga remains today, more than a century and a half after its foundation, actively supported by its foundation iwi, respected by other Maori throughout the country, and acknowledged by our English Queen (somewhat ahead of her Pakeha New Zealand subjects). In retrospect, we might wonder what all the fuss was about since the Maori King and his supporters always had a limited objective, summed up in the early refrain: 'The King on his piece; the Queen on her piece; God over both; and love binding them to each other.'[19] The trouble was that the Pakeha wanted too much of the King's piece.

The King movement was not the only attempt by Maori to found a national organisation. The prophet movements — Pai Marire, Ringatu and Ratana (discussed briefly in chapter 8, 'Colonial Rule and Local Response') — had similar ambitions. So did the Kotahitanga movement, founded from the ranks of the Kupapa tribes and led by young Maori represented in Parliament. They made several attempts in the late nineteenth century to establish a separate Maori parliament, but they failed, particularly because the Pakeha parliament in Wellington refused to pass legislation that would have recognised the Maori parliament. The establishment of separate Maori authorities has continued beyond the movements discussed in chapter 8, notably with the creation of a New Zealand Maori Council in 1962, and the founding of a National Maori Congress in 1990. It is discussed in Lindsay Cox's book *Kotahitanga: The Search for Maori Political Unity*.[20]

Though such bodies have had little influence on the Pakeha government, Maori elected to Parliament have been more influential, as discussed at length in chapter 9. Members of the Young Maori Party, who usually held at least two of the four Maori seats, were particularly influential, and notably Sir Maui Pomare and Sir Apirana Ngata held Cabinet office for much of the inter-war period. Later, as Labour gradually captured the four seats, several of their Maori members were also in Cabinet. Since 1948, Maori members have regularly held Cabinet rank, particularly as Minister of Maori Affairs, irrespective of the Pakeha party in power. One reason that separate Maori representation has existed for so long was that Maori strongly supported it and Pakeha have acquiesced. Although the 1986 Report of the Royal Commission on the Electoral

System favoured the abolition of the Maori seats and the establishment of a common roll, it also recommended that such a decision be postponed until the country decided, by referendum, on a system of proportional representation.[21] The country voted in favour of a mixed member proportional (MMP) system which was introduced for the 1996 election. However, the Maori seats were retained on the assumption that they would rise or fall on the basis of enrolments on the Maori roll, as counted at each census. As a result the number of Maori seats increased to five in 1996, to six in 1999, and to seven in 2002. Since then, the move to the Maori roll has slowed — at the recent census 9817 Maori joined the Maori roll, against 4142 who joined the General roll. A Constitutional Advisory Panel with Maori representation is currently examining the role of the Maori seats, along with other constitutional arrangements. The MMP system has brought additional political benefits for Maori since the main parties have usually placed several Maori candidates high on their party lists. That further increased Maori representation in Parliament.

Despite their increased representation, the course of Maori politics at the national level has not run smoothly. For much of the time since the first Labour government lost office in 1949, the party maintained its 'Maori mandate' on the Maori seats, thanks largely to the alliance with the Ratana movement. But there was a severe rift in 2004 when Helen Clark's fifth Labour government subverted Maori rights in asserting title to the seabed. One of the Labour ministers, Tariana Turia, withdrew from Cabinet and with other Maori leaders such as Professor Whatarangi Winiata formed a new Maori Party. The party won four of the seven Maori seats in the 2008 election. The National Party won that election and two of the Maori Party's members, Turia and Pita Sharples, were invited to join the Cabinet — Sharples as Minister of Maori Affairs. In all of this there was much that was reminiscent of times past — for instance, when Maui Pomare, one of the stalwarts of the Young Maori Party, deserted the Liberals in 1912 and became a minister in the incoming Reform government. It was reminiscent also of an even longer tradition whereby some Maori, serving their own interests, became Kupapa; originally as allies of the government forces in the New Zealand wars. That might not have helped the Maori nationalist cause but there is no reason to regard that behaviour as dishonourable. Since Maori defeat and Pakeha domination were inevitable, some Maori recognised that they had to participate in government as best they could. As Pita Sharples keeps saying, 'they needed to be at the table'. But supping at the Pakeha table may not give Maori a decent kai. It was that possibility that led one Maori Party member, Hone Harawira, to withdraw and form the Mana Party (officially the

Mana Movement). Although he held his seat at a by-election, the party has made no further progress, apart from coming second to Labour in the 2013 Ikaroa-Rawhiti by-election.

Besides Maori political activity on a national level, there has been a reassertion of tribal authority. Iwi authorities were given a brief impetus by the Labour government's Runanga Iwi Act 1990, though this was repealed by National in 1991. Nevertheless, iwi have gained more extended influence through Treaty claims and settlements, either through the Waitangi Tribunal, or by direct negotiation with the Crown. Some iwi authorities such as Ngai Tahu and Tainui have obtained large settlements, invested substantially in land, and become economic powerhouses. Other Maori authorities have obtained substantial resources in forestry and fishing quotas.

The final group of chapters relate in one way or another to revived interest in the Treaty and Treaty settlements. As I indicated in the Introduction, much of my Treaty work, including the essays published here, was a consequence of my involvement in the activities of the Waitangi Tribunal. The essays reflected the intellectual ferment that was generated by the Tribunal and the scholars who nourished it. The Tribunal was well informed on the international context for indigenous claims settlements, particularly in relation to previous hearings of Native American claims in the United States (through the Indian Claims Commission) and by the courts in Canada. It was able to draw particularly on the work of the Cambridge-based but New Zealand-connected legal historian Paul McHugh, a son of Deputy Chief Judge and deputy chairman of the Waitangi Tribunal Ashley McHugh. Paul McHugh's Cambridge PhD, subsequently published in much revised form as *The Maori Magna Carta: New Zealand Law and the Treaty of Waitangi*,[22] was a landmark in the legal contextualisation of the Treaty.

Another development, discussed in my four concluding essays, was the application of the Maori text of the Treaty. This too was promoted by the Tribunal and also in notable works by historians. Ruth Ross's landmark 1972 essay, 'Te Tiriti o Waitangi: Texts and Translations',[23] was the first examination of the meaning of the much-neglected Maori text of the Treaty. Claudia Orange took it up in her PhD thesis, published in 1987 as *The Treaty of Waitangi*.[24] This also provided the first comprehensive examination of the subsequent Maori history of that text of the Treaty. Though the Treaty may have been consigned to oblivion for many years by Chief Justice Prendergast's statement that it was a 'nullity',[25] it was gradually rescued in the twentieth century, first to celebrate its centenary in 1940 — though that was largely a celebration of the English text — and more thoroughly in the work of the Tribunal and scholars working in its wake.

The Tribunal was given retrospective jurisdiction by the Treaty of Waitangi Amendment Act 1985 to examine claims by Maori that the Crown had breached the principles of the Treaty at any time since the Treaty was signed in 1840. That amendment laid the basis for a veritable flood of claims. In examining claims, the Tribunal was required to consider both texts of the Treaty and it tended to concentrate on the Maori text since that was the one that was signed by all but 39 of the 512 signatories. According to international jurisprudence, and notably the 1899 United States case *Jones v Meehan*,[26] treaties were to be interpreted as they would have been understood by the indigenous signatories. That precedent led the Tribunal to consider the relationship of the guarantee to Maori of their rangatiratanga in the second article of the Treaty as opposed to the cession to the Crown of sovereignty in the first article. It is that relationship and its implications that I have examined in chapter 11, 'Giving Better Effect to the Treaty' — my contribution to the navel-gazing associated with the 1990 sesquicentennial.

Chapter 10, 'The Role of the Waitangi Tribunal', deals with early Tribunal reports, and chapters 12 and 13 are my general assessments of the progress of Tribunal inquiries and the Crown in the settlement of Treaty claims, though they carry that story only so far as 1998. A great deal has been achieved since then. The Tribunal, according to its in-house magazine *Te Manutukutuku* for May 2012, had completed seventeen of its proposed 37 district inquiries, covering some 76 per cent of the surface area of New Zealand, while another twelve districts were under inquiry or being prepared for inquiry, and eight more had been settled by direct negotiation.[27] That bare list of statistics provides little indication of the importance of the Tribunal's reports which often run to several fat volumes. Indeed, it could be said that the Tribunal's published reports constitute the largest exercise in public history ever undertaken in New Zealand. In my view, they excel the various centennial histories produced around (and sometimes well after) 1940; the numerous war histories produced after the Second World War; and the *Dictionary of New Zealand Biography*, published in five volumes between 1990 and 2000.

Yet, for all their panache, the Tribunal reports have some limitations. They are necessarily restricted to Crown acquisition of Maori land through purchase, confiscation and public works takings. Private acquisitions by purchase and lease under the Native Lands Acts are excluded from the Tribunal's jurisdiction, though they were often as acrimonious, litigious and fraudulent as Crown purchases. The matter is investigated more fully in my Master's thesis and referred to briefly, especially in relation to Hawke's Bay transactions, in chapter 5, 'Land Purchase Methods'.

The Tribunal processes have also stimulated numerous independent publications. Two of the essays reprinted here as chapters 2, 'Treaties in British Colonial Policy', and 10, 'The Role of the Waitangi Tribunal', began life as contributions to collections of Tribunal-related essays. Several other notable collections have been published, including *The Waitangi Tribunal: Te Roopu Whakamana i te Tiriti o Waitangi*, edited by Janine Hayward and Nicola R. Wheen.[28] Other scholars have published accomplished books, including Andrew Sharp's *Justice and the Maori: The Philosophy and Practice of Maori Claims in New Zealand since the 1870s*;[29] Michael Belgrave's *Historical Frictions: Maori Claims & Reinvented Histories*;[30] Richard Boast's *Buying the Land, Selling the Land: Governments and Maori Land in the North Island 1865–1921*;[31] and a two-volume work by Richard Hill, *State Authority, Indigenous Autonomy: Crown–Maori Relations in New Zealand/Aotearoa 1900–1950* and *1950–2000*.[32] Clearly, the 'Treaty industry' is alive and well.

But that 'industry' has not been without its critics. Some historians, and notably W. H. Oliver and Giselle Byrnes,[33] have complained that in its historical reports the Tribunal has been writing 'presentist' history. I have some sympathy with this view since, as I noted in the Introduction to this book, it is impossible for historians to achieve the ideal of the nineteenth-century German historian, von Ranke, and write completely objective history; or to empty their minds of the intellectual influences that have nurtured and surround them. In addition to that, it has to be acknowledged that the Tribunal is a creature of statute. As more fully explained in chapters 10 to 13, the 1975 Treaty of Waitangi Act required the Tribunal to investigate Maori claims that the Crown, in its dealings with them, had breached the principles of the Treaty of Waitangi; and the 1985 amendment of that Act required the Tribunal to investigate such claims all the way back to when the Treaty was signed in 1840. The principles of the Treaty were not defined in the legislation and somehow the Tribunal, and the courts when involved in related litigation, had to devise principles from the somewhat ambiguous provisions of the English and Maori texts of the Treaty. In doing so, neither the Tribunal nor the courts confined their investigations to 'presentist' notions. Indeed, as I have demonstrated in several of my chapters, there was an exhaustive search of contemporary documents for New Zealand and related overseas colonies as the Tribunal constructed a narrative and analysis of the Crown's treatment of

Maori who were the subject of claims. That is evident in each elaborately documented Tribunal historical report.

The Tribunal is a commission of inquiry and appoints panels selected from its members to report on a claim or group of claims. But it is not possible to accurately detail the contribution of particular individuals to the writing of the reports. All members of the panel sign the reports, although all do not contribute equally to their writing. The Chief Judge of the Maori Land Court, who is also chairperson of the Tribunal, often acts as the presiding officer of a Tribunal inquiry, although other Maori Land Court judges may do so, as well as other Tribunal members who are lawyers of seven years' standing. As with reports of other commissions of inquiry, a chairperson might well write most of a report, with some assistance from Tribunal staff (often able young historians). The arrangement is analogous to that in a High Court where judges make a majority or unanimous decision but only one of them (often assisted by a law clerk) writes up their judgment. It is well known that many of the early reports of the Tribunal, including the ones discussed in my chapter 10, 'The Role of the Waitangi Tribunal', were written mainly by the chairperson, Eddie Durie (as he then was). A little later, some important reports were crafted by Professor Gordon Orr, a former Secretary for Justice and Dean of the Victoria University Law School. I had the privilege to sit with both men on several of those panels and readily acknowledge that I contributed little to the writing of 'their' reports. I did make a larger contribution to some later reports, though I leave it to others, who claim to know my style, to identify anything that I may have written.

However, there is one report where my contribution is fairly evident: *The Radio Spectrum Management and Development Final Report*.[34] We were a three-member panel. Two of us were responsible for the majority report; the third member, who was the presiding officer, wrote a minority report. To put the matter briefly, the majority report supported the claimants' case to be allocated some radio spectrum that the government was then offering. The minority report disagreed. In what I believe was a unique decision, the government of the day rejected the majority report; but, to my wry satisfaction, proceeded to allocate some spectrum to the claimants, which was all that we had recommended.

We can be reasonably sure that the Tribunal's reports will remain enduring monuments to what has already been the most significant inquiry in our history into the alienation of Maori land and other resources. They lay a basis for a fuller appreciation by Maori and Pakeha of our bilateral destiny as a nation.

Clearly, the Treaty settlement process will be an ongoing saga which, with goodwill from both sides, will eventually be completed, at least for the historical claims. The Labour government placed a date limit of 1 September 2008 for the registration of new historical claims. This provoked a flood of more than 1800 claims before the deadline applied. Many of the new claims were added to the Tribunal's programme of district inquiries.[35] Once the Tribunal completes its hearing of these and other registered claims, or they are settled independently, the process of hearing and settling historical claims should be at an end. As historical claims are settled, each settlement is incorporated in legislation which also precludes further claims, ostensibly for evermore. Perhaps that is optimistic, since Parliament in New Zealand is sovereign, and there is nothing to stop future parliaments from overturning previous legislation.

The Tribunal-related settlements are not by any means the first 'full and final' settlements of Maori claims. Indeed there have been many previous claims inquiries and settlements relating to Crown acquisitions of Maori land, some of them dating from the time of the acquisitions. These included claims relating to the confiscation of Maori land during the wars of the 1860s, under the New Zealand Settlements Acts, which were investigated by the 1927 Royal Commission headed by Mr Justice Sim. The Commission recommended compensation for most of the confiscations. Compensation was eventually negotiated and paid — as a 'full and final' settlement — but the amounts were considered by the claimants to be too low and were eventually revised upwards. The claims were renewed again when the Tribunal got its retrospective jurisdiction in 1985 and settled again, in yet more 'full and final' settlements, following Tribunal hearings or direct negotiations with the Crown.

Whether or not a cap has finally been put on historical claims, it is still possible for Maori to lodge claims relating to contemporary breaches of the principles of the Treaty, and they continue to do so to the Tribunal. It could be hoped that further such claims will be infrequent, on the ground that the Crown, aware of its Treaty obligations, will refrain from actions that breach the principles of the Treaty. But it would be naive to assume that this will always be the case, given the likely continuation of aggressive behaviour by large corporations or wealthy individuals in seeking access to Crown land and other resources. It is also to be expected that Maori authorities who have obtained Treaty settlements will use their new resources in productive ways. If so, it is likely that old grievances will be set aside.[36] Maybe, but there is a danger that the benefits will be restricted to a small coterie associated with the tribal authorities and that many Maori, more especially the large number of young Maori, will remain 'detribalised', not listed on tribal registers, and will therefore miss out on benefits. They could remain a predominantly urban proletariat, largely unemployed, especially during periods of recession.

Yet there are also hopeful signs. The Tribunal has been at the forefront of improved relations between Maori and Pakeha, as much by its processes as its findings. Since hearings are public affairs and usually held on the claimants' marae, local Pakeha, who are always made welcome, hear Maori claimants unburdening themselves of long-held grievances. Though many of those Pakeha have close connections with the Maori claimants, through intermarriage, work and play, they seldom anticipate the degree of hurt buried in the hearts of the Maori claimants that gets revealed as hearings proceed.

As pointed out in chapter 13, 'Waitangi: Ka Whawhai Tonu Matou', the settlement of Maori Treaty claims has become a bipartisan business, in which National ministers charged with Treaty settlements, particularly Douglas Graham and Christopher Finlayson, have been equally as effective as Labour's Michael Cullen. The settlements have generally been accepted by Pakeha New Zealand, though a good many continue to ask: 'When will it ever end?' My answer is usually, 'Maybe never', but that needs to be qualified. After all, as I've just pointed out, there have been previous inquiries and 'final settlements' and it is appropriate to ask whether the Tribunal-inspired settlements will be any better. Only, as I've also suggested above, if the settlements are effectively applied — though we should not assume that the wisdom of our generation is any better than that of previous generations.

Although it seems evident that New Zealand will remain a nation with two peoples, Maori and Pakeha, there is a danger that our much-improved race relations could be compromised if the significant inequality that prevails today persists. New Zealand is a fragile nation. We have had difficulty forging a common nationality out of the wars that were fought between Maori and Pakeha in the mid-nineteenth century, or in the world wars we fought in together (though in separate units) in the early twentieth century. We have the strange belief that we forged a nation out of our defeat at Gallipoli. We only seem to know who we are when we win a big rugby match, or go overseas and manage to persuade people that we are not Australians. We have adopted as a national symbol a bird that works mainly in the dark and is almost extinct. But we muddle along, often talking past one another, but occasionally meeting, kanohi ki kanohi, eye to eye, when we begin to understand one another.

Notes

INTRODUCTION

1. According to the Google Scholar Citations Index, it was cited 82 times, compared with the next most cited essay, 'Maori Representation in Parliament', cited 40 times.
2. Keith Sinclair, 'Why are Race Relations in New Zealand Better than in South Africa, South Australia or South Dakota?', *The New Zealand Journal of History* [hereafter *NZJH*], vol. 5, no. 2 (1971), pp. 121–7.
3. M. P. K. Sorrenson, ed., *Na To Hoa Aroha (From Your Dear Friend): The Correspondence between Sir Apirana Ngata and Sir Peter Buck, 1925–1950*, 3 vols, Auckland University Press, Auckland, vol. I (1986), vol. II (1987) and vol. III (1988).
4. Ngata to Buck, 2 June 1928, ibid., vol. I, p. 96; Buck to Ngata, 9 November 1929, ibid., p. 267; A. T. Ngata, 'Land Development Report', *Appendices to the Journals of the House of Representatives* [hereafter *AJHR*], 1931, G-10, p. 18.
5. M. P. K. Sorrenson, *Maori Origins and Migrations: The Genesis of Some Pakeha Myths and Legends*, Auckland University Press, Auckland, 1979; reprinted 1983, 1990.
6. Simon During, 'What Was the West? Some Relations between Modernity, Colonisation and Writing', *Meanjin*, vol. 48, no. 4 (1989), p. 775.
7. *Na To Hoa Aroha*, op. cit.

1 THE WHENCE OF THE MAORI

1. Bernard Smith, *European Vision and the South Pacific, 1768–1850: A Study in the History of Art and Ideas*, Clarendon Press, Oxford, 1960, p. 7.
2. John Hawkesworth, *An Account of the Voyages . . . by Commander Byron, Captain Wallis, Captain Carteret and Captain Cook*, 3 vols, Strahan & Cadell, London, 1773, vol. II, p. 287.
3. Ibid., vol. III, pp. 69–70.
4. Ibid., vol. III, p. 73.
5. Sydney Parkinson, *A Journal of a Voyage to the South Seas in H.M.S. Endeavour*, Stanfield Parkinson, London, 1773, p. 125.
6. George Forster, *A Voyage Round the World in H.M.S. Resolution . . .*, 2 vols, White, Robson, Elmsley and Robinson, London, 1777.
7. J. R. Forster, *Observations made during a Voyage round the World . . .*, Robinson, London, 1778, p. ii.
8. Ibid., p. 257 (Forster's italics).
9. Ibid., pp. 287–8, 303–4.
10. Ibid., p. 360.
11. J. F. Blumenbach, *The Anthropological Treatises of Johan Friedrich Blumenbach*, trs. T. Bendyshe, Longman Green, London, 1865, p. viii.
12. Ibid., p. 210.
13. J. M. Crozet, *Crozet's Voyage to Tasmania, New Zealand, the Ladrone Islands and the Philippines*, trs. H. Ling Roth, Truslove and Shirley, London, 1891, p. 28.
14. Ibid., pp. 66–67.
15. Ibid., p. 28.
16. J. L. Nicholas, *Narrative of a Voyage to New Zealand*, 2 vols, James Black & Son, London, 1817, vol. I, p. 38.
17. Judith Binney, *The Legacy of Guilt: A Life of Thomas Kendall*, Auckland University Press, Auckland, 1968, pp. 44–45, 92–98.
18. Smith, op. cit., pp. 105–9.
19. A. T. Yarwood, 'The Missionary Marsden: An Australian View', *NZJH*, vol. 4, no. 1 (1970), p. 27.
20. R. H. W. Reece, *Aborigines and Colonists: Aborigines and Colonial Society in New South Wales in the 1830s and 1840s*, Sydney University Press, Sydney, 1974, p. 74.
21. J. R. Elder, *The Letters and Journals of Samuel Marsden, 1765–1838*, Coulls Somerville Wilkie, Dunedin, 1932, pp. 219–20.
22. Nicholas, op. cit., vol. II, pp. 267, 286–7.
23. Ibid., p. 288.

24 G. L. Craik, *The New Zealanders*, Charles Knight, London, 1830, pp. 159, 235; W. B. Marshall, *A Personal Narrative of Two Visits to New Zealand*, James Nisbet & Co., London, 1836, pp. 68–69; Robert FitzRoy, *Narrative of the Surveying Voyages of H.M.S Adventure and Beagle, 1826–1836*, 4 vols, Henry Colburn, London, 1839, vol. II, p. 650; J. L. Polack, *New Zealand*, 2 vols, Richard Bentley, London, 1838, vol. I, pp. 358, 385; E. Dieffenbach, *Travels in New Zealand*, 2 vols, John Murray, London, vol. II, pp. 98–99; and G. C. Mundy, *Our Antipodes*, 2 vols, Richard Bentley, London, 1852, vol. II, p. 256.

25 Richard Taylor, *Te Ika a Maui*, Wertheim & Macintosh, London, 1855, p. vi.

26 Ibid., pp. 6–8.

27 Joseph Jones, *The Cradle of Erewhon: Samuel Butler in New Zealand*, University of Texas Press, Austin, 1959, pp. 99–108.

28 J. W. Burrow, *Evolution and Society: A Study of Victorian Social Theory*, Cambridge University Press, Cambridge, 1966, pp. 12–14.

29 J. M. Booth, 'A History of New Zealand Anthropology during the Nineteenth Century', MA thesis, University of Otago, 1949, p. 17.

30 Polack, op. cit., vol. I, pp. 359–62.

31 Dieffenbach, op. cit., vol. II, pp. 4, 7. For further comment on the so-called 'Caucasian' features, see also F. von Hochstetter, *New Zealand*, trs. E. Sauter, Cotta, Stuttgart, 1867, p. 201.

32 William Brown, *New Zealand and its Aborigines*, J. and A. Darling, London, 1845, p. 94; FitzRoy, op. cit., vol. II, pp. 569, 640.

33 A. S. Thomson, *The Story of New Zealand: Past and Present — Savage and Civilized*, 2 vols, John Murray, London, 1859, vol. I, p. 81.

34 Thomas F. Gossett, *Race: The History of an Idea in America*, Shoken, New York, 1968, pp. 73–75.

35 Thomson, op. cit., vol. I, p. 73.

36 J. H. Scott, 'Contribution to the Osteology of the Aborigines of New Zealand and the Chatham Islands', *Transactions and Proceedings of the New Zealand Institute* [hereafter *T&PNZI*], vol. 26 (1893), pp. 1–64.

37 S. Percy Smith, *Hawaiki: The Original Home of the Maori*, 3rd ed., Whitcombe & Tombs, Christchurch, 1910, p. 18.

38 Te Rangi Hiroa (P. H. Buck), 'Maori Somatology', *The Journal of the Polynesian Society* [hereafter *JPS*], vol. 21 (1922), pp. 37–44, 145–53, 159–69; vol. 22 (1923), pp. 21–28, 189–99.

39 John Ledyard, *Journal of Captain Cook's Last Voyage to the Pacific Ocean*, Newbery, London, 1781, p. 15.

40 E. Shortland, *Traditions and Superstitions of the New Zealanders with Illustrations of their Manners and Customs*, Longman Brown, London, 1854, p. v.

41 Ibid., p. 59.

42 J. Hamlin, 'On the Mythology of the New Zealanders', *Tasmanian Journal of Natural Science*, vol. 1 (1842), pp. 254–64, 342–58.

43 H. Hale, *The United States Exploring Expedition . . . 1838–1842*, Vol. VII: *Ethnography and Philology*, Lee & Blanchard, Philadelphia, 1846, pp. 146–7.

44 J. D. Lang, *View of the Origin and Migrations of the Polynesian Nation*, Cochrane and McCrone, London, 1834, pp. 58–62; A. Sharp, *Ancient Voyagers of the Pacific*, The Polynesian Society, Wellington, 1956.

45 Dieffenbach, op. cit., vol. II, p. 85.

46 E. Shortland, *The Southern Districts of New Zealand*, Longman Brown, London, 1851, pp. 94–95.

47 Shortland, *Traditions and Superstitions of the New Zealanders . . .*, p. 29.

48 Sir George Grey, *Polynesian Mythology and the Ancient Traditional History of the New Zealand Race*, John Murray, London, 1855, p. iii.

49 R. M. Dorson, *The British Folklorists: A History*, Routledge & Kegan Paul, London, 1968, pp. 169, 372–4.

50 Grey, op. cit., p. xiii.

51 Taylor, op. cit., p. 12.

52 Ibid., pp. 123–4.

53 Thomson, op. cit., vol. I, p. 120.

54 Ibid., vol. I, p. 67.

55 Hochstetter, op. cit., pp. 205–8; C. Schirren, *Die Wandersagen der Neuseelander und der Maui-Mythos*, Kymmel, Riga, 1856.

56 Julius von Haast, 'Moas and Moa Hunters', *T&PNZI*, vol. 4 (1871), pp. 66–107.

57   Roger Duff, *The Moa-Hunter Period of Maori Culture*, Government Printer, Wellington, 1950, pp. 282-328.
58   In his unpublished History of New Zealand Archaeology which he kindly allowed me to read.
59   Edward Shortland, 'A Short Sketch of the Maori Races', *T&PNZI*, vol. 1 (1868), p. 4.
60   M. P. K. Sorrenson, 'The Purchase of Maori Lands, 1865-1892', MA thesis, Auckland University College, 1955, pp. 25-26.
61   W. E. Gudgeon, 'Maori Migrations to New Zealand', *JPS*, vol. 1 (1892), pp. 212-32; vol. 3 (1894), pp. 46-51; 'The Whence of the Maori', *JPS*, vol. 11 (1902), pp. 179-89; vol. 12 (1903), pp. 51-61, 120-30.
62   S. Percy Smith, 'Hawaiki: The Whence of the Maori', *JPS*, vol. 7 (1898), pp. 137-77, 185-223; vol. 8 (1899), pp. 1-48; *Lore of the Whare Wananga*, Polynesian Society, Wellington, 1913-1915.
63   J. F. H. Wohlers, 'The Mythology and Traditions of the Maori in New Zealand', *T&PNZI*, vol. 7 (1874), pp. 3-53; vol. 8 (1875), pp. 108-23.
64   William Colenso, 'On the Maori Races of New Zealand', *T&PNZI*, vol. 1 (1868), pp. 54, 59.
65   W. T. L. Travers, 'Notes upon the Historical Value of the *Traditions of the New Zealanders as collected by Sir George Grey*', *T&PNZI*, vol. 4 (1872), pp. 51-62.
66   Smith, *Hawaiki: The Original Home of the Maori*, p. 5.
67   Ibid., p. 19.
68   D. R. Simmons, 'A New Zealand Myth: Kupe, Toi and the "Fleet"', *NZJH*, vol. 3 (1969), p. 18.
69   Ibid., pp. 14-31.
70   Smith quoted in support Fornander, Fenton, Dr Wyatt Gill, Tregear, Dr John Fraser, William Churchill, and Gudgeon. Smith, *Hawaiki: The Original Home of the Maori*, p. 86.
71   Ibid., pp. 15-16, 104.
72   Te Rangi Hiroa (P. H. Buck), *The Coming of the Maori*, Whitcombe & Tombs, Wellington, 1958, p. 11.
73   Edward Tregear, 'The Moriori', *T&PNZI*, vol. 22 (1889), pp. 75-79.
74   Duff, op. cit., p. 14.
75   Edward Tregear, *The Aryan Maori*, Government Printer, Wellington, 1885, p. 1.
76   W. H. Blyth, 'On "The Whence of the Maori"', *T&PNZI*, vol. 19 (1886), pp. 515-49.
77   Tregear, *The Aryan Maori*, p. 39.
78   Edward Tregear, 'The Maori in Asia', *T&PNZI*, vol. 18 (1885), pp. 3-24; 'Asiatic Gods in the Pacific', *JPS*, vol. 2 (1893), pp. 129-46; 'Myths of Observation', *T&PNZI*, vol. 27 (1894), pp. 579-93; 'Thoughts on Comparative Mythology', *T&PNZI*, vol. 30 (1894), pp. 50-65.
79   Smith, *Hawaiki: The Original Home of the Maori*, p. 93.
80   J. Macmillan Brown, *Maori and Polynesian*, J. and A. Darling, London, 1907, p. 121.
81   Tregear, *The Aryan Maori*, p. 1.
82   Blyth, op. cit., p. 44.
83   Lang, op. cit., p. 29.
84   Colenso, 'On the Maori Races of New Zealand', p. 49.
85   Tregear, *The Aryan Maori*, p. 104.
86   Ibid., p. 38.
87   A. S. Atkinson, 'The Aryo-Semitic Maori', *T&PNZI*, vol. 19 (1886), pp. 552-76.
88   Ibid., p. 556.
89   Ibid., p. 558.
90   Ibid., pp. 560-1.
91   Edward Tregear, 'The Aryo-Semitic Maori: A Reply', *T&PNZI*, vol. 20 (1887), pp. 400-13.
92   C. B. K. Smithyman, 'Attitudes to Immigration in New Zealand', MA thesis, University of Auckland, 1971; N. Harrison, 'The Formation of the White New Zealand Policy between the years 1890 and 1907', MA thesis, Victoria University of Wellington, 1995.
93   Tregear, *The Aryan Maori*, p. 103.
94   Ibid., p. 105.
95   Te Rangi Hiroa, *The Coming of the Maori*, pp. 9-60.

2   TREATIES IN BRITISH COLONIAL POLICY

1   *New Zealand Herald*, 6 February 1990.
2   Ibid., 22 February 1990.
3   *Report of the Committee on Aborigines*, GBPP (HC), 1837, p. 40.
4   Paul McHugh, 'The Aboriginal Rights of New Zealand Maori at Common Law', PhD thesis, University of Cambridge, 1987, especially chs 2 & 4.

5   Sir Kenneth Keith, 'Handling and Settling Disputes Arising From the Treaty of Waitangi', *9th Commonwealth Law Conference Papers*, CCH, Auckland, 1990, p. 244. The Convention is in E. Hertslet, *The Map of Africa by Treaty*, Cass, London, 1967, vol. I, pp. 31–32.
6   *Hertslet's Commercial Treaties*, Butterworth, London, 1840, vol. I, p. 13.
7   The treaties are in *Hertslet's Commercial Treaties*, vol. IX.
8   Quoted in McHugh, op. cit., p. 14.
9   F. D. Lugard, *The Dual Mandate in Tropical Africa*, Frank Cass & Co., London, 1965, p. 15.
10 Ibid., pp. 15–16.
11 Tom Bennion, 'Treaty-Making in the Pacific in the Nineteenth Century', research paper for Administrative Law (LLM), Victoria University of Wellington, 1987.
12 See especially ch. 2.
13 In *Cherokee Nation v State of Georgia* (1831) 30 US (5 Peters) 1 (SC).
14 CO 5/65.
15 Enclosure in Lords of Trade to Earl of Halifax, 4 October 1763, CO 5/65.
16 McHugh, op. cit., pp. 200–2.
17 Ibid., p. 205.
18 *Johnson v M'Intosh* (1823) 21 US (8 Wheat) 543 (SC).
19 *R v Symonds* (1847) NZPCC 387 (SC).
20 Ibid., p. 227. The extract is quoted by McHugh from the *Southern Cross*, 15 June 1858.
21 *AJHR*, 1861, E-2, p. 70.
22 Quoted in Wilcomb E. Washburn, *The American Indians and the United States: A Documentary History*, Random House, New York, 1973, 1974, vol. IV, p. 2543.
23 McHugh, op. cit., p. 228.
24 Quoted in Washburn, op. cit., vol. IV, p. 2544.
25 The report is in CO 42/516.
26 More especially, Henry Reynolds, *The Law of the Land*, Penguin, Ringwood, 1987; Alan Frost, 'New South Wales as *Terra Nullius*: The British Denial of Aboriginal Land Rights', *Historical Studies*, vol. 19, no. 72 (1981), pp. 513–23; and Robert King, 'Terra Australis: Terra Nullius aut Terra Aboriginum?', *Journal of the Royal Australian Historical Society*, vol. 72, no. 2 (October 1986), pp. 75–91.
27 Portland to King, 26 February 1800, CO 202/5.
28 Glyndwr Williams, '"Far more Happier than we Europeans": Reactions to the Australian Aborigines on Cook's Voyage', *Historical Studies*, vol. 19, no. 77 (October 1981), pp. 499–512.
29 Quoted in King, op. cit.
30 Proposals for establishing a settlement in New South Wales, 23 August 1783, CO 201/1.
31 King, op. cit., p. 75.
32 Ibid., p. 80.
33 Quoted in Reynolds, op. cit., p. 70.
34 Phillip to Lord Sydney, 15 May 1788, CO 201/3.
35 Instructions to Governor Phillip, 25 April 1787, CO 201/1.
36 Robert Hall, Secretary for the South Australia Commissioners, to Sir George Grey, 23 July 1835, CO 13/3.
37 Ibid.
38 Grey to Torrens, 15 December 1835, CO 13/3.
39 Ibid
40 Ibid.
41 Torrens to Grey, – December 1835, CO 13/3.
42 Stephen to Colonization Commissioners, 27 October 1836, CO 396/1.
43 Cited in J. M. Bennett and A. C. Castle, *A Source Book of Australian Legal History*, Law Book Co., Sydney, 1979, p. 260.
44 Quoted in Sir William Martin, *England and the New Zealanders*, College Press, Auckland, 1847, p. 25.
45 *Hertslet's Commercial Treaties*, vol. VIII.
46 G. C. Henderson, *The Evolution of Government in Fiji*, Angus & Robertson, Sydney, 1935, p. 92.

3 HOW TO CIVILISE SAVAGES

1   H.C. 425, 1837, p. 76.
2   See J. C. Beaglehole's note to Banks's comment on the Chain of Being, *The Endeavour Journal of Joseph Banks, 1768–1771*, Angus & Robertson, Sydney, 1962, vol. II, p. 20; Augustus Earle, *Narrative of a Residence in New Zealand*, ed. E. H. McCormick, Oxford University Press, Oxford, 1966, p. 187; [E. G. Wakefield and J. Ward], *The British Colonization of*

New Zealand, John W. Parker, London, 1837, p. 276; and J. B. Marsden, *Memoirs of the Life and Letters of the Rev. Samuel Marsden*, The Religious Tract Society, London, 1857, p. 79, who noted that Drs Gall and Spurzheim had applied the phrenological system to some Aborigines' skulls and caused people 'to wonder whether the Creator had brought into existence a whole race of idiots'.

3   W. Brown, *New Zealand and its Aborigines*, Smith, Elder & Co., London, 1845, p. 294; S. M. D. Martin, *New Zealand ...*, Simmonds & Ward, London, 1845, p. 294; Aborigines Protection Society, *On the British Colonization of New Zealand*, Smith, Elder & Co., London, 1846, p. 1; Edward Shortland, *Traditions and Superstitions of the New Zealanders*, Longman & Brown, London, 1854, p. 196. Maori were commonly regarded as superior to other savages on grounds of physique, lighter skin colour, intellect and so on.

4   Marsden Journal, 7 November 1819, *The Letters and Journals of Samuel Marsden*, ed. J. R. Elder, Coulls Somerville Wilkie and A. H. Reed, Dunedin, 1932, p. 219; J. L. Nicholas, *Narrative of a Voyage to New Zealand*, James Black & Sons, London, 1817, vol. II, p. 286; R. FitzRoy, *Narrative of the Surveying Voyages of H.M.S.* Adventure and Beagle, *1826–1836*, 4 vols, Henry Colburn, London, 1839, vol. II, p. 650; W. B. Marshall, *A Personal Narrative of Two Visits to New Zealand*, James Nisbet & Co., London, 1836, p. 68; G. C. Mundy, *Our Antipodes*, Richard Bentley & Co., London, 1852, p. 256; R. Taylor, *Te Ika a Maui*, Wertheim & Macintosh, London, 1855, pp. 8, 190; W. Swainson, *New Zealand*, Smith, Elder & Co., London, 1856, p. 37. Others — Ernst Dieffenbach (*Travels in New Zealand*, John Murray, London, 1843, vol. II) was probably the first — traced Maori on linguistic grounds back to the pre-Aryan inhabitants of India. In the later nineteenth century this quest in comparative philology was encouraged by the works of Max Müller and others — as discussed in chapter 2 of the present volume.

5   R. H. W. Reece, *Aborigines and Colonists: Aborigines and Colonial Society in New South Wales in the 1830s and 1840s*, Sydney University Press, Sydney, 1974, p. 74.

6   Bernard Smith, *European Vision and the South Pacific, 1768–1850: A Study in the History of Art and Ideas*, Clarendon Press, Oxford, 1960, pp. 24–26.

7   J. W. Davidson, 'European Penetration of the South Pacific, 1779–1842', PhD thesis, University of Cambridge, 1942, p. 16.

8   See, for instance, the descriptions of Cook and Banks: J. C. Beaglehole, ed., *The Journals of James Cook*, Hakluyt Society, Cambridge, vol. I, 1955, pp. 273–94; and *The Endeavour Journal of Joseph Banks 1768–1771*, Angus & Robertson, Sydney, vol. II, pp. 1–38.

9   Beaglehole, *Journals of James Cook*, vol. I, pp. 236, 282; vol. II, pp. 293–4; *Journal of Joseph Banks*, vol. II, pp. 19, 29.

10 Beaglehole, *Journals of James Cook*, vol. II, p. 578.

11 Elder, ed., op. cit., p. 170.

12 Earle, op. cit., p. 67.

13 J. S. Polack, *Manners and Customs of the New Zealanders*, 2 vols, Madden, London, 1840, vol. I, p. 187.

14 Ibid., p. 183.

15 R. G. Jameson, *New Zealand, South Australia and New South Wales*, Smith, Elder & Co., London, 1842, p. 235.

16 Keith Sinclair, *The Origins of the Maori Wars*, New Zealand University Press, Wellington, 1957, p. 42.

17 A. S. Thomson, *The Story of New Zealand: Past and Present — Savage and Civilized*, 2 vols, John Murray, London, 1859, vol. II, pp. 298–9.

18 Earle, op. cit., p. 86.

19 J. B. Marsden, op. cit., p. 79; also *Report of the Parliamentary Select Committee on Aboriginal Tribes*, reprinted by the Aborigines Protection Society, London, 1837, p. 54, quoting a New Zealand missionary.

20 Herman Merivale, *Lectures on Colonization and Colonies*, Longman, London, 1841, p. 123.

21 G. L. Craik, *The New Zealanders*, Charles Knight, London, 1830, p. 419.

22 M. Russell, *Polynesia*, Oliver & Boyd, Edinburgh, 1842, p. 372, had an almost identical sentence.

23 Marshall, op. cit., p. 308; FitzRoy, op. cit., vol. II, p. 573. Others, like Polack (op. cit., vol. II, p. 328) and Thomson (op. cit., vol. I, p. 239), took their lessons from the Roman civilisation of the Britons.
24 See, for example, Charles Darwin's description of the Bay of Islands in 1835 in FitzRoy, op. cit., vol. III, pp. 491–509.
25 William Yate, *An Account of New Zealand . . .*, Seeley & Burnside, London, 1835, pp. 294, 304.
26 G. F. Angas, *Savage Life and Scenes in Australia and New Zealand . . .*, Smith, Elder & Co., London, 1847, vol. I, p. 337.
27 See, for example, Harrison M. Wright, *New Zealand, 1769–1840*, Harvard University Press, Cambridge, Massachusetts, 1959; J. M. R. Owens, 'Christianity and the Maoris to 1840', *NZJH*, vol. 2, no. 1 (1968), pp. 18–40; and Judith Binney, 'Christianity and the Maoris', ibid., vol. 3, no. 2 (1969), pp. 143–65.
28 Michael D. Jackson, 'Literacy, Communication and Social Change', in I. H. Kawharu, ed., *Conflict and Compromise*: *Essays on the Maori since Colonisation*, A. H. & A. W. Reed, Wellington, 1975, pp. 27–54.
29 J. D. Lang, *New Zealand in 1839 . . .*, Smith, Elder & Co., London, 1839, p. 7.
30 FitzRoy, op. cit., vol. II, p. 580.
31 Earle, op. cit., p. 139.
32 W. Brodie, *Remarks on the Past and Present State of New Zealand . . .*, Whittaker & Co., London, 1845, p. 71.
33 Thomson, op. cit., vol. I, pp. 296, 297, 303.
34 Advocates included: Angas, op. cit., vol. I, p. 292; Brown, op. cit., pp. 41–42; L. A. Chamerovzow, *The New Zealand Question and the Rights of Aborigines*, T. C. Newby, London, 1848, p. 216; Dieffenbach, op. cit., vol. II, p. 42; Martin, op. cit., p. 67; and publicists for the New Zealand Company.
35 E. G. Wakefield and John Ward, op. cit, pp. 27–28.
36 E. J. Wakefield, *Adventure in New Zealand from 1839 to 1844 . . .*, John Murray, London, 1845, vol. I, p. 43.
37 Ibid., vol. II, p. 451.
38 Wakefield and Ward, op. cit., p. 29.
39 E. J. Wakefield, op. cit., vol. I, p. 41.
40 Dieffenbach, op. cit., vol. II, p. 83, estimated the Maori population at 114,890 in 1843.
41 John Miller, *Early Victorian New Zealand: A Study of Racial Tension and Social Attitudes, 1839–1852*, Oxford University Press, London, 1958, pp. 42–69.
42 Sinclair, op. cit., pp. 110–225.
43 M. P. K. Sorrenson, 'The Purchase of Maori Lands, 1862–1892', MA thesis, Auckland University College, 1955, passim.
44 R. W. S. Fargher, 'Donald McLean, Chief Purchase Agent (1846–1861) and Native Secretary (1856–1861)', MA thesis, Auckland University College, 1947, pp. 19–48.
45 Memorandum of 5 October 1863, *AJHR*, 1863, A-84, p. 11.
46 A. D. Ward, 'The Origins of the Anglo-Maori Wars: A Reconsideration', *NZJH*, vol. 1, no. 2 (1967), pp. 148–70.
47 For a fuller discussion, see Alan Ward, *A Show of Justice: Racial 'Amalgamation' in Nineteenth Century New Zealand*, Australian National University Press, Canberra, 1974, especially ch. xiv.
48 *New Zealand Parliamentary Debates* [hereafter *NZPD*], vol. IX (1870), p. 361.
49 Ibid., vol. XXIV (1877), pp. 253–4.
50 Ward, 'The Origins of the Anglo-Maori Wars', op. cit., p. 167.
51 Quoted by T. L. Buick, *The Treaty of Waitangi*, Avery, New Plymouth, 1933, p. 160.
52 R. T. Lange, 'The Revival of a Dying Race', MA thesis, University of Auckland, 1972, passim.

4 FOLKLAND TO BOOKLAND

1 I. H. Kawharu, *Maori Land Tenure: Studies of a Changing Institution*, Clarendon Press, Oxford, 1977; David V. Williams, *'Te Kooti Tango Whenua': The Native Land Court 1864–1909*, Huia Publishers, Wellington, 1999.
2 M. P. K. Sorrenson, 'The Purchase of Maori Lands, 1865–1892', MA thesis, Auckland University College, 1955, p. 24.
3 Two Tribunal reports in particular have lengthy discussions: *Turanga Tangata Turanga Whenua: The Report on the Turanganui a Kiwa Claims* (*Gisborne Report*), Legislation Direct, Wellington,

2004, vol. II, pp. 395–494; and *The Hauraki Report*, Legislation Direct, Wellington, 2006, vol. II, pp. 657–777. Both make extensive use of the published work of Alan Ward and a Crown-commissioned report by Donald Loveridge that I also use and cite frequently below. Two overviews prepared for the Tribunal's Rangahau Whanui National Themes are also relevant: Hazel Riseborough and John Hutton, 'The Crown's Engagement with Customary Tenure in the Nineteenth Century', Theme C, 1997; and Tom Bennion and Judi Boyd, 'Succession to Maori Land, 1900–52', Theme P, 1997.
4   Particularly his *A Show of Justice: Racial 'Amalgamation' in Nineteenth Century New Zealand*, Australian National University Press, Canberra, 1974; and *An Unsettled History: Treaty Claims in New Zealand Today*, Bridget Williams Books, Wellington, 1999.
5   F. D. Fenton to Mother, 14 November 1850, Fenton Papers, Alexander Turnbull Library, Wellington [hereafter ATL], micro 708. Subsequent letters refer merely to Fenton's domestic affairs and make no reference to his later career as chief judge of the Native Land Court.
6   James Cowan, *The New Zealand Wars. A History of the Maori Campaigns and the Pioneering Period*, Government Printer, Wellington, 1955 reprint, vol. I, p. 262.
7   W. L. Renwick, *Dictionary of New Zealand Biography*, Allen & Unwin/Department of Internal Affairs, Wellington, 1990, vol. I, pp. 121–3.
8   F. D. Fenton, *Observations on the State of the Aboriginal Inhabitants of New Zealand*, W. C. Wilson for New Zealand Government, Auckland, 1859, p. 41.
9   Ibid., p. 42.
10 M. P. K. Sorrenson, 'The Maori King Movement, 1858–1885', in Robert Chapman and Keith Sinclair, eds, *Studies of a Small Democracy: Essays in Honour of Willis Airey*, Paul's Book Arcade, Hamilton & Auckland, 1963, pp. 38–44. The essay is reprinted as chapter 6 of the present volume. For Fenton's Waikato journals, see *AJHR*, 1860, E-1c, pp. 14–35.
11 Ward, *A Show of Justice*, op. cit., p. 107.
12 D. M. Loveridge, 'The Origins of the Native Lands Acts and Native Land Court in New Zealand', Wai-686, P1, Wellington, October 2000, p. 88.
13 Fenton, *Observations . . .*, op. cit., pp. 43–44.
14 For discussion on the role of juries in the management of enclosures in England, see J. M. Neeson, *Commoners: Common Right, Enclosure and Social Change in England, 1700–1820*, Cambridge University Press, Cambridge, 1993, pp. 2, 9, 124–6, 134, 144, 319, 324–5.
15 John Prebble, *The Highland Clearances*, Penguin Books, London, 1963.
16 Allan Kulikoff, *From British Peasants to Colonial American Farmers*, University of North Carolina Press, Chapel Hill, 2000, pp. 17–18.
17 E. P. Thompson, *Customs in Common: Studies in Traditional Popular Culture*, Merlin Press, London, 1991, p. 109.
18 Ibid., p. 121.
19 Ibid., p. 137.
20 Kulikoff, op. cit., p. 75.
21 Neeson, op. cit., p. 107.
22 Quoted by Thompson, op. cit., p. 164.
23 Ibid.
24 Sewell, *NZPD*, vol. 9, 1870, p. 361.
25 Fenton, *Observations . . .*, op. cit., pp. 41, 76.
26 Sir William Martin, *The Taranaki Question*, reprinted in *AJHR*, 1861, E-2, pp. 2–3 (Martin's italics).
27 Kaitorete judgment, in F. D. Fenton, *Important Judgments delivered in the Compensation Court and the Native Land Court 1866–1879*, published under the direction of the Chief Judge, Native Land Court, Auckland, 1879, p. 34.
28 F. E. Maning to Fenton, 24 June 1867, *AJHR*, 1867, A-10, pp. 7–8.
29 Letter to *Aucklander*, 17 September 1862, and Christchurch *Press*, 11 October 1862, quoted by Loveridge, op. cit., pp. 254–7.
30 'Report . . . as to Native Affairs in the Waikato District', *AJHR*, 1860, E-1c, pp. 18–36.
31 William Cronon, *Changes in the Land: Indians, Colonists, and the Ecology of New England*, Hill & Wang, New York, 2003, pp. 30–38.
32 Ward, *A Show of Justice*, op. cit., p. 107.
33 Loveridge, op. cit., p. 89.
34 Ibid., pp. 156–69.

35 Ward, *A Show of Justice*, op. cit., p. 51.
36 Renwick, *Dictionary of New Zealand Biography*, vol. I, p. 122.
37 Ward, *A Show of Justice*, op. cit., p. 80.
38 Richard Boast, *Buying the Land, Selling the Land: Governments and Maori Land in the North Island 1865–1921*, Victoria University Press, Wellington, 2008, p. 66, fn. 75.
39 Loveridge, op. cit., pp. 202–4.
40 Alexander F. G. Brown, 'A Humanitarian Institution? Francis Dart Fenton and the Origins of the Native Land Court, 1850–1865', BA (Hons) thesis, University of Otago, 1998.
41 *NZPD*, 1861–1863, pp. 608–15.
42 Sorrenson, 'The Purchase of Maori Lands', op. cit., pp. 15–18.
43 Loveridge, op. cit., pp. 208–38, 268.
44 Ibid., pp. 268–74. The hearings are recorded in the Native Land Court Hauraki Minute Books, vols 2–6, and the Kaipara Minute Book, vol. 2 (reprints in the University of Auckland Library); see also the Waitangi Tribunal's *Hauraki Report*, vol. II, pp. 681–3.
45 Quoted by Loveridge, op. cit., p. 277.
46 Fenton to W. Mantell, 1 December 1879, quoted by Ward, *A Show of Justice*, op. cit., p. 180.
47 *AJHR*, 1885, I-2B, p. 31.
48 Williams, op. cit., pp. 36–37.
49 Ibid., p. 39.
50 Renwick, *Dictionary of New Zealand Biography*, vol. I, p. 122.
51 Ward, *An Unsettled History . . .*, op. cit., p. 132; Waitangi Tribunal, *Hauraki Report*, vol. II, pp. 668–9.
52 Boast, op. cit., p. 66.
53 Loveridge, op. cit., p. 288.
54 *AJHR*, 1885, I-2B, p. 31.
55 F. D. Fenton, evidence, Native Land Laws Commission, 18 March 1891, *AJHR*, 1891, G-1, p. 45.
56 Ward, *A Show of Justice*, op. cit., p. 188.
57 *NZPD*, 1864–1866, pp. 321–5.
58 Ward, *A Show of Justice*, op. cit., p. 180.
59 Ibid., p. 155.
60 Ibid., p. 180.
61 Williams, op. cit., pp. 150–2. Williams cites Ward and Vincent O'Malley in support.
62 Enclosure in Fenton to Native Land Laws Commissioner, 6 April 1891, *AJHR*, 1891, G-1, p. 86.
63 Fenton to Native Minister (J. C. Richmond), 11 July 1867, *AJHR* 1867, A-10, p. 4.
64 *AJHR*, 1873, G-7. The two Maori commissioners wrote an alternative report that was far more critical of the transactions.
65 Fenton to D. McLean, 28 August 1871, *AJHR*, 1871, A-2A, p. 10.
66 Ibid.
67 The consequences are discussed at greater length in my thesis, 'The Purchase of Maori Lands', op. cit., pp. 44–60.
68 Fenton, *Important Judgments*, op. cit., pp. 19–20; Waitangi Tribunal, *Hauraki Report*, op. cit., vol. II, pp. 688–93.
69 Primogeniture was not universally applied in England and it was common for smallholders to divide their property among heirs, who frequently made arrangements to consolidate the land in the hands of one of them. See G. E. Mingay, *Enclosure and the Small Farmer in the Age of the Industrial Revolution*, Macmillan, London, 1968, p. 27.
70 Minutes of Evidence, Native Land Laws Commission, 1891, *AJHR*, 1891, G-1, p. 47.
71 Ibid.
72 Ward, *A Show of Justice*, op. cit., p. 216; Native Land Court Auckland Minute Book No. 2, pp. 8–9.
73 For instance, Native Land Court Kaipara Minute Book No. 2, p. 40.
74 *NZPD*, vol. 6, 1869, p. 180.
75 *AJHR*, 1891, G-7, p. 47.
76 Waitangi Tribunal, *Hauraki Report*, op. cit., vol. II, pp. 702–3.
77 *AJHR*, 1891, G-1, p. 170. The Act is discussed at length in the Tribunal's *Gisborne Report*, vol. II, pp. 426–46 and *Hauraki Report*, op. cit., vol. II, pp. 713–49.
78 Boast, op. cit., p.140.
79 Ward, *A Show of Justice*, op. cit., p. 255.
80 *AJHR*, 1890, G-1, p. 170.
81 Ward, *A Show of Justice*, op. cit., p. 255.
82 Ward, entry on McLean, *Dictionary of New Zealand Biography*, vol. I, p. 255; see also Ray Fargher, *The Best Man Who Ever Served the Crown? A Life of Donald McLean*, Victoria University Press, Wellington, 2007.
83 For a contextual discussion, see my book, *Maori Origins and Migrations: The Genesis of Some Pakeha Myths and Legends*,

Auckland University Press, Auckland, 1979, pp. 11–33.
84 For the King Country, see my thesis, 'The Purchase of Maori Lands', pp. 98–113; for Te Urewera, see Judith Binney, *Encircled Lands: Te Urewera, 1820–1921*, Bridget Williams Books, Wellington, 2009.
85 Fenton, *Important Judgments*, op. cit., p. 59.
86 Norman Smith, *Native Custom Affecting Land*, Maori Purposes Fund Board, Wellington, 1942, pp. 47–48.
87 Quoted in Ward, *An Unsettled History*, op. cit., p. 129.
88 Neeson, op. cit., pp. 18, 25, 177, 204–8.

5 LAND PURCHASE METHODS AND THEIR EFFECT ON MAORI POPULATION, 1865–1901

1 G. R. Lewthwaite, 'The Population of Aotearoa: Its Number and Distribution', *New Zealand Geographer*, vol. 71, no. 1, p. 49. Cook's estimate was 100,000 but Lewthwaite cites evidence for his higher figure.
2 Selected estimates cited by Lewthwaite (ibid., p. 37) were as follows: Nicholas (1817) 150,000; Williams (1834) 200,000; New Zealand Company (1840) 100,000; and McLean (1853) 60,000. The 1857 census estimate was 56,049, but this was probably too low. See Nancy G. Pearce, 'The Size and Location of the Maori Population, 1857–1896', MA thesis, Victoria University College, 1952, p. 206.
3 Ibid.
4 I. L. G. Sutherland, *The Maori Situation*, H. H. Tombs, Wellington, 1935, pp. 33–35. See also R. Firth, *The Primitive Economics of the New Zealand Maori*, Routledge & Sons, London, 1929, pp. 465–8; and F. M. Keesing, *The Changing Maori*, Thos. Avery & Sons, New Plymouth, 1928, p. 65.
5 Sutherland recognises the damaging effect of land dealings but, by over-emphasising 'psychological reaction', he misses the vital point: that the opposition of the defeated groups was primarily an attempt to prevent further alienation and social disorganisation.
6 Report of the Native Land Laws Commission, *AJHR*, 1891, G-1, VII.
7 R. W. S. Fargher, 'Donald McLean, Chief Land Purchase Agent (1846–1861) and Native Secretary (1856–1861)', MA thesis, Auckland University College, 1947, pp. 20–21, 70–86.
8 The Native Land Administration Act 1886 prohibited direct private negotiations but was repealed in 1888; and the Native Land Court Act 1894 prohibited private purchase, but the following year the Governor-in-Council was empowered to lift this restriction and did so frequently. Report of the Native Lands Commission, *AJHR*, 1907, G-1c, p. 4.
9 R. A. MacDonald, *Te Hekenga: Reminiscences of Early Horowhenua*, Bennett, Palmerston North, 1929, p. 191 — a stinging attack on the 'callous indifference of . . . Parliament'.
10 *NZPD*, vol. 9, 1870, p. 361.
11 *NZPD*, vol. 24, 1877, p. 254.
12 John Sheehan, evidence on petition of Piripi Whatuaio, *AJHR*, 1883, I-2A, p. 18.
13 See, for example, 96 Maori complaints against two Hawke's Bay storekeepers, Report of Hawke's Bay Native Lands Alienation Commission, *AJHR*, 1873, G-7, pp. 1–17. For further comments on liquor and sales, see G. S. Whitmore, *NZPD*, vol. 9, 1870, p. 364; and court sittings in public houses, John Lundon, *NZPD*, vol. 37, 1880, p. 52.
14 John Sheehan, *NZPD*, vol. 19, 1875, pp. 210–11; W. T. L. Travers, *NZPD*, vol. 24, 1877, p. 392.
15 P. J. Coleman, 'The Native Lands Acts and Hawkes Bay; Some Considerations on the Alienation of Maori Land in the Provincial Period of Hawkes Bay Government', MA thesis, Victoria University College, 1949, p. 48; Robert Stout, Memorandum, Owhaoko and Kaimanawa Native Lands, *AJHR*, 1886, G-9, p. 14.
16 MacDonald to John Bryce, 26 May 1883, *AJHR*, 1883, G-5, p. 2.
17 James Bryce, *NZPD*, vol. 45, 1883, p. 458.
18 George Hart, *NZPD*, vol. 25, 1877, p. 404.
19 *New Zealand Herald*, 8 December 1888.
20 Kawana Ropiha, evidence, Native Land Laws Commission, *AJHR*, 1891, G-1, p. 47.
21 W. L. Rees, ibid., p. 57.
22 Accounts of Renata Kawepo, Walter Buller Papers, ATL.

23 MacDonald, op. cit., pp. 172–204.
24 Quoted ibid., p. 204.
25 The purchase is fully reported by the Hawke's Bay Native Lands Alienation Commission, *AJHR*, 1873, G-7, pp. 17–29. See also John Sheehan, *NZPD*, vol. 25, 1877, pp. 315–17. It is also discussed at greater length in my thesis, op. cit., pp. 46–51.
26 The 1848 Sale of Spirits Ordinance, prohibiting the sale of liquor to Maori, was still in force, but it was a dead letter. Nevertheless, the Hawke's Bay Commission and the Supreme Court upheld land purchases in Hawke's Bay that had been paid for by sales of liquor to Maori. See Robert Stout, *NZPD*, vol. 25, 1877, p. 363; and John Sheehan, *NZPD*, vol. 29, 1878, p. 643.
27 Ormond's name was included as one of the plaintiffs.
28 The attempt by a European party led by E. B. Walker to occupy land on the King party side of the border led to the murder of Sullivan, one of Walker's employees, in 1873. Walker had negotiated with the land-selling faction of Ngati Haua and concluded a lease after the Court had awarded the land to this group. Purukutu, who was alleged to have committed the murder, was the leader of the non-selling faction of Ngati Haua, a supporter of the King movement, and boycotted the Court sitting. The murder was an attempt to prevent further sales of land across the border, but it was the last resort to violence in the region. *New Zealand Herald*, 23 May 1873.
29 The Maungatautari block was a typical example. Hearings were started in the Court in 1883, but some sub-divisions were not completed until the end of 1889. *New Zealand Herald*, 12 December 1889.
30 Joseph Ivess, *NZPD*, vol. 46, 1883, p. 124. Ivess owned a newspaper in Cambridge and attacked the abuses, but the commercial community in the town boycotted the paper.
31 *New Zealand Herald*, 2 March 1883. See also Hirini Taiwhanga, *NZPD*, vol. 63, 1888, p. 449.
32 *New Zealand Herald*, 27 May 1885. See also reports on the Patetere negotiations, *AJHR*, 1880, G-1; 1881, G-13; and 1883, G-6.
33 Sheehan, evidence on Piripi Whatuaio's petition re Patetere judgment, *AJHR*, 1883, I-2A, p. 17.
34 F. J. Moss, *NZPD*, vol. 46, 1883, p. 110; *New Zealand Herald*, 24 February and 18 March 1882.
35 *NZPD*, vol. 19, 1875, p. 82.
36 James Mackay to T. B. Gillies, 20 March 1872, *AJHR*, 1873, G-5, p. 20.
37 E. G. B. Moss, *Native Lands and their Incidents*, Wilson & Horton, Auckland, 1888, p. 6.
38 J. C. Batkin, Report on Young's transactions, *AJHR*, 1880, G-5, p. 15.
39 Ibid., p. 13.
40 Audit Inspector Churton, quoted in *Bay of Plenty Times*, 2 March 1880.
41 'Occasional Correspondent', Letter No. 2, in Anon., *How the Native Land Court and Land Purchase Department Behave on the East Coast*, W. Atkin, Auckland, 1877, p. 13.
42 Sir George Grey, *NZPD*, vol. 45, 1883, p. 513. See also MacDonald, op. cit., pp. 179–82. Significantly, that chapter is headed 'The Land Court Wrecks the Tribe'.
43 R. C. Bruce, *NZPD*, vol. 52, 1885, p. 515.
44 *New Zealand Herald*, 18 March 1882.
45 Ibid., 26 May 1891.
46 *Reports of the Census of New Zealand* at the below dates. The decrease in the 1896 census was probably not a natural decrease. There was widespread Maori opposition to this census and considerable numbers were probably omitted. *AJHR*, 1896, H-13B. There were no widespread epidemics between 1891 and 1896.
47 *Reports of the Census of New Zealand* at the above dates. Figures for Ngati Awa are from Pearce, op. cit., p. 130, and include only the Taranaki section of the tribe. Three Taranaki tribes — Ngati Ruanui, Taranaki and Ngati Awa — are included. In Taranaki little land was purchased since most of it had been confiscated during the wars. However, Taranaki Maori had reoccupied much of the confiscated land and, under the leadership of Te Whiti at Parihaka, resisted European attempts to occupy it until Parihaka was invaded in 1881 and most of his followers were detained or dispersed.
48 Pearce, op. cit., p. 68.
49 Ibid., p. 130.
50 W. H. Grace, Enumerator for the Maori

Census, to the Department of Justice, *AJHR*, 1896, H-13B, No. 4, p. 3.
51   Under the Native Lands Alienation Restriction Act 1884.
52   Debate on 'Liquor in the King Country', 8 December 1900, quoted in *Report of Fifth Conference of the Te Aute Students' Association*, p. 10.
53   G. T. Wilkinson, Native Agent, Otorohanga, to the Under-Secretary, Native Department, *AJHR*, 1890, G-2, No. 4, pp. 2–6.
54   *New Zealand Herald*, 21 April 1897.
55   *AJHR*, 1872, F-3, pp. 7–9; 1874, G-2, p. 9 and G-2B, p. 2; 1875, G-1, p. 9 and G-1A, p. 19; 1878, G-1, p. 6; and 1881, G-3, p. 3.
56   *New Zealand Herald*, 3 May 1877.
57   Ibid., 9 May 1878.
58   Special correspondent, *New Zealand Herald*, 19 March 1880.
59   Ibid.
60   R. M. Burdon, *New Zealand Notables*, First Series, Caxton Press, Christchurch, 1941, p. 100.
61   *AJHR*, 1885, G-2A, pp. 11–12.
62   Ibid., 1874, G-2, p. 21.
63   Ibid.
64   *New Zealand Herald*, 28 March 1891.
65   Keesing, op. cit., p. 65; James Cowan, *The Old Frontier*, Waipa Post, Te Awamutu, 1922, p. 84, pictured the King party as 'inimical, sullen, waiting, for well-nigh twenty years after the final shots of the Waikato war'; Firth, op. cit., pp. 465–7, 'The Mood of Reaction'.
66   In 1875 Mair, when stressing the friendship of the King party chiefs, noted that a European from the Armed Constabulary had been allowed to travel through the King Country to visit friends in Taranaki. *AJHR*, 1875, G-1A, p. 2.
67   Mair's Reports on King Country, *AJHR*, 1872, F-3, pp. 7–9; 1876, G-1A, p. 19; 1878, G-1, pp. 6–7.
68   Literally, 'The Morning Star'.
69   R. S. Bush to McLean, 12 October 1875, *AJHR*, 1876, G-1, p. 6.
70   It could be argued that living in large nucleated settlements and the continuance of many communal customs aggravated the spread of infectious diseases. There is some substance in this argument but the emphasis of the King party on social order, sanitation and abstinence from liquor meant that the less fatal illnesses at least were not so destructive. Mair, for example, reported in 1878 that there was less influenza among the King party than among Europeans in the Waikato. *AJHR*, 1878, G-1, p. 7.
71   G. W. Rusden, ed., *Aureretanga: Groans of the Maoris*, William Ridgeway, London, 1888, p. 87.
72   Burdon, op. cit., p.101.

6   THE MAORI KING MOVEMENT, 1858–1885

1   *Southern Cross*, 21 November 1870. Manuhiri was a younger brother of Potatau, the first Maori King, and was also known as Tamati Ngapora.
2   K. Sinclair, *The Origins of the Maori Wars*, New Zealand University Press, Wellington, 1957, pp. 103–4.
3   Gore Browne's proclamation to the King party, *AJHR*, 1861, E-1B, pp. 11–12.
4   *AJHR*, 1860, F-3, for the views of the Waikato Committee.
5   *Southern Cross*, 5 May 1857.
6   J. E. Gorst, *The Maori King; or, the Story of our Quarrel with the Natives of New Zealand*, Macmillan & Co., London and Cambridge, 1864, p. 39.
7   *The Origins of the Maori Wars* and his introduction to the second edition of Gorst's *Maori King*, Paul's Book Arcade, Hamilton & Auckland, 1959, pp. ix–xxv.
8   Gorst, op. cit., p. 66.
9   Sinclair, *The Origins of the Maori Wars*, pp. 75–76, 78–82.
10   *Southern Cross*, 5 June 1857.
11   Sinclair, *The Origins of the Maori Wars*, p. 80.
12   Ibid., p. 77. See also Raymond Firth, *The Economics of the New Zealand Maori*, 2nd edition, Government Printer, Wellington, 1959, pp. 455–7, on 'The Mood of Reaction' after the wars.
13   There is no exact equivalent in English. Mana can also mean prestige, influence and psychic power. See Firth, op. cit., pp. 255, 392.
14   Paora Tuhaere of Ngati Whatua at the Rangiriri meeting, quoted in the *New Zealander*, 6 June 1857.

15 'Curiosus' quoted in ibid., 3 July 1858.
16 R. W. S. Fargher, 'Donald McLean, Chief Land Purchase Agent (1846–61) and Native Secretary (1856–61)', MA thesis, Auckland University College, 1947, pp. 79–86; and Sinclair, *The Origins of the Maori Wars*, pp. 58–59.
17 Sinclair, *The Origins of the Maori Wars*, p. 72.
18 K. Sinclair, *The Maori Land League: An Examination into the Source of a New Zealand Myth*, Auckland University College Bulletin No. 37, History Series No. 4, 1950.
19 Tamihana to Gore Browne, 7 June 1861, quoted in [M. Winiata], *History of the King Movement*, Centennial Celebration pamphlet on the Founding of the Maori King Movement, North Waikato Printing Co. Ltd, Ngaruawahia, 1958, unpaged.
20 Sinclair, introductory note to the appendix in the 2nd edition of Gorst's *Maori King*, p. 263. The appendix consists of two letters written by Tamihana and published in the *Southern Cross* (on 3 and 6 August 1858) describing the Ngaruawahia and Rangiaowhia meetings. A further description by the Rev. R. Burrows was published in the *Southern Cross* on 11 June 1858.
21 Burrows' translation of the question.
22 Tamihana's account in Sinclair's edition of Gorst's *Maori King*, Appendix, p. 267.
23 *New Zealander*, 3 July 1858.
24 J. A. Smith's census figures, prepared for W. Brown, superintendent of the Auckland Province, ibid., 2 May 1855. There is an incomplete list of Europeans squatting on Maori land in the Waikato in *AJHR*, 1863, E-16, p. 5.
25 *Votes and Proceedings of the House of Representatives*, 1855, unpaged, recording 308 acres purchased for J. Armitage and 170 acres for Heather; and *AJHR*, 1856, C-7, recording payments for homesteads for Armitage, Cheetham and Dr Harsant.
26 *Southern Cross*, 28 November 1856.
27 Ibid., 25 February, 8, 22, 25 March, 8 April, 31 May, 10, 17, 24 June, 16 August 1859; cf. *New Zealander*, 21 May 1859, which attacks the agitation.
28 Account of Nixon's expedition, Auckland Provincial Council MSS, Sess. XI (1859); and accounts of Firth's expedition, *New Zealander*, 17, 24 December 1859, and 21 and 28 January 1860. The accounts note strong Maori opposition to dealing with land.
29 'A Nobody' in *New Zealander*, 26 March 1856; W. Aitken, ibid., 2 June 1858; and 'An Old Hauraki Settler', ibid., 5 October 1859.
30 Ibid., 28 May 1859.
31 *Te Hokioi*, 10 November 1862, quoted in *AJHR*, 1863, E-12, p. 15.
32 The phrase is Sinclair's: *The Origins of the Maori Wars*, p. 77.
33 *Southern Cross*, 22 June 1860, 26 May 1862.
34 Sinclair, *The Origins of the Maori Wars*, p. 106; Gorst, op. cit., pp. 62–63.
35 *Acts and Proceedings, Auckland Provincial Council*, Sess. V, 1856, A-23 (licences granted to J. V. Cowell and P. Brosman); *New Zealander*, 8 February 1860 (noting that Cheetham held a licence for a public house at Rangiaowhia).
36 Speaking at King party meeting in June 1857, quoted by Gorst, op. cit., pp. 60–61.
37 Ibid.
38 Fenton's evidence before the Waikato Committee, *AJHR*, 1860, F-3, p. 1.
39 See, for examples, his reports to the *Southern Cross*, 26 February 1858 and 19 April 1859.
40 Ibid., 5 May, 5, 16 June 1857, 5 February, 20 April 1858, 24 May 1859. On the other hand, the rival Auckland newspaper, the *New Zealander*, usually supported the Government and maintained that the King movement was 'a piece of Maori folly, fostered by knavish Europeans, who have their own individual interests to attain' (28 May 1859) — a charge that may have contained a grain of truth.
41 The Journals of both trips (July–August 1857 and February–March 1858) were printed in *AJHR*, 1860, E-1C, encl. 3, pp. 14–35.
42 Taupari was near the mouth of the Waikato river and should not be confused with Taupiri, a Maori kainga and mountain higher up the river.
43 Fenton's Journals, op. cit., 20 July 1857.
44 Ibid., 31 July 1857.
45 Ibid., 20 August 1857.
46 Ibid., 4 March 1858.
47 Ibid., 11 August 1857.
48 Gorst, op. cit., p. 116.

49 Winiata, *History of the King Movement*, op. cit., unpaged.
50 *Southern Cross*, 19, 22 November 1861, and 23 June 1862 (a letter from R. Ormsby, a squatter, appealing to the Government to protect the squatters).
51 Sinclair, *The Origins of the Maori Wars*, p. 76; Gorst, op. cit., pp. 267–85.
52 Gorst, op. cit., p. 113, admits that the loyalty of Fenton's Maori supporters (the Queen's party) 'was far more a love of prospective gifts and salaries than law and order'.
53 'Tribal Organisation' in I. L. G. Sutherland, ed., *The Maori People Today: A General Survey*, Whitcombe & Tombs, Christchurch, 1940, p. 178.
54 Pei Te H. Jones, *An Account of the Life of Potatau Te Wherowhero, the First Maori King*, Polynesian Society, Wellington, [1960], p. 37.
55 'Souvenir Booklet on the *Poukai* Celebrations and the Visit of the Prime Minister to Tamatepokaiwhenua Meeting House', [Judea, Tauranga], 1958, p. 11. My italics.
56 The story is told in more detail in Winiata's pamphlet, *History of the King Movement*, from which the statement which follows on Potatau's qualifications is taken; and in Jones, op. cit., pp.183–266.
57 Jones, op. cit., p. 37, suggests that Potatau accepted the Kingship because the idea appealed to his priestly ego.
58 Meaning the sovereignty, the prestige, the cultural integrity of the Maori people.
59 Quoted in Gorst, op. cit., p. 94.
60 Quoted in Tamihana's letter to the *Southern Cross*, reproduced in Sinclair's edition of Gorst's *The Maori King*, p. 270. The explanation of the metaphorical statements is in the original letter.
61 Ibid., p. 271.
62 Winiata, *History of the King Movement*, op. cit., p. 14 (my pagination).
63 Gorst, op. cit., pp. 267–85.
64 See M. Winiata, 'Leadership in Pre-European Maori Society', *JPS*, vol. 65, no. 3 (1956), pp. 212–14, for an account of the *waka* organisation.
65 S. Percy Smith, *Maori Wars of the Nineteenth Century*, 2nd edition, Whitcombe & Tombs, Christchurch, 1910, pp. 224–37; and Jones, op. cit., pp. 114–32, 148–54.
66 Sinclair, *The Origins of the Maori Wars*, p. 75.
67 For the origins, see especially Sinclair, *The Origins of the Maori Wars*; and for the course of the wars, see James Cowan, *The New Zealand Wars: A History of the Maori Campaigns and the Pioneering Period*, 2 vols, Government Printer, Wellington, 1922–3.
68 Discussed in more detail in my MA thesis, 'The Purchase of Maori Lands, 1865–1892', Auckland University College, 1955, pp. 98–113, 216–20.
69 The phrases are from Keith Sinclair, *A History of New Zealand*, Penguin Books, Harmondsworth, 1959, p. 142; and F. M. Keesing, *The Changing Maori*, The Board of Maori Ethnological Research, New Plymouth, 1928, p. 65. Most other writers who mention the King party in this period use similar terms.
70 Quoted by 'An Occasional Correspondent' in the *Southern Cross*, 29 March 1872.
71 Norman Smith, *The Maori People and Us*, A. H. & A. W. Reed, Wellington, pp. 164–7. Of this area, 1,202,172 acres were in the Waikato; 314,264 acres were subsequently returned. In 1927 a Royal Commission concluded that the confiscations had been excessive and, so far as the Waikato tribes were concerned, recommended an annual compensation payment of £3,000. Several years later the Government doubled the award.
72 Ibid., p. 72.
73 Report of Judge Mair's decision in the Rohepotae case before the Native Land Court, *New Zealand Herald*, 26 October 1886.
74 Reports of Native Land Court hearings re the J. C. Firth lease, *Southern Cross*, 24 October, 8 and 21 November 1866. The last report admits that the Kingite section of the tribe, who had boycotted the hearings, was left out of the Court's award for the land leased to Firth.
75 Ibid., 20 March, 8 November 1866.
76 Ibid., 20 May 1873.
77 Ibid., 12, 14 February 1872 reporting comments by J. Cash and A. Erskine, who had been prospecting with Lyons in 1870.
78 Ibid., 29, 30 November 1870.

79 The affray was extensively reported in the press between 26 April and 28 June 1873. It was generally assumed that Porokutu had performed the deed or instigated it, but he was never brought to trial, although Donald McLean sent James Mackay into the King Country where he made an unsuccessful attempt to arrest Porokutu. Whether Porokutu was acting on Tawhiao's instructions remains uncertain. Porokutu had been chosen as one of the 'keepers of the *aukati* [boundary]' and, according to one report (*Southern Cross*, 20 May 1873), Tawhiao had told him: 'If you see a [praying] mantis ... upon a manuka bush pick it off carefully. But if you see a reptile crawling across the road, you are to kill it and eat it' — i.e. stray European travellers were not to be harmed, but surveyors and other Europeans working on land across the border were to be killed.
80 Proclamations were published in the *Southern Cross* on 17 February, 10 August 1868, 7 May 1869 and 24 May 1873.
81 Manuhiri to C. O. Davis, 26 August 1870, printed in *Southern Cross*, 21 November 1870.
82 *Southern Cross*, 22 February 1868.
83 *New Zealand Herald*, 3 May 1877.
84 See his reports on the King Country, *AJHR*, 1872, F-3, pp. 7–9; 1875, G-1A, p. 19; and 1878, G-1, pp. 6–7.
85 *Southern Cross*, 6 January 1875.
86 Ibid., 29 December 1873, 5 March 1874.
87 Ibid., 3 March 1868.
88 Ibid., 29 December 1875.
89 Ibid., 3 November, 8 December 1875.
90 Ibid., 4 September 1872.
91 Ibid., 24 June 1873.
92 R. S. Bush to McLean, 12 October 1875, *AJHR*, 1876, G-1, p. 6.
93 The meetings were reported by Mair and other officials and published in *AJHR*, G-1 of each year, and in the Auckland and Waikato press.
94 Quoted in the *New Zealand Herald*, 17 May 1882.
95 *AJHR*, 1883, G-6, pp. 7–8; *New Zealand Herald*, 27 May 1885.
96 *New Zealand Herald*, 22 December 1882.
97 *AJHR*, 1888, G-4A, pp. 2–5.
98 *New Zealand Herald*, 13 November 1883.

7 POLYNESIAN CORPUSCLES AND PACIFIC ANTHROPOLOGY

1 Ramsden Papers, MS Papers 196/310, ATL. All of the quotations below are taken from my edition of this collection, M. P. K. Sorrenson, *Na To Hoa Aroha, From Your Dear Friend: The correspondence between Sir Apirana Ngata and Sir Peter Buck 1925–50*, 3 vols, Auckland University Press, Auckland, 1986, 1987, 1988.
2 *Na Toa Hoa Aroha*, vol. I, p. 48.
3 Ibid., p. 96.
4 Ibid., vol. II, p. 245.
5 J. B. Condliffe, *Te Rangi Hiroa: The Life of Sir Peter Buck*, Whitcombe & Tombs, Christchurch, 1971, pp. 63–73; G. V. Butterworth, 'The Politics of Adaptation: The Career of Sir Apirana Ngata, 1874–1928', MA thesis, Victoria University of Wellington, 1969, pp. 16–21.
6 Some of Ngata's term results and lecture notes are in the Maori Purposes Fund Board Papers, MS Papers 189/94, ATL; some of Buck's results are in the Ramsden Papers, MS Papers 196/337, ATL.
7 J. H. Scott, 'Contribution to the Osteology of the Aborigines of New Zealand and the Chatham Islands', *T&PNZI*, vol. 26 (1893), pp. 1–64.
8 *JPS*, vol. 31 (1922), pp. 37–44, 145–53, 159–69; vol. 32 (1923), pp. 21–28, 189–99.
9 P. H. Buck, 'Medicine Amongst the Maoris in Ancient and Modern Times', MD thesis, University of Otago, 1910.
10 Buck to Ngata, May 18, 1909, MA 31/42, National Archives of New Zealand [hereafter NA].
11 P. H. Buck, 'On the Maori Art of Weaving Cloaks, Capes, and Kilts'; 'Some Notes on the Small Outrigger Canoes in Niue-fekai'; 'Some Tattoo Patterns from Mangaia'; and 'Aitutaki Moko: Some Tattoo Patterns from Aitutaki', *Dominion Museum Bulletin*, no. 3, pp. 69–98.
12 A. T. Ngata, 'Draft Statement of the Aims and Objectives of the Young Maori Party', Maori Purposes Fund Board Papers, MS Papers 189/11, ATL.
13 A. T. Ngata, *Songs, Haka and Ruri*, Government Printer, Wellington, 1914.
14 Condliffe, op. cit., p. 106.
15 *Na To Hoa Aroha*, vol. I, p. 48.

16 Condliffe, op. cit., p. 98.
17 M. P. K. Sorrenson, *Maori Origins and Migrations*, Auckland University Press, Auckland, 1979, pp. 18–33.
18 *Na To Hoa Aroha*, vol. III, p. 66.
19 Ibid., p. 79.
20 H. W. Williams, 'The Maruiwi Myth', *JPS*, vol. 46 (1937), pp. 105–22.
21 P. H. Buck, *The Coming of the Maori*, Maori Purposes Fund Board, Wellington, 1949, p. 51.
22 Ngata to Buck, 27 November 1949, *Na To Hoa Aroha*, vol. III, p. 249.
23 P. H. Buck, review of *The Racial History of Man* by R. D. Dixon, *JPS*, vol. 32 (1923), pp. 248–9.
24 Buck to Ngata, 5 June 1928, *Na Toa Hoa Aroha*, vol. I, p. 101.
25 Buck to Ngata, 24 September 1928, ibid., p. 133.
26 Buck to Ngata, 19 August 1931, ibid., vol. II, p. 203.
27 Buck to Ngata, 3 December 1933, ibid., vol. III, p. 123.
28 Buck to Ngata, 29 July 1928, ibid., vol. I, pp. 115–22; Buck to Ngata, 9 November 1929, ibid., p. 267; Buck to Ngata, 4 November 1930, ibid., vol. II, p. 73; Buck to Ngata, 16 December 1930, ibid., p. 90. The works cited by Buck were: Clark Wissler, *An Introduction to Social Anthropology*, Holt, New York, 1929; R. H. Lowie, *Primitive Society*, Routledge, London, 1920; and A. M. Tozzer, *Social Origins and Social Continuities*, Macmillan, London, 1925.
29 Ngata to Buck, 23 June 1928, *Na To Hoa Aroha*, vol. I, p. 102.
30 A. T. Ngata, 'The Genealogical Method as Applied to the Early History of New Zealand', a paper read before the Wellington Branch of the Historical Association, typescript, ATL.
31 The actual title of the paper by W. H. R. Rivers was 'On the function of the maternal uncle in Torres Straits', *Man*, vol. 1 (1901), pp. 171–2.
32 Ngata to Buck, 23 June 1928, *Na To Hoa Aroha*, vol. I, p. 103.
33 Buck to Ngata, ibid., p. 110.
34 Ibid.
35 A. T. Ngata, 'Anthropology and the Government of Native Races in the Pacific', *The Australasian Journal of Psychology and Philosophy*, vol. VI, no. 1 (1928), pp. 1–14.
36 Ngata to Buck, 7 June 1929, *Na Toa Hoa Aroha*, vol. I, p. 201.
37 I. L. G. Sutherland, 'The Study of the Native Mind', *JPS*, vol. 38, (1929), pp. 127–47.
38 Ngata to Buck, 7 June 1929, *Na To Hoa Aroha*, vol. I, p. 201.
39 G. H. L. Pitt-Rivers, 'A visit to a Maori village', *JPS*, vol. 33 (1924), pp. 48–65; and *The Clash of Culture and the Contact of Races ... Depopulation of the Pacific and the Government of Subject Races*, Routledge, London, 1927, ch. XII, pp. 217–28; the thanks to Buck is on page xiii of the Preface.
40 Buck to Ngata, 29 July 1928, *Na To Hoa Aroha*, vol. I, p. 120; and Ngata to Buck, ibid., p. 123.
41 Ibid., p. 123.
42 Buck to Ngata, 24 September 1928, ibid., p. 133.
43 F. M. Keesing, *The Changing Maori*, Board of Maori Ethnological Research, Wellington, 1928, p. vii.
44 F. M. Keesing, 'Maori Progress on the East Coast of New Zealand', *Te Wananga*, vol. I, no. 1 (1929), pp. 10–56; and no. 2 (1930), pp. 92–127.
45 Ngata to Buck, 2 June 1928, *Na To Hoa Aroha*, vol. I, p. 96.
46 Ibid., p. 267.
47 Buck to Ngata, 9 November 1929, ibid.
48 Buck to Ngata, 22 October 1930, ibid., vol. II, p. 71.
49 Ngata to Buck, 20 September 1930, ibid., p. 57.
50 A. T. Ngata, 'Land Development Report', *AJHR*, 1931, G-10, p. 18.
51 Ngata to Buck, 6 February 1931, *Na To Hoa Aroha*, vol. II, pp. 110–11.
52 Ngata, 'Anthropology and the Government of Native Races', op. cit., pp. 1–14.
53 Ibid.
54 Buck to Ngata, 12 March 1928, *Na To Hoa Aroha*, vol. I, p. 74.
55 Buck to Ngata, 13 January 1931, ibid., vol. II, pp. 103–6.
56 Ngata to Buck, 8 March 1931, ibid., p. 121.
57 Ngata to Buck, 11 January 1931, p. 97.
58 Buck to Ngata, 25 August 1931, ibid., p. 209.
59 R. Firth, 'The Economic Aspect of Culture Change', *The Primitive Economics of the*

    New Zealand Maori, Routledge & Sons, London, 1929, p. 472.
60 A. T. Ngata, 'Land Development Report', op. cit., p. ix.
61 Ibid., pp. ix, xi, xiii, xiv.
62 Ibid., p. xiv.
63 Buck to Ngata, 15 December 1931, *Na To Hoa Aroha*, vol. II, pp. 242–3.
64 Buck to Ngata, 19 October 1931, ibid., p. 230.
65 D. Smith, 'Report of the Native Affairs Commission of Inquiry', *AJHR*, 1934, G-11, p. 56.
66 Ibid., p. 39.
67 Ngata to Buck, 27 November 1933, *Na To Hoa Aroha*, vol. III, p. 119.
68 Buck to Ngata, 11 February 1934, ibid., p. 126.
69 Ngata to Buck, 29 October 1934, ibid., p. 168.
70 Buck to Ngata, 11 February 1934, ibid., p. 177.
71 Buck to Ngata, 11 November 1936, ibid., pp. 241–2.
72 Buck to Ngata, 26 June 1937, ibid., p. 243.
73 Ngata to Buck, 15 July 1940, ibid., p. 245.
74 Buck to Ramsden, 6 November 1940 (Ramsden Papers, MS Papers 196/318, ATL) says that he wrote 'a warm and friendly letter' to Ngata, who did not reply.
75 Quoted in Ramsden to Buck, 19 July 1940, Ramsden Papers, MS Papers 196/318, ATL. The author of the statement was not named but was said to have been from the Ngati Kahungunu tribe.
76 P. H. Buck, 'The Passing of the Maori', *T&PNZI*, vol. 55 (1924), pp. 363–75.
77 P. H. Buck, *The Coming of the Maori*, op. cit., p. 538.
78 Katherine Luomala, 'Necrology: Peter Henry Buck (Te Rangi Hiroa)', Bernice P. Bishop Museum Bulletin, no. 208 (1951), p. 39.

8 COLONIAL RULE AND LOCAL RESPONSE

1 C. D. Rowley, *The Remote Aborigines*, Australian National University Press, Canberra, 1970, pp. 1–26.
2 Quoted by Alan Ward, *A Show of Justice: Racial 'Amalgamation' in Nineteenth Century New Zealand*, Australian National University Press, Canberra, 1974, p. 208.
3 J. G. A. Pocock, *The Maori and New Zealand Politics*, Blackwood & Janet Paul, Hamilton & Auckland, 1965, p. 8.
4 See, in particular, T. O. Ranger, 'Connexions between "Primary Resistance" Movements and Modern Mass Nationalism in East and Central Africa', *Journal of African History*, vol. IX, nos 3 and 4 (1968), pp. 437–53, 631–41.
5 Quoted by T. L. Buick, *The Treaty of Waitangi*, Avery, New Plymouth, 1933, p. 160.
6 'Curiosus', *New Zealander*, 3 July 1858.
7 C. D. Rowley, *The Destruction of Aboriginal Society*, Penguin Books, Ringwood, 1970, pp. 187 et seq.; D. Welsh, *The Roots of Segregation: Native Policy in Colonial Natal 1845–1910*, Oxford University Press, Cape Town, 1971, pp. 217–34.
8 M. P. K. Sorrenson, 'The Purchase of Maori Lands, 1865–1892', MA thesis, Auckland University College, 1955, passim.
9 M. P. K. Sorrenson, 'The Maori King Movement, 1858–1885', in *Studies of a Small Democracy: Essays in Honour of Willis Airey*, ed. R. M. Chapman and K. Sinclair, Paul's Book Arcade, Hamilton & Auckland, 1963, pp. 33–55.
10 J. A. Williams, *Politics of the New Zealand Maori: Protest and Co-operation, 1891–1909*, University of Washington Press, Seattle, 1969, pp. 44–47.
11 See P. J. A. Clark, 'Prospect of Peace: Te Ua and Pai Marire, 1862–1865', MA thesis, University of Auckland, 1974.
12 There is no satisfactory recent study. For a useful account of the religion, see W. Greenwood, 'The Upraised Hand', *JPS*, vol. 51, no. 1 (1942), pp. 1–80.
13 Dick Scott, *The Parihaka Story*, Southern Cross Books, Auckland, 1954.
14 Williams, op. cit., pp. 132–4.
15 Alan D. Ward, 'The Origins of the Anglo-Maori Wars: A Reconsideration', *NZJH*, vol. 1, no. 2 (1967), p. 167.
16 See, for instance, J. M. Henderson, 'The Ratana Movement', in *The Maori and New Zealand Politics*, ed. J. G. A. Pocock, Blackwood & Janet Paul, Hamilton & Auckland, pp. 62–67.
17 The most interesting recent examination

is by W. H. Oliver and Jane M. Thomson, *Challenge and Response: A Study of the Development of the Gisborne East Coast Region*, The East Coast Development Research Association, Gisborne, 1971, pp. 80–94, though this is confined to Poverty Bay.
18   Sorrenson, 'The Purchase of Maori Lands', op. cit., pp. 44–51.
19   Ibid., pp. 224–7.
20   Williams, op. cit., pp. 48–67.
21   J. M. Henderson, *Ratana: The Origins and Story of the Movement*, Polynesian Society Memoir, vol. 36, New Plymouth, 1963.

9 MAORI REPRESENTATION IN PARLIAMENT

1   P. Adams, *Fatal Necessity: British Intervention in New Zealand, 1830–1847*, Auckland University Press, Auckland, 1977, pp. 52–53.
2   C. J. Orange, 'The Treaty of Waitangi: A Study of its Making, Interpretation and Role in New Zealand History', PhD thesis, University of Auckland, 1984, pp. 77–83.
3   Ibid., pp. 83–94.
4   A. H. McLintock, *Crown Colony Government in New Zealand*, Government Printer, Wellington, 1958, pp. 54–55.
5   Orange, op. cit., pp. 452–3.
6   R. M. Ross, 'Te Tiriti o Waitangi: Texts and Translations', *NZJH*, vol. 6, no. 2 (1972), p. 154.
7   Orange, op. cit., pp. 145–6.
8   Ross, op. cit., p. 141.
9   Quoted by Adams, op. cit., p. 184.
10 Ibid., pp. 185–6.
11 Ibid., p. 187.
12 Orange, op. cit., pp. 310, 320–32.
13 McLintock, op. cit., p. 101.
14 Ibid., p. 287.
15 Governor Grey to Earl Grey, 3 May 1847, GBPP Cmd. 892, 1847–8, p. 44.
16 M. P. K. Sorrenson, 'The Maori King Movement, 1858–1885', in Robert Chapman and Keith Sinclair, eds., *Studies of a Small Democracy: Essays in Honour of Willis Airey*, Paul's Book Arcade, Hamilton & Auckland, 1963, pp. 38–39, reprinted as chapter 6 above.
17 Ibid., pp. 33–34.
18 Quoted by 'Curiosus', *New Zealander*, 3 July 1858.
19 Quoted in J. E. Gorst, *The Maori King; or, the Story of our Quarrel with the Natives of New Zealand*, Macmillan & Co., London and Cambridge, 1864, p. 324.
20 Enclosure in Newcastle to Browne, 19 December 1859, *AJHR*, 1860, E-2, pp. 7–8.
21 *NZPD*, 1861–1863, pp. 483–513.
22 W. K. Jackson and G. A. Wood, 'The New Zealand Parliament and Maori Representation', *Historical Studies, Australia and New Zealand*, October 1964, p. 386.
23 Alan Ward, *A Show of Justice: Racial 'Amalgamation' in Nineteenth Century New Zealand*, Australian National University Press, Canberra, 1974, p. 188.
24 *NZPD*, vol. 2, 1867, p. 336.
25 Ibid., p. 461.
26 Ibid., p. 463; also James Paterson, ibid., p. 465.
27 Ibid., p. 655.
28 Ibid., p. 813.
29 Ibid., p. 812.
30 Ibid., p. 814.
31 Ibid., p. 815.
32 Ibid.
33 Ibid., p. 816.
34 Ibid., pp. 975–7.
35 Ward, op. cit., p. 209.
36 Sheila McLean, 'Maori Representation, 1905–1948', MA thesis, Auckland University College, 1949, p. 5.
37 *New Zealand Herald*, 30 August 1867.
38 *Daily Southern Cross*, 2, 9 September 1867.
39 Rolleston to McLean, 17 December 1867. I am grateful to Alan Ward for providing me with a copy of this letter from the McLean Papers, MSS 362, ATL.
40 *The New Zealand Gazette*, 1868, pp. 103–4.
41 Ibid., p. 111.
42 Quoted by Ward, op. cit., p. 210.
43 Ibid.
44 Ibid.
45 Ibid.
46 Williams to D. McLean, 15 February 1871, *AJHR*, 1871, F-6A, p. 11: and Ward, op. cit., p. 344.
47 *NZPD*, vol. 10, 1871, pp. 471–6.
48 Ibid., vol. 22, 1876, p. 230.
49 *AJHR*, 1876, J-6, pp. 1–2; for recent pleas,

50 Jackson and Wood, op. cit., p. 389.
51 Ibid., p. 388.
52 *The New Zealand Gazette*, 1875, p. 799.
53 Ibid., pp. 1032–3.
54 G. T. Wilkinson to T. W. Lewis, 19 May 1887, *AJHR*, 1887, vol. II, G-1, p. 5.
55 Ibid., 1887, vol. II, G-1, p. 1033.
56 Enclosure in G. Preece to T. W. Lewis, 16 December 1890, MA 23/15, NA.
57 Ward, op. cit., p. 344.
58 M. P. K. Sorrenson, 'The Purchase of Maori Lands, 1865–1892', MA thesis, Auckland University College, 1955, p. 229.
59 Ward, op. cit., p. 271.
60 Quoted by John A. Williams, *Politics of the New Zealand Maori*, University of Washington Press, Seattle, 1969, p. 43.
61 Quoted ibid., p. 45.
62 Ibid., p. 50.
63 Ward, op. cit., p. 291.
64 *NZPD*, vol. 63, 1888, pp. 448–51.
65 G. V. Butterworth, 'Maori Land Legislation: The Work of Carroll and Ngata', *The New Zealand Law Journal*, August 1985, pp. 242–9.
66 *NZPD*, vol. 134, 1905, p. 37.
67 A. T. Ngata to P. H. Buck, 29 June 1931, Ramsden Papers, MS Papers 196/312, ATL.
68 P. H. Buck, 'He Poroporoaki — A Farewell Message', in E. Ramsden, ed., *Sir Apirana Ngata Memorial Tribute*, Polynesian Society, Wellington, 1951, p. 63.
69 The fullest discussion is in Sheila McClean, op. cit., pp. 11–89.
70 *NZPD*, vol. 167, 1913, p. 413.
71 T. E. Y. Seddon to E. Ramsden, 4 April 1953, Ramsden Papers, MS Papers 196/333, ATL.
72 *NZPD*, vol. 167, 1913, p. 825.
73 Ibid., p. 412.
74 Ibid., pp. 407–8, 412.
75 Sheila McClean, op. cit., p. 36.
76 Ngata to Buck, 20 September 1930, Ramsden Papers, MS Papers 196/312, ATL.
77 Ngata to Buck, 16 July 1930; and Buck to Ngata, August mm [sic] 1930, Ramsden Papers, MS Papers 196/312, ATL.
78 Seddon to Ramsden, 4 April 1953, Ramsden Papers, MS Papers 196/333, ATL.
79 Butterworth, op. cit., p. 248.
80 Ibid.
81 *New Zealand Herald*, 4 November 1925, quoted by Sheila McClean, op. cit., p. 59.
82 Ngata to Buck, 17 December 1928, Ramsden Papers, MS Papers 196/310, ATL.
83 Ibid.
84 *NZPD*, vol. 225, 1930, p. 684.
85 Report of the Native Affairs Commission of Inquiry, *AJHR*, 1934, G-11, p. 39.
86 Ngata to Buck, 27 November 1933, Ramsden Papers, MS Papers 196/313, ATL.
87 Ngata to Buck, 11 February 1934, Ramsden Papers, MS Papers 196/313, ATL.
88 Buck to Ngata, 29 November 1934, Ramsden Papers, MS Papers 196/313, ATL.
89 See I. L. G. Sutherland, *The Maori Situation*, Harry H. Tombs, Wellington, 1935, pp. 76–85.
90 *New Zealand Herald*, 1 November 1934.
91 *NZPD*, vol. 134, 1905, p. 37.
92 Ibid., pp. 34–37.
93 J. Hislop to Massey, 19 July 1920, EL 19/15/3, NA.
94 Hislop to Massey, 20 October 1920, EL 19/15/3, NA; reply prepared by G. G. Hodgkins to question by H. E. Holland in House, 8 September 1928, EL 19/6, NA.
95 Hodgkins to Forbes, 23 July 1934, and Ngata to Forbes, 31 July 1934, EL 19/6, NA.
96 *NZPD*, vol. 153, 1910, p. 656.
97 Ibid., p. 663.
98 Williams, op. cit., p. 60.
99 Quoted ibid., p. 51. Significantly, Arawa had not signed the Treaty.
100 Quoted ibid., p. 46.
101 Ibid., pp. 55–56.
102 For assessments of Ratana, see J. M. Henderson, *Ratana: The Man, the Church, the Political Movement*, A. H. & A. W. Reed, Wellington, 1963; and R. Ngatata Love, 'Policies of Frustration: the Growth of Maori Politics; The Ratana/Labour Era', PhD thesis, Victoria University of Wellington, 1977.
103 Love, op. cit., p. 229.
104 Ngata to Buck, 17 December 1928, Ramsden Papers, MS Papers 196/310, ATL.
105 Love, op. cit., pp. 289–91.
106 R. M. Chapman, quoted by David Tabacoff, 'The Role of the Maori M.P. in Contemporary New Zealand Politics',

in S. Levine, ed., *New Zealand Politics: A Reader*, Melbourne, 1975, p. 376.
107 Quoted by Joan Metge, *The Maoris of New Zealand*, Routledge & Kegan Paul, London, 1967, p. 59.
108 Ibid.
109 Quoted in J. B. Condliffe, *Te Rangi Hiroa: The Life of Sir Peter Buck*, Whitcombe & Tombs, Christchurch, 1971, pp. 111–12.
110 Jones to Ngata, 15 September 1930, MA 31/56, NA.
111 Jones to Ngata, 20 September 1930, MA 31/56, NA.
112 Mick Jones to Ngata, 24 September 1930, MA 31/56, NA.
113 *Hawera Star*, 23 September 1930.
114 Love, op. cit., p. 295.
115 Jackson and Wood, op. cit., p. 393.
116 A. G. Harper to Fraser, 13 November 1944, 10 June 1949, and Harper to T. T. Ropiha, 9 November 1949, EL 19/15/3, NA.
117 Orange, op. cit., pp. 63–64, 105–110.
118 Ibid., p. 116.
119 Ibid., p. 118.
120 On Paikea's death in 1943, Tirikatene took over both responsibilities.
121 Orange, op. cit., p. 135.
122 Quoted by Love, op. cit., p. 361.
123 Ibid., p. 400.
124 Ibid., p. 396.
125 A. J. McCracken, 'Maori Voting and Non-Voting: 1928 to 1969', MA thesis, University of Auckland, 1971, pp. 235–7.
126 R. M. Chapman, Graph 1, Report of the Royal Commission on the Electoral System, *Towards a Better Democracy*, AJHR, 1986, H-3, B 108.
127 Love, op. cit., pp. 407–8.
128 Ngata to Ramsden, 12 October 1947, quoted by Orange, op. cit., p. 167.
129 Ibid.
130 See Orange, op. cit., pp. 160–2, for samples.
131 Ibid., p. 209.
132 Quoted from the Nash Papers by Augie Fleras, 'From Social Control towards Political Self-Determination? Maori Seats and the Politics of Separate Maori Representation in New Zealand', *Canadian Journal of Political Science*, vol. 18 (1985), p. 562.
133 Love, op. cit., p. 433.
134 Ngata to Ramsden, 1 January 1950, Ramsden Papers, MS Papers 196/377, ATL.
135 *New Zealand Herald*, 27 August 1951.
136 See Chapman Annex, Graphs 1 & 7.
137 Quoted in Corbett to J. R. Marshall, 29 July 1957, EL 19/15/3, NA.
138 Corbett to Marshall, 7 September 1954, EL 19/15/3, NA.
139 L. Irwin to Corbett, 13 June 1957, and Corbett to Marshall, 26 June 1957, EL 19/15/3, NA.
140 Corbett to Marshall, 29 July 1957, EL 19/15/3, NA.
141 Love, op. cit., pp. 440–2; and Appendices 1 & 2.
142 See Chapman Annex, Graph 1.
143 Keith Sinclair, *Walter Nash*, Auckland University Press, Auckland, 1976, p. 340.
144 J. K. Hunn, *Report on Department of Maori Affairs*, Government Printer, Wellington, 1960, p. 13.
145 Love, op. cit., pp. 477–8.
146 Ibid., p. 478.
147 Ibid., p. 488.
148 See Chapman, op. cit., Appendix 4.
149 Hunn, op. cit., p. 15.
150 See, for instance, *A Maori View of the Hunn Report*, published for the Maori synod of the Presbyterian Church, Christchurch, 1961.
151 Hunn, op. cit., p. 77.
152 Ibid., p. 78.
153 *Thursday Magazine*, 24 July 1969, p. 36.
154 NZPD, vol. 328, 1961, p. 2199.
155 Ibid., vol. 344, 1965, p. 2708.
156 Ibid.
157 NZPD, vol. 353, 1967, p. 3264.
158 Appendix 4.
159 See, for instance, his statement reported in *Te Maori*, June–July 1970, pp. 53–54.
160 Rata to Mira Szaszy, 7 November 1968, Rata Papers, 2/23, NA.
161 Tom Newnham, *Apartheid is not a Game: The Inside Story of New Zealand's Struggle against Apartheid Sport*, Graphic Publications, Auckland, 1975, p. 36.
162 Chapman Annex, Graph 1.
163 W. L. Rowling, NZPD, vol. 401, 1975, p. 4547.
164 Appendix 4.
165 NZPD, vol. 406, 1976, pp. 2848–9.
166 Quoted in E. M. McLeay, 'Political Argument about Representation: The Case of the Maori Seats', *Political Studies*, vol. 28 (1980), p. 48.

167 Appendix 4.
168 Chapman Annex, Graph 1 & Appendix 4.
169 Chapman Annex, Graph 1.
170 Ngata to Buck, 15 July 1940, Ramsden Papers, MS Papers 196/310, ATL.
171 Quoted by Bernard Kernot, 'Maori Strategies: Ethnic Politics in New Zealand', in Levine, ed., op. cit., p. 233.
172 S. K. Jackson, 'Politics in the Eastern Maori Electorate, 1928–69', MA thesis, University of Auckland, 1977, pp. 132–50.
173 Tabacoff, in Levine, ed., op. cit., p. 377.
174 Ibid.
175 Rata Papers, Series 1, Boxes 1–5, NA.
176 Jackson, op. cit., pp. 185–212.
177 Quoted ibid., p. 196.
178 Fleras, op. cit., p. 26.
179 See Appendix 4.
180 Labour Party submissions to the Royal Commission on the Electoral System.
181 Personal communication, R. M. Chapman, 28 March 1986.
182 See Appendix 6.
183 Final submissions of the National Party to the Royal Commission on the Electoral System.
184 See 'Korero', *New Zealand Listener*, 1 February 1986; see also Donna Awatere, *Maori Sovereignty*, Broadsheet, Auckland, 1985.
185 In fact both arguments can be supported by statistics. See Appendices 1 & 2.
186 R. Mahuta, 'Maori Political Representation: A Case for Change', in Evelyn Stokes, ed., *Maori Representation in Parliament*, University of Waikato, Hamilton, 1981, p. 25.
187 Fleras, op. cit., p. 26.
188 See Appendix 7.
189 Ibid.
190 Fleras, op. cit., p. 34.
191 A. C. Simpson, *Redistributing the Maori Vote, 1972–84*, Department of Politics, University of Waikato, 1985.
192 See Chapman Annex, Graph 7.
193 See Appendix 4.
194 Fleras, op. cit., p. 36.

10 TOWARDS A RADICAL REINTERPRETATION OF NEW ZEALAND HISTORY

1 For example, by Donna Awatere, *Maori Sovereignty*, Broadsheet, Auckland, 1985; Ranginui Walker, *New Zealand Listener*, 1 February 1986.
2 Ruth Ross, 'The Treaty of Waitangi: Texts and Interpretations', *NZJH*, vol. 6, no. 2 (1972), pp. 129–57.
3 D. F. McKenzie, *Oral Culture, Literacy & Print in Early New Zealand: The Treaty of Waitangi*, Victoria University Press, Wellington, 1985.
4 Claudia Orange, 'The Treaty of Waitangi: A Study of its Making, Interpretation and Role in New Zealand History', PhD thesis, University of Auckland, 1984; published as *The Treaty of Waitangi*, Allen & Unwin, Wellington, 1987.
5 H. F. von Haast, 'The Treaty of Waitangi: Its Consideration by the Courts', *New Zealand Law Journal*, vol. X, no. 2 (1934), pp. 20–21; 'The Effect of the Treaty of Waitangi on Subsequent Legislation', ibid., pp. 13–15, 25–27.
6 James Rutherford, *The Treaty of Waitangi and the Acquisition of British Sovereignty in New Zealand, 1840*, Auckland University College Bulletin No. 36, History Series No. 3, 1949.
7 F. M. Auburn, 'Te Tiriti o Waitangi', *New Zealand University Law Reports*, vol. IV (1971), pp. 309–11.
8 W. A. McKean, 'The Treaty of Waitangi Revisited', in G. A. Wood and P. S. O'Connor, eds, *W. P. Morrell: A Tribute*, University of Otago Press, Dunedin, 1973, pp. 237–49.
9 P. G. McHugh, *Maori Land Laws of New Zealand*, University of Saskatchewan Native Law Centre, Saskatoon, 1983; 'The Aboriginal Rights of the New Zealand Maori at Common Law', Ph.D. thesis, Cambridge University, 1987.
10 D. V. Williams, 'The Use of Law in the Process of Colonization', PhD thesis, University of Dar es Salaam, 1983; see also his essay in Kawharu, ed., op. cit., pp. 64–91.
11 A month later, in February 1978, the Tribunal had begun to hear a claim by T. E. Kirkwood and others objecting to the Electricity Department's proposal to site a gas-powered station near Waiau Pā, on the Manukau Harbour. The proposal was abandoned before the hearing was completed.

12 *Report of the Waitangi Tribunal on the Motunui-Waitara Claim*, Wai-6, Waitangi Tribunal, Wellington, 1983.
13 'Treaty Interpretation in the English Courts', *International and Comparative Law Quarterly*, vol. XII (1963), p. 508, cited in ibid., pp. 56–57.
14 Ibid., p. 58.
15 Ibid., p. 55.
16 Ibid., p. 61.
17 E. T. J. Durie, 'The Waitangi Experiment', 26 September 1986, p. 1, unpublished typescript in possession of the author.
18 Ibid.
19 E. T. J. Durie, 'Address to the Race Relations Class', Auckland University, 8 October 1986, p. 1, unpublished typescript in possession of the author.
20 Ibid., p. 4.
21 *Report . . . on the Motunui-Waitara Claim*, op. cit., p. 59.
22 Ibid., pp. 59–60.
23 Ibid., p. 6.
24 B. Ainsley, 'Settling Up', *New Zealand Listener*, 6 August 1988, p. 18.
25 I. H. Kawharu, quoted in the *Report of the Waitangi Tribunal on the Kaituna River Claim*, Wai-4, Waitangi Tribunal, Wellington, 1984, pp. 18–19.
26 Ibid., p. 20.
27 In *Wi Parata v Bishop of Wellington* (1877) 3 NZ Jur (NS) 72 (SC).
28 *Report . . . on the Kaituna River Claim*, op. cit., p. 23.
29 Ibid., p. 25.
30 Ibid., p. 24.
31 Ibid., p. 26.
32 Ibid. It might be noted that the warning was not heeded by the law draftsmen in the instance of the State Enterprises Bill 1986, as was discovered by the reconstituted Waitangi Tribunal during the first stage of the Muriwhenua hearing in December 1986.
33 *Report of the Waitangi Tribunal on the Manukau Claim*, Wai-8, Waitangi Tribunal, Wellington, 1985, p. 8.
34 Ibid., p. 29.
35 Ibid., pp. 46–47.
36 Ibid., pp. 9–10.
37 Ibid., p. 48.
38 Ibid., p. 49.
39 Ibid., p. 53.

40 Ibid., p. 60.
41 Ibid., p. 111.
42 Ibid., p. 112.
43 Ibid., p. 114.
44 Ibid., p. 112 (my italics).
45 Ibid.
46 Ibid., pp. 77–78.
47 Ibid., p. 100.
48 Ibid.
49 Ibid., p. 130.
50 Ainsley, op. cit., p. 18.
51 *Report of the Waitangi Tribunal on the Te Reo Maori Claim*, Wai-11, Waitangi Tribunal, Wellington, 1986, p. 11.
52 Ibid.
53 Ibid., p. 5.
54 Ibid., p. 26.
55 Ibid., p. 28.
56 The Treaty made no such promise; presumably the Tribunal was stretching the meaning of the third article which promised Māori 'the rights and privileges of British subjects'.
57 *Finding . . . Relating to Te Reo Maori*, op. cit., p. 46.
58 Ibid., p. 50.
59 *Report of the Waitangi Tribunal on the Orakei Claim*, Wai-9, Waitangi Tribunal, Wellington, 1987.
60 Ibid., p. 180.
61 Ibid., pp. 196–8.
62 This statement is based on a Treasury paper of 13 May 1988 for the Minister of Finance.
63 *Report of the Waitangi Tribunal on the Muriwhenua Fishing Claim*, Wai-22, Waitangi Tribunal, Wellington, 1988.
64 Ibid., p. 9.
65 Ibid., pp. 196–7.
66 Ibid., p. 202.
67 Ibid., p. 118.
68 Ibid., p. 224.

11 GIVING BETTER EFFECT TO THE TREATY

1 *Jones v Meehan* (1899) 175 US 1 (SC).
2 *Report of the Waitangi Tribunal on the Motunui-Waitara Claim*, Wai-6, Waitangi Tribunal, Wellington, 1983, p. 49.
3 D. F. McKenzie, *Oral Culture, Literacy and Print in Early New Zealand: The Treaty*

of *Waitangi*, Victoria University Press, Wellington, 1985, p. 34.
4   R. M. Ross, 'Te Tiriti o Waitangi: Texts and Translations', *NZJH*, vol. 6, no. 2 (1972), pp. 129–57; Bruce Biggs, 'Humpty-Dumpty and the Treaty of Waitangi', in I. H. Kawharu, ed., *Waitangi: Maori and Pakeha Perspectives of the Treaty of Waitangi*, Oxford University Press, Auckland, 1989, pp. 300–12.
5   For one recent essay, see Judith Binney, 'The Maori and the Signing of the Treaty of Waitangi', in J. O. C. Phillips, ed., *Towards 1990*, Wellington, 1989, pp. 20–31.
6   Quoted in Claudia Orange, *The Treaty of Waitangi*, Allen & Unwin, Wellington, 1987, p. 38.
7   *Wi Parata v Bishop of Wellington* (1877) 3 NZ Jur (NS) 72 (SC).
8   Orange, *The Treaty of Waitangi*, op. cit.
9   From Lewis Carroll, quoted by Biggs in Kawharu, op. cit., p. 304.
10 M. P. K. Sorrenson, 'The Purchase of Maori Lands, 1865–1892', MA thesis, Auckland University College, 1955.
11 *Report of the Waitangi Tribunal on the Waiheke Island Claim*, Wai-10, Waitangi Tribunal, Wellington, 1987, pp. 39–40; *Report of the Waitangi Tribunal on the Orakei Claim*, Wai-9, Waitangi Tribunal, Wellington, 1987, pp. 149–50.
12 *Report of the Waitangi Tribunal on the Kaituna River Claim*, Wai-4, Waitangi Tribunal, Wellington, 1984, p. 14.
13 'Curiosus', *New Zealander*, 3 July 1858.
14 Alan Ward, *A Show of Justice: Racial 'Amalgamation' in Nineteenth Century New Zealand*, Australian National University Press, Canberra, 1974, pp. 61–62.
15 *Report . . . on the Kaituna River Claim*, op. cit., p. 19.
16 Reprinted as F. M. Brookfield, 'The New Zealand Constitution: the search for legitimacy', in Kawharu, op. cit., pp. 1–24.
17 *New Zealand Maori Council v Attorney-General* [1987] 1 NZLR 641 (HC & CA).
18 Moana Jackson, *The Maori and the Criminal Justice System*, Part 2, Department of Justice, Wellington, 1989, p. 3.
19 M. P. K. Sorrrenson, 'Towards a Radical Reinterpretation of New Zealand History: the role of the Waitangi Tribunal', in Kawharu, op. cit., pp. 158–78; and chapter 10 of the present volume.
20 G. Orr, 'Principles Emerging from Waitangi Tribunal and Court Decisions', unpublished paper, 13 March 1989.
21 *Report . . . on the Orakei Claim*, op. cit., p. 149.
22 Orr, 'Principles', op. cit., p. 3.
23 Brookfield in Kawharu, op. cit., p. 7.
24 Ibid., p. 14.
25 P. G. McHugh, 'Constitutional Theory and Maori Claims', in Kawharu, op. cit., pp. 42–46.
26 For a fuller discussion of the whole issue, see my 'A History of Maori Representation in Parliament', in Report of the Royal Commission on the Electoral System, *Towards a Better Democracy*, AJHR, 1986, H-3, Appendix B, reprinted as chapter 9 of the present volume.
27 *NZPD*, vol. 167, 1913, p. 413.
28 *New Zealand Herald*, 7 February 1990.
29 McHugh in Kawharu, op. cit., p. 50.
30 *Te Weehi v Regional Fisheries Officer* (1986) 1 NZLR 680.
31 Benedict Kingsbury, 'The Treaty of Waitangi: some international law aspects', ibid., pp. 121–57.

12 THE WAITANGI TRIBUNAL AND THE RESOLUTION OF MAORI GRIEVANCES

1   Ralph Hanan, 29 June 1965, quoted by Tom Newnham, *Apartheid is not a Game: The Inside Story of New Zealand's Struggle against Apartheid Sport*, Graphic Publications, Auckland, 1975, p. 30.
2   'Historical Treaty Claims: more haste less speed?', *Evening Post*, 14 January 1994.
3   For a fuller discussion of the early Tribunal reports, see chapter 10, 'Towards a Radical Reinterpretation of New Zealand History: The Role of the Waitangi Tribunal', of the present volume.
4   Personal communication from Richard Hill, Chief Historian, Treaty of Waitangi Policy Unit, 10 March 1994.
5   See chapter 10 of the present volume.
6   *Jones v Meehan* (1899) 175 US 1 (SC).
7   *Report of the Waitangi Tribunal on the Motunui-Waitara Claim*, Wai-6, Waitangi Tribunal, Wellington, 1983, pp. 56–57.

8. Ibid., p. 61.
9. Ibid., p. 6.
10. *Report of the Waitangi Tribunal on the Manukau Claim*, Wai-8, Waitangi Tribunal, Wellington, 1985, p. 78.
11. The term is used by W. Renwick in 'Decolonising Ourselves from Within', *The British Review of New Zealand Studies*, no. 6 (1993), p. 37.
12. *Report of the Waitangi Tribunal on the Muriwhenua Fishing Claim*, Wai 22, Waitangi Tribunal, Wellington, 1988.
13. Ibid.
14. It is more fully discussed in Tom Bennion, 'Protecting Fishing Rights — Recent Fisheries Settlements in New Zealand', a paper prepared for the Conference on Indigenous Peoples and Sea Rights, Northern Territory University, 14–16 July 1993.
15. *The Fisheries Settlement Report*, Wai-307, Waitangi Tribunal, Wellington, 1992; for a critical commentary on the settlement, see A. L. Mikaere, 'Maori Issues', in *New Zealand Law Review*, 1993, pp. 308–12.
16. *Te Ika Whenua — Energy Assets Report*, Wai-213, Waitangi Tribunal, Wellington, 1993; *Ngawha Geothermal Resource Report*, Wai-304, Waitangi Tribunal, Wellington, 1993; and *Preliminary Report on the Te Arawa Representative Geothermal Resource Claims*, Wai-153, Waitangi Tribunal, Wellington, 1993.
17. *New Zealand Maori Council v Attorney-General* [1987] 1 NZLR 641 (HC & CA); for commentary see Carrie Wainwright, 'Report to the Waitangi Tribunal on the Current State of Treaty Jurisprudence', 1992, p. 9.
18. *Ngawha Geothermal Resource Report*, op. cit., pp. 145, 147; *Preliminary Report on the Te Arawa Representative Geothermal Resource Claims*, op. cit., p. 35; see also Mikaere, op. cit., p. 322.
19. Jane Kelsey, *A Question of Honour? Labour and the Treaty, 1984–1989*, Allen & Unwin, Wellington, 1990, p. 144; and *Te Ika Whenua-Energy Assets Report*, Wai-212, op. cit., p. 21.
20. *The Te Roroa Report*, Wai-38, Waitangi Tribunal, Wellington, 1992, p. 292.
21. Judge E. T. J. Durie, '"The Outstanding Business": The Waitangi Tribunal and Maori Treaty Claims', paper to International Conference of Women Judges, Wellington, 14 September 1993, pp. 11–12.
22. Chief Judge Durie to Minister of Maori Affairs, 30 November 1993, Appendix 2.
23. W. H. Oliver, *Claims to the Waitangi Tribunal*, Waitangi Tribunal Division, Department of Justice, Wellington, 1991, Appendix 2, pp. 94–100.
24. Personal communication, Richard Hill, 10 March 1994.
25. Oliver, op. cit., Appendix 2, pp. 94–95.
26. *New Zealand Herald*, 13 January 1994.
27. Personal communication, Richard Hill, 10 March 1994.
28. *Report on South Auckland Railway Lands*, Wai-264, Waitangi Tribunal, Wellington, 1993, pp. 910.
29. The early stages of the negotiation, more especially in relation to coal, are discussed in Kelsey, op. cit., pp. 154–61.
30. *New Zealand Herald*, 13 January 1994.
31. *Report of the Waitangi Tribunal on the Te Reo Maori Claim*, Wai 11, Waitangi Tribunal, Wellington, 1986.
32. For a fuller discussion of this, see my essay 'Giving Better Effect to the Treaty: Some Thoughts for 1990', *NZJH*, October 1990, pp. 135–49, reprinted as chapter 11 of the present volume.
33. See my 'A History of Maori Representation in Parliament', in Report of the Royal Commission on the Electoral System, *Towards a Better Democracy*, AJHR, 1986, H-3, Appendix B, reprinted as chapter 9 of the present volume.
34. As reported in the *New Zealand Herald*, 17 March 1994.
35. For discussion of the conflict over aboriginal title in New Zealand, see P. G. McHugh, *The Maori Magna Carta: New Zealand Law and the Treaty of Waitangi*, Oxford University Press, Auckland, 1991, pp. 117–26.
36. Claudia Orange, *The Treaty of Waitangi*, Allen & Unwin, Wellington, 1987, pp. 205–16, 228, 232.
37. Quoted by Judge Durie in 'Waitangi, Justice and Reconciliation', Second David Unaipon Lecture, Adelaide, 10 October 1991, p. 7.
38. Sorrenson, 'Giving Better Effect to the Treaty', op. cit., p. 147.

39 For fuller discussion, see Benedict Kingsbury, 'The Treaty of Waitangi: some international law aspects', in Kawharu, op. cit., pp. 121–57.
40 K. J. Keith, 'Race Relations and the Law in New Zealand', in W. A. McKean, ed., *Essays on Race Relations and the Law in New Zealand*, Sweet & Maxwell, Wellington, 1971, pp. 329–68.
41 *Report . . . on the Muriwhenua Fishing Claim*, p. 235.
42 Kingsbury in Kawharu, op. cit., pp. 143–8.
43 For a discussion, see Joe Williams, 'Indigenous "Human" Rights in New Zealand from an International Perspective', paper prepared for Aotearoa/New Zealand and Human Rights Policy Conference, Wellington, 26–28 May 1989, pp. 9–10.

13 WAITANGI

1 All speeches as reported in the *New Zealand Herald*, 7 February 1990.
2 K. Stam, J. Williams, R. Peffer and E. Watkin, *Washington DC & the Capital Region — A Lonely Planet Travel Survival Kit*, Lonely Planet Publications, Hawthorn, 1997, p. 61.
3 *Cherokee Nation v State of Georgia* (1831) 30 US (5 Peters) 1 (SC).
4 A reference to the nineteenth-century English legal philosopher John Austin. For a discussion of his influence on New Zealand law, see Paul McHugh, *The Maori Magna Carta: New Zealand Law and the Treaty of Waitangi*, Oxford University Press, Auckland, 1991, pp. 115–16, 376, 381–2.
5 Discussed more fully in chapter 11, 'Giving Better Effect to the Treaty', of the present volume.
6 For fuller discussion, see Bruce Biggs, 'Humpty-Dumpty and the Treaty of Waitangi', in I. H. Kawharu, ed., *Waitangi: Maori and Pakeha Perspectives of the Treaty of Waitangi*, Oxford University Press, Auckland, 1989, pp. 300–12; and Claudia Orange, *The Treaty of Waitangi*, Allen & Unwin, Wellington, 1987, pp. 36–43.
7 *Jones v Meehan* (1899) 175 US 1 (SC).
8 Quoted by Michael H. Fletcher, *Washington Post*, 15 January 1998.
9 As discussed more fully in chapter 9, 'Maori Representation in Parliament', of the present volume.
10 Quoted in Orange, op. cit., p. 53.
11 In Kawharu, op. cit., pp. 300–12.
12 See chapter 12, 'The Waitangi Tribunal and the Resolution of Maori Grievances', of the present volume.
13 For a general discussion, see Jane Kelsey, *A Question of Honour? Labour and the Treaty, 1984–1989*, Allen & Unwin, Wellington, 1990.
14 *New Zealand Maori Council v Attorney-General* [1987] 1 NZLR 641 (HC & CA) [*Lands* case].
15 D. Graham, *Trick or Treaty?*, Institute of Policy Studies, Victoria University of Wellington, 1997, p. 17.
16 *The Te Roroa Report*, Wai-38, Waitangi Tribunal, Wellington, 1992, p. 292.
17 *National Overview*, vol. I, Waitangi Tribunal Rangahaua Whanui Series, Waitangi Tribunal, Wellington, 1997, p. 147.

EPILOGUE

1 M. P. K. Sorrenson, *Maori Origins and Migrations: The Genesis of Some Pakeha Myths and Legends*, Auckland University Press, Auckland, 1979; reprinted 1983, 1990.
2 K. R. Howe, *The Quest for Origins: Who First Discovered and Settled New Zealand and the Pacific Islands?*, Penguin, Auckland, 2003.
3 J. Darwin, *After Tamerlane: The Global History of Empire since 1405*, Bloomsbury Press, London, 2007.
4 J. Belich, *Replenishing the Earth: The Settler Revolution and the Rise of the Anglo-World, 1783–1939*, Oxford University Press, Oxford, 2009.
5 J. K. Hunn, *Report on Department of Maori Affairs*, 24 August 1960, Government Printer, Wellington, 1961, p. 15.
6 See, for instance, *A Maori View of the Hunn Report*, published for the Maori Synod of the Presbyterian Church of New Zealand, Whakatane, 1961.
7 The best discussion of these terms I have seen is in Joan Metge, *The Maoris of New Zealand: Rautahi*, revised edition,

8   Ian Pool, *Te Iwi Maori: A New Zealand Population, Past, Present & Projected*, Auckland University Press, Auckland, 1991, p. 62.
9   Pool, op. cit.
10 R. Lange, *May the People Live: A History of Maori Health Development 1900–1920*, Auckland University Press, Auckland, 1999.
11 Particularly in *A Show of Justice: Racial 'Amalgamation' in Nineteenth Century New Zealand*, Australian National University Press, Canberra, 1974; and his *National Overview*, 3 vols, 1997, prepared for the Waitangi Tribunal's Rangahau Whanui Series.
12 M. P. K. Sorrenson, 'Modern Maori: The Young Maori Party to Mana Motuhake', in Keith Sinclair, ed., *The Oxford Illustrated History of New Zealand*, Oxford University Press, Auckland, 1990, pp. 323–51.
13 M. P. K. Sorrenson, *Na To Hoa Aroha, From Your Dear Friend: The correspondence between Sir Apirana Ngata and Sir Peter Buck 1925–50*, 3 vols, Auckland University Press, Auckland, 1986, 1987, 1988.
14 Hunn, op. cit.
15 *Progress Towards Closing Social and Economic Gaps Between Maori and Non-Maori: A report to the Minister of Maori Affairs*, Te Puni Kokiri (Ministry of Maori Development), Wellington, 1998.
16 Richard S. Hill, *Maori and the State: Crown–Maori Relations in New Zealand/Aotearoa, 1950–2000*, Victoria University Press, Wellington, 2009, p. 273.
17 James Cowan, *The New Zealand Wars: A History of the Maori Campaigns and the Pioneering Period*, 2 vols, Government Printer, Wellington, 1922; Keith Sinclair, *The Origins of the Maori Wars*, New Zealand University Press, Wellington, 1957; James Belich, *The New Zealand Wars and the Victorian Interpretation of Racial Conflict*, Auckland University Press, Auckland, 1986.
18 Michael King, *Te Puea: A Biography*, Hodder & Stoughton, Auckland, 1977.
19 'Curiosus', *New Zealander*, 3 July 1858.
20 L. Cox, *Kotahitanga: The Search for Maori Political Unity*, Oxford University Press, Auckland, 1993.

Routledge & Kegan Paul, London, 1976, pp. 289–331.

21 Royal Commission on the Electoral System, *Towards a Better Democracy*, AJHR, 1986, H-3.
22 P. McHugh, *The Maori Magna Carta: New Zealand Law and the Treaty of Waitangi*, Oxford University Press, Auckland, 1991.
23 R. Ross, 'Te Tiriti o Waitangi: Texts and Translations', *NZJH*, vol. 6, no. 2 (1972), pp. 129–57.
24 C. Orange, *The Treaty of Waitangi*, Allen & Unwin, Wellington, 1987.
25 *Wi Parata v Bishop of Wellington* (1877) 3 NZ Jur (NS) 72 (SC).
26 *Jones v Meehan* (1899) 175 US 1 (SC).
27 *Te Manutukutuku*, issue 64, May 2012, p. 8.
28 *The Waitangi Tribunal: Te Roopu Whakamana i te Tiriti o Waitangi*, J. Hayward and R. Wheen, eds, Bridget Williams Books, Wellington, 2004.
29 A. Sharp, *Justice and the Maori: The Philosophy and Practice of Maori Claims in New Zealand since the 1970s*, Oxford University Press, Auckland, 1990.
30 M. Belgrave, *Historical Frictions: Maori Claims & Reinvented Histories*, Auckland University Press, Auckland, 2005.
31 R. Boast, *Buying the Land, Selling the Land: Governments and Maori Land in the North Island 1865–1921*, Victoria University Press, Wellington, 2008.
32 R. Hill, *State Authority, Indigenous Autonomy: Crown–Maori Relations in New Zealand/Aotearoa 1900–1950* and *1950–2000*, Victoria University Press, Wellington, 2004, 2009.
33 W. H. Oliver, 'The future behind us: The Waitangi Tribunal's retrospective utopia', in Andrew Sharp and Paul McHugh, eds, *Histories, Power and Loss: Uses of the Past — a New Zealand Commentary*, Bridget Williams Books, Wellington, 2001, pp. 9–29; Giselle Byrnes, *The Waitangi Tribunal and New Zealand History*, Oxford University Press, Melbourne, 2004, passim.
34 *The Radio Spectrum Management and Development Final Report*, Wai-776, Waitangi Tribunal, Wellington, 1999.
35 *Te Manutukutuku*, op. cit., p. 9.
36 As Chief Judge Eddie Durie once remarked in a private discussion, after a Tribunal hearing.

Index

Aborigines' Protection Society, 172
African Americans, 275
Airey, Willis, 3, 5
All Blacks, *see* rugby contacts with South Africa
Allotment Act 1887, 279
American Association for the Advancement of Science (Anthropological Section), 130
American Indian Claims Commission, 268, 286, 291, 298
American Indian treaties, 258, 271, 276, 280
American Indians, 6, 245–6, 250, 276, 279, 298
Andersen, Johannes, 135
Angas, G. F., 60
Anglo-Maori wars, *see* New Zealand wars
anthropology, 9, 12, 129–34, 136–8, 142, 144
Arawa canoe, 21
archaeology, 9, 17, 26–27
Archey, Gilbert, 132
Armitage, James, 113–14, 115
Aryan Maori, 16, 23–24, 28, 31, 32, 34–37, 38, 39
Asher, David, 3
Atkinson, A. S., 36–37, 170
Auburn, F. M., 219
Austin, J., 277
Austin, Rex, 205, 211
Australasian Association for the Advancement of Science, 134
Australian Aborigines, 15, 48–53, 56, 63, 145, 254, 276

Ballance, John, 125
Balneavis, H. R. H., 129
Banks, Joseph, 10–12, 21, 49, 57
Batman, John, 52–53
Beaglehole, Ernest, 127, 130, 142
Beaglehole, John, 5, 126
Beauchamp Committee on Transportation 1785, 49
Belgrave, Michael, 300
Belich, James, 293, 295
Bell, F. D., 77–78
Bennett, Charles, 223
Bennett, Manuhia, 40
Bennion, Tom, 44
Bentinck, W. H. C., 49
Berlin Conference on Africa 1884–85, 44

Best, Elsdon, 28, 29, 31–32, 126–7, 128, 129, 131, 132, 134
Biggs, Bruce, 239–40, 243, 284
Bill of Rights 1990, 246, 262, 271
Binney, Judith, 2
Bishop Museum, Honolulu, 127, 129
Blumenbach, J. F., 11, 12, 18
Blyth, W. H., 32–33
Boas, Franz, 130
Boast, Richard, 77, 79, 85, 300
Bolger, James, 289
Bourke, Richard, 53
British-Sherbo agreement 1825, 42
Brodie, W., 61
Brookfield, F. M., 246, 250
Brown, Alexander, 78
Brown, J. M., 3, 24, 33–34, 38
Brown, William, 19
Browne, Thomas Gore, 64, 88, 107, 165–6, 245
Bryce, John, 101–2, 124–5, 151, 165, 179
Buck, Peter (also known as Te Rangi Hiroa): and Apirana Ngata, 1, 2, 5, 126–44 *passim*, 187, 191, 294; and Maori oral traditions, 39; and Maori somatology, 21; and 'vikings' of the Pacific, 34; and Young Maori Party, 154; as expatriate anthropologist, 154; as Medical Officer for Maori Pioneer Battalion, 183; education, 192; on Maui Pomare, 184; parliamentary career, 182–3, 192, 251
Buckland, W. T., 120
Buddle, Thomas, 14
Buganda agreement, 1900, 44
Buller, Walter, 94
Burdon, R. M., 102
Busby, James, 42, 47, 54, 159, 160, 171, 189, 244
Byrnes, Giselle, 300

Cadman, A. J., 190
Cameron, Duncan, 167
Canadian Indian reserves, 63
Carleton, Hugh, 107, 108, 111, 113, 171
Carroll, James, 128, 137, 154, 179, 180–2, 184–5, 188, 191, 192, 207, 210, 211, 213, 282–3
Carroll, Turi, 202, 207
Center for Australian and New Zealand Studies, Georgetown University, 6, 7
Chambers, Robert, 74

329

Chapman, H. S., 47
Chapman, R. M., 106, 157, 215
Chinnery, E. W. P., 137
Church Missionary Society, 158
Citizens' Association for Racial Equality, 6
Clark, Helen, 297
Clarke, George, 59
Clarke, George, jnr, 79
Clarke, H. T., 85
Coalcorp, 287
Coates, Gordon, 183, 185, 196, 210, 289
Colenso, William, 14, 29, 32, 35
Columbus, Christopher, 276
Combo, King of the Gambia, 42
Commission on Indian Affairs 1842, 48
Commonwealth Games, 203
Condliffe, J. B., 129, 135
Conservation Act 1987, 261
Cook Islands administration, 137, 138, 183
Cook, James, 10–11, 13, 20, 21, 25, 48–49, 50, 56–57, 90, 158, 235, 240, 276
Cooke, Robin (Lord Cooke of Thorndon), 246
Corbett, E. B., 143, 197–8, 201
Couch, Ben, 204, 205, 211
Court of Appeal, 94, 153, 246–7, 249, 261, 274, 278–9
Cowan, James, 135, 295
Cox, Lindsay, 296
Craik, G. L., 16, 60
Crown-Congress Joint Working Party, 266–7, 289
Crown Forestry Rental Trust, 288
Crozet, M., 13, 18
Cullen, Michael, 303
Curnin, John, 85

Daldy, W. C., 111
Darwin, Charles, 9, 16, 17, 20, 56, 74, 128
Darwin, John, 293
Davis, C. O., 106
Declaration of Independence 1835, 159, 244
de Surville, Marion, 13
de Thierry, Charles, 159
Dieffenbach, Ernst, 16, 18–19, 22
Dixon, Roland, 131–2
Domett, Alfred, 65, 77
Douglas, Roger, 286, 295
Douglas, Thomas, 120
du Fresne, M., 13, 56, 57
Duff, Roger, 27, 39
Durie, E. T. J., 40, 220–2, 285, 301
D'Urban, Benjamin, 43
Dutch East India Company, 42

During, Simon, 3
D'Urville, Dumont, 18

Earle, Augustus, 58, 59, 61
East India Company, 41; *see also* Dutch East India Company
Electoral Amendment Act 1876, 205, 210
Electoral Amendment Act 1967, 201
Electoral Amendment Act 1975, 204, 210
Elizabeth II, Queen, 252, 270–1, 273–5, 282, 296
enclosure: English 68, 71–75, 76, 79, 85, 88–89; of Maori land, 68, 69, 70–72, 75–6, 78, 79, 81–82, 85, 87–89; *see also* Highland clearances; Irish confiscations; Maori: land alienation
Energy Companies Act 1992, 262
Environment Act 1986, 261

Fage, J. D., 4
Fairgray Report 1988, 236
Federated Maori Assembly Empowering Bill 1893, 190
Fenton, F. D., 28, 68–89, 107; attitude to Hawke's Bay native land transactions, 82; chief judge, Native Land Court, 68, 79, 293; legal training of, 69; Native Land Act 1865, 81–84; Native Lands Act 1873, 87; *Observations on the State of Aboriginal Inhabitants of New Zealand*, 70; official positions of, 69–70, 165, 167; on juries, 79; operation of the Native Land Court, 80–81; *Orakei* judgment, 87; *Papakura – Claim of Succession* judgment, 83; precedent of English enclosures, 71–72, 75; role in drafting Native Land Acts, 79–80; 'Scheme for the Partition and Enfranchisement of Lands held under Native Tenure', 70–71; 'squatter' in Waikato, 69; Waikato circuits, 75–76, 113–15
Fiji, 22, 30, 31, 44, 54
Finlayson, Christopher, 303
Firth, J. C., 111, 120
Firth, Raymond, 2, 127, 135, 138–9
Fisheries Act 1983, 227, 228, 234
Fitzgerald, J. E., 80, 169–70
FitzRoy, Robert, 16, 19, 61, 64, 76, 162, 241
folklore, 9, 21–27
Forbes, G. W., 140, 184, 186, 189
Forestcorp, 286, 288, 291
Fornander, A., 30
Forster, G., 11
Forster, J. R., 11–13, 18, 25
Fox, William, 77, 79, 107, 167
Fraser, Peter, 142, 143, 194, 196–7

Frauds Prevention Acts, 243
Freeman, J. S., 54, 160
Freud, Sigmund, 133
Freyberg, Bernard, 143
Furneaux, Tobias, 56

Gallagher, J. A., 5, 55
Gallipoli, 128, 303
Gandhi, Mahatma, 151
Gipps, George, 48, 53, 160
Glenelg, C. G., 43
Godfrey, E. L., 22
Goldsmith, Charles, 140
Golson, Jack, 90
Gorst, John, 107–8, 112, 113, 167, 226
Graham, Douglas, 283, 289–90, 303
Graham, George, 169
Gregory, Bruce, 205
Gregory, Herbert E., 129, 143
Greig, Mr Justice, 234
Grey, Earl, 163–4
Grey, George, 3, 52, 69; and Hawke's Bay land transaction, 153; and Native Land Acts, 7–8; and New Zealand constitution, 163–5; and New Zealand wars, 167; ends Northern and Cook Strait conflicts, 58–59; introduces civil institutions, 115, 167, 195; negotiations with King movement, 101, 115, 124, 153, 195; on Maori myths and legends, 23–24, 27; on McLean's land purchase system, 165, 195; resumes Crown pre-emption, 64, 76, 162, 241
Groube, L. M., 27
Gudgeon, W. E., 28
Gulliver, Lemuel, 29

Hale, Horatio, 21–22, 25
Hall, William, 14
Hamilton, Augustus, 128
Hamlin brothers, 95
Hamlin, John, 21
Hanan, J. R., 200–1, 256
Harawira, Hone, 297
Harris, J. H., 171
Harris, Paul, 157
Hart, H. E., 138
Hau Hau movement, 67, 108, 123, 150, 168; see also Pai Marire
Hawaii, 44, 126, 135, 140
Hawaiians, 139
Hawaiki, 21, 23, 25, 29, 39
Hawke, Joseph, 220
Hawke's Bay Native Lands Alienation Commission, 1872, 82, 84–85, 153

Hayward, Janine, 300
Hector, James, 27, 143
Heke, Hone, 58, 162–3, 180, 244, 281
Henare, J. C., 196, 207
Henare, Tau, 207
Heretaunga block, 82, 95
Herries, W. H., 183
Hettit, Louis, 122
Heyerdahl, Thor, 292
Highland clearances, 72–73, 86
Hika, Hongi, 58, 158
Hill, Richard, 295, 300
Hira, 30
Hobson, William: as Lieutenant-Governor and Governor of New Zealand, 159–60, 161, 163; early career, 41, 47; inquiry into New Zealand Company claims, 162; negotiation of the Treaty of Waitangi, 42, 53, 54, 67, 147, 159, 160, 167, 216, 218, 222, 230, 238, 241, 244, 252, 280, 283–4; proclamation of, 30 January 1840, 48, 240
Hohepa, 113
Holland, S. G., 196, 197
Holyoake, K. J., 200, 201, 203
Horouta canoe, 21
House of Commons Committee on Aborigines 1837, 40
House of Commons Committee on New Zealand 1844, 162
Hoturoa, 118
Howe, Kerry, 292
Hughes, Helen, 264
Hunn Report, 200–1
Hunn, J. K., 199, 200, 293, 295
Hunter, Thomas, 133
Hutton, James, 27

influenza epidemic 1918, 155
International Convention on the Elimination of All Forms of Racial Discrimination 1966, 271
Irish confiscations, 72

Jackson, Moana, 246
Jackson, S. K., 208
Jackson, W. K., 176
Jones, Joshua, 124
Jones, M. R., 196
Jones, Pei Te Hurinui, 115–16, 193, 202, 208
Jones v Meehan 1899, 239, 258, 281, 284, 299
Journal of the Polynesian Society, 6, 9, 28, 32, 39, 90, 126, 128, 131, 133, 134
Jury, Whatahoro, 31, 131

Kaihau, Henare, 191
Kaihau, Kerei, 190
Kaituna claim, 223–5, 227, 257–8; see also Waitangi Tribunal reports
Kamehameha monarchy, 281
Katene, Wi, 174, 175
Kauhanganui, see Maori King movement
Kawepo, Renata, 94
Kawharu, I. H., 68, 217, 223–4, 243
Keesing, Felix, 2, 127, 135
Keith, Kenneth, 42
Kemp, Major (Te Rangihiwinui), 94
Kendall, Thomas, 14, 59
Kerr, John, 253
King Country, 67, 86, 95, 96, 100–1, 119–25, 149, 150, 151, 168, 176, 177–8, 210, 281, 296; see also Maori King movement
King, John, 14
King, Michael, 296
King, P. G., 49
King, Robert, 49
Kingi, Wiremu, 109, 119, 243
Kingitanga, see Maori King movement
Kingsbury, Benedict, 253
Kirk, Norman, 201, 203–4
Kohere, Mokena, 174, 175
Kohere, R. T., 194
Kohimarama Conference, 179, 189, 245
Kotahitanga, 67, 150, 153–5, 180–1, 190–1, 202–3, 212, 213, 245, 269, 282, 296
Kupapa, 148, 150, 152–3, 154, 174, 176, 179, 190, 213, 245, 296, 297
Kupe, 23, 29, 30, 31, 34
Kurahaupo canoe, 21

Landcorp, 259, 267, 286, 291
Lang, J. D., 22
Lange, David, 206, 286, 295
Lange, Raeburn, 294
Langstone, F., 195
Large, J. T., 176
Latimer, Graham, 202, 220, 267, 274, 285
Ledyard, John, 21
Legislative Amendment Act 1910, 189
Leopold II, King of the Belgians, 43
Lévy-Bruhl, Lucien, 133
Linnaeus, Carolus, 18
Locke, John, 73–74
Locke, Samuel, 102
Love, Ngatata, 195, 200
Loveridge, Donald, 76, 77–80
Lowie, R. W., 132
loyalist troops, see Kupapa

Lugard, F. D., 43–44, 137–8
Luomala, Katherine, 144
Lyell, Charles, 19

MacDonald, J. E., 94
Mackay, James, jnr, 97
Magna Carta, 272, 291
Mahuta, see Te Wherowhero, Mahuta Tawhaio Potatau
Mahuta, Robert, 214
Maine, Henry, 75
Mair, W. G., 101, 122
Makauri case, 94
Maketu, 162
Malinowski, Bronislaw, 130, 132, 134, 136
mana motuhake, 7
Mana Motuhake party, 205–6, 213
Maniapoto, Rewi, 118, 125
Maning, F. E., 61, 75, 82
Mantell, W. B. D., 26, 27, 171
Manukau claim, 225–9, 230, 257–9; see also Waitangi Tribunal reports
Manukau Harbour Control Act 1911, 227
Maori Advisory Committee of the National Party, 211
Maori Affairs Amendment Act 1967, 203, 209
Maori Affairs Amendment Act 1974, 204
Maori: agriculture, 56, 110–11, 122–3; assimilation, 147, 217, 280, 293; autonomy, 7, 275; benefits, 194–5, 206–7, 214; Christianity, 59–60, 110–11, 158; commerce, 57, 59; electoral rolls and electorates, 172–3, 188–9, 194, 198–9, 204, 214–16, 269, 283, 297; ethnology, 11–12, 14, 18–19; fishing, 56–9, 110–11; fleet, 25, 30, 32, 39; land alienation, 91–9, 250–1, 254 (see also Native Land Court; Native Land Acts); land confiscation, 100–1, 226 (see also New Zealand Settlements Act 1863); land consolidation and development, 186, 294; language, 10, 14, 23, 35–36, 66, 203, 221, 229–31; literacy, 60; mandate, 155; myths and legends, 21, 23, 25, 32; nationalism, 146, 149, 155–6; origins and migrations, 2–3, 9–39, 86, 130, 292; population, 65, 67, 90–105, 146–7, 166, 188, 294; psychology, 123; relationships with Pakeha, 1, 5, 272, 274; religion, 14–16 (see also Pai Marire; Ratana church; Ringatu); representation in Parliament, 164, 169–216; self-rule, 147, 203 (see also Kotahitanga); social and economic conditions, 91, 94, 96, 98–105, 132, 274–5, 295; urbanisation, 295
Maori Battalion, 21, 195; see also Maori Pioneer Battalion

Maori Bible, 143
Maori Councils Act 1900, 180–1, 191, 213
Maori Education Foundation, 200
Maori elections: 1868, 173; 1875, 176; 1879, 175; 1886 (by-election), 176; 1887, 176–7; 1938, 194; 1946, 196; 1957, 199; 1960, 200; 1967, 209; 1972, 203; 1975, 204; 1981, 205–6; 1984, 206, 216; 2008, 297; Ikaroa-Rawhiti (by-election), 298; *see also* Maori: electoral rolls and electorates
Maori Fisheries Act 1989, 252, 260, 265
Maori King movement (or Kingitanga), 3, 5, 7, 70, 101–2, 106–25, 189, 212, 269; agriculture and trade, 110, 121; attitude to introduction of law, 112–15, 120, 124–5; attitude to land transactions, 96, 111–12, 243; continuing significance of, 282; 'election' of first Maori King, 106, 165–7, 281; exercise of autonomy by, 65, 67, 121, 124–5, 147, 149–50, 155, 190, 177–8, 244–5, 250; hui, 117–8, 123, 179; in King Country, 67, 101–4, 177–8, 296; institutions, 115–16, 118; Kauhanganui, 150, 153, 155, 190, 191; Maori 'nationalism', 146; objectives, 107–10, 281; participation in elections, 176, 213; population, 91; Queen Elizabeth's visit to Ngaruawahia, 252, 271; religion, 123; view of Aborigines' Protection Society, 172; Waikato war and land confiscation, 119, 165–8
Maori Land Boards, 186
Maori Land Court, 220, 301; *see also* Native Land Court
Maori Lands Administration Act 1900, 181
Maori Organisation for Human Rights, 202
Maori Organising Committee (later Maori Advisory Committee) of Labour Party, 194, 199
Maori Parliament, *see* Kotahitanga
Maori Pioneer Battalion, 128, 183
Maori Representation Act 1867, 65–6, 148, 169–73, 279, 282
Maori Social and Economic Advancement Act 1945, 195
Maori tribes: Ngai Tahu, 182, 195, 197, 237, 240, 251, 257, 264, 266, 278, 286, 288, 290, 298; Ngai Takoto, 234; Ngai Te Rangi, 119, 149, 168, 295; Ngati Awa, 100, 109, 119; Ngati Haua, 106, 118–20, 158, 166; Ngati Kahu, 234; Ngati Kahungunu, 96, 99, 153, 174, 175; Ngati Kuri, 234; Ngati Mahuta, 118; Ngati Maniapoto, 100, 106, 118–19, 120, 122, 124–5, 149–50, 176, 177–8, 193, 296; Ngati Pikiao, 223, 225; Ngati Porou, 104, 174, 185, 208–9, 254; Ngati Pukenga, 2, 3; Ngati Raukawa, 120, 124, 176; Ngati Ruanui, 100, 119; Ngati Toa, 158; Ngati Tuwharetoa, 106, 124, 166, 289, 295; Ngati Whatua, 79, 158, 174, 179, 220, 226, 232–4, 245, 254; Tainui, 118–19, 146, 158, 225, 226, 264, 279, 282, 287, 289–90, 291, 295–6, 298; Taranaki, 100, 158; Te Arawa, 158, 189, 240; Te Aupouri, 234; Te Atiawa, 32, 221, 223; Te Rarawa, 175, 234; Tuhoe, 100–3, 178, 295; Waikato, 100, 106, 118, 124–5, 158, 166, 225; Whakatohea, 197, 290
Maori Union of Waitangi, 179, 189
Maori War Effort Organisation, 195, 213
Maori Women's Welfare League, 196, 202, 247, 251, 269, 282
Maoritanga, 103–5, 125, 155–6, 192, 203, 272
Marquesans, 31
Marsden, Samuel, 13–16, 57–58, 59, 60, 61, 253
Marshall, J. R., 198, 203
Marshall, Justice John, 45, 47, 48, 276
Marshall, W. B., 16
Massey, W. F., 183, 189
Martin, William, 47, 74–75, 85, 107, 293
Matahoura canoe, 22
Mataatua canoe, 21, 22, 23
Matra, James, 49
Matutaera, *see* Tawhiao
Mau resistance movement, 137, 138
Mawhete, Rangi, 194
McHugh, Ashley, 298
McHugh, Paul, 41, 46–48, 219, 224, 250, 252–3, 298
McIntyre, Duncan, 202, 215
McKean, W. A., 219
McKenzie, D. F., 218, 239
McLean, Donald, 64, 82, 85–86, 95, 107, 113, 114, 121, 124, 165, 170, 173, 174, 175
McLeay, Elizabeth, 205
McLeod, Isaac, 79
McLeod, John, 79, 253
McNair, Lord, 221
Melanesians, 12, 31, 32
Menzies, J. A., 171
Merivale, Herman, 60
Micronesians, 18
Minhinnick, Gordon, 197
Minhinnick, Nganeko, 225
Ministry of Agriculture and Fisheries, 234, 236
Mitchell, Henry Taiporutu (Tai), 129
moa (*Dinornithiformes*), 26
moa-hunter Maori, 27, 39
Morgan, J., 60
Moriori, 30, 31, 32
Motonui claim, 221–3, 227, 257–9; *see also* Waitangi Tribunal reports
Motonui Syngas plant, 221

Motunui–Waitara Report, 239; *see also* Waitangi Tribunal reports
Muldoon, R. D., 204, 205, 285
Muller, Max, 23, 32, 33
Munchausen, K. F., 29
Mundy, G. C., 16
Muriwhenua Fisheries Claim, 234–7; Report, 266; *see also* Waitangi Tribunal, Waitangi Tribunal reports
Murray, Hubert, 137

Nash, Walter, 194, 197, 199
National Expenditure Commission, 186
National Maori Congress, 251, 267, 269, 282, 289, 296
Native Affairs Commission of Inquiry 1934, 140–2, 143, 186–8
Native Affairs Committee, 177, 184
Native Americans, *see* American Indians
Native District Circuit Courts Act 1858, 70, 76
Native Districts Regulation Act 1858, 70, 76
Native Land Act 1888, 180
Native Land Act 1909, 184–5
Native Land Amendment Bill 1913, 183
Native Land Court, 4, 25, 27, 64, 68, 79, 86, 88–89, 92–96, 98–102, 120–3, 124, 149, 150, 168, 178, 179, 186, 278, 293
Native Land Court judges, 66
Native Land Court minute books, 28, 87
Native Land Laws Commission 1891, 88
Native Land Partition Bill 1859, 77
Native Land Purchase Ordinance 1846, 111
Native Lands Act 1862, 64, 75, 77, 78, 79, 80–83, 86, 92, 111, 112, 168, 170, 242, 278
Native Lands Act 1865, 64, 66, 79, 80–83, 85, 88, 95–96, 119, 120, 148, 149, 153, 170, 171, 232
Native Lands Act 1867, 83–84, 87, 88, 232
Native Lands Act 1869, 84–85, 87
Native Lands Act 1873, 85–89
Native Lands Acts, 4, 66, 67, 80, 86, 93–98, 177, 279, 293, 299
Native Medical Officers, 66
Native Rights Act 1865, 65, 80, 148, 242, 279
Native Rights Bill 1894, 190
Native Schools Act 1867, 66
Native Territorial Rights Bill 1858, 71, 76, 77, 111, 165, 242, 252
Nelson, O. F., 138
New Caledonia, 44
Newcastle, Henry Pelham, 77, 178
New Zealand Association, 53, 159
New Zealand Company, 18, 53, 62–64, 159, 162, 163; tenths system, 63–64

New Zealand Constitution Act 1846, 163–4
New Zealand Constitution Act 1852, 65–66, 162–3, 164–6, 178, 181, 191, 212, 241, 246, 281–2
New Zealand Constitution Act 1986, 246, 250, 269
New Zealand Maori Council: authority, 213, 253, 267; creation, 213, 247, 251, 296; Electoral Option claim to Tribunal, 269; involvement in negotiation of fishing quota, 234, 237, 248, 287; *New Zealand Maori Council v Attorney-General* 1987, 246, 287–8; orientation, 196, 202, 282; role of chairman (Sir Graham Latimer), 220, 274; state-owned enterprises case in Court of Appeal, 261; sidelined for Crown-Congress Joint Working Party, 289
New Zealand sesquicentennial, 273
New Zealand Settlements Act 1863, 65, 148, 168, 226, 232, 242, 279
New Zealand Settlements Acts, 72, 302
New Zealand Steel slurry pipeline, 226–8
New Zealand wars, 4, 147–8, 149, 152, 166, 167–8, 177; *see also* Grey, George; Heke, Hone
Nga Kaiwhakapumau i te Reo (Wellington Board of Maori Language), 229–30; *see also* Te Reo Maori claim; Waitangi Tribunal reports
Nga Tamatoa, 202–3
Ngahue, 23, 30
Ngai Tahu purchase, 278
Ngai Tahu Trust Board, 251
Ngata, Apirana: and Board of Maori Ethnological Research, 129; and Cook Islands and Samoa, 137–8; and I. L. G. Sutherland; and Maori rights, 2, 126–44, 154, 181–2, 187–8, 189, 191–2; and National Government's Maori policy, 197; and Pei Te Hurinui Jones, 193; and Peter Buck, 1–2, 5, 126–44 *passim*, 294; and Young Maori Party, 182, 188, 189, 192; as Native Minister, 127–38, 140–2, 154, 212, 282–3, 284; as parliamentarian, 128, 142, 181–2, 183–5, 187, 192, 194, 196, 206, 210; education, 127–8, 143; Land Development Report 1931, 138–40; promotes land consolidation, incorporation and development, 88–89, 181–8, 206; views on anthropologists, 2, 126–44 *passim*; views on Maori King movement, 115; views on Maori Parliament, 191
Ngata, Henare, 143, 207, 208–9
Ngata, Reire Arihia Kane, née Tamati, 143
Ngatata, Wiremu, 175
Ngati Whatua Trust Board, 233
Nicholas, J. L., 16
Nixon, M. G., 111

Nopera Panakareo, 239, 244
North American treaties, 44–5, 276, 277; *see also* American Indians
Nyerere, Julius, 204

O'Carroll, P. J., 102
Oliver, Roland, 4
Oliver, W. H., 264–5, 300
Omana, Tiaki, 194, 196
Onslow, W. H., 102–3
Orakei claim, 232–4, 265; *see also* Waitangi Tribunal reports
Orange, Claudia, 195, 218, 240, 278, 298
Ormond, J. D., 95
Orr, Gordon, 247–8, 250, 301
Outlying Districts Police Act 1865, 80, 242

Paetahi, Mete Kingi, 174
Paikea, T. P., 194, 195, 196, 207
Paikea, Tipi, 207
Pai Marire, 150–1, 296; *see also* Hau Hau movement
Pakeha-Maori, 61, 62
Pakeha: as colonists, 1, 2, 69, 71, 89; control of government, 76, 89, 112, 144, 156, 153–216 *passim*, 245, 246, 251, 252; defined, 1, 2, 144, 155, 157; effects of their diseases on Maori, 62, 103; in Department of Maori Affairs, 140–2; including Peter Buck and Apirana Ngata, 126–38 *passim*; viewed by Maori, 117, 129, 141, 142, 150, 276; views on: Maori assimilation 39, 127, 135, 139, 144, 217; Maori autonomy, 179, 255, 269, 296; Maori representation in Parliament, 7, 153–216 *passim*, 212; New Zealand history, 217; race relations, 1, 135, 136, 138, 147, 155, 188, 222, 238, 241, 245, 251, 252, 258, 271, 272, 274, 280; Treaty of Waitangi, 54, 218, 219, 223, 258, 272; Treaty settlements, 267, 272, 274, 276, 283, 291, 293, 303; Tribunal findings, 231
Palmer, Geoffrey, 246, 250, 261, 274
Papua New Guinea, 13, 31
Papuans, 44
Parihaka, 104, 151, 178–9, 190, 193
Park, Robert E., 140, 144
Parkinson, Sydney, 11
Patetere block, 96, 124
Patterson, John, 174
Pearce, Nancy, 90
Pere, Wi, 180, 181
Perry, W. J., 130, 131
Peters, Winston, 205, 211, 283
Peti, Hone, 175

Petrocorp, 262, 288
phrenology, 17, 18, 19
Phillip, Arthur, 49, 50
Pilate, Pontius, 161, 243, 280
Piniha, 123
Pitt Rivers Museum, Oxford, 132
Pitt-Rivers, G. H. L., 134–6, 136
Pocock, J. G. A., 146
Pohuhu, Nepia, 31, 39
Polack, J. L., 16, 18, 26, 58
Pollen, Daniel, 97
Polynesia, 12, 25, 33, 38, 157
Polynesians, 2, 12, 13, 18, 20, 23, 26–32, 34–6, 38, 56, 116, 126, 130–1; monarchs, 281
Polynesian Society, 1, 6, 9, 12, 13, 28, 30, 33, 126–8, 133, 134, 139, 190
Pomare, Maui, 128, 154–5, 182–4, 191, 193, 296, 297
Pool, Ian, 294
Porokutu, 120–1
Portland, 3rd Duke of, *see* Bentinck, W. H. C.
Potatau, *see* Te Wherowhero, Potatau
Potiki, Paul, 207
Prendergast, James, 84, 219, 224, 240, 298
Preliminary Report on the Te Arawa Representative Geothermal Resource Claims, 262
Pritchard-Waetford Report, 200
Public Accounts Committee, 186
Puke, Hare, 263–4, 269

Race Relations Act 1971, 271
Radcliffe-Brown, A., 130, 132
Radin, Paul, 133–4
Rakuraku, Mohi, 94
Ramsden, Eric, 143
Ranger, T. O., 146, 152
Rangitakaiwaho, H. M., 175
Rankin, Hone Heke, 154, 180, 181, 183, 188, 190, 192
Rarotongans, 31
Rata, Matiu, 203–4, 205, 207–8, 213, 219, 234
Ratana church, 155, 156, 191–2, 206, 208, 245, 296
Ratana–Labour alliance, 155, 194–8, 200, 202, 207, 210
Ratana political movement, 142, 155, 156, 191–200, 202, 204, 205–6, 207–8, 210, 213, 245, 296–7
Ratana, Iriaka, 207
Ratana, Matiu, 196, 202–4, 205, 207
Ratana, T. W., 142, 152, 155, 156, 191–2, 195, 213, 245

Ratana, Tokouru, 191–4, 195, 207
Reagan, Ronald, 286
Renwick, W. L., 77, 79
Report of the House of Commons Committee on Aborigines 1837, 40–41, 54
Report on Maori Affairs 1960, *see* Hunn Report
Repudiation Movement, 153
Resource Management Bill 1989, 246, 261–2
Resource Management Act 1991, 261–2, 265
Rewiti, Paroane, 202, 207, 208–9
Richardson, J. L. C., 171
Richmond, C. W., 71, 76, 82, 84–5, 166
Richmond, J. C. 84, 146
Ringatu, 150–1, 178, 296
Rivers, W. H. R., 132
Rochon, Abbe, 13
Rodwell, Harold, 4
Rogan, J., 79, 84
Rohepotae judgment, 178
Rolleston, William, 173–4
Ropiha, Tipi, 197
Ross, Ruth, 161, 218, 239, 284, 298
Roth, H. Ling, 13
Rowley, C. D., 145
Rowling, W. L., 204
Royal Commission of Inquiry on Confiscated Native Lands and Other Grievances 1926–27, 183, 226, 232, 265, 267–8, 279, 302
Royal Commission on the Electoral System 1986, 7, 157, 283, 296–7
Royal Proclamation [for British North America] 1763, 46–47, 48
Rua Kenana, 151–2, 155, 191
rugby contacts with South Africa, 5–6, 199, 203, 204, 205
Runanga Iwi Act 1990, 298
Russell, A. H., 170
Russell, F. N., 174
Russell, H. R., 175
Rutherford, James, 3, 4, 219

Salmond, John, 185
Samoa, 44, 137–8
Sanderson, G. N., 5, 145
Sandwich Islands, 23, 54; *see also* Hawaii
Sanscrit, 16, 23, 24, 33–6
Savage, John, 13–14
Savage, Michael Joseph, 194
Savaii, 22
Schirren, C., 25
Scott, J. H., 20, 128
Scott, K. G., 220
Scottish enlightenment philosophers, 74

Sealord, 260, 266, 287
Seddon, Tom, 184
Semitic Maori, 15, 16, 17, 28, 36, 39, 56
Servant, Louis Catherin, 14
Sewell, Henry, 66, 74, 77, 79, 89, 92
Sharp, Andrew, 22, 39, 300
Sharples, Pita, 297
Shepherd, G. P., 197
Sherbo, 42, 54
Shortland, Edward, 21, 22–23, 27
Sim, Justice, 302
Simmons, D. R., 31
Sinclair, I. M., 221
Sinclair, Keith, 1, 4, 5, 40, 41, 107, 108, 226, 277, 295
Skinner, H. D., 38, 127
slave trade, Atlantic, 41
Smith, David, 140, 143, 186
Smith, Elliot, 130, 131
Smith, Harry, 43
Smith, Norman, 88
Smith, S. P., 20, 24, 25, 28, 29–32, 33, 35, 37, 38, 127–32, 143
Somes, Joseph, 162
South Africa, 42, 43, 63, 145, 148, 151, 199, 203, 205, 211, 271, 277
South Australia Association, 51–52
Southwick, L. H., 220
Stafford, E. W., 165, 174
State-Owned Enterprises Act 1986, 261, 265, 287–8
Stephen, James, 50, 51–53
Stirling, James, 51
Stout, Robert, 125
Stout-Ngata Commission 1907, 181
Strockenstrom, Andries, 43
Sullivan, Timothy, 120–1, 123
Suppression of Rebellion Act 1863, 65, 168, 242, 279
Surplus Lands Commission 1948, 232
Sutherland, I. L. G., 91, 100, 127, 133–4, 143, 187
Swainson, William, 246

Tabacoff, David, 207
Taiaroa, H. K., 174, 175
Tainui canoe, 21, 118, 149, 166
Tainui Raupatu claim, 267
Tainui Trust Board, 267
Taipa claim, 232
Taipua, Hoani, 176
Taiwhanga, Hirini, 179–80
Takaanini, Erina, 83
Takaanini, Ihaka, 83

INDEX

Takaanini, Te Wirihana, 83
Takamoana, Henare, 95
Takamoana, Karaitiana, 95, 174, 175
Takitimu canoe, 21
Tamihana, Wiremu, 109–10, 112, 117–19, 120 166, 170
Tane, 33
Tanner, Thomas, 95
Tapsell, Peter, 206, 207
Tapsell, Phillip, 62
Taranaki Trust Board, 251
Taranaki war, 77, 119, 147, 149, 167; see also Waitara purchase; New Zealand wars
Taylor, Aila, 221
Tariao faith, 103, 123
Tasman, Abel, 10, 48, 52, 56
Tauroa, Hiwi, 214
Taylor, Griffith, 131
Taylor, Richard, 14, 16–17, 24, 26, 27, 32
Tawhaki, 32
Tawhiao (Matutaera), 103–4, 118, 119–25, 151, 168, 176, 177–8, 180, 190, 191
Te Ahuru, Paora, 112
Te Akerautangi, Wiremu, 117–18
Te Arawa Trust Board, 251
Te Ariki-tara-are, 29
Te Atairangikahu, Queen, 282
Te Atirau, Katerina, 2
Te Aute College, 127, 181
Te Aute College Students Association, 128
Te Awarahi, 118
Te Hapua, 42; Incorporation, 234
Te Hau, Matiu, 211
Te Heu Heu, Hepi, 289
Te Heu Heu, Iwikau, 166
Te Kooti Rikirangi, 95, 96, 150–1, 153, 168, 178
Te Matarohanga, 31, 39, 131
Te Moananui, Tareha, 174, 175
Temm, Paul, 220, 285
Te Otene, 79
Te Pouhere Korero, 3
Te Puea Herangi, 150, 186, 193, 296
Te Rangi Hiroa, *see* Buck, Peter
Te Rata Te Wherowhero, 191, 193
Te Rauparaha, 158
Te Rauparaha, Tamihana, 166
Te Reo Maori claim, 229–31
Te Roroa Report, 262
Te Tomo, Taite, 193–4
Te Ture Whenua Maori Act 1993, 85, 294
Te Ua Haumene, 150
Te Waharoa, 158
Te Whakaunua, Hetaraka, 176–7

Te Weehi v Regional Fisheries Officer 1986, 253
Te Wheoro, Wiremu, 176, 191, 213
Te Wherowhero, Mahuta Tawhiao Potatau, 70, 191
Te Wherowhero, Potatau, 106, 109, 114–17, 149, 158, 165–6, 240, 244
Te Whiti o Rongomai, 100, 101, 102, 103, 104, 151, 155, 178–9, 184, 190
Te Whiwhi, Matene, 116, 166
Thatcher, Margaret, 286
Thermal Springs Act 1881, 96–97
Thompson, E. P., 73–74
Thomson, A. S., 19–20, 24–25, 30, 59, 61–62
Tirikatene, Eruera, 191–2, 194–6, 199, 201, 203, 207, 213
Tirikatene-Sullivan, Whetu, 204, 207, 208
Titokowaru, Riwha, 168
Tohu Kakahi, 179
Toi, 30
Tonga, 22
Torrens, Robert, 51–52
Torres Straits Islanders, 132
Tozzer, A. M., 132
Travers, W. T. L., 29
Treaty of Waitangi: and 'sovereignty', 212–13; as 'Maori Magna Carta', 222, 298; celebrations, 273–5; English versus Maori text, 217–18, 238–44, 245–6, 258, 272, 277–80, 298–9; 'fourth article', 244; guarantee of Maori resources, 237; interpreted by courts, 246; interpreted by Waitangi Tribunal, 222, 236; Maori 'signatures' on, 1, 239–40, 276; negotiated by Hobson, 160–2; pre-emptive clause, 76; principles, 219, 221, 225, 229, 246, 257, 300–1; related to other treaties, 40–44, 54, 276–7, 283, 292–3; rights and privileges of British subjects under, 148, 168; transfer of sovereignty, 65
Treaty of Waitangi Act 1975, 160, 219–20, 231, 238–9, 257–8, 284–5, 300
Treaty of Waitangi Amendment Act 1985, 219, 231, 247, 259, 286, 299, 300
Treaty of Waitangi Amendment Act 1993, 262
Treaty of Waitangi (Fisheries Claims) Settlement Act 1992, 260–1
Treaty of Waitangi Policy Unit, 263, 265
Treaty of Waitangi (State Enterprises) Act 1988, 261–2, 265, 288
Tregear, Edward, 24, 32, 33, 34, 38, 127, 130, 131
Tuamotuans, 31
Tuhaere, Paora, 123–4, 174, 179, 189, 245
Tui Viti, 54
Tumana, 30
Turia, Tariana, 297

Tuwharetoa Trust Board, 251
Tylor, E. B., 23, 130

United Nations, 271
UN Declaration on the Rights of Indigenous Peoples, 272

Vattel, E., 50
Vercoe, Whakahuihui, 274, 276
Victoria, Queen, 252, 270, 273
Vogel, Julius, 86, 94, 124
von Haast, H. F., 219
von Haast, Julius, 27
von Hochstetter, F., 25
von Ranke, Leopold, 7, 300

Wahanui, 125
Waikato confiscation, 64–65, 100–1, 113, 120, 123, 150, 177–8, 226
Waikato war, 64–65, 69, 119, 147, 149–50, 167
Waikerepuru, Huirangi, 229
Waitangi Day, 204
Waitangi Tribunal: associations, 2, 6; jurisdiction, 6, 68–69, 219–20, 238–9, 247, 285–6, 299
Waitangi Tribunal reports, 247–8, 263–4, 299–300; *Electoral Options*, 269; *Hauraki*, 85; *Kaituna*, 220, 223–5, 257, 259; *Manukau*, 221, 257, 259; *Motunui*, 220–3, 257, 259; *Muriwhenua Fishing*, 221, 234–7, 239, 248, 260–1, 287; *Ngai Tahu*, 240, 288; Ngawha Geothermal Resource Report 1993, 262; *Orakei*, 221, 232–4, 249, 254; *Radio Spectrum Management and Development*, 301; *Te Reo*, 221, 229–31, 268–9; *Taranaki*, 288; *Te Roroa*, 290; *see also* names of individual claims
Waitara purchase, 64–65, 77, 92, 109, 111, 112, 166, 278
Waka Nene, Tamati, 163
Wakefield, E. G., 51, 53, 61, 62–64, 159, 279
Wakefield, E. J., 63
Wakefield, William, 159

Walker, E. B., 120
Walker, Ranginui, 213
Wallace, John, 7, 157
Ward, Alan, 69, 71, 76–77, 79, 80, 85, 146, 171, 177, 180, 256, 266, 289, 291, 294
Ward, John, 62
Ward, Joseph, 189
Watene, Apanui, 207
Watene, Steve, 202, 207
Weld, Frederick, 79, 170
Wetere, Koro, 206, 219
Wheen, Nicola R., 300
Whewell, W., 55
Whiro (also Hiro, Iro), 30
Whitaker, Frederick, 66, 79, 92–93
White, John, 22
White, W. B., 79
Whitlam, Gough, 253
Whitmore, G. S., 171
Wilkinson, D., 54
William the Conqueror, 25
Williams, David V., 68, 77, 81, 219
Williams, E. M., 175
Williams, Edward, 160, 280
Williams, Henry, 59, 158, 160, 161, 224, 239, 243–4, 280–1
Williams, Herbert, 131, 132
Williams, Joe, 272
Williams, Samuel, 95
Williams, William, 59–60
Williamson, J., 253
Wilson, J. A., 28
Winiata, Maharaia, 116
Winiata, Whatarangi, 297
Wissler, Clark, 132
Wohlers, J. F. H., 29
Wood, G. A., 176

Yate, William, 14, 60
Young Maori Party, 104–5, 128, 154–6, 181–2, 183, 188–9, 191–2, 193, 210, 213, 296
Young, J. C., 97